Hitler's Spies

Hitler's Spies

Lena and the Prelude to Operation Sealion

Mel Kavanagh

The true story of four men who, as pathfinders for Operation Sealion – the proposed invasion of Britain – came to England in 1940 to spy for the Germans.

Operation Lena was the codename. This is their story.

Pen & Sword
MILITARY

First published in Great Britain in 2020 by
Pen & Sword Military
An imprint of
Pen & Sword Books Ltd
Yorkshire – Philadelphia

Copyright © Mel Kavanagh 2020

ISBN 978 1 52676 872 8

Typeset by Mac Style
Printed and bound in the UK by TJ Books Ltd,
Padstow, Cornwall.

MIX
Paper from
responsible sources
FSC® C013056

Pen & Sword Books Limited incorporates the imprints of Atlas, Archaeology, Aviation, Discovery, Family History, Fiction, History, Maritime, Military, Military Classics, Politics, Select, Transport, True Crime, Air World, Frontline Publishing, Leo Cooper, Remember When, Seaforth Publishing, The Praetorian Press, Wharncliffe Local History, Wharncliffe Transport, Wharncliffe True Crime and White Owl.

For a complete list of Pen & Sword titles please contact

PEN & SWORD BOOKS LIMITED
47 Church Street, Barnsley, South Yorkshire, S70 2AS, England
E-mail: enquiries@pen-and-sword.co.uk
Website: www.pen-and-sword.co.uk

Or

PEN AND SWORD BOOKS
1950 Lawrence Rd, Havertown, PA 19083, USA
E-mail: Uspen-and-sword@casematepublishers.com
Website: www.penandswordbooks.com

Contents

Operation Lena: The Ascension to Heaven?

After their victory in France and the Low Countries, the German military was on the crest of a wave and only Britain stood in their way. Britain was Germany's first major stumbling block, the only major European power not to have fallen to the Nazis. It was said that Hitler was prepared to offer Britain generous peace terms and, if not accepted, then the country could, he believed, be successfully invaded. Hitler had initially planned an economic war, but this would have taken too long to be effective.

The amount of food the British Government imported had already been cut back as German submarines started attacking British supply ships. After petrol (rationed in September 1939), rationing of foodstuffs was introduced on 8 January 1940, with bacon and butter – both limited to 2oz – and sugar, capped at 12oz per person, per week. That was followed in March by the rationing of meat, dealt with by price rather than weight.

On 21 May, the commander-in-chief of the Kriegsmarine (the German Navy), Grand Admiral Erich Raeder, had advised Hitler about a plan to invade Britain and the Führer was apparently impressed by the proposal. It was felt that a military conquest of Britain would be quick and decisive; the military success of the Germans since September 1939 seemed to confirm, at least in Hitler's mind, that a demoralized British Army could be swiftly dealt with. Hitler hoped that the British would realize the futility of further resistance. His goal was a British 'Vichy', which would allow him to focus on events in continental Europe. Since the end of 1939, the Wehrmacht had produced a report favouring a surprise attack on England, but the German Navy knew that this plan would involve them not only protecting the landing fleet but also having to fight the Royal Navy.

The Luftwaffe, in turn, stated that to provide effective cover they needed good weather for the duration of the invasion. The problems of an invasion were patently obvious to all three branches of the German military, namely:

• Control of the Channel would be needed.
• Control of the skies would be needed.
• Good weather would be needed.

It is unclear how serious Hitler was about an invasion. His plans may have been half-hearted, and it would have been an extremely difficult operation to carry out. Without doubt, Hitler's biggest problem was the Channel. On 17 June 1940, the Kriegsmarine received the following communiqué:

> 'With regard to the landing in Britain the Führer has not up to now expressed such an intention, as he fully appreciates the unusual difficulties of such an operation. Therefore, even at this time, no preparatory work of any kind has been carried out in the Wehrmacht High Command.'[1]

Four days later, the German Army informed the Navy that they were unconcerned about invading England, as they considered the task an impossible one. Hitler's position on this matter was obviously crucial, as without his support no invasion would be possible. It was thought that Hitler believed a peaceful solution could still be possible, with Britain forced to recognize Germany's position regarding mainland Europe. The Führer was known to be an admirer of the British Empire, and a cheap victory would have suited Hitler best. Furthermore, it would have created the conditions to make possible his desired great drive to the East, and would also probably keep the United States out of any involvement in the war. Hitler's primary interest was thus to force the British to the bargaining table.

Only when it became abundantly clear to him that Britain would not sign peace terms did Hitler change his position and give the first indication of a possible invasion. On Tuesday, 2 July 1940, Hitler stated that, 'A landing in England is possible, providing that air superiority can be attained and certain other necessary conditions fulfilled ... all the preparations must be made on the basis that the invasion is still only a plan, and has not yet been decided upon.'[2]

Prior to Hitler implying that a landing in England was entirely possible, Prime Minister Winston Churchill may well have been sceptical about the chances of invasion. In June 1940, in an upbeat mood, he told the House of Commons, 'It seems to me that as far as seaborne invasion on a great scale is concerned, we are far more capable of meeting it today than we were at many points in the last war and during the early months of this war.' Privately, he told his staff that he hoped 'to drown the bulk of them in the salt sea'.[3]

By 8 July, Churchill was not quite so optimistic. In a memo to the Minister of Aircraft Production, Lord Beaverbrook, the Prime Minister stated:

> 'When I look around to see how we can win the war I see that there is only one sure path. We have no Continental army which can defeat the German military power ... there is one thing that will bring him down, and that is an absolutely devastating, exterminating attack by very heavy bombers from this country upon the Nazi Homeland. We must be able

to overwhelm them by this means, without which I do not see a way through.'[4]

Hitler's exasperation at Britain's continuing defiance was amplified when, on 14 July in a BBC radio broadcast, Churchill prepared the British people for a possible German attack:

'And now it has come to us to stand alone in the breach, and face the worst that the tyrant's might and enmity can do. Bearing ourselves humbly before God, but conscious that we serve an unfolding purpose, we are ready to defend our native land against the invasion by which it is threatened. We are fighting by ourselves alone; but we are not fighting for ourselves alone. Here in this strong City of Refuge which enshrines the title-deeds of human progress and is of deep consequence to Christian civilization; here, girt about by the seas and oceans where the Navy reigns; shielded from above by the prowess and devotion of our airmen we await undismayed the impending assault. Perhaps it will come tonight. Perhaps it will come next week. Perhaps it will never come. We must show ourselves equally capable of meeting a sudden violent shock or – what is perhaps a harder test – a prolonged vigil. But be the ordeal sharp or long, or both, we shall seek no terms, we shall tolerate no parley; we may show mercy – we shall ask for none.'[5]

Two days later, Hitler signed and issued Directive 16. Marked 'TOP SECRET By Hand Of Officer Only', the document outlined the terms of Hitler's proposed invasion of Britain. All three branches of the German military were assigned responsibilities, but overall control remained with Hitler. The landing was to take the form of a surprise attack along a broad front. The following[6] is a translation:

TOP SECRET   The Führer's H.Q.
By Hand Of Officer Only. 16th July, 1940.
Directive No. 16
The preparations for a landing operation against Britain.

As Britain shows no readiness to come to terms, although her military position is hopeless, I have decided to make preparations for a landing operation against Britain, and, if necessary, to carry it out.

It is the purpose of this operation to eliminate the British home country as a base for prosecuting the war against Germany and if necessary it is to be completely occupied.

For this purpose I order the following:

1. The <u>landing</u> must be carried out in the form of a surprise crossing on a broad front approximately from Ramsgate as far as the area west of the Isle of Wight.

    Parts of the Luftwaffe will have to perform the functions of artillery and parts of the Navy will have to function as engineers.

    All branches of the Armed Forces are to report to me whether it is practicable to carry out smaller scale operations such as the occupation of the Isle of Wight or the Duchy of Cornwall, prior to the main crossing.

    I reserve to myself the decision on this point.

    Preparations for the whole operation must be completed by the <u>middle of August.</u>

2. These preparations include also the creation of conditions which make a landing in Britain possible:

    (a) Both morally and materially the R.A.F. must be eliminated sufficiently to prevent it from offering any effective resistance to the German landing.

    (b) Mine-free channels must be created.

    (c) Both <u>flanks</u> of the Straights [*sic*] of Dover as well as the Western entrance of the Channel (approximately along the line Alderney–Portland) must be closed by minefields.

    (d) Powerful coastal artillery must be used to dominate and seal off the coastal area.

    (e) It is desirable to confine the British Naval Forces in the North Sea as well as in the Mediterranean (by the Italians) shortly before the crossing. From now on attempts must be made to weaken the British Naval Forces in Home Waters as much as possible through air and torpedo attacks.

3. <u>Organisation of Command and of preparations.</u>

    Under my command and according to my general directives the Commander-in-Chief will <u>direct the forces taking part.</u>

    From 1st August onwards the staffs of the Commander-in-Chief, Army, Commander-in-Chief, Navy and Commander-in-Chief, Luftwaffe must be not more than 50km from my headquarters (Ziegenberg). It seems to me desirable to accommodate the personal staffs of the Army and Navy Commanders-in-Chief alongside each other at Giessen.

    It will thus be necessary for the Commander-in-Chief, Army to use an Army group to command the landing troops.

    The operation will be given the cover name '*SEALION*'[(*Seelöwe*].

During the preparations and actual execution of the operation the Armed Forces will have the following tasks:-

(a) <u>Army.</u>

The Army will begin by working out plans for the operation and the plans for all troops to be embarked in the first wave.

The Anti-aircraft Artillery which will cross with the first wave will be subordinated to the various assault groups of the Army until such time as it is possible to divide the functions into support and protection of ground forces, protection of the disembarkation harbours and protection of the air bases to be occupied.

Furthermore, it will be the task of the Army to allocate shipping space to the various assault groups to determine the places of embarkation and disembarkation in co-operation with the Navy.

(b) <u>Navy.</u>

The Navy is to secure the necessary shipping spaces and conforming to the Army's wishes as far as practicable, is to be governed by nautical considerations in directing the ships to the various embarkation areas. Ships of conquered enemy states are to be used to the fullest possible extent.

The Navy will station at every crossing point the staff necessary to advise on naval matters and will provide the necessary escort and screening forces.

The Navy in conjunction with the units detailed by the Luftwaffe will protect both flanks of the whole crossing area.

Orders relating to the chain of command during the crossing will follow.

Furthermore, it is the task of the Navy to organise the coastal artillery i.e. all batteries – Military or Naval – which can be used to engage targets at sea, and to organise the fire control as a whole.

As much <u>heavy artillery</u> as possible is to be made ready in the shortest time to protect the crossing and to screen the flanks against enemy attacks from the sea. For this purpose railway guns using railway turntables may also be employed (supplemented by all available captured guns) but not those batteries destined for engaging targets on the British mainland.

Apart from these, the heaviest available fixed gun emplacements are to be constructed under concrete opposite the straights [*sic*] of Dover in such a way that they will be able to withstand the heaviest air attack and will thus be able to dominate the Straights [*sic*] of Dover.

The technical work will be undertaken by the organisation Todt [civil and military engineering group].

(c) <u>It is the task of the Luftwaffe:</u>

To prevent the enemy air force from operating. To destroy coastal fortifications which could operate against the landing points, to break the first resistance of enemy ground forces and to annihilate approaching reserves. For this purpose the closest co-operation between the various units of the Luftwaffe and the Army groups is necessary.

Roads which are important for the transport of reserves are to be destroyed and enemy naval forces approaching the landing area are to be attacked well before reaching the crossing area.

I request that proposals be submitted to me on the use of parachute and airborne troops. The question is to be examined in co-operation with the Army whether it is advisable to keep the parachute and airborne troops as a <u>reserve</u>, to be thrown in quickly in case of emergency.

4. The necessary preparations for communications between France and England will be made by the Head of Army Communications.

The construction of the remaining 80km of East Prussian cable is to be planned in co-operation with the Navy.

I request the Commanders-in-Chief to submit the following information as soon as possible:

(a) The intentions of the Navy and Luftwaffe regarding the creation of conditions for a crossing of the Channel (see No. 2).

(b) The construction of coastal barriers in detail.

(c) An estimate of the ships to be used (Navy) and the method of getting them ready and equipped. Participation of civil authorities (Navy).

(d) The organisation of air raid protection in the assembly areas for invasion troops and ships (Luftwaffe).

(e) The invasion and operation plan of the Army formation and equipment for the first wave.

(g) [*sic*] Proposals for the use of parachute and airborne troops and for the subordination and command of the Anti-aircraft Artillery after sufficient space has been gained on British territory (Luftwaffe).

(h) Proposals for suitable Headquarters for the Commander-in-Chief, Army, and Commander-in-Chief, Navy.

(i) A statement from the Army, Navy and Luftwaffe as to whether – and which – preliminary actions should be carried out <u>before</u> the main landing.

(k) [*sic*] Proposal from the Army and Navy concerning the chain of command during the crossing.

(Signed)   Adolf Hitler

Only seven copies of Directive 16 were prepared: one for each of the supreme commanders of the Army, Navy and Air Force; one for General Jodl, head of the OKW (Oberkommando der Wehrmacht or High Command of the Armed Forces); two for Section L (the Landesverteidigung or National Defence); with the seventh and last copy locked up in Hitler's own files.

By issuing Directive 16, Hitler formally gave the order for the German military to make plans for the invasion of Britain. Time was of the essence, as preparations for the entire operation had to be completed by mid–August, four weeks after the issue of the Directive. Hitler wanted *Sealion* to be over by mid–September.

The whole plan relied on Germany having complete control of the English Channel, which in turn meant that the Luftwaffe had to have control of the skies, neutralizing the Royal Air Force so it could not attack German ships crossing the Channel.

Hitler, at a meeting with his service chiefs on 21 July, made it plain that he recognized the dangers in the plan, but was keen to continue so that he could turn his attention to Russia, once Britain had been defeated.

Even before the Directive was issued, the Wehrmacht began assembling troops in Channel ports and preparing craft for the crossing.

Operation *Sealion* looked simple in theory. Britain should have been an easy target. The Luftwaffe was very experienced in modern warfare, the Wehrmacht had achieved astonishing success since the attack on Poland and the British had lost a vast amount of military hardware on the beaches at Dunkirk. After Dunkirk, virtually the only fully armed division in Britain was the 1st Canadian Division. US President Franklin D. Roosevelt had rushed arms to the British, and the British munitions factories worked non–stop to try to make good the losses on the Continent. But the RAF and the Army in Britain looked weak; only the Royal Navy seemed to offer Britain some semblance of protection.

Despite his defiant speech on 14 July, Churchill's mood became more sombre. 'The scene has darkened swiftly,' he wrote to Roosevelt. 'We expect to be attacked here ourselves, both from the air and by parachute and airborne troops in the near future and we are getting ready for them.'[7]

Three days after Hitler issued Directive 16, while addressing a session of the German Reichstag, he gave a bullish if not a somewhat deluded speech entitled 'A Last Appeal to Reason', in which he appeared to offer Britain a solution for final peace. He tried to convey to what was already a converted audience that Germany were the innocents and, more importantly, that he, the Führer, was the appeaser:

'And Mr Churchill should make an exception and place trust in me when as a prophet I now proclaim: A great world empire will be destroyed. A world empire which I never had the ambition to destroy or as much as harm. Alas, I am fully aware that the continuation of this war will end only in the complete shattering of one of the two warring parties. Mr Churchill may believe this to be Germany. I know it to be England!

'In this hour I feel compelled, standing before my conscience, to direct yet another appeal to reason in England. I believe I can do this as I am not asking for something as the vanquished, but rather, as the victor! I am speaking in the name of reason! I see no compelling reason which could force the continuation of this war!

'I regret the sacrifices it will demand. I would like to spare my *Volk* [people]. I know the hearts of millions of men and boys aglow at the thought of finally being allowed to wage battle against an enemy who has, without reasonable cause, declared war on us a second time!

'But I also know of the women and mothers at home whose hearts, despite their willingness to sacrifice to the last, hang onto this last with all their might.

'Mr Churchill may well belittle my declaration again, crying that it was nothing other than a symptom of my fear, or my doubts of the final victory.

'Still I will have an easy conscience in view of things to come!'[8]

The next day, 20 July, so-called 'peace leaflets', written in English, were dropped over London. The four-page booklet was a copy of Hitler's speech to the Reichstag and railed over the 'injustices', as Hitler saw it, that were inflicted upon Germany after the Great War of 1914–18, with warnings of the machinations of the 'Jewish warmongers' and their henchmen. The leaflet closed with Hitler's plea to call off the war. The speech was also arranged to be broadcast on hundreds of radio stations across Europe.

Unsurprisingly, this blatant German propaganda was received with disdain by the British civilian population and the military.

Despite the call for appeasement, Hitler was confident that his stormtroopers would soon be marching down Whitehall, and a list of prominent Britons to be arrested by the Gestapo was drawn up at the Abwehr headquarters in Berlin. The list included Churchill, of course, but also the likes of Noël Coward and Virginia Woolf. Furthermore, all males aged between 17 and 45 would be sent to the Continent.

Hitler's naval chiefs, however, believed that any invasion could not start until mid-September. Admiral Raeder supplied a list of reasons why it could not go ahead before this date, including the clearance of mines from shipping lanes and getting invasion barges ready, and he won the support of the Army. Hitler ordered that so long as Germany controlled the skies, Operation *Sealion* would start on 15 September. The invasion, therefore, depended entirely on whether Hermann Göring's Luftwaffe could defeat the RAF.

The RAF's Spitfire fighter plane was revered by the British public and feared by the Germans. When Göring asked his Luftwaffe commanders what they needed to defeat the RAF, the alleged reply from one of them was 'a squadron of Spitfires', much to the ire of the <u>Reichsmarschall</u>.

Before any invasion could commence, however, the Nazis needed to infiltrate England. The simple truth was that the Abwehr had singularly failed to recruit an effective team of spies in Britain to enable Operation *Sealion* to be successful. To rectify this situation, the German secret service swung into action with a vengeance.

In 1939 and 1940, MI5 (Britain's Military Intelligence) had no idea of the extent of any German espionage penetration in Britain. In reality, there was none to speak of, but this would change after the Fall of France.

Between September and November 1940, it is estimated that at least twenty-one Abwehr agents were despatched to Britain. They came by rubber dinghy, U-boat, seaplane and parachute; they came disguised as refugees and seamen. Some came armed with the latest wireless transmitters and carefully forged documents; others arrived with nothing more than the clothes they stood up in. The agents' brief was simple and somewhat predictable: to report on troop movements, identify and sabotage targets vital to Britain's defence, prepare for the imminent invasion and then mingle with the retreating British Army.[9] These spies were to be the forward scouts carrying out reconnaissance work and acting as guides for the impending invasion force. These pathfinders would warn the Wehrmacht about the lie of the land in Kent (the target for the prospective invasion), helping the invasion force navigate through the signpost-less country lanes and quintessential English villages.

The Abwehr spies were an eclectic bunch. Some were Nazi ideologues, but most were opportunists, criminals and fantasists. The vast majority of these 'invasion spies' had one thing in common: they were amateurs. Many spoke English badly or not at all. Few had received anything more than rudimentary training, and they were ignorant of English life. One, for example, was arrested after he tried to pay £10 and six shillings (£10 6/-) for a train ticket costing 'ten and six' (10/6).[10]

To get these agents into Britain and to operate effectively, Operation *Lena* was born. This was the codename for the Abwehr's contribution to Hitler's invasion plan. Unofficially, the spymasters considered the mission so hazardous that they called it *Himmelfahrt* ('the ascension to heaven').

At this time, with a climate of fear of invasion, Britain was gripped by spy paranoia. People believed enemy agents, infiltrators and collaborators were everywhere. Rumours abounded of spies recently arrived on Dunkirk evacuation ships, of lamps being flashed at low-flying Dorniers in the Home Counties or of a Lincolnshire vicar arrested for transmitting wireless messages from his vicarage.[11]

In July 1940, a 25-year-old aircraftwoman was arrested for starting false rumours about a German invasion. A man claimed he heard her say in a cafe that German parachutists had landed in England. Despite the rumours being false, the woman was found guilty and sentenced to three months in prison.[12]

Whether the stories were true or not, fear and suspicion fuelled the belief that the Germans were coming; and the precursor to the invasion, Operation *Lena*, was one of the most outrageous, important but least-known German missions of the Second World War.

Chapter One

'Where on Earth are we going to get hold of that many would-be suicides?'

Before Operation *Sealion* could commence, a network of spies in Britain was a priority. Like *Sealion* itself, Operation *Lena* necessitated indecent haste because of the very tight timescale – thirty days or so to recruit, train and brief agents before sending them into Britain.

There were several high-ranking men entrusted with the responsibility of finding the agents for this hazardous mission.

General Alfred Josef Ferdinand Jodl, Chief of the Operations Staff of the OKW (Armed Forces High Command):

The man responsible for formulating the plans for the German invasion of Britain was Hitler's chief military advisor, General Alfred Jodl.

Jodl, one of the youngest among Hitler's inner circle, was a general who, as head of the Wehrmacht's operations staff, helped plan and conduct most of Germany's military campaigns during the Second World War.

He was born on 10 May 1890 in Würzburg, Bavaria, as Alfred Baumgärtler, son of the Bavarian Hauptmann der Artillerie Johannes Jodl and Therese Baumgärtler. His parents were not married, partly because Johannes Jodl's family considered a farmer's daughter not good enough for someone from a military family.

Primarily a staff officer during and after the First World War, Jodl served as head of the Department of National Defence in the War Ministry from 1935. A competent staff officer and, most importantly, a faithful servant to Adolf Hitler, Jodl was named Chief of Operations of the Oberkommando der Wehrmacht on 23 August 1939, just before the invasion of Poland. He became a key figure in Hitler's central military command.

Jodl was a man of contrasts to those who knew him, Some believed that, as Chief of the Operations Staff, he had signed many orders for the shooting of hostages and other acts contrary to international law; they also believed that there was no doubting his loyalty to Hitler.

Jodl, however, did not follow his Führer's orders slavishly. Eckhard Christian – Jodl's personal General Staff Officer between 15 January 1941 and 31 August 1943 – would later testify that, at the end of August 1942, a quarrel ensued between Jodl and Hitler regarding waging war against Russia in the Caucasus. Jodl pointed out to the Führer that the war had gone astray owing to his (Hitler's) orders. Hitler felt aggrieved because this demonstration took place in front of a large gathering; therefore, the quarrel continued and did not end until 30 January 1943.

When describing a different scenario, Christian said that documentary evidence had shown that German prisoners were shackled around their throats by Canadians on the beach during the raid at Dieppe in August 1942 and the lower part of their legs bent back, leading to several prisoners allegedly choking. At least one Todt construction worker had been found dead on the beach, shackled.

As a result, the Führer ordered Jodl to draw up a proclamation in which the British were called upon to give a command that German prisoners were no longer to be shackled. Until this was done, 1,000 Canadians taken prisoner at Dieppe would be shackled. Far from being the author of atrocities for Hitler, Jodl's point of view, according to Christian, was that the shackling of Canadians was only a threat if the British refused to issue the order demanded.

Christian, however, reported Hitler's response: 'He had no use for this putty-like democratic form; it was not a matter of <u>threatening</u> to shackle 1,000 Canadian prisoners but of saying this had been done and will continue to be done until the British gave out the command demanded and informed us of it.'[1]

Christian would later confirm that on 7 October 1942, Hitler issued a communiqué that ordered Allied commandos to be killed rather than be taken prisoner. This followed commando operations in Norway and against the Channel Islands, striking at radar establishments and damaging other military installations. The Führer believed that such commando operations must be inseparably connected with violent measures, with no prisoners taken, and that such measures must be brought to the attention of the enemy. Jodl declared that Hitler's so-called 'Commando Order' was contrary to the rights of nations and refused provisionally to carry it out. He ordered a professor, Dr Kipp (of the Quartermaster Department of the Armed Forces Operation Staff), to make enquiries as to the legality in international law for such a command.

Jodl refused to make a draft for the command to be handed over to Hitler, and successfully initiated a delay of eleven days before it was eventually signed by Hitler and released.

Jodl was a very busy man. Conferences with Hitler, for example, could last up to eight hours a day, and there were also lengthy meetings with General Staff officers.

Oberstleutnant IG Heinz Waizenegger, adjutant to Jodl from November 1942 until 28 February 1945, later testified that he was present at most of the conferences that Jodl had with Hitler, and that during these meetings, the annihilation of the Jews or atrocities in the concentration camps were never mentioned. Waizenegger believed only the Reichsführer-SS, Heinrich Himmler, and SS-Gruppenführer Fegelein – brother-in-law of Eva Braun, Hitler's long-term companion – had meetings with the Führer in which such questions were discussed. Waizenegger thought it impossible that Jodl knew about these atrocities, which were treated as top secret in the headquarters. In the two-and-a-half years that he worked for Jodl, the adjutant knew his boss as a 'good soldier with a great sense of justice'.[2] He was convinced that Jodl would have disapproved of the atrocities in the concentration camps against the Jews, had he known about them.

Following the Fall of France, Jodl was optimistic about Germany's success over Britain. On 30 June 1940 he wrote, 'The final German victory over England is now only a question of time.'[3] Just twelve days later, Jodl issued a paper entitled 'First Deliberations Regarding a Landing in England',[4] in which he admitted that 'landing in England would be difficult' because of Britain's command of the sea and the vulnerability of any transport fleet to RAF bombing. Neither factor would make an invasion impossible, however.

The paper suggested, 'It will be necessary to land the assault elements of seven divisions simultaneously between Bournemouth and Dover', a front stretching over 143 miles.

The Navy would allocate disembarkation harbours and be responsible for laying two long mine barriers to protect the invasion force, one on the left flank between Alderney and Portland, the other on the right flank between Calais and Ramsgate.

The Luftwaffe, meanwhile, would need to ensure that it overcame coastal defences which could operate against landing points; broke the resistance of the ground troops and annihilated the reserves; and destroyed the most important lines of transport necessary for bringing up reinforcements.

Clearly, a significant amount of planning had already been carried out for *Sealion*, with details that had been incorporated into Hitler's Directive 16.

Admiral Wilhelm Canaris, head of the Abwehr:
Canaris was born on 1 January 1887 in the village of Aplerbeck, near Dortmund, the son of Carl Canaris, a wealthy industrialist, and his wife Auguste.

As part of his planning for *Sealion*, Jodl spoke to Canaris of the need for a network of spies to be ensconced in Britain. Since 1935, Canaris had been Chief of the Abwehr and responsible for running Germany's network of spies. Reputedly one of Mata Hari's lovers during the First World War, he was just 5ft 5in and was known as the 'little admiral', being a slight figure, prematurely white-haired with a pale, ashen complexion. He spoke hesitantly and with a lisp, walked with a stoop with his hands clasped firmly behind his back, but was well educated. He could speak English (fluently), French and Russian,[5] as well as Italian and Spanish. To some he was a timid, nervous and oversensitive individual who looked older than his years, and was an outsider in every respect; in his bearing and manner he was a most unmilitary person.[6] Canaris hated violence and had human qualities that placed him above the usual German military bureaucrat. Major General Erwin Lahousen, formerly on Admiral Canaris' staff, would reveal after the war that his chief 'hated Hitler, his system and his methods. He hated war. He was a human being.' Canaris not only held Hitler in utter contempt, he also hated Heinrich Himmler and the entire Nazi system as a political phenomenon.

Wilhelm Canaris led a double life, and he remains to this day the number one mystery man of the Nazi regime. On the one hand, he maintained close ties with the German resistance and highly protected and motivated the opponents of the regime in a dangerous plot to eliminate Hitler and make a separate peace with the Allies. At the same time, he was responsible for running the Nazi secret service and hunting his associates as conspirators – a contradiction he was forced to live with in order to stay in control of the Abwehr. He was confused and uncomfortable in his double role.

As the plan to send spies to the south of England unfolded, Canaris, clearly doubtful about the project, was reported to have asked, 'Where on Earth are we going to get hold of that many would-be suicides?'[7]

Canaris was a subtle, shrewd and brilliant spymaster who ran the Abwehr as his personal fiefdom. He built his staff up from 150 to just under 1,000 within three years, and its premises steadily grew from a rambling building in Berlin to taking over several buildings to the west of the city.

Canaris had been in the espionage business for most of his adult life. During the First World War, he had been one of Kaiser Wilhelm's most cagey and highly productive spies. He was dubbed by Russian military intelligence as the most dangerous intelligence man in the world.[8] This likeable, cultured spymaster had eyes and ears everywhere, and he had files full of damning evidence against the leading Nazis, among them Reinhard Heydrich and Heinrich Himmler – some sort of incriminating evidence that made them afraid to cross the Admiral. For years, Himmler went on protecting Canaris.

The admiral had personal traits considered by many to be peculiar at the very least. For example, no matter where this master spy travelled, at home or abroad, it was his habit to telephone his headquarters in Berlin on a daily basis to inquire into the state of the health of his two beloved dachshunds; an aide would give him a detailed briefing as to his dogs' eating habits and bodily functions. When the animals were ill, Canaris plunged into depression.[9] While he was very attached to his dogs, Canaris also had a wife and two daughters but took little part in family life. Walter Schellenberg, head of the unified German secret services after the arrest of Canaris, recalled, 'Canaris was a highly intelligent and sensitive man with many likeable qualities. He loved his dogs and his horse almost more than any other living creatures. He often said to me, "Schellenberg, always remember the goodness of animals. You see, my dachshund is discreet and will never betray me – I cannot say that of any human being."'

Canaris surrounded himself with dog-lovers, and any ambitious officer's promotion plans would be thwarted had he spoken a disparaging word about dogs!

As soon as Britain declared war on Germany in 1939, personnel from MI5 and Scotland Yard wasted no time in scouring the country rounding up German spies. Over 250 agents had been operating under cover in Great Britain, some for several years. Pretty much all were apprehended, as well as many others who were suspected of spying for Germany.

Jodl appeared oblivious to this. He probed Canaris about the number of agents the Abwehr had in England, but the admiral could not reveal the shocking truth, so he lied. Being a quick thinker, he told Jodl that the Abwehr had spies in place throughout Britain and boasted of the valuable work that these non-existent agents were doing. This seemed to placate Jodl. As *Sealion* was planned for 15 September, Jodl told Canaris that the Wehrmacht wanted a stable of British-based agents to act as scouts in advance of the invasion, giving him a deadline of 15 August to have the new spies in situ. He wanted these spies to relay the state of British defences and what beaches were suitable for a landing, and to guide advancing troops inland. When asked whether he could manage this, Canaris replied, 'Undoubtedly'. The Abwehr chief was fuming, believing Jodl's orders reflected Hitler's absurd and unrealistic wishes. Canaris knew that the thirty days he had been given was an impossible target. To do the job properly and establish new effective espionage networks would take many months, perhaps years.[10]

Canaris realized the futility of his task and would not care if every one of his spies was compromised; he just wanted to inform the German High Command that his agents in Britain were reporting on a regular basis.

He appointed men around him who were loyal to him rather than to the Nazi Party, giving them a large degree of autonomy. The historian Hugh Trevor-Roper wrote:

'In effect the operational officers of the Abwehr sat in Paris and Athens, in Biarritz and Estoril, enjoying the opportunities for self-indulgence provided by these resorts, undisturbed so long as a quota of reports was sent in. Whether these reports were true or false was unimportant, since there was no centralized evaluation.'

According to Trevor-Roper, under Canaris the Abwehr became 'not only a nest of spies but a nest of conspirators'.[11]

The Abwehr had penetrated the British Secret Service, MI6, and had broken some of its ciphers. Canaris, very much anti-war, was in touch with MI6, though the British were understandably suspicious of the motives of this powerful military man.[12]

In the summer of 1943, Canaris met secretly with General Stuart Menzies, Chief of British Intelligence, and William J. Donovan, head of the Office of Strategic Services (OSS), at Santander in Spain. Canaris presented Menzies and Donovan with his peace plan: a ceasefire in the West, Hitler to be eliminated or handed over and a continuation of the war in the East.

Although Donovan, Menzies and Canaris reached an agreement on the basis of Canaris' proposal, President Roosevelt flatly declined to negotiate with 'these East German Junkers' and called his presumptuous OSS chief to heel. Canaris' peace offer was rejected.

It came to the attention of Canaris that a friend of one of his officers suggested working with British Intelligence to bring down Hitler. Canaris, however, thought such an action ill-advised.

He added that anyone working for British Intelligence would, at some point, be mentioned in a cipher, and that these messages could be broken. He believed the British Secret Service, if they had the 'least suspicion, they will not hesitate to betray you to me or to my colleagues of the Reich Security Service'.[13]

Appointed by Hitler himself, Canaris was initially a vociferous supporter of the Führer and a patriotic German. But he was never a member of the Nazi Party and was a careful opponent of Hitler and Nazism. He was dubbed the 'Hamlet of conservative resistance' by Trevor-Roper.[14]

However, Canaris became increasingly anti-Nazi. After the <u>Anschluss</u> in 1938, he recruited Erwin von Lahousen-Vivremont from Austria's intelligence services. He warned the Austrian, 'You may not, under any pretext, admit to this section ... or take on your staff any member of the NSDAP, the Storm Troopers or the SS, or even an officer who sympathises with the Party.'[15]

Also by 1938, he had shifted to work against the regime, fearing that Hitler was embarking on a path that would eventually destroy Germany as a nation.

In September of that year, Canaris and other senior military officers hatched a plan to assassinate Hitler. They were ready to take action in order to prevent an invasion of Czechoslovakia. However, British Prime Minister Neville Chamberlain gave in to the dictator's demands that the Allies agree that the Czechs hand over the Sudetenland – the area bordering Germany – to the Reich. Czechoslovakia was eventually occupied without a shot being fired, and the immediate risk of war was averted. The conspirators were forced to abandon their plot.

Another example of the duplicity of Canaris happened when, in the hearing of the admiral, a young Luftwaffe pilot said that the RAF would crumple within six weeks. Straining to keep a straight face, Canaris said, 'The Führer is said to give them only fifteen days and the Führer is always right.'[16]

Hitler sent Canaris to Spain in 1938 to try to persuade General Franco to join forces with Germany in his plans for world domination. In reality, Canaris told Franco that he was convinced Germany could not win the war, and encouraged the Spanish dictator to maintain Spain's neutrality. Following Canaris' advice, Franco denied the Germans access to Gibraltar via Spain.

As if to exemplify his utter contempt for the Führer, on one of his trips to Spain, Canaris sprang to attention in his open car and raised his arm in the Nazi salute every time he drove past a herd of sheep. 'You never know,' Canaris said, 'whether one of the party bigwigs might be in the crowd.'

By 1940, Canaris felt Nazism 'was not only a political disaster: it was also a moral pestilence'.[17] He also expressed contempt for the generals who absolved themselves from responsibility that allowed the SS to carry out mass murder with unfettered freedom.

This contempt was exasperated when, on 10 September 1939, Canaris travelled to the front to watch the German Army in action. Wherever he went, his Intelligence officers told him of an 'orgy of massacre'. He was an eyewitness to the killing of civilians in Poland. At Bedzin, SS troops pushed 200 Jews into a synagogue and then set it aflame; the occupants all burned to death. Canaris was shocked. Two days later, he went to Hitler's headquarters train in Upper Silesia, the *Amerika*, to protest. He first saw General Wilhelm Keitel, Chief of the Armed Forces High Command. 'I have information,' Canaris told Keitel, 'that mass executions are being planned in Poland and those members of the Polish nobility and the clergy have been singled out for extermination. The world will one day hold the Wehrmacht responsible for these methods since these things are taking place under its nose'. Keitel urged Canaris to take the matter no further.

Soon the Vatican began to receive regular, detailed reports of Nazi atrocities in Poland. The information had been gathered by agents of the Abwehr by order of Canaris, who passed them on to Dr Josef Muller, a devout Catholic and a leading figure in the Catholic resistance to Hitler. Muller got the reports safely to Rome. He met Pope Pius XII on several occasions, but all attempts to get help from the Pope ended in failure.

Canaris sent another of his colleagues, Pastor Dietrich Bonhoeffer – who worked for the resistance movement under the cover of employment in Germany's Military Intelligence Department – on a flight to Sweden to meet secretly with Bishop Bell of Chichester. Bonhoeffer told Bell of the crimes his nation was committing, and assured the bishop of growing resistance in Germany to such acts.

While Canaris was anti-Nazi, he also had a deep hatred of communism. He was a monarchist, nationalist and a Franco sympathizer, and it was he who persuaded

Hitler to support the fascists during the Spanish Civil War. Yet Canaris was also a Christian and opposed to Hitler's aggressive foreign policy and the horrors of Nazism, although he was believed by some to be one of the architects of some of the Nazis' atrocities. However, in direct contrast to Nazi practice, he employed Jews in the Abwehr, aided others to escape and is rumoured to have provided intelligence to the Allies revealing German intentions.[18]

In one instance he saved seven Jews from being sent to a concentration camp and certain death by going personally to Himmler, complaining that his Gestapo was arresting his agents. The seven were turned over to the Abwehr, taught a few codes and then smuggled out of Germany.

Admiral Canaris constantly talked of treason, putting up projects for seizing power, for kidnapping and imprisoning Hitler, and for concluding a separate peace with England. Canaris, in July 1944, joined other high-ranking German officers in a dangerous plot to eliminate Hitler and make a separate peace with the Allies, an act that would ultimately seal his fate.

It only became clear to Hitler that Canaris was misleading him after the conspirators attempted to assassinate him on 20 July 1944. Canaris and many others were arrested. The principal prisoners were confined in Gestapo cellars at Prinz Albrechtstrasse in Berlin, where Canaris was kept chained in solitary confinement. His cell door was permanently open and the light burned continually, day and night. He was given only one-third of the normal prison rations, and as winter set in his starved body suffered cruelly from the cold. Occasionally he was humiliated by being forced to do menial jobs, such as scrubbing the prison floor while SS men mocked him.

On 7 February 1945, Canaris was taken to the Flossenburg concentration camp, but he was still ill-treated and often endured having his face slapped by the SS guards. For months, Canaris baffled his SS interrogators with one ruse after another, and he denied all personal complicity in the conspiracy to assassinate Hitler. He never betrayed his fellow participants in the resistance movement.

On 9 April 1945, gallows were erected hastily in the courtyard. Canaris and pastor Dietrich Bonhoeffer, amongst others, were ordered to remove their clothing and led down the steps, under trees to the secluded place of execution before the gloating SS guards. Under the scaffold, naked, they knelt for the last time to pray before being hanged, their corpses left to rot.

Two weeks later the camp was liberated by American troops.

The Nuremberg War Crimes Trials, held between November 1945 and October 1946, revealed Canaris' strenuous efforts in trying to put a stop to the war crimes and genocide committed by the Nazis. It also revealed that Canaris prevented the killing of captured French officers in Tunisia, just as he saved hundreds of Jews.

Captain Herbert Christian Oscar Otto Wichmann (alias Wegener, Wiesinger, Wolf, Weber or Werner), officer in charge of the Hamburg intelligence unit:
Naval Captain Herbert Christian Oscar Otto Wichmann was born in Hamburg on 18 April 1894, to Oscar and Emma Wichmann.

Of slim build, he was 5ft 7in tall, weighed about 10st 3lb and had brown hair going grey at temples, blue eyes, sharp features and an oval face with creases running from his nose to his mouth. He wore glasses, occasionally a monocle, and had a duelling scar. He appeared a 'typical officer, self-assured'.[19]

Canaris gave the unenviable task of creating new espionage networks in England to Wichmann, his Abwehr chief at Hamburg, who had directed operations against Britain (and later the US). Wichmann was earmarked for head of the London branch of Abwehr should the invasion prove successful.

Wichmann spoke Spanish and English, was conscientious, loyal but not one of the more intellectual officers. He was heavy-set, alert but heavy-handed. Intellectually, he seemed a perfect foil for Canaris, although not too distant morally from the admiral himself.

All attempts to spy on England were, up to the outbreak of war, disappointing, and despite their efforts, the Germans achieved nothing. Canaris, in 1939, was most 'displeased' with the results of the previous two years of work.

Under pressure, Wichmann's efforts to establish a new intelligence presence began in Eire with, somewhat bizarrely, Ernst Weber-Drohl, an ageing circus performer who had appeared throughout Europe for thirty-five years as 'Atlas the Iron Giant' and the 'World's Strongest Man'.[20]

Presumably not a man to go unnoticed, Weber-Drohl stole ashore by submarine and was told to start his cover in a chiropractic practice. However, he had other ideas and took it upon himself to find his two 'relatives' – illegitimate children from a mistress thirty years ago. The search for these resulted in his arrest by the Irish police as a vagrant. He was fined, released and eventually rejected by his 'children': 'Broke, fearful of being apprehended and charged with being a spy, Weber-Drohl contacted authorities at the British embassy, identified himself, and to avoid being jailed, agreed to work against Germany as a "turned spy".'[21]

Without Wichmann's knowledge, his superiors sent a man to win over some members of the crews of British steamers sailing weekly to Hamburg before the outbreak of war, but without success.

Then a young Dutch art dealer, named Reich, made two trips to England in 1938 to try to recruit agents who might supply information, but he fared no better.

Newspaper advertisements were studied, both German and English (*The Times*). The German newspapers were scoured for firms or individuals who had connections with and had travelled to England, and might be willing to accept missions. *The Times* was read for similar advertisements asking for people who may have German connections.

Firms were set up in Hamburg to answer the advertisements. They did no trade whatsoever, merely occupying a single room with a doorplate.

Hilmar Dierks, a First World War spymaster who was in charge of recruiting agents, received one report from Britain. It came from an agent called Jesse Jordan, whom Wichmann claimed he had never seen, and it concerned storage tank installations on the Firth of Forth in Scotland. Wichmann believed that Jordan lived near Dundee. This agent, however, proved fruitless, and she was arrested by the British authorities.

Wichmann also understood that Dierks received a report on the port of Sheerness in Kent, from a man whose name Wichmann never knew, but who had travelled to England. There was a paucity of information sharing amongst the spy recruiters.

Before the war, MI5 had the vision to penetrate the NSDAP, the Nazi Party, in Britain. British-based pastors, seamen, merchants, actresses, prostitutes, domestics, crooks, Germans and Austrians had been dragged into the Nazi Party net. If a German was antagonistic to the Nazi creed, they would be hounded out of employment. Some were as zealous as they were pompous, but others were blackmailed and became blackmailers in turn. As a consequence, Plan *Snuffbox* was born. The object was the liquidation of the Nazis in Britain upon the outbreak of war. Unbelievable as it may seem, that final duty was allocated to just one officer and one secretary, and she was extremely young. Strength lay, however, in the co-operation of the Chief Constables, and secrecy was preserved.

In August 1939, some 600 party members prudently fled the country. That still left 800, and by the outbreak of the war, approximately 700 were safely in jail. In effect, the German Fifth Column had been brought to an abrupt halt, which proved to be an incalculable gain as Britain, alone in Europe, was to remain singularly free of this cancerous influence, possibly for the rest of the war.

Any smug satisfaction was short-lived, however. Many Germans were naturalized as British, and eminent Englishmen advocated the release of eminent Germans. However, in a bid to apprehend 'illegal aliens', Special Branch at Scotland Yard undertook raids by day and night, everywhere from the vestry of the German Church in Dalston, East London, to shabby apartments in Notting Hill Gate. There was a pied-a-terre where two Irish sisters sheltered a man wanted by the authorities; a rubbish dump in Victoria where Nazi Party records had been jettisoned by an incautious German; and a pastor was arrested for sending a hacksaw in a cake to a parishioner in internment. German agents in seamen's homes in ports such as Hull were also taken in, while another only evaded arrest because of his ordination as a Church of England priest.

The Registrar General was induced to prevent a marriage whose suspected aim was to gain British nationality. The Public Prosecutor was persuaded to proceed against a gardener with bigamy charges because he had spuriously married a woman of 'great beauty' from UFA (Universum Film-Aktien Gesellschaft, a German motion-picture production company) for a fee.

The safe of the German Air Attaché was traced to The Pall Mall Safe Deposit, where it was blown open by a crook who gave his services to the Crown for nothing. The reaction of the proprietor would have been reasonable in peacetime, but he asked whether next time it would be acceptable to call after office hours, as this sort of thing had a bearing on the confidential nature of his business.

An RAF officer in 'Ops' was arrested for having German connections and holding the King's commission under a false name. There was also a dentist in Seaton, Devon, with an anglicised name. In peacetime, he made a strange living by selling ready-made teeth in standard sizes to replace those lost by holidaymakers in the sea. In wartime, he was bribed by the internees until he became an internee himself.

Virtually all of the spies had been apprehended by MI5, but back in Germany, Wichmann had no idea of this. With his spy network in Britain behind bars in prisons such as Wormwood Scrubs, messages were being transmitted to him by the British Secret Service, imitating precisely the individual touch of the German agents.

The British thought that once the Germans realized that most of their spies had been apprehended, they would introduce professional spies on a major scale. The hope was that preparation would be indifferent for lack of time, and if only the first spies could be caught and 'turned', they would supply an increasing flow of information on Nazi intentions.

Wichmann feared that an attack on England would fail, at great cost to Germany, and would ultimately lead to a full-scale world war. To avoid such devastation and the loss of thousands of German lives, Wichmann planned to despatch as spies citizens with low levels of intelligence but a resounding enthusiasm for National Socialism. Many of these individuals were petty criminals and members of far-right organizations in the Netherlands, Belgium and Denmark, and they received only cursory training.

MI5 described Wichmann and his group of agents as 'good Germans, but bad Nazis'.[22]

Major Nikolaus Fritz Adolf Ritter (alias Dr Norbert Rantzau, Hansen or Renkin, Dr Rankin, Jantzen, Nicolaus Reinhardt or Davidson), Chief of Air Intelligence in the Abwehr:

> 'Having lived in the United States, subject thought to make use of some of his contacts there for the benefit of the Abwehr.'
>
> (FBI report on Nikolaus Ritter, 2 September 1945)[23]

A protégé of Canaris, Nikolaus Fritz Adolf Ritter was born on 8 January 1899 at Rheydt in the Rhineland, the eldest of six children.

Weighing about 165–170lb, he was 5ft 8in tall, of chunky build, with straight dark brown hair, partly bald, clean shaven and with an oval face. Ritter sported a prominent gold tooth, had a friendly, full-faced countenance and a patter that seemed to have seeped from a B-movie.[24] He was fluent in English but, due to his time spent in the United States, spoke it with an American accent. He barely drank, did not talk excessively but seemed to command respect from those around him.

A pampered descendant of a dour aristocratic family, Ritter bore the arrogance of a man who refused to take orders from anyone whom he considered his social inferior. He was subjected to an upbringing of discipline, duty and honour. Despite this straight-laced background, the Ritter family were prone to bouts of fun and eccentricity, such as the male members of the family holding 'pissing' contests to see who could urinate the furthest.[25]

After studying at a Prussian military academy, Ritter joined the infantry in 1917 as an officer and served until the end of the Great War. However, it was also reported that Ritter served in the German Air Force and saw fighting in the Ostend Nieuwpoort sector. He later served on the military attaché's staff in America in an unknown capacity.

From the time of his discharge until 1921, he worked in the textile industry. The subsequent catastrophic economics of Germany prompted Ritter, at the age of 24, to move to the United States on an immigration visa, arriving on 1 January 1924. He gave his destination as in the care of his uncle, Julius Ritter, of 2101 Amsterdam Avenue, New York City, and his birthplace – wrongly – as Verden in Germany.

He married, in 1926, a hard-working, God-fearing American citizen of Irish extraction, Mary Aurora Evans, who was born on 30 October 1900 at White Oak Springs, Alabama. They eventually had two children, Nikolaus (called Klaus) and Katharina.

Ritter's family travelled with him when he returned to Germany. Impressed with Hitler's rise to power and having received an invitation for his services in his High Command, 'He simply could not resist the temptation of adventure',[26] his daughter would later reveal.

On 31 July 1930, sailing on the SS *Bremen*, Ritter arrived back in the US under a re-entry permit and gave his destination as 60 West 120th Street, New York City. His wife was with him, and he now gave his birthplace, correctly, as Rheydt, Germany. In 1933, with his brother Hans, he formed a company known as the Brush Importing Company, located at 70 East 11th Street, New York City.

The FBI would later report that 'between 1918 and 1933 Ritter was actively engaged in espionage'.

On 14 October 1935, Ritter again returned to the United States, on the SS *Europa*, this time giving his destination as the home of a friend, Mr A. Brandts, at 120 West 87th Street, New York City. With William Meyer he then formed a partnership to operate a small loan business. This lasted for six months, at which time Meyer loaned about $300 to facilitate Ritter's return to Germany.

On 15 June 1936, Ritter signed a promissory note for $210 payable to the Consumer's Credit Corporation. Both Ritter and his brother, Hans, worked as salesmen for the Consumer's Credit Corporation in New York City.

Ritter returned to Germany in August 1936, shortly after which he was reinstated as an officer in the German Army and assigned to the Secret Service Branch, operating out of Hamburg and Bremen. In autumn 1936, Ritter and his family were living in Bremen, where he served as a staff officer for the Wehrmacht.

The following February, Ritter became part of Ast Hamburg with Herbert Wichmann, the chief of Gruppe I. Ritter was given the assignment of organizing Referat (department) IL, which had previously not existed at Hamburg. The only officer in IL, he had no previous experience or available information on which to base his work.

Initially crestfallen about his surroundings, Ritter determinedly immersed himself in the business of espionage: he learned to create tiny documents, used 'invisible ink' in apparently routine letters, combed English-language newspapers and periodicals for news on the aircraft industry and took research trips to Luftwaffe installations.

Having lived in the United States, Ritter thought to make use of some of his contacts there for the benefit of the Abwehr. He thus took over control of the Air Force Section of German Intelligence at Hamburg, collecting information of interest to the Luftwaffe regarding Great Britain, Ireland and the United States. He also had a subsidiary interest in sabotage.

He received information from the USA about the aircraft industry from agents who forwarded letters by mail, sometimes written in invisible ink. Ritter spent a few days in New York between 1937 and 1939. On 29 October 1937, he obtained a visitor's visa to return to the United States. On 11 November 1937, he entered the United States on a temporary non-immigration visa via the SS *Europa*, at which time he gave his destination as in the care of Colonel Ullrich

Thompson at 130 Washington Avenue, Hastings, New York. His intention was to stay there until 27 December 1937. His occupation given on the visa was that of an engineer, although at that time he was actually an army officer.

He stated that he intended to live in Germany and was visiting the US to arrange business matters there. He gave Colonel Thompson as a reference.

Ritter was also required to submit a letter from his wife, who wrote that on 29 October 1937 her husband intended to visit the United States on business and pleasure, and intended to return to Germany before Christmas. She stated that she was remaining in Germany and that 'to the best of my knowledge, my husband is not connected to any subservient movement and is not a member of the National Socialistic Party'.[27]

The FBI reported that a 'Nicolous [*sic*] Ritter' left the United States on 16 December 1937 from the port of New York, his destination being Verden, Germany, with an indication that he was going to make his permanent residence in Germany.

In the summer of 1938, Ritter expressed dissatisfaction with the work of his organization in America and proposed that one of his agents should travel there to set up a new information service and to convey a code to the chief of the existing network.

At this time it dawned upon Ritter that being married to a foreigner would not sit comfortably with the Nazi hierarchy. He caught the eye of one of his clerical assistants, 22-year-old Irmgard von Klitzing, whose lineage appealed to Ritter's self-aggrandizement, plus she was a member of the Nazi Party. 'He looked so American ... shook hands with everybody ... raced through the hallway in his light-coloured raincoat and frightfully bright-grey Stetson hat,'[28] she cooed. His marriage was doomed.

Nikolaus and Mary divorced in Hamburg in 1938. Mary had custody of the children but Ritter was permitted to see them when on leave, and had temporary custody during the summer months. Ritter and Irmgard married in Hamburg in 1939 and they had one child, Karin.

After the divorce, Mary obtained employment at the American Consulate in Hamburg, but Ritter later indicated that this had no significance as far as his Abwehr activities were concerned. Furthermore, he frustrated his ex-wife's attempts to return to America.

Mary was privy to her husband's covert affairs. She stated that on his last trip to the United States, he visited all the important airplane factories there, where he was aided by his perfect knowledge of English. She added that his sole reason for going to the United States was to visit the agents planted in such factories, and that he was the contact man for his service in Hamburg and Bremen.

As a senior member of German Air Intelligence, Major Ritter was charged with the task of sending spies to Britain, although he had the tendency to be something of a 'Walter Mitty' character. For example, he claimed to have escaped from a tight spot by stealing a biplane from a US military airfield and flying it to Mexico.

He was also reported as saying, 'I got a note from Canaris telling me that I was one of his best officers. All he could say was that I was better than excellent.'[29] Ritter appeared to have a passion for the epithet 'doctor', as can be seen from his contact names: Doktor Rantzau, Dr Renken, Dr Weber, Dr Rheinhardt, Dr Leonhardt or Dr Jantzen.

Oberleutnant Walter Henry Praetorius (alias Walter Thomas), Abwehr officer:
Ritter, needing a 'talent scout', gave the job to SS-Oberleutnant Walter Praetorius, also known as 'The Pied Piper'[30] (for his past success in recruiting agents), to search for, find and quickly train the renegades needed to initiate a successful invasion. Ritter had set quite a narrow limit on the people he wanted for the mission: individuals who were English-speaking, aged between 20 and 30, charming, of good physical health and possessing some technical knowledge. It was not an easy task.

However, Praetorius' recruiting talents did not always bode well. He vouched for a Sudetenlander who was a trained agent, although several officers considered this agent hopeless and not apt for the task. Praetorius intervened, got his way, and the agent was later dropped over England. But he never worked his wireless and was soon picked up by the British.

Praetorius was born in Warsaw on 25 June 1911, and was of Russian nationality until his father's naturalization in Berlin in 1920. He was the holder of a German passport, issued in Berlin on 11 May 1932.

He was 5ft 9in, had straight fair hair, coarse blue eyes and a very fresh complexion. Of medium build, he spoke German and English and had a high-pitched voice.

It is believed that his family's experience in Russia inclined them to readily sympathize with the anti-communist tendencies of the Nazi Party, of which Praetorius was a member. Praetorius himself was a committed and dedicated Nazi politically, but also a confirmed Anglophile due to his lineage, his mother being of Scots origin.

His maternal great-grandfather had been a Scottish flax merchant who emigrated from Dundee to Riga and married a German woman. Praetorius was fiercely proud of his British roots and liked to remind anyone who would listen that he was a scion of the 'Chiefly line of Clan McThomas'.[31]

As a student at Berlin University, the young Praetorius wanted to become a teacher. He landed at Harwich in Essex on 29 September 1933 and a month later, on a German state scholarship, the 22-year-old spent a year at Southampton University as part of an Anglo-German exchange scheme. He was, in fact, the last German student at Southampton University not appointed by the Nazi Government. At the university, Praetorius registered as 'Walter Henry', but in his alien's registration he was recorded simply as 'Walter'.

Praetorius was nicknamed 'Rusty' by his fellow students due to the reddish tinge to his receding hair. He played the flute, rowed for the university and sported the clothes and airs of an English gentleman. He learned the reels and sword dances from his Scottish heritage, 'but above all he fell in love with Morris dancing'.[32] He cycled around England photographing folk dances and analysing the dance steps. After months of careful study, he pronounced Morris dancing to be the root of all dancing in the world and hence a foundation of world culture.[33]

He spoke English fluently and without an accent, no doubt due to his British mother, and was, 'for a German, remarkably well-dressed in British style'.[34] Someone who had considerable contact with him felt that, of all the German students who attended Southampton University, Praetorius could most easily pass as an Englishman: 'His manners and appearance were pleasant in an English fashion.'[35]

He was very friendly with an Englishman who visited Praetorius' home in Germany, and may have had knowledge of his Scottish relatives. This man was Kenneth Cottam, who would later become a captain in the Intelligence Corps.

On 28 August 1934, Praetorius returned to Germany from Dundee, where he had visited relatives.

It was reported that Praetorius' mother was a 'rabid Nazi', and the young Praetorius embraced his mother's beliefs. He was an idealist type of Nazi and embraced the Nazi ideology, especially regarding the superiority of the German and Anglo-Saxon races over all others.

Upon his return to Germany, Praetorius' passion for folk dancing was usurped by an even greater passion for fascism. His beliefs, however, may well have been fuelled by personal factors: living abroad and the death of his brother Hans in Poland during the early years of the war only increased his fervour for the party, and he became a committed, unquestioning Nazi.

With the Nazi occupation of much of Europe, there was a plentiful supply of potential agents. Praetorius began his recruiting task in Belgium and Holland, an obvious starting point; refugees from these occupied countries were constantly travelling to Britain, where the British authorities would not be suspicious of such sudden arrivals. The Abwehr tried to focus on young men who were physically fit, daring and exhibited some technical experience, which was vital for using radio transmitters. That was the ideal; the reality was very different. Praetorius drew up a list and gave it to Ritter, who proceeded to choose his favourites. It is fair to say that the agents put forward were low-grade and not overburdened with brains; they had either been blackmailed or attracted to espionage by greed, thrills or a misplaced sense of loyalty.

This book will primarily concentrate on four of the men who were chosen as the very first[36] batch of invasion spies to be successfully sent over the Channel and arrived in wartime Britain: a conspicuous half-Dutch, half-Japanese hotel receptionist who spoke English hesitantly; a German-born Dutchman who spoke English with an American accent; an unemployed ex-Dutch Army ambulance driver who, by his own admission, spoke less than perfect English; and a German, brought up as a Frenchman, who spoke no English at all. They were, respectively, Charles Albert van den Kieboom, Carl Heinrich Cornelius Meier, Sjoerd Pons and Jose Rudolf Waldberg, collectively known by MI5 as the 'Brussels Four'.

Chapter Two

The Brussels Four

Charles Albert van den Kieboom (Dutch); spy-name 'Kirche'

Charles Albert van den Kieboom was born in Takarazuka, Japan, on 6 September 1914, to a Dutch father and Japanese mother. His mother died when he was an infant and he was subsequently educated at an English Mission School in Japan, where he spoke mainly English.

He arrived in Belgium with his father in 1927, and was sent to a boarding school in Boom, near Antwerp, where he learned to speak French, German and Dutch. Despite speaking English well, he claimed to only understand it if spoken slowly; he also professed to know very little Japanese in spite of spending the first thirteen years of his life in Japan.

In 1932, his father was unable to continue to pay for his son's education and so returned to Japan, leaving Charles in the care of friends. Kieboom was sent to Hilversum, to an acquaintance of his father named Mieuwenhuys, a director of Van Ommeren, Rotterdam. Kieboom was then sent to Finland and worked for the Java–China–Japan shipping line.

He then began work as a lift-boy at the Carlton Hotel in Amsterdam, and later became a reception clerk and telephone operator. During his time at the hotel, he made the acquaintance of a man named Punsley, a former British agent in Holland.

In 1933/34, Kieboom was conscripted into the Dutch Army with the 7th Dutch Infantry Regiment at Harderwijk. He served for nine months, attaining the rank of sergeant.

The following year, after his conscription ended, he was taken on at the Victoria Hotel, Amsterdam, as a junior reception clerk. The hotel was known to be closely associated with the activities of the German Nachrichtendienst (Intelligence Agency). Kieboom knew the Victoria to be a 'German hotel'.

During 1936, Kieboom lost his job at the Victoria and returned to the Carlton Hotel, where he stayed for six months. He was then asked to go back to the Victoria as a reception clerk at a monthly salary of 100 Fl (Guilders), plus a weekly average of 30 Fl for 'perks', but no tips. He stayed there until 1939, when he found himself unemployed after being caught embezzling money. He then went to work for a short period as a clerk in a church hostel. It is clear that in the years leading to the outbreak of the Second World War, the mild-mannered

Kieboom led a somewhat unsettled life. This was emphasized when, in August or September that year, he was again called up for military service, this time with the second company of the 6th Motor Transport (Red Cross) Battalion at Zeist. Here he met and served with Sjoerd Pons, a future compatriot and spy.

In June 1940, with Holland having capitulated to the Germans, demobilization loomed for Kieboom. He was given the choice of remaining in the service and being incorporated into the Opbouwdienst (something like the Arbeitsdienst, the Reich Labour Service) or returning to civilian life. He chose the latter, and went to live with friends in Amsterdam. Kieboom applied for a job to a former porter, who was now director at the Victoria Hotel, but to no avail.

Unable to find employment, Kieboom learned that the Germans were offering work to Dutchmen as drivers, apparently transporting the wounded and refugees in France and Belgium. He volunteered, gave his name but heard nothing for some time.

Around 20 July he was approached by a Dutchman, or at least a man who spoke fluent Dutch, who did not give his name. He professed to come from Kieboom's late company commander, and to be acting as a go-between on the instructions of a German colonel named Meyer, also known as Kurt Mirow, to join the German Secret Service, ostensibly as a chauffeur, but more likely to conduct English translation. However, at this stage it was not made clear just what was expected of him. Kieboom was somewhat menacingly informed that they knew everything about him. Kieboom said he would be willing under certain circumstances, and when the Germans told him that he would be employed in an office in Brussels, he readily, if naively, accepted.

Two days later, Colonel Meyer took Kieboom to dinner at the Victoria Hotel. After sizing him up, Meyer formally offered Kieboom (and Sjoerd Pons) employment in Brussels. After learning the true nature of the work, Kieboom initially declined. Meyer told him that the German authorities knew he had smuggled money out of Germany, and he was thus given a choice: accept the job or be sent to a concentration camp for currency offences. Since 1936, the penalty for smuggling was death.[1] He was told to forget about escape, as he knew too much dangerous information and would not be allowed to go scot-free. Fearing for his future, he relented and chose to work for the Germans. Both he and Pons were taken to Brussels on 26 July.

When questioned, Kieboom maintained never to have been a member of the National Socialist Party or of any youth movement; he was 'interested only in motor cycling'.[2]

In his private life he was engaged to a Miss Bien de Vries, a Dutch subject, aged about 29, who lived in Amsterdam and was fully aware of her fiancé's work with the Germans.

As if to reinforce how naive he was, Kieboom had previously had contact with a Polish Jew by the name of Bach, who allegedly tricked him into advancing him 300 Fl from hotel funds, after which Bach disappeared and Kieboom had to pay back 10 Fl a month out of his sergeant's monthly salary of 90 Fl. When the German invasion of Holland began, Kieboom claimed he had already paid back 170 Fl. When Bach was subsequently arrested, none of the money was found on him.

Another contact of Kieboom's was a Michael Holzmann, who stayed for long periods at the Victoria Hotel, spending large sums on cars, clothing and hotel bills. He was said to have been interested in gun-running in Spain through a centre in Paris.

There was also a 45-year-old Frenchman named Letellier, said to be a 'shady' friend of Holzmann's, and a 'Potato' Jones, whom Kieboom recollected as having stayed at the Victoria.

Finally, there was Miss Petersen, a hairdresser at the hotel who was frequently absent from duty. She had many regular visitors, but she pretended not to know any of their names.

Carl Heinrich Cornelius Ernst Meier (Dutch); spy-name 'Milch'

Carl Meier was born on 18 October 1916 in Koblenz, Germany, to a German father and Dutch mother. After his father died in 1921, he was taken by his mother, who regained her Dutch nationality, to Holland, where Carl was educated and automatically naturalized as Dutch.

Cultured and educated, Meier was 6ft 2in tall, weighed 12st 7lb and had blond hair and blue eyes; pretty much an ideal Aryan type in the eyes of the Nazis, except that he lost some height due to a pronounced stoop.

Meier was educated in Holland until his 17th birthday, considered himself 'a thoroughbred Dutchman and didn't feel German in the least'.[3] For five years he studied at a school in Flushing, improving and polishing his English.

Meier's mother remarried a W.C.F.A. van Waltmeyer, who was said by Meier himself to have been an enthusiastic admirer of the German Army. Meier's new stepfather was a captain of the Maréchaussée (Dutch military police) and a district commandant at Maastricht from 1935, having formerly served at Flushing.

After a round-trip to America in 1934 on the freighter *Delfshaven*, owned by a Rotterdam firm, Meier said that it was his 'sincerest wish' to return to the United States and, if possible, stay there. Meier was related to certain members of the freighter company, whom he claimed were anti-Nazi, although admitting he knew very little of them.

Meier was smitten with America; he loved the feeling of freedom, space and the opportunities for wealth. He would later recount, 'The wide open spaces got to me … there is nothing to compare with the Midwestern corn fields when they're ripe. America is my country as it has my heart and I'd never allow anyone to slight it.'[4]

Meier inherited money from his father and grandfather (who was also German), which was held in trust for him by his uncle, Karl Ernst Meier of Freiburg, to pay for his studies in German universities. This enabled him to enrol as a medical student at Freiburg University in autumn 1934 upon his return from his freighter journey. He chose Germany to study because part of the family inheritance had gone to Holland, where his mother gained access to it. She was not financially astute and lost most of the money when the global financial market crashed in 1929. However, the German side of his inheritance thrived under the watchful eye of his uncle, and was given to Meier as and when he should need it.

It was at medical school in Frieburg, in 1936, that Meier met his future fiancée, Margaret Moseley, a 23-year-old American exchange-student. According to a statement from Meier, 'since 1936 we know each other and inofficially [sic] she's my fiancée. I use "inofficially" because although I've always received encouragement from her parents my finances do not allow an official engagement. Although we promised to marry each other, we could of course, not name a date for the marriage to take place.'[5]

Meier was described by a fellow student as 'irresponsible, easy-going and rather a weak character, but very good-natured and quite intelligent. Everybody liked him and he got on equally well with Dutch, American and German students.'[6] The student lived in the same Berlin hostel as Meier between April and July 1937.

The student also stated that Meier spent a fair amount of free time in his and Margaret Moseley's company. Meier got on well with people irrespective of their nationality or background. He was a great admirer of all things American and spoke English with a strong American accent; he was happy to be mistaken for an American, something that often happened. He displayed neither pro-Nazi nor anti-British feelings, though his student friend reported that there were several violently anti-British students in the hostel, including Boers. It appeared, however, that Meier took no active part in any of their discussions. He regarded himself as an American and therefore detached from any problem, political or otherwise, which did not concern America.

In spring 1937, he continued his medical studies in Berlin after following Margaret there. When she returned to America later that year, Meier stayed in Berlin. He did not have enough money to complete his studies, so he applied for an immigration visa to the USA in the summer of 1938. He was so sure that he would get on the Dutch quota that he arranged everything for his departure, including buying his ticket for the passage. However, in Rotterdam he learned that he could not get on the quota as he was born in Germany. Up until he was 5 he had German nationality, even though he had been educated until the age of 17 in Holland and he considered himself a 'thoroughbred' Dutchman, not German in the least. Indeed, he would later say, 'the German disregard for other nations' achievements, the boorish manner in which they gave expression to their contempt for other people but Germans, have irked me always and from time to time I've downright hated them.'[7]

Eventually he obtained an affidavit from Margaret Moseley's father, but then Meier realized that he needed to get on the German quota to obtain his visa and that he required the affidavit of a relative. Meier was in despair, believing his dream of moving to America was over.

He became tired of Berlin and its atmosphere, moving to Innsbruck in Austria, where, on 8 November, he was issued with a passport. In February 1939, in desperation, he applied for a visitor's visa to the US, which he got immediately as Mr Moseley had sent Meier an affidavit to go to America as a visitor.

After arriving in America, he lived off the money he got out of Germany and by selling German cameras and binoculars to Americans. During the six months he was allowed to stay in the States, he spent his time productively. He managed to get a half-scholarship for the spring-quarter at the University of Chicago, believing that training for a degree in economics would help him go into business with Mr Moseley and get a job.[8] The next step, he planned, would be to get married, as having a job as well as being married to an American would enhance the chances of his dream of US citizenship.

Perhaps out of desperation and to bolster his American citizenship, Meier visited the US Army offices in Chicago in June 1939 and enquired whether he could enlist as a volunteer. He was accompanied by a Chicago-based friend of his, a Belgian named de Roover. Meier was unsuccessful, the reason given being that 'they don't take foreigners'.[9]

By July, Meier had everything ready to change his visitor status to that of a student, which would allow him to work his way through college. However, in the middle of July, Meier received a postcard from his mother, which had initially been sent to her from the American Consulate in Rotterdam, telling him to appear before them at the end of the month. He went to the immigration office in Chicago, showed them the postcard, and they advised him to change his plans and go to Rotterdam, as his immigration visa was waiting for him there.

Meier immediately returned to Europe. When he arrived in Hamburg, however, he decided not to go straight to Holland but to 'see something of Europe before I'd leave it forever'.[10] He rented a car with an American he'd met on the boat from the US. They took a trip through Germany and Austria, and in Innsbruck he went to see the Dutch Consul, Mr Eigl, to get a paper stating his good conduct during his time in the city. He would need that for the American Consulate, as 'they require such papers over the last five years in threefold'.[11]

Meier eventually reached Holland in September 1939. Having known he couldn't get to the consulate for the appointed date, he had written to them whilst in America. When Meier finally arrived at the American Consulate, he discovered that applying for his visitor's visa had automatically cancelled his application for immigration; he would have to start all over again. He was told that this would take approximately eight years, unless he could get on the preference quota. He would have been distraught. What didn't help his American cause was that with war having broken out, Meier was medically examined for military service in early October 1939 but was deemed unfit.

He decided taking regular work might help his cause, and on 11 October 1939 he became a clerk in the Dutch Government Food Control Department in Bezuidenhout, The Hague. His thinking was that if he worked hard for a year, he might be able to start in business, make enough money to marry and get on the preference quota that way. Fate, however, had other ideas.

On Friday, 10 May 1940, German troops invaded the Netherlands, ending Meier's hopes of getting out of the country. With the Nazis sweeping to victory in France and the Low Countries, Meier thought the best thing he could do was to play the 'good German'.[12]

Meanwhile, working at the same desk as Meier in the Food Control Department was a member of the NSNAP (Nationaal-Socialistische Nederlandsche Arbeiders-Partij, the Dutch Nazi Party), a man called Koos Vorrink. The NSNAP had been in existence for five years, although its activities had been suspended by the Netherlands Government. When Holland was invaded, the party sprang back into life, favouring strong links with Germany. However, the NSNAP was not under the wing of any member of the Nazi Party, nor was it financed from Germany.

Vorrink knew of Meier's weakness for the US. He also knew that Meier had been in Germany, and Vorrink himself had recently been in Berlin. Having common ground to talk about, their chats became more intimate, both men complaining about the low wages at the Food Control Department.

Attempting to get Meier to work for Germany, Vorrink told him of the good jobs he might get with the Germans, 'a life-position in store for me and all that stuff'.[13] Vorrink then told him what the work was: 'Go to England by plane, land by parachute and send messages by radio.'[14] Meier was told that his chances of getting such a job would be enhanced if he became a member of the party, and he should meet the group leader. He was all for it, seeing it as an opportunity to get away.

Meier joined the NSNAP, and even signed up for the SA (Sturmabteilung, the German Storm Troopers or Brown Shirts). In a confused way, Meier thought that his membership of the NSNAP might help him eventually reach America.

On Wednesday, 19 June 1940, Meier visited Maastricht by bicycle and learned that his stepfather, Waltmeyer, had been arrested; he was released three days later. Meier also heard from his mother that the Germans had taken to Germany the British Vice Consul for Maastricht, a Mr Driessen, and the Belgian Consul, a man named Hustinx.

On Saturday, 13 July, Vorrink introduced Meier to Goyvaerts, The Hague Group Leader of the NSNAP and liaison for the German Secret Service. Goyvaerts, a Dutch national of Belgian origin, spoke Dutch, German and probably French.

On Friday, 26 July, Goyvaerts invited Meier to spend the evening at his flat in The Hague and suggested that he work for Germany, in a job requiring knowledge of English and involving some risk. It would mean learning Morse code and listening in to radio messages, perhaps in France. Meier readily accepted the offer.

The following day, Meier met Vorrink, who said that he too had been approached, but had refused because he suspected that the volunteers would be sent to England with wireless transmitting apparatus.

On Sunday, 28 July, Meier again visited Goyvaert's flat. Also there were Goyvaert's wife, a man named de Vreede – a 19-year-old American from New York – and Klein Nagelvoort from The Hague. The latter two had been recruited for their knowledge of English, and both lived in the HTO building, Rijswijkseweg, The Hague. De Vreede had been sent to Holland for commercial training by his father, who was in the flower bulb business in the US. He spoke English and Dutch, had no real Nazi sympathies and was a Theosophist, a mystical line of thought not appreciated in Nazi Germany. Nagelvoort was a lawyer by profession, and was also a member of the NSNAP.

Meier, de Vreede and Nagelvoort were introduced to Kapitan Mirow, a German 'talent scout', and his assistant, Dr Erfurt, who was there for his knowledge of Dutch. Kurt Mirow wore a Rittmeister's uniform, that of a commissioned cavalry officer, and he sported a 1939 Iron Cross.

Mirow repeated Goyvaert's original enquiry as to whether Meier would work for the German Army, but again nothing specific was said, save that again it would be a risky job which would involve learning how to use Morse code and listening in to messages. When asked whether he was afraid of flying, Meier replied 'No', but admitted to being air-sick once. Meier thought that it was an interesting proposal, and again he agreed to accept the work.

Vorrink refused a similar offer, as the job involved speaking English as well as learning Morse code. Not realizing what the work would entail, Meier said, 'You want me to go to England and send information by radio?' Goyvaerts confirmed that was the case. At this stage, monetary payment for the venture had not been offered; despite that, Meier was still interested.

On Tuesday, 30 July, Meier, de Vreede and Mirow left for Brussels in a small orange 1938 car, possibly an Opel. The others followed over the next two days, as they could not get a bigger vehicle.

Passports were made ready so they could cross the Belgian frontier. They stopped twice on the way to Brussels, once at Breda and again at the frontier.

Meier's connection with the Germans simply came about because they were looking for people in The Hague who were willing to take on several kinds of risky jobs, which included going to England to perform acts of sabotage or to spy by means of a small radio transmitter. Now Meier was told that he would be 'well paid' for the daring undertaking, or so he was promised.

Sjoerd Pons (Dutch); spy-name 'Pleite'

Sjoerd Pons was born 5 June 1912 in Amsterdam, of Dutch parents. He learnt English at school in Amsterdam but, by his own admission, 'There are many faults in it'.[15] Pons was 5ft 10in tall, with brown hair, grey/blue eyes, pale complexion and weighed 12st.

He worked for his father, as a commercial traveller in the building trade – registered with the Amsterdam Chamber of Commerce – and, prior to the outbreak of war, visited Belgium, France and French Morocco on business. There is evidence of him visiting Germany, apparently for the purpose of smuggling money and jewellery into Holland. On one occasion, he was involved in the smuggling of stones and gold from a garage in Köln (Cologne). Pons received instructions by post to meet a man at Köln Cathedral, and was to be recognized by his car. Then a large, clean-shaven man with dark hair handed him a parcel to deliver. Payment was upon delivery. Pons made at least three such smuggling trips.

Pons was a member of the Nationalist Socialist Dutch Workers Party (NSNAP), and expressed anti-Semitic views as well as admiration for German efficiency. He was conscripted into the Dutch Fifth Regiment of Infantry in 1933, and in 1939 was again called up for military service, serving with the 3rd Lichte Verbandplaats Afd Red Cross at Zeist, achieving the rank of sergeant.

He married, early in 1940, a 24-year-old Dutch woman, Katherina van Slingerlandt. They had no children.

During the night of 9/10 May 1940, he was transferred to the Central Red Cross Depot at Driebergen. He went from there to Bodegraven in southern

Holland. As a Red Cross man, Pons did not see much fighting during the German invasion. It was while doing military service that he first met Charles Albert van den Kieboom, who tried to help Pons speak English.

On Friday, 14 June, Pons was demobilized and returned to Amsterdam to try to take up his old business. A month later, on 15 July, he was visited by an anonymous Dutch-speaking man who said, 'You are Sjoerd Pons', before asking him several questions and threatening him with the consequences of his smuggling jewellery and currency from Germany to Holland if he did not work for Germany or go to England as a spy. Pons knew that the penalty for smuggling from Germany was death.

The mystery man knew a lot about Pons; where he served, which company and battalion he was in. Pons believed that he was betrayed by someone he knew in the Dutch Army, as he used to speak to Kieboom about things and thought they may have overheard. The mystery man said to Pons, 'We have a job for you to do. If you are willing to do it perhaps we will forget what you have done against Germany.' Pons was then asked if he spoke English, to which he replied, 'Yes, I understand English but I do not speak very well English.'[16]

He was told the job was something to do with translations and that he would have to go to Brussels. Pons, concerned about leaving his wife, was reassured that he could return home every three months. He agreed to the work, and a few days later he was taken, along with his friend Kieboom, to the Victoria Hotel in Amsterdam, where they were met by a German Rittmeister.

Both men were taken to Brussels after they agreed to go to England. Pons lodged in the city in Rue Gretry, before they were sent to Rue Stevin, 4 for military training. At this point, Pons had no experience at all of spying or intelligence work.

Jose Rudolf Waldberg (German); also known as Dubois and Henri Lassudry); spy-name 'Dubois'

Born on 15 July 1918 in Mainz, Germany, Jose Waldberg had a German father and French mother. Waldberg's father, Heinrich, who was a courier between embassies in Berlin and Paris, died in 1935. His mother, Maria, remarried a Frenchman named Dubois. Waldberg was brought up as a Frenchman in Strassbourg, Pontoise, Lille, Mobeuge and Sedan. He attended a private boarding school near Paris between 1926 and 1935. He spoke fluent but uneducated French and managed some German with a strong dialect, but virtually no English. He would later describe himself as 'a German citizen but rather more of a Frenchman'.[17]

Soon after his father's death, a certain Edmund Mueller – also known as 'Mr Edmund' – a friend of his father, took Waldberg from school to St Julien in Doubs, eastern France, where he lived with his mother for about a year. In either 1936 or 1937, a stranger arrived at St Julien with a special police order to take both mother and son back to Germany. Waldberg thought this order might have been due to anti-Nazi sentiments expressed by his mother. She refused to go, but Waldberg was taken to Wiesbaden, where he was questioned by the police for three days.

He was sent back to St Julien to persuade his mother to return to Germany, but she would not change her mind. In May 1937, Waldberg was taken back to Wiesbaden, this time by a man named Müller. He received brief instruction on industrial espionage before being told to return to France to work for Germany, collecting information on factories and the political situation. He was allotted the Paris, Oise and Seine districts, and his pay was fixed at 10 Marks a day, but in addition he drew on Müller for considerable sums. He was also provided with false papers as a French citizen.

Waldberg remained in France in this capacity from July 1937 until 4 April 1938, when he received an unsigned letter summoning him to return to Wiesbaden.

Remaining there from April 1938 until June 1939, Waldberg acted as an office messenger, delivering incoming coded telegrams, and was given general instruction in matters such as the English and French road systems. The staff at Wiesbaden numbered between 400 and 500, under the command of a general, but Waldberg was never allowed to set foot in the offices of the senior officers.

Waldberg's various accounts of the SS at Wiesbaden were inconsistent at best, nebulous at worst. According to Waldberg's recollections, some officers appeared to belong to more than one section:

General Kuhn	Hitlerstrasse, 8 Wiesbaden: Head of Centre.

<u>Section I</u>	
Oberleutnant Werner	Co-ordinated and directed work of the
Alias WERNER UHLN	entire centre. Various sections were
Oberleutnant Weber	independent of each other but some
alias ROSY/	were subordinate to Section I. The
DUVREUIL	higher staff communicated with each other
Werner's deputy	in writing or under cover
	of sobriquets: for example, Weber had the
	alias of Rosy and Duvreuil.
	The senior lieutenant of each section was
	an ex-officio member.

Oberleutnant Paul Koch	Formerly of Java, San Sebastian and Britain, where he worked in a hotel. He had three sets of papers in different names. Waldberg thought Koch would be dropped by parachute into Norfolk or Suffolk.

Section II

Colonel Meyer (titular head) alias REUYE	Recruited, trained and despatched agents to Britain. Interested in economic and military questions.
Major Seynsburg	Effective head.
Werner	Women members reported to Werner.

Section III

This section dealt with countries with German minorities – Poland, Austria, Czechoslovakia, etc.

The other sections dealt with anti-Russian activities and the Ukraine.

According to Waldberg, the sections were based in various locations. The central head office was in Wiesbaden, while Brussels was responsible for all occupied countries and Cherbourg subordinate to Brussels; Hamburg was possibly just one of the offices in all the major towns.

There was Chateau Wimille, which was a mere 'jumping-off' place: Waldberg said Major Seynsburg was never there, and there was no one there of apparent authority. Paris Plage was Seynsburg's residence. It was a large bungalow with rustic architecture and a large, round garden.

In 1938, Waldberg maintained that Captain Herbert Wichmann was an SS agent. Although he never saw him at Wiesbaden, he heard his name and thought that he may have been at Chateau Wimille.

After initial training at Wiesbaden, where he learnt Morse code, Waldberg was smuggled into France in June 1939, this time to obtain information on war preparations, the political situation and general morale. He was issued with false French papers, but in his own name. He travelled throughout northern France – including Paris, Rouen and Le Havre – in a car, accompanied by a German, being left at each place for two or three days. He was instructed to note the names of boats arriving and leaving, to find out the opinions of people about the looming war and to pick up information as to whether Britain would enter into the conflict. He reported his findings to his German companion, whom he only knew as Hermann. He carried out these and other instructions sent to him until 15 August, when, after a brief holiday, he joined Müller again and went to Brussels. He remained there from 9 September 1939 until 23 August 1940. During this time, he lived at the house of the German Commercial Attaché at Place d'Arrego, and sent reports to Wiesbaden on the state of public opinion in Belgium, also visiting Wetteren, Namur and Charleroi. He also reported regularly at the German Embassy. He received free lodging and 80 Marks a week for this work.

Between 28 March and 12 June 1940, Waldberg was posted as a secretary for the interrogation of French PoW officers at an internment camp at Mainz, reporting to a Major Schmidt. Waldberg never performed any military service in the German Army, nor had he received any military training, but at Mainz he wore a German military uniform with the rank of private, with a small dagger and star on the left sleeve.

It was while at Mainz that Waldberg was told that he was to undertake a special mission for Germany in England. Any disinclination he may have felt for such work was dispelled by the fact that he believed two of his friends at Wiesbaden, Metzger and Wetterhofer, were summarily shot for refusing to go to England.

He returned to Brussels on 14/15 June to begin training for his special mission. He stayed first in the Rue du Consiel and, after trying two guesthouses, stayed with Oberleutnant Koch, whom he believed was a member of Section I at Wiesbaden, in a requisitioned house in Avenue Gribaumont.

Whilst Waldberg was not married, he was attached to a Helene Ceuppens, whom he would later claim was molested by the Gestapo, an inference that she may have been sexually assaulted.

Waldberg was the only one of the four agents about to be sent to England who had any previous experience of spying (in France); he was also a committed Nazi.

Second World War timeline

Friday, 1 September 1939:
Germany invades Poland.
The great evacuation of London schoolchildren begins.
Fearing the worst and in readiness, British Armed Forces are mobilized.

Sunday, 3 September 1939:
Britain declares war on Germany.
A little after 11.15 am, in a live broadcast from Downing Street, the British Prime Minister Neville Chamberlain addresses the British people: 'This morning the British Ambassador in Berlin handed the German Government a final note stating that unless

we heard from them by 11 o'clock that they were prepared to withdraw their troops from Poland, a state of war would exist between us. I have to tell you that no such undertaking has been received and that consequently this country is at war with Germany.'

Wasting little time, Parliament passes the National Services (Armed Forces) Act, which imposes conscription on all males aged between 18 and 41, who have to register for service.

Those medically unfit are exempted, as are key industry workers such as those in baking, farming, medicine and engineering.

Tuesday, 5 September 1939:
The National Registration Act receives Royal Assent.

Friday, 29 September 1939:
National Registration Day: The Government needs to know how many people there are in the UK who need to be fed, so everyone is asked to fill in a form giving details such as name, address, date of birth, sex, marital status and occupation. This is required to be done at 6.30 pm precisely. Servicemen and women are exempt.

Monday, 16 October 1939:
First air raid on Britain: The war, still in its infancy, does not make Scotland immune from enemy action. At 2.30 pm, the Luftwaffe targets ships in the Firth of Forth. Damage is inflicted on HMS *Southampton* (cruiser), HMS *Edinburgh* (light cruiser) and HMS *Mohawk* (Tribal-class destroyer).

Friday, 8 December 1939:
The first Polish pilots reach Britain, arriving at Eastchurch in Kent after their departure from France two days previously.

Saturday, 9 December 1939:
The first British soldier killed in action in Europe is 27-year-old Corporal Thomas Priday, of the King's Shropshire Light Infantry. Corporal Priday died when he stepped on a land mine during a night patrol in France.

Thursday, 4 April 1940:
Lord Woolton is appointed Minister of Food. One of his first jobs is to draft his initial speech, making the following notes:

'He who touches the nation's food is courting trouble. Minister for Food is likely to displease everybody. Nation's Housewife: If it's alright then nothing is said; if it isn't then everything is said.

My plan will be to give security. I don't promise perfection. I promise that I will do all I can to keep you fed during the worst that may come and whilst I wish things are going well we will experiment, try things out, and slowly improve.'

Tuesday, 9 April 1940:
Germany invades Norway and Denmark.

Wednesday, 8 May 1940:
Hitler orders an attack on Holland and Belgium to commence at 5.35 am on 10 May.

Friday, 10 May 1940:
Chamberlain resigns and Winston Churchill is appointed as wartime Prime Minister.

A genuine coalition is formed under Churchill. Two out of five members of the War Cabinet are Labour politicians, one is National and two are Conservatives. Domestic political fighting is put on hold and all three parties strive to work together with the common aim of defeating Nazi Germany.

At 1 pm, a meeting of the War Cabinet is held in the First Lord's Room in the Admiralty. Churchill invites attention to a Belgian proposal which had been addressed to the French and British Governments for the issue of an announcement that the bombing of open towns in Belgium would be regarded as if open towns in France and England were being bombed. This reserves the right to take any action that is considered appropriate in the event of bombing by the enemy of civil populations, whether in France, the United Kingdom or in countries assisted by France.

At 6.30 pm, a further meeting of the War Cabinet is held, with Oliver G. Stanley, MP, Secretary of State for War, in the Chair.

Members are informed that the Commander-in-Chief, the Nore (covering the East Coast), has asked that the existing scheme for the evacuation of children and expectant mothers from Sheerness, Rochester, Chatham and Gillingham be carried out forthwith; and immediate consideration should be given to the evacuation of the aged and invalids from these towns. The evacuation would not only be in the interests of those affected, but would also help create sufficient air-raid shelter accommodation for the rest of the population.

Germany invades France and the Low Countries. At 5.35 am, two Army Groups under Colonel Generals von Rundstedt and von Bock launch the attack. It is their mission, along the entire front from the River Moselle to the North Sea, to break through enemy lines along the frontier; to occupy the Netherlands; to move against Antwerp and the troops stationed at Dyle; to take Liege; and above all, to reach the left flank along the River Meuse with massive forces for the attack, to force a crossing between Namur and Carignan, with a main thrust of the tank and motorized divisions at Sedan, and to push onward, along the system of canals and rivers between the Aisne and the Somme, to the sea.

Saturday, 11 May 1940:
Former Prime Minister Neville Chamberlain is appointed Lord President of the Council; Clement Attlee is appointed Lord Privy Seal; Arthur Greenwood is appointed Minister without Portfolio. All three men are members of the War Cabinet.

Wednesday, 15 May 1940:
Holland surrenders.

Monday, 27 May 1940:
7pm, 10 Downing Street. A meeting of Ministers and Chiefs of Staff hear from the Prime Minister of the critical and desperate situation facing the British Expeditionary Force in France and the Low Countries. Their only choice is to force their way back to the port of Dunkirk. Army stores now accumulated at Le Havre, particularly guns and ammunition, are to be got back to England as rapidly as possible, while the Advance Air Striking Force was to be moved back to the Le Mans area as soon as possible.

Operation *Dynamo* – the codename given to evacuating the British, French and Belgian forces from the beaches at Dunkirk – swings into action.

Tuesday, 28 May 1940:
Belgium capitulates.

Thursday, 30 May 1940:
A meeting of Ministers and Chiefs of Staff at the Admiralty is told that strenuous efforts are being made on the beaches east of Dunkirk. The limiting factor is small craft for getting the men from the beaches to the bigger ships. There are, if anything, too many of the latter, and they are forced to remain for long periods in danger off the coast, waiting for their capacity to be filled.

Tuesday, 4 June 1940:
The call for smaller ships results in hundreds of such craft helping to evacuate the bulk of the BEF, plus some French units (some 338,000 men in total), from Dunkirk and back to Britain. John Edward Atkins, aged 15, from Gravesend, Kent, a cook and third mate on *Lady Rosemary*, a Thames sailing barge, is thought to be the youngest Briton to die during the evacuation.

Monday, 10 June 1940:
Norway surrenders; Italy declares war on Britain and France.

Friday, 14 June 1940:
German forces take control of Paris.

Chapter Three

Shaking Hands with the Devil

Sunday, 16 June 1940:
France surrenders to Germany. Despite pleas from both France and Britain, the US Congress continues to refuse to intervene in Europe, with some legislators going so far as to suggest that England surrender to Hitler.

The decision is made to evacuate the remaining BEF from ports in north-western France: some 136,963 British and 38,500 Allied troops are transported across the English Channel.

Waldberg was the first of the spies-in-training to arrive in Brussels. He was initially taken to Rue du Conseil before being taken to an empty house at 36 Avenue Gribaumont. Here he was in the company of Oberleutnant Koch, a German SS officer whom he first met at Wiesbaden. Waldberg occasionally had to report to the Belgian Ministry Ravitaillement, at 63 Rue de la Loi, where the German main offices for the SS were situated. No 48 Rue Josef II and Rue Stevin, 4, an empty red brick house, were the main training centres for German agents. Rue Stevin became the establishment for the training of spies who were to be sent to England.

Sunday, 30 June 1940:
German troops occupy Guernsey.

Friday, 26 July 1940:
At 11.30 am, during a meeting of the War Cabinet and Defence Committee (Operations) in the Upper War Room at the Admiralty, the Prime Minister discusses the action which should be taken to improve the system of protection for Channel convoys against air attack. The previous day, the convoys experienced a large number of casualties, which were not sustainable. Air Chief Marshal Sir Hugh Dowding, Air Officer Commanding, Fighter Command, says the problem is the strength of the enemy formations attacking the convoys. At times there are more than 100 aircraft over the Channel – RAF fighters are kept busy engaging enemy fighters, so the bombers often have a comparatively straightforward task.

After much discussion it is agreed that the Naval Staff, in consultation with the Air Staff, Ministry of Transport and Ministry of Shipping, should work out the traffic which could be passed through the Channel on the basis of one convoy every six days – the convoys not to be unduly large, and to sail as a tactical operation with the best protection that could be provided.

Kieboom and Pons arrived together in Brussels and were lodged at Rue Grétry. They were told to report every morning for a month to the training centre at Rue Stevin to study Morse code, and for military training, in a top-floor room. The place was empty save for a few chairs, tables and shake-down beds.

Meier arrived in Brussels on Wednesday, 31 July, the last of the four to arrive in the Belgian capital. He stayed at the Hotel Metropole before being moved to the Hotel Les Ambassadeurs. The men were to be lavishly entertained for two weeks. It was during this time that Meier met two further spies: Robert Heidenreich and Hoogeboom (Christian name unknown).

Heidenreich was officially joint manager of a large garage in Amsterdam. In his late 30s, he was 5ft 9in tall, with a 'normal' figure, brown eyes, hair that was smoothed and greying with a parting on one side and clean-shaven, revealing an oval face. He was well dressed, often in brown. Unusually for a would-be spy, he was highly strung. He had visited the Dutch East Indies, and he spoke Dutch, German and French (it is not known whether he spoke English). He lived with a woman who was not his wife, and experienced financial difficulties.

Hoogeboom, an ex-student of the University of Utrecht, was a Dutch national. Aged about 27, he was 6ft tall, of slender build but not thin, with fair hair worn in a mop with a side parting, blue eyes, was clean-shaven and had a long face with a pointed chin and a 'fanatical' expression. He dressed in plus-four suits. He spoke German, Dutch and a smattering of French.

Throughout August, the would-be agents underwent limited training, familiarizing themselves with the south-east of England and 'English ways'. Hoogeboom and Heidenreich were not in Meier's group, but were with Klein Naglevoort.

The training was initially at Rue Stevin. It was here that the Gestapo showed its hand, confronting Meier with his criminal dossier. The document stated that while at Freiburg, Meier was not averse to smuggling money and jewellery out of Germany. He was also reminded that the penalty for smuggling was death. Meier could not deny what the dossier revealed, as he had taken a substantial amount of money out of Germany when he went to the United States. The Gestapo told him that they had overrun Belgium and Holland, and would do the same to England, so it was in his interest to go to England as a spy. After the invasion of Britain, they promised him 'plenty of money and a good job'.

What didn't help Meier's cause was that the Dutch press had recently published an article which stated, 'Conditions in Holland since Germany occupied it can be very unpleasant for any Dutchman who has committed an offence, or what the Germans think of as an offence, against Germany.'

If a man had committed an offence, the Gestapo had the right to waive any prosecution, provided the man did something they wanted him to; what might be described as official blackmail: 'Either you do what we ask you to do or you go to Germany.' This was a veiled threat that the concentration camps awaited anyone falling foul of the Germans, and possibly death.

The men began their training learning Morse code and wireless receiving (no more than forty letters a minute was required) and transmitting (fifty letters a minute) from two soldiers from the Engineer Corps. During training, the instructor, sitting beside the pupil, kept transmitting while they had to take down the messages. They also had to practice sending messages.

Meier, along with Nagelvoort and deVreede, were asked to sign a *Sonderauftrag* (special order/mission) accepting commissions to carry out espionage and sabotage in England. Nagelvoort and de Vreede both refused to sign, and were sent to The Hague and Berlin, respectively, to work for the Germans. Meier, on the other hand, did sign. The paper that he put his signature to simply stated, 'I accept the mission to England.'[1] He would later claim that he added to his signature, 'I am not a confirmed Nazi.'

He was told that by signing the document, there was no way back; should he 'squeal', as they put it, retribution would be rapid as soon as the Germans arrived in England.

Even after signing the *Sonderauftrag*, Meier still received no real clear explanation of what was expected of him. However, it went through his mind that by going to England it might be possible to get from there to his beloved America.

By signing the document, Meier had actually undertaken to go to England and send back information on the food situation and civilian morale in the face of air attacks. When he arrived in England, he was not to 'stir-up revolution' or furnish any military information, thus, ostensibly, avoiding the fatal penalties of spying. It was explained to the men that it would take too long to introduce them into England via another European city, such as Lisbon, in the guise of neutral tourists. Meier was led to believe that the German Army would invade England very soon after his arrival. But they were also told that if they found the population in a state of real panic, the invasion would be unnecessary. After signing the paper, Kapitan Mirow made it very clear to Meier that it would be 'very painful' for him if he now did not go to England. This threat to Meier only came after he had signed the document. However, he was told that he would be well paid.

'Well, how do you mean, well paid?' he asked. 'We will take care that you get a good job afterwards and you will be paid some more; it depends on the work you do,'[2] was the answer. It was payment by results, as far as the German authorities were concerned.

At this stage, neither Kieboom nor Pons, unlike Meier, had signed the *Sonderauftrag*. Despite its exotic-sounding name, the *Sonderauftrag* that Kieboom, in particular, was asked to sign was simply a plain piece of notepaper with 'I accept this mission voluntarily to go to England' written on it. Those men who signed the *Sonderauftrag* had, effectively, shaken hands with the Devil.

Meier was told that his companions had refused to sign the document. Heidenreich, despite his financial problems, found the proposed work so badly remunerated that he refused to sign. Hoogeboom, although strongly sympathetic to the Nazi cause, declined to sign because he felt temperamentally unsuitable for such work.

Meier was not the only one to have had his hand forced. Kieboom found out that the Germans knew all about him, including his past employment, military service, where he was born, how old he was and other similar information. They told him that he would go to Brussels and be employed in an office. Kieboom thought that, due to his knowledge of English, it would probably be a translating job. Before he left Amsterdam for Brussels, he asked his German masters whether the work incorporated working against the English, and whether it was an aggressive form of work, distinct from translating. The Germans assured him with a resounding 'no!'

Even after being in Brussels and being taught to use Morse, Kieboom still thought that he would only listen-in to English radio messages, despite the fact that, over a period of about three weeks, he desperately tried to find out more about his new task but was constantly rebuffed.

When Kieboom again asked for an explanation as to the purpose of the instruction which they received, the matter was referred to Meyer. Kieboom was eventually told by Meyer that he was due to go to England. He immediately refused. A few days later, a German officer he had previously met in Amsterdam proffered options to him: he was told that it was known that he had smuggled currency between Holland and Germany, and if he did not agree to go to England, then he would, to all intents and purposes, be sent to a concentration camp.

Kieboom knew that, since 1936, the penalty in the German Military Code for smuggling was death. He was given time to think it over, but it was made clear that he knew too much already, and it would be useless to try to escape from Brussels. Kieboom was confronted with Hobson's choice: either be sent to a concentration camp or spy for his German masters. Kieboom, not surprisingly, chose to take his chances by going on the mission to England.

Jose Waldberg, despite his relatively small flirtation with the armed forces, and having never performed any military service with the German Army or received any military training, had been given access to German SS Headquarters at Rue de la Loi, Brussels. Part of the organization of this centre was as follows:

Oberleutnant Weber: (alias Rosy, Duvreuil)	Instructor at Rue Joseph – II. Age about 35, approx. 5ft 10in tall, thickset, wore glasses, had fair hair which was cropped very short with a small parting on the left side, grey-green eyes, stern expression, clean-shaven, one gold tooth, reddish face, a very smart upright stance. He spoke English, Dutch and some French. Gave instructions in using secret ink. Rumoured to have English friends in diplomatic circles. Seen by Waldberg at Wiesbaden and Mainz.
Dr Kohler: (alias Dr Kuehn)	Gave general instruction on information required. Worked at Brussels and Chateau Wimille. 5ft 11in tall, age 39, 'kinky' black bristly hair, glasses, bad teeth and very thin. Spoke French. Supplied information as to the composition of the British Army, the various kinds of weapons employed, coached the spies in map reading, particularly of the south coast of England. Supplied the individual pairs' detailed instructions regarding the sending of messages and the kind of information to be supplied.
Oberleutnant Werner Uhln: (alias Werner)	General instructor at Rue Joseph. Waldberg claimed he was the principal assistant to Major Seynsburg, who had visited Chateau Wimille. Age 31, 5ft 9in tall, athletic figure, brown hair brushed back, weather-beaten face, wore glasses. Gave instruction in the use of invisible ink. Spoke French, English, Italian, Spanish and Malay. (Reported to have left Norfolk by air at the end of August or beginning of September 1940).
Kapitan Meyer (alias Kurt Mirow)	Recruiter of agents. Age approx. 50, short grey hair, clean-shaven, round face, 'typically German in appearance'.[3]
Schnacke (alias Schnake)	Morse instructor at Rue Stevin. Age 35–37, height 5ft 11in, athletic and powerful figure, gold-filled teeth on one side of his mouth, black hair, very dark brown eyes, swarthy, married, artisan class, careless dresser and slow mover, spoke French very well.

Schrie (alias Schree)   Morse instructor at Rue Stevin. 5ft 7in tall, thinning
                          hair, clean-shaven, often dressed in brown sports suit,
                          spoke French and German, age≈35.

                          Schrie and later Schnacke gave lessons in Morse
                          and in transmitting messages, for one or two hours a
                          day, in a top-floor room at Rue Stevin. Meier believed
                          that the messages they would send from England
                          would be received in Brussels.

                          Werner gave five or six lessons during the course of
                          a week on the organization of the British Army and the
                          kind of information they were to send from England.
                          Kohler handed out English money to the spies to use
                          after landing and he also informed the agents, as a form
                          of morale-building, that several spies had already gone
                          to England with great success; they 'had experienced
                          no difficulty in landing'.[4]

There was uncertainty in planning and decision-making with the German
authorities. Kapitan Meyer told Meier that he, Meier, would be going to England
as a refugee. The next day, the scheme was abandoned. Suddenly, posing as a
refugee was deemed unworkable.

The men were told that the guard was not strong on the English coast where
they were to land, and that it would be quite possible for them to move about
unhindered without being found. However, this was quite unfeasible when an
invasion was expected to land on the south coast.

Meier was teamed with Waldberg. He was surprized by the suggestion that
his new companion had been in the employ of the German military for two
years. Meier assumed that the reason he had been grouped with Waldberg was
due to Waldberg's ignorance of the English language. Even though Waldberg
had rudimentary experience of military life (at Wiesbaden), they were to be
considered equals; neither was given authority over the other.

Kohler eventually told Meier the kind of information that he was required
to send. Despite previously being informed that he was not required to supply
military information, things had again changed. Kohler now gave Meier
individual instruction on the general organization of the British Army – the
composition of divisions and brigades. Meier was told the Germans needed to
know where battalions were situated and how he would recognize them. He was
also instructed to find out about the economic situation in England, how much
foodstuffs such as butter were available. He was told to go to cafes and listen;
soldiers always talk, so he was to make conversation with them. Furthermore, if
he saw any military vehicles, he was to note their exact number if possible, and

also information about any troops marching through towns, remembering their direction and, if known, their destination. As far as the RAF was concerned, the Germans wanted to know where any new aerodromes were, along with the location and calibre of anti-aircraft guns, and the type and number of aircraft at the airfield.

To sum up, the Germans wanted to know the following:

- the position of reserves;
- new aerodromes;
- number and type of planes;
- anti aircraft defences – fixed or mobile, light or heavy;
- damaged ships in ports, extent of damage and if they are being repaired;
- road mines for certain areas. Also information on the line passing from London through Oxford, Northampton, King's Lynn, Peterborough, Norwich, Ipswich, Colchester and back to London. Kohl particularly wanted details of reserves stationed along the Croydon–Aldershot–Andover–Salisbury line.

They were also interested in troop numbers along the London–Bristol line. This development, the type of information now wanted, put the four men into the realm of being spies, should they be caught.

As to the means of obtaining information, Meier and Waldberg were told to try to ascertain the numbers used by signal corps, which would match the divisional numbers. It was suggested that these numbers might be found by obtaining military notepaper in hotels which had been used by soldiers. Another item of information required was the original letters and numbers of Army cars. It was presumed that these letters and numbers would not be completely obliterated, and this information would indicate which regiment the cars belonged to. The spies were also to listen to conversations between soldiers, though it was not specified how this was to be done. As Waldberg did not understand German, the instructions were subsequently repeated to him in French. As listening to conversations between soldiers in England would have proved somewhat difficult, if not impossible, for the non-English-speaking Waldberg, this task would be left for Meier.

Once that work was completed, Meier and Waldberg were to fall back to Ashford to collect information regarding movements on the Dover–Canterbury–Whitstable railway lines. Kieboom and Pons were to cover the area between Dungeness, Hythe and Folkestone, eventually working to Ashford.

They were all told, possibly for reassurance, 'You don't need to go near the coast, because we know there are troops there; we want to know where the reserves stand though'.[5] This was contradictory to what they had been told earlier – that the guard on the English coast was not strong and they would be able to move about freely without being found.

If no further information could be gleaned, Pons and Kieboom were to get in touch with the German invading force, which was expected in England two weeks after the spies arrived.

Kapitan Meyer issued Kieboom with contact names and addresses in England, should he get into difficulty:

David Bankes-Price	128 Churchill Avenue, Coventry.
Herbert Reynolds Barfoot	Lloyds Building, Leadenhall Street, London.
Arthur Butterworth	11 Leadenhall Street, London.
Alfred Doleman	143 Huddersfield Road, Halifax.
Robert Wade	8 Warren Road, Purley, Surrey & 25 Eastcheap, EC.
Percy Walter Snow	Hillcrest Road, London, SE 26.

There were also some Dutch addresses issued to Kieboom: B. Houwert, Boeht Oosterdiep 21, Veendam, and the somewhat bizarrely named Granny, Kerkstr. 5, Assen. The names came from the books of the Victoria Hotel, Amsterdam, and the addresses were procured later. If he got into difficulties, Kieboom was to use those names and addresses and try to make contact.

There were no German contacts in England. It was deemed unnecessary; the Germans were confident that an invasion would take place a couple of weeks after the 'Brussels Four' had arrived on the south coast of England.

Between August 26 and August 31, Messrs Meier, Waldberg, Pons, Kieboom and another man, Peter Schroeder, left Brussels and were taken to Boulogne.

Peter Schroeder (aka Schneider) was about 21 years old, 5ft 6in tall, broad, strongly built, with dark eyes, black hair brushed back, a pointed nose, broad flat face, big hands and short neck, and he smoked cigarettes. He originated from Malmedy in Belgium. He did not speak English, but spoke French very well and, according to Meier, 'speaks German like a man from Luxembourg'.

The five men were hardly allowed any social intercourse together. All training was taken separately, save for Pons and Kieboom, who already knew one another.

They all arrived at a villa known as Chateau de Wimille to await further orders or a passage to England. The chateau was a large, 15–20 roomed, two-storey mansion of white stone and brick facings, with a dark slate roof and a terrace on one side. This substantial building stood in an isolated position quite close to a secondary road, some distance from the village of Wimille itself.

About 600 yards along this road there was a cafe, which stood by itself and was recognized as the first building in the village. There was no protective barbed wire around the chateau or the grounds, but there was a certain amount of parkland and woodland. The estate had a resident guard that consisted of a Feldwebel (sergeant), two privates and two sailors. In the immediate vicinity of the chateau was a platoon of troops, possibly to furnish the guard.

All water for the chateau was sourced from the River Denacre because the electric pump of the building's artesian well was not functioning. There was a transceiver set up in the garden, which transmitted during daylight hours at irregular times, but not before 8.30 am.

No officer lived at the chateau, but a naval captain, Korvettenkapitan Klapps, came every day and instructed the future spies in the geography of the English coast. Klapps was in his early to mid-40s, 5ft 10in tall and his hair colour was said to be uncertain but definitely not dark. He wore a naval uniform which sported three medal ribbons. Although Klapps knew the English coast well, Pons was of the opinion that this officer had not actually been to England, but had only observed the coast frequently from the sea. He was a Naval Reserve Officer who, before the war, had been in the Merchant Service.

The German SS staff seen at the chateau comprised the following:

Major Seynsburg	Visited the chateau just once while the spies were there.
Korvettenkapitan Klapps	Appeared to be in charge; visited for short periods every day. Did not sleep at the chateau.
Dr Kohler	Instructed the spies on the exact topography of the area where they were to land.
Oberleutnant Werner	
Oberleutnant Weber	Kuhert NCO W/T operator. Operated the wireless set in communication with the Brussels SS station which was believed to be in or near Rue de la Loi. Age 24, 5ft 6in tall, thin, dark parted hair, fair skin, heavy lidded eyes, long thin fingers, long neck.
Hasselbrinck	W/T operator
Schmidt and Siegmann	German sailors

Training at the chateau consisted of short lesson of 20–30 minutes, given by Dr Kohler. Waldberg had some practice in transmitting messages to Rue de la Loi. During the group's week-long stay at the chateau, time was of the essence and all their lessons were very patchy and rudimentary as they tried to fit in as much training as the short timescale allowed.

Meals were not taken at the villa but at the nearby cafe, which was formerly a mill. The men were under constant supervision, with Schroeder and a German naval officer in charge of them.

It was at the cafe that Meier first thought that Waldberg was Swiss. When asked, Waldberg replied, 'Yes, I come from Berne.' When Meier then said that Waldberg should speak German, Waldberg replied, 'I am not from Berne itself but the French-speaking side of the Canton.'

The agents reported being given a good time, where 'money was burned for their entertainment'.[6] The idea was to keep them from brooding about what lay ahead.

Friday, 2 August 1940:
Lord Beaverbrook is appointed Minister of Aircraft Production.

Saturday, 31 August 1940:
Early morning: Hurricanes from No. 56 squadron, operating from North Weald in Essex, are scrambled. At 15,000ft, the squadron attacks a large formation of enemy bombers over Colchester, Essex. One of the pilots, 21-year-old Flight Lieutenant Maurice Mounsdon, engages one of the escorting fighters and registers some hits. As he pulls away, a Messerschmitt Bf 109 opens fire on him from behind and shoots down his Hurricane. Mounsdon is wounded in the leg and bullets hit the gravity petrol tank behind the instrument panel, which explodes, blowing petrol into the cockpit, which instantly catches fire. 'Up it went,' recalled the officer, 'and I was sitting in a blowlamp … I was on fire. There was only one thing to do, and that was to get out as fast as possible … I was badly burned, but I rotated the aircraft over and came down by parachute from 14,000ft.'

He lands in a field a mile outside the village of High Easter in Essex, with little left of his clothing, which is burnt away.

Farmers come over with pitchforks in hand and at first he has some trouble convincing them he is not a German. The local ARP (Air Raid Precaution) warden comes to his aid, however, and rushes him into hospital at Black Notley near Braintree, Essex. He is treated for severe burns to his arms and legs.

Mounsdon later recounted: 'The dogfights were pretty frightening. Everyone was firing at the same time. It was a matter of luck if you survived or not … But at the end of it all it was the happiest time of my life, though I lost a lot of good friends.'

Sunday, 1 September 1940:
The great evacuation of schoolchildren from London begins at 7.30 am.

During a period of 'down-time', Meier was told of Goering's boast that, 'By the 10th September not a house will be standing in England.'[7]

After the men had been at the chateau for several days and generally had a great time, it was time for them to prepare to leave for a new destination.

Monday, 2 September 1940:

At 12 noon a meeting of the War Cabinet is held at 10 Downing Street. The Prime Minister, Winston Churchill, states that on 31 August he had visited the Fighter Command during one of the big German air attacks. He had found it very instructive to watch officers of the Fighter Command deploying their forces and building up a front at the threatened points.

Churchill then reviews the results of the last month of hard air fighting, saying that they had every right to be satisfied with the results. The Prime Minister says he was tempted to ask why the enemy should continue on this heavy scale – which included some days as many as 700 aircraft – if it did not represent something like their maximum effort. This might not, of course, be the explanation. But the Royal Air Force was stronger than ever and there was every reason to be optimistic about the 1940 Air Battle of Britain.

The Cabinet is informed of the civilian air raid casualties for August, with approximately 700 killed and 781 seriously injured.

The Prime Minister says that he proposes to make a statement to Parliament on 5 September, in which he would say the following:

He would propose to make a guarded statement on the progress of the air battle, indicating that the results were generally satisfactory.

Next he hoped it would be possible to make some statement as to compensations for air raid victims.

Thirdly, he would mention the internment of aliens. At a time of the country's greatest danger, the War Cabinet had decided that, as an act of high policy, large numbers of aliens must be interned, notwithstanding the great hardships involved. However, Churchill says the country is now in a stronger position and can afford to release aliens quickly, even though this might involve some risk.

So dawned the day of their departure for England.

At 8 am, the four spies left Wimille in two cars en-route for Paris-Plage (Le Touquet), a journey of about one-and-a-half hours, in the company of Korvettenkapitan Klapps.

Shortly after reaching Le Touquet, they crossed a bridge over the river Canche at Etaples, and while crossing, Pons spotted two aeroplanes landing on the Le Touquet side. The aerodrome itself was hidden from view by a high dyke or fence on the river side and on the other side by the forest of Le Touquet. Had he not seen the aircraft landing, Pons would not have been aware of the existence of an aerodrome.

Ten minutes after crossing the bridge, the cars stopped in front of a villa in the centre of the town, next door to the headquarters of the German invasion troops. The villa was of quite modest dimensions and ordinary in appearance, standing about 20 yards from the roadway, separated by a hedge, and had a small garden around it. It seemed to be occupied as a residence, because in one room a woman was seen cooking. There was no guard at the front, but there were a number of soldiers around the back. The spies were taken into the villa by Klapps and handed over to Major Seynsburg, who was treated by Klapps with some respect.

Seynsburg was about 40–45 years old, 5ft 10in tall, of medium build, bald, clean-shaven, wore no glasses and bore no visible scars. He had a long, sharp face and a long, sharp and slightly twisted nose. He wore an Army uniform and sported, like Klapps, three medal ribbons. In the room with Seynsburg were seven or eight other officers, including three naval officers; one or two of the Army officers wore the Iron Cross, but none of the naval officers. The spies believed the villa may have been Seynsburg's private residence-cum-office.

Ninety minutes before departing Paris Plage, Major Seynsburg gave them their final instructions, speaking to each spy separately for about ten minutes and indicating, on a map, the point on the English coast at which they were to land and the area where they were to operate. While one spy was instructed, the others remained in the garden.

Each pair were given definitive instructions as to where they were going to land. The instructions were generally to work the Dungeness peninsula to the military canal, after which they were to fall back to Ashford and ascertain if the railway lines at Folkestone, Dover–Canterbury and Whitstable were fortified. The main interest was the peninsula of Dungeness. More specifically, Waldberg and Meier were to take the western part, and Pons and Kieboom the eastern. Maps of the regions, along with code patterns, were rolled around a stone, which the men were instructed to throw away if they found themselves in danger. If they could do this where there was deep water, it would ensure that no incriminating evidence would be found.

During the early stages of training, the men were given to understand that military information would not be expected and they would therefore escape the penalties of spying. Waldberg, possibly because of his elementary military experience, was under the impression that he would be treated as a prisoner of war by the English should he be caught. However, despite previous instructions, Seynsburg revised the information that he required the group to obtain. This now comprised the following:

- distribution and frequency of patrols, movements and armament of troops;
- new aerodromes, numbers and types of aircraft;
- anti-aircraft defences;
- damaged ships in port;
- names of ships in harbour;
- morale of the civilian population.

Once again, all instructions were translated into French for Waldberg's benefit.

Kieboom's specific instruction for work in England was to report the whereabouts of gun batteries, street batteries, whether the southern part of England was evacuated or not and the morale of the civilian population.

For noting down valuable information, the four men were to write using 'invisible ink', which was supplied to them. While not 'invisible ink' per se, they were given a reagent substance to make visible what was written with water or lemon juice.

Once established in England, the spies were to send a 'false' message that would induce the Germans to invade in the areas the men were allocated; this would be the phrase 'weak coastal dispositions'. Strong forces on the canal would not affect the issue. A report that the coast was strongly held, on the other hand, would result in abandonment of an attack in that area, but would not prevent a proposed landing on the east coast of England from Aldborough (Suffolk) as far as, but not including, the Wash (between Norfolk and Lincolnshire), as German Intelligence believed the Wash to be heavily mined.

The agents were initially told that after the invasion had started, they should retire with the population and continue sending messages, giving details of the results of air attacks. If this was not possible, then they should surrender to the advancing German soldiers.

To facilitate the latter, each spy had been issued with special instructions to signal to any approaching German forces by waving a handkerchief over his head. He had then to contact an officer and say, '*Ich bin hier mit einem Sonderauftrag für Deutschen Wehrmann*' (roughly translated as 'I am here with a special order for German military man'), to be followed by the password 'Elizabeth'.[8]

They were told that they would find widespread havoc as a result of air raids. In the event of their arrest, Klapps told them to say that they had come from Brest in north-west France.

Meier and Kieboom were told that they would be well looked after upon the completion of their jobs. Any promises of payment to Waldberg and Pons were vague.

Waldberg was taken into his German masters' confidence and told that the invasion would take place between 3 and 15 September 1940. He was also told that the Germans intend to attack:

a. East and south from Dungeness and north and east from Norfolk.
b. They would use their guns on the coast in France along with lots of speedy boats, bombers and parachutists.[9]

Furthermore, a special mission was entrusted to Waldberg but kept secret from the other three. While he was at Paris Plage, Waldberg was informed that, shortly after his arrival in England, he was to commandeer a motor-boat, put out to sea and make for Boulogne, where he would be picked up by the Germans and towed across the Channel. He was to stay a day in Boulogne and return the following night in the company of Oberleutnant Werner, landing again on the Dungeness coast. Werner, who was said to have visited England in August 1939, would then contact an Englishman in London and send direct word to Wiesbaden. Waldberg thought Werner's visit to be the precursor to the invasion of England.

Meier, along with his other two comrades, did not know the exact date of the invasion. As he had been given food for approximately ten to fourteen days, he assumed that the invasion would occur before that time was up. He did notice that there were many mountain troops with mules at Le Touquet. Meier, with no evidence to back it up, thought that the invasion would take place in small boats, although he did not see any such craft. He also thought that they would await a misty day.

Kieboom grandly assumed that his work alone was to facilitate an invasion. This was reinforced by the fact that each pair had provisions for no more than fourteen days, while Kieboom and his companion had just £60 with which to buy food. They were told that if the team ran short of provisions, they could report this by wireless and a plane would drop a new supply near the place where they had originally landed.

Communication with Germany was to be via a wireless set, for which each pair of spies was issued with two black thick leather cases – albeit not waterproof – with carrying straps. The first case measured 11in x 6in x 3¾in, weighed 7lb and contained three 90v HT batteries, two 4½v LT dry batteries and connecting wire. The second case was 8½in x 7¾in x 4in, weighed 4lb and contained the transmitter, spare valve, key and aerial equipment. The transmitter was contained in a metal box measuring 5½in x 4½in x 3in. The key plugged in on a 4ft length of cord, a multiple battery lead was attached, and plugs for ground antenna completed the external attachment. Each set contained two aerials.

The equipment consisted of an on-off battery switch, key plugs, plug-in crystal in a sealed holder, two tuning controls, a lamp indicator and aerial taps for adjustment purposes. The apparatus was low-powered and required exceptional conditions to work over 100 miles. A reliable range would more realistically be 50 miles, particularly on the higher frequency end of the range; yet the receiving station was Wiesbaden, over 400 miles from the Kent coast! The large batteries had a life of three months and the smaller batteries one month.

The sets – which rather fortuitously for the four spies, required no technical knowledge to operate – were packed into the fenders of the rowing boats without being seen by the men who were to operate them, although all four had practised on similar sets. One fender contained a transmitter, the other the batteries.

The fenders were not together, and when Meier went to collect a fender where he thought his W/T set was held, he picked the wrong one and was promptly told, 'No, they belong to the other party.'[10]

A daily call was to be made, and if there were no messages of importance to transmit, weather reports were to be sent instead. Messages, signed by spy-names, were to be transmitted between 5 pm and 8 pm, and 10 pm and 2 am (Central European Time).

The codes were handed over to the agents by Hasselbrinck (the W/T operator at Chateau Wimille). He had a number of codes ready, and Meier, in particular, assumed them to be different, although Meier was only familiar with two codes.

Two codes were provided: a circular code and an emergency code, a simple transposition of the key words '*Rangierbahnhof*' ('marshalling yard', for Waldberg and Meier) and '*Zinkbadewanne*' ('zinc bath', for Pons and Kieboom). The letter 'P' in the preamble of the message indicated that the emergency code was being used, and 'T' was the final letter.[11]

Waldberg was told he would be able to send a message to Germany, which would result in him contacting a Messerschmitt by signalling with a sheet and handkerchief, to which the aeroplane would reply with a burst of machine-gun fire. Thereafter, other instructions would follow.

The four recruits were reassured that their precarious stay in England would be a short one. They were told the invading German armies would soon rescue them.

With interviews and formalities over, a special farewell lunch was laid on. There was plenty of drink to give the group encouragement, offering, somewhat appropriately, 'Dutch courage'. The champagne flowed freely in toasts to success and to 'The Invasion'. A photograph was taken, and it proved to be a merry party. The choice of a lunch instead of dinner for the send-off spree was a considered one, as it enabled heads to be clear before final embarkation for Boulogne later that night.

After lunch, the spies were taken on a five-minute journey by car, via the seafront, to a small jetty on the river estuary, where a motor-boat was waiting for them. Lying out in the river, about 200 yards away on the left-hand side of the stream – which at this point was about three-quarters of a mile across – were five fishing smacks moored at intervals of about 70 yards from each other. Kapitan Klapps supervised the departure of the expedition. Pons and Kieboom were taken in a motor-boat to one of the fishing smacks by Klapps, who then returned to the jetty to take Meier and Waldberg to board another vessel. The five smacks were all small single-masters of the same type and approximately the same size – about 40ft in length. The boat taking Waldberg and Meier to England was called *La Mascotte*, while Kieboom and Pons were aboard the *Rose du Carmel*. The latter boat initially flew a German flag, on top of which was a white flag, as used by French fishing vessels from the occupied territory.

La Mascotte had a captain and a crew of four or five, which was thought to consist of at least three Russians and a Latvian, and was a little larger than the *Rose du Carmel*, which had a Norwegian captain and two crew – a Norwegian engineer and Russian deckhand. In conversation, Pons learned from the captain of the *Rose du Carmel* that he had already made one trip to the English coast and 'dropped people' there. Exactly when and where this had happened, Pons did not enquire; he only knew that the trip had been made from some point on the French coast, and he gathered that the same boat and crew had been used.

Early that afternoon, at about 2 pm, the two single-masted, diesel-engine fishing boats set sail from Le Touquet and proceeded under their own power, doing 3 or 4 knots. They headed for Boulogne, about five hours' sailing time away.

Before they reached the port of Boulogne, they stopped about 3 miles out. After a wait of about 90 minutes, they were escorted by armed German minesweepers and taken, at about 8 knots, in a westerly direction across the Channel toward the English coast.

Chapter Four

Champagne Cider and a Bath

Tuesday, 3 September 1940:
At 7 pm, Prime Minister Winston Churchill chairs a meeting of the War Cabinet and Defence Committee (Operations). During the meeting, Churchill stresses 'the importance of giving the Home Guard a clearly defined status as part of the authorized and regular forces of the Crown'. If this was done there would be no danger of the Home Guard being taken for *franc-tireurs* [irregular soldiers]. Churchill says it might be advisable to issue a Royal Proclamation so that this force would be completely legal in every respect. Certain points needed consideration, such as the introduction of ranks for officers and of saluting. The Secretary of State for War (Anthony Eden) is invited to examine the status of the Home Guard with a view to regularizing the position of this 'valuable force'.[1]

I n the early hours, with the small flotilla within 5 miles of the English coast, south of Dungeness, the minesweepers returned to France and the fishing boats sailed on for another two hours in the same westerly direction, until they were about half a mile from the shore. Two rowing boats were put out, and into these scrambled Waldberg and Meier from *La Mascotte* and Kieboom and Pons from *Rose du Carmel*.

There was very little light and the sea, which was dead calm, was at full tide. Visibility was poor, which was advantageous in enabling the rowing boats to approach the shore without being seen. The German Command had chosen a good night.

Pons and Kieboom paddled to the beach and landed near Dymchurch Redoubt. The first thing for them to do was to rescue the wireless set from the fenders. Kieboom carried one of the black leather cases, Pons the other. Kieboom quickly ordered Pons to find a place where they could hide the cases, as he knew that the contents would be incriminating if found in their possession. The search for a hiding place for the cases initially proved fruitless. They then moved up from the beach, where they climbed over a sea wall, crossed the coast road and spotted a relatively safe place to hide the cases – a large layer of rushes behind a dyke. They hid the cases about 75 yards apart and brushed the rushes over them. Kieboom went back to the boat to get a spade, with the intention of burying the cases. He returned and, about a yard from the road, tried to dig a hole but found the ground too hard. In the meantime, Pons was nowhere to be seen.

Waldberg and Meier had still not landed. As they drew nearer to the coast, they spotted a patrol boat approaching about 200 yards in the distance. As the boat drew nearer, they feared trouble. The pair threw overboard a weighted package, which contained the circular code and two maps; Waldberg panicked and also threw his automatic pistol into the water before they continued to row. They were not spotted, but the two men still had to negotiate minefields and the full tide carried them over barbed-wire entanglements. They did, however, bump into steel spikes and tram rails that were embedded in the sand just below the high water mark. But with no further mishaps, they landed on the beach between Dungeness Lighthouse and Lydd coastguard station. They should have landed about 6 miles from Dungeness, but actually found themselves just 1¼ miles from there, and almost 8 miles from Pons and Kieboom.

Meier and Waldberg lightly fastened their boat before unloading their hand luggage, then unpacked their wireless transmitter and hid it under an overturned advertising board before rescuing a sack of food, which was far too heavy to carry any distance. Fortunately, they spotted a small upturned lifeboat nearby. This was from the *Normandie* and it had drifted ashore shortly after the evacuation of Dunkirk. The duo dragged the food sack up the beach and hid it in the lifeboat.

Each man had a suitcase containing clothing and other necessities. Meier had a raincoat; Waldberg did not, but 'he had his swimming vest' (life jacket).[2] They unfastened their boat, having been told that it would eventually be washed out by the receding tide and leave no trace of their arrival. Unfortunately for them, this did not happen.

Both men had a small spade, about 1½ft long, and like their compatriots, their intention was to dig a hole to hide the transmitting set. The spades instead were leant up against the wall of a wooden house. Against this house were roof tiles which afforded a little protection against the elements. They then went for the fenders, which still contained the radio and associated equipment. They took their personal bags, Meier also getting his raincoat and Waldberg his swimming vest. It was still early morning, and to escape detection from military patrols and coastguards they hid behind two bungalows, slumped against the garage doors and tried to sleep.

At 4.45 am, 24-year-old Private Sidney Charles Tollervey of 'D' Company, 6th Battalion, Somerset Light Infantry, and another soldier from the same regiment, Private Pearce, were sent out by their platoon commander for general observation duties. They patrolled at Romney Marsh along a sea wall that was built between the coastal road and the beach, offering a silhouette of their bodies against the early morning sky. The sea wall ran from south-west to north-east, and Tollervey's patrol extended from a house called *SeaWrack* to a roadblock at the Grand Redoubt, West Hythe. They were to keep a lookout for any 'suspicious circumstances',[3] and if necessary, contact the Royal Engineers stationed at the roadblock.

Tollervey thought he heard what sounded like someone moving on the land side of the coastal road. Both soldiers stopped to listen. It was about three-quarters of an hour from being light enough to see anything clearly. After a few seconds, they saw the vague, shadowy figure of a man, who ran across the road from the fields in the direction of the sea and and flung himself flat into some tall grass on the sea wall bank.

Private Pearce, who was now on the sea wall, covered the man with his rifle, while Tollervey moved forward and shouted, 'Halt, who goes there?' The man, about 15–20 yards away, raised himself up from the bank and replied, in good English, 'I do not know your codeword.'

'Have you any means of identification?' asked Tollervey. 'I don't understand what you mean,' was the stranger's reply. 'Advance and let me see you,' ordered the soldier. The man approached with his hands up. This struck Tollervey as being suspicious; the man had raised his hands without being ordered to do so.

As he got closer, it became clear that, slung around the stranger's neck, was a pair of binoculars, that had the word 'Praha' ('Prague') inscribed on them, as well as a pair of spare shoes.

'I have come across the water. I am a Dutch refugee and if I can see an officer I will explain my position,'[4] exclaimed the man, rather nervously. At this point there was no mention of a companion or that there was anyone else involved.

It was now 5.15 am, and Tollervey escorted the man to his platoon headquarters and handed him over to his platoon commander, 2nd Lieutenant Eric Arnold Batten.

Tollervey explained to his officer that he had found the man hiding nearby. When asked by Batten who he was, the man reiterated that he was a Dutch refugee. He then produced a Dutch passport in the name of Charles Albert van den Kieboom. The passport had expired on 5 April 1940, making it, by September that year, a useless document! Batten asked Kieboom if he was armed, to which he replied 'Yes', and produced a loaded pistol, of Belgian make, from a pocket. The pistol contained a clip of nine cartridges in the butt. Batten took the weapon, as well as the binoculars. The prisoner was asked where he had come from. 'Brest, France,' he replied. Kieboom added that he had been rowing since half past midnight, but again made no mention of a second person. Kieboom, who was wearing civilian clothes and white canvas shoes, asked if he could change into his spare shoes, as those he was wearing were wet.

The location where Kieboom and his companion landed happened to be the only place in the area where there were no wire defences, and had the only steps up from the beach within 150 yards. The area where Kieboom was found was a restricted one, the coast and many miles inland being heavily patrolled. Consequently, it would have been very difficult for anyone to go very far before being challenged.

At 5.25 am, Lance Corporal Robert Henry North of the Royal Engineers, Stevedore Battalion, stationed at Morle Tower, Hythe, was on guard duty at No. 1 Support Post, West Hythe, which faced seawards. Between the sea and his post there was a meadow and a canal. He noticed a figure moving in a field about 150 yards away. It was not quite daylight, and he did not recognize anything about the figure.

He shouted at him to stop and stand still, then called out to him, 'What are you doing there?' 'I am a Dutchman,' came the reply. North, thinking that the man might run away, commanded him to stand still while at the same time he directed two other soldiers to assist him by surrounding the man. North was forced to cross the canal to approach the man, who was then about 500 yards away. The stranger made no effort to escape, so North promptly arrested him and took him to a nearby hut. The man was wearing a dirty white polo sweater, grey flannel trousers, and his clothes and shoes were very wet. The soldier asked him to explain his presence.

'I am a refugee from the Germans, who are looking for me for trying to evade the currency laws,' he replied. 'I have a companion and we crossed from Brest in a fishing boat, and when a few miles from the shore we were cast off in a small boat.'

'Who is your companion and why hasn't he come with you?' asked Lance Corporal North. 'He left the boat before me and perhaps he has been shot,' the man answered.[5]

North searched the man and found, amongst other things, a compass and a Dutch passport (issued in Amsterdam on 17 April 1939) in the names of Sjoerd Pons and his wife, Catherina.

North transported Pons, under close guard, to Seabrook police station. Unknown to Pons, Kieboom was already at the police station; they noticed one another, but did not exchange words. Pons was given some food, and his wet clothes were dried. A patrol was immediately sent out to search for Pons' companion and their boat.

Both Pons and Kieboom were quickly apprehended due to the vigilance of the soldiers on patrol. Everyone was on alert because of the threat of invasion, so in theory the hunt was on even before they had arrived. Once Kieboom was discovered, the hunt had intensified and it was not long before both men were under lock and key. They had not succeeded in getting their radio set into action, having been apprehended almost as soon as they landed.

Meanwhile, at about 7 am, Meier and Waldberg went to look for a better place to hide their radio.

The pair crept across an open stretch of land to a ditch, and found a better hiding place for themselves and their equipment in a small clump of trees that offered shelter. The boughs of one of the trees came down to the ground, providing good cover to hide the wireless sets and the novice spies. The hideout also afforded them a good view of the surrounding countryside.

Meier and Waldberg now started planning their campaign in earnest. Waldberg, being the brains and natural leader of the pair, really did all of the planning. He was working for his country, not just for money like the renegade Meier, who was rather in fear of his overbearing colleague. Even though they were risking their lives with one another, they did not get on well together. Each had a separate espionage role: Meier, with his excellent English – spoken with an American accent embellished with some US slang – was to be the collector of information. He was to frequent pubs, cafes and railway stations to pick up information. He was especially instructed to get into conversation with soldiers, having been told by his German masters that soldiers always talked a lot about things that were better left unsaid in public places during wartime. Waldberg's role, meanwhile, was to get any useful information collected by his companion back across the Channel to the German secret police.

At 8 am, 2nd Lieutenant Batten decided to have the whole beach searched to see if a boat could be found, sending out Private Richard Chappell and another soldier to comb the area. They went to the sea wall opposite the Beach Holiday Camp, where a small rowing boat, bearing the name *St Joseph*, was spotted floating at the edge of the water. The boat was searched, and although nothing was found it was immediately made secure. As Private Chappell walked across the beach, away from the sea, he noticed, under some steps leading up the sea wall, a sack and some other articles.

Chappell returned to his platoon headquarters and handed over to 2nd Lieutenant Batten the items he had found; a sack, blanket, mackintosh and large leather case. The sack contained various tins of food, biscuits, some cigarettes, a bottle of brandy and a length of rope. Chappell informed Kieboom that he had found the boat and told him of the things he had brought back. The private remarked to Kieboom that the sack was very heavy, asking if it was his and whether he carried it himself. 'Yes,' replied Kieboom.

Amazingly, Kieboom still had some very incriminating items in his possession and he realized he needed to dispose of them, and fast. An opportunity presented itself when Kieboom asked one of the soldiers to be allowed to visit the lavatory as a matter of urgency.

In Kieboom's pocket was a sheet of paper containing a secret code wrapped around a stone, along with a map and a reagent for secret ink. He screwed the paper up and flushed it down the toilet, along with the map and reagent, thus ridding himself of the incriminating evidence. He laid the stone next to the pan, and casually left.

Kieboom was eventually handed over by 2nd Lieutenant Batten to Police Sergeant Frank George Robertson of the Kent County Constabulary. At 9.30 am, the police at Seabrook received a message from Sergeant Robertson that he had Kieboom and Pons in his custody.

Both Waldberg and Meier were still at liberty. Waldberg complained of thirst, and Meier, being the only one of the pair to speak English, was sent into Lydd to bring back a drink for his leader.

At about 8.30 am, Meier left behind his raincoat and bag and, wearing a reefer jacket, walked across the shingle to Lydd on his first sortie of their mission. Meier, a good-looking, cultured and educated man, would have been very tall but his pronounced stoop made him look shorter than he actually was. There was nothing about him that would arouse suspicion. He reached Lydd, which was a prohibited area, unchallenged and went to the local pub, the *Rising Sun*. He knocked on the door of the pub and, when it was answered, asked for a drink. Unfortunately for him, the church clock had only just struck nine, a time when no Englishman would have expected to be served. The woman who answered the door, Mabel Cole, told him to come back at opening time, 10.30 am. Before heeding her advice, Meier asked for a bath! This was a strange-sounding request for a small public house. He was told that there were no facilities for a bath to members of the public.

If Meier had any doubts about going through with his task, and if he really wanted to leave Waldberg, then surely this would have been his opportunity to give himself up. He realized, however, that if he went to the police and told them his story, a record would be made of this, and consequently, the Germans would know everything when the invasion came. Meier was convinced that the Germans would be in England within a few days' time.

Meier returned to the pub at opening time and ordered a 'champagne cider'. This request, once again and not surprisingly, set Mabel Cole wondering. After deliberating, Meier finally decided on half a pint of mild and bitter, and lingered as he waited for his military 'contacts' to turn up. But Lydd was no hub of cosmopolitan activity, and Meier – with his foreign accent, ignorance of pub etiquette and lack of knowledge of the customs and conventions of British society – was soon under suspicion. Mrs Cole encouraged him to talk, and when she made a remark about how the Germans were starving because of the Royal Navy's blockade, Meier snapped, 'How do you know they are?'[6]

Satisfied that he was a person who required further investigation, Mrs Cole went to the pub's four-ale (public) bar, where there were men playing darts, and invited one of them into the saloon bar to talk to the stranger there. She whispered her suspicions to him. The darts player was Horace Rendal Mansfield, a 24-year-old aircraft examiner originally from Esher, Surrey, but at the time was residing at 58 Sutton Road, Maidstone, Kent. Mansfield was recuperating at Lydd from shock and minor injuries he received during bombing raids on Short's factory near Rochester.

Mansfield entered the saloon bar and started a conversation with Meier. Somewhat incompetently over-zealous, Meier soon began to make enquiries as to the disposition and numbers of British troops in the area. Meier then decided to leave, but before doing so he put half-a-crown (2/6d) on the bar counter and asked if that was enough for his half a pint. Meier was somewhat surprised to learn that the price was only 4½d – about one-sixth of the price he tried to pay. Knowing nothing about the price of beer proved a fatal blunder. As Meier left the pub, desperately trying not to draw more attention to himself, he knocked an electric light bulb from the passageway ceiling.

Mansfield decided to follow Meier, who, about a quarter of a mile down the road towards Dungeness, entered a small grocers shop to buy cream crackers, butter and a packet of cigarettes, before asking directions for Dungeness. He was asked by the proprietor whether he was rationed there. Of course, he was not, so he could not have the butter. Meier said that he would have the crackers anyway.

As he left the shop and walked away, Meier got a tap on the shoulder. It was Mansfield, who produced his own Air Ministry pass and said to Meier, 'Excuse me, can I see your Identity Card or your Permit?' He specifically asked for a permit because Meier was in a prohibited area.[7]

All things considered, Meier took the shock very well: calmly, if somewhat impertinently. He asked why he should show anything, and was told that he was in a prohibited area. Meier blandly admitted that he had no registration card and was a Dutch refugee who had just arrived in England. He reached into a pocket to produce his passport and another pocket to get several bank notes, which he tried to hand over to Mansfield.

Without provocation, Meier suddenly started to explain how he had escaped from Holland through France, and had then sailed from Brest to Dungeness. Whether by accident or design, he went on to say, '<u>We</u> arrived here last night', thus disclosing the arrival of other members of the party. Mansfield's suspicions were sufficiently aroused by the stranger's foreign accent and by what he said to ask Meier to go with him to Lydd Police Station. At this point they were joined by another man, an R.M. Silvester. Mansfield drove them all to the police station in his car.

On duty at Lydd Police Station when Mansfield brought in Carl Meier at 10.45 am was Police Sergeant Joseph Tye – who was attached to the Kent County Constabulary – along with Police Constable Frank Pearman. Meier answered the description of a person about whom Sergeant Tye had earlier received information. Meier was asked to empty his pockets in the presence of PC Pearman. On the table he put, amongst other things, seven £5 Bank of England notes, nine £1 Bank of England notes, one ten shilling note, six shillings in silver and 7½d in bronze, along with a passport. Pearman paid no attention to the passport, but asked the prisoner, 'How is it you have so much English money?' There was £44.16/7½d in total.

Meier replied that he had been sent it by friends in Scotland, and that with other money that he possessed he had paid for a boat to bring him from Brest to England to escape Nazi rule. Sergeant Tye then asked Meier who he was and where he was from. 'I am a Dutch subject and landed on the beach in a small boat. I have come from France,' was the reply. Without further questioning, he volunteered, 'I have left a sack of food in a boat on the beach.' Again without being prompted, he added, 'I can show you the boat.'[8]

Meier complained that he was hungry, so the officers gave him breakfast, including eggs from their own hens. He returned the compliment by handing around cigarettes and sharing his bottle of brandy. As he ate, he talked, and the more he talked, the more the police realized that something big was afoot. He dropped the Brest story and mentioned Boulogne, and how he had been intimidated by the Germans into coming across the Channel. Meier mentioned the existence of not only his immediate colleague, Waldberg, but another pair who landed the same morning in the Dymchurch area. He made it clear that he did not mind what happened to himself; he just did not want to go back to Germany.

Unsurprisingly, Meier was told that he would be detained. He had smoked so much during the interrogation that his supply of cigarettes was now exhausted, so he gave Mansfield £1 to buy some more. The police officers then telephoned Dymchurch to tell them of the couple in their area, and they were asked to bring Meier over immediately. It was only at this point that Meier was relieved of his revolver.

The police, Meier and Mansfield set off by car for Dungeness. Their route took them close to Waldberg's hideout, and Meier's accomplice, who had no doubt been anxiously awaiting his colleague's return with a wad of military information, saw him instead being driven past in a car with the police. He was left in no doubt as to what had happened, so he packed up his radio set and moved further afield into hiding.

At about noon, Dennis Henry Hayles, a 17-year-old labourer, was strolling along the beach between the Coastguard and Lifeboat Stations at Lydd-on-Sea.

About halfway between the two, he spotted a rowing boat a few yards out on the sea. It had a black bottom with a white band around it, and also had a number. Hayles waded out and got into the boat. Inside he found four new oars, so he rowed the boat to the Coastguard Station.

Hayles returned along the beach to a spot where he was aware that there was a wrecked lifeboat, which he knew had been there for some considerable time. He looked into the boat and in the stern he found a sack. Upon investigation, he found that it contained some loaves of bread and tinned foodstuffs. Hayles took the sack and walked off.

Meanwhile, between Dungeness and Lade, Sergeant Tye spotted a large boat on the beach. Meier, seemingly eager to please his captors, pointed to the boat and cried out, 'That looks like the boat I put the sack in.' Tye searched the vessel but found nothing.

The policeman then spotted Hayles with a sack, upon which Meier, again without prompting, said, 'That's the sack I put in the boat.' Tye stopped the young labourer and took possession of the sack before returning to Seabrook Police Station, where the contents were examined. The sack contained the following:

Ten tins of pork and beans packed in Belgium.
Eighteen 1lb tins of corned beef (American).
Two tins of condensed milk (British).
Fourteen packets of eating chocolate (Belgian).
Twelve 2oz round packets of biscuits in bag.
Twenty-three 2oz square packets of biscuits in bag.
One packet of Jacob's Cream Crackers.
Five packets of Belgian cigarettes.
Three loaves of bread.
One bottle of brandy.
An empty bottle labelled grapefruit juice.
Approximately 1lb of sugar.

The provisions were to last for about ten days. Most of the food was left behind by the retreating Allied armies, abandoned out of necessity, picked up and redistributed by the Germans.

During a three-and-a-half-hour interrogation at Seabrook Police Station, Meier prevaricated, although the interrogators were able to elicit the following information:

After leaving medical school in Germany, Meier said he had got a job back in Holland with the Central Distribution Office in Bezuidenhout. He had not seen much of German activities during the invasion of Holland, as most of the time he was on duty as a member of the fire brigade in the Central Distribution Office building. Nobody had been able to work, telephone lines were cut and he only knew of the capitulation after he saw German soldiers entering the town.

He said that he received from his aunt Van't Hof sufficient money for travelling, as he was sure that the Germans were looking for him. He had intended to go to America and remain there. He had asked for dismissal from the Central Distribution Office, left The Hague on his bicycle and, via Breda, arrived at Brussels. Meier claimed to have stayed there for one month, trying to find an opportunity to come to England first. He made acquaintance in cafes of people who told him to leave for Brest, as there he was sure to find someone who would be willing to take him over to England. He said he did so, and there he found a Russian skipper, paid him 20,000 French Francs, and this man brought him to England, together with a French subject who called himself Dubois (Waldberg). They landed near Dungeness. After his arrest, Meier claimed to be a Dutch refugee. He said his fellow passenger had already left him, and he did not know where he could be.

Toward the end of the questioning, Meier relented and told his interrogators the place where Waldberg could be found. Waldberg was in possession of the wireless transmitter, the code for which, Meier said, had been thrown overboard, along with a revolver which was given to them at Brest.

Unsurprisingly, the interrogators were not impressed. Meier was told to return to his cell and to write down his own story, but this time telling the truth!

Meanwhile, at 3 pm, as a consequence of instructions received, 2nd Lieutenant Batten ordered some men from his platoon to search an area on the landward side of the sea wall running between *SeaWrack* house and the Grand Redoubt, near where Kieboom had been apprehended.

About 50 yards from the road adjoining the sea wall, in a field, Private James McDonnell from Batten's 'D' Company spotted that some rushes in a dry ditch – 50 yards on the land side of the road – had been disturbed. McDonnell followed the track for a few yards and found a parcel, well hidden and wrapped in a khaki cover. He unwrapped it and found a black leather case. McDonnell returned to his headquarters and handed over his find to 2nd Lieutenant Batten. When the case was opened, it revealed a number of Pertinax dry batteries and a Morse key on a lead.

When Sergeant Robertson had received Kieboom into custody from 2nd Lieutenant Batten, the police officer asked for some identification. Kieboom produced a passport along with a Dutch military driving licence form dated 15 February 1939 for Charles v.d. Kieboom. Robertson searched his prisoner, and among other property he found:

Ten £5 Bank of England notes.
Eleven £1 notes.
One 10/- Bank of England note.
5/6 in silver.
One 1,000 (Belgian) Franc note.
Two electric torches in a case.

When Sergeant Robertson first saw Kieboom, the prisoner claimed, 'I am a Dutch refugee. I came across from Brest several days ago. I gave a French fisherman 5,000 Francs to smuggle me across. We cruised up and down the Channel for two or three days, [then] I was dropped overboard in a boat with some stores about midnight. It is my intention to proceed to Canada as a refugee from Nazi oppression in Holland.'[9]

The area in which Kieboom was arrested was a restricted one, where no one was allowed without a permit or a pass. Kieboom could never have got very far in that area without being challenged, as every yard of the coast there was patrolled. In fact, 'for many miles inland there is a watch kept of all suspicious movements of any living thing.'[10]

By 3.30 pm, Waldberg was still at liberty. A German plane had flown over and signalled to him. The plane dived down and Waldberg signalled to the pilot by waving his handkerchief and laying his bathing towel on the ground; it showed up to the pilot as a square.

A telephone message was received from the Regional Police Staff Officer (RPSO), Tunbridge Wells, at 4.25 pm, stating that three men (Kieboom, Pons and Meier) had landed from Brest in France. Their story was that they had served in the Dutch Army until 13 June, when Holland capitulated. They had been seeking employment in Amsterdam but without success, so then went to Brussels. The message continued:

'In conversation with some refugees these men were told that if they could reach Brest they would be able to bribe some fishermen to get them over to England. They made their way to Brest where they were successful in bribing some fishermen and left there about midnight on Sunday 1 September. The fishing boat took them within a mile of the English Coast when they transferred into rowing boats and rowed themselves ashore. They landed about 4 am on Tuesday 3 September between Lydd and Dymchurch and were arrested, individually, by military authorities about 1½ hours later.

'It was their intention, they stated, to travel by night and hide during the daytime and make their way to a port to board a vessel en-route to

Canada. One of the boats in which these men landed contained a sack with chocolates, biscuits and blankets.

'No. 1 [Kieboom] had in his possession approx. £60 in English money; a loaded revolver and a pair of binoculars.

'No. 3 [Meier] had about £40 in English money; some of the money was in £5 Bank of England notes.

'No. 1 speaks English without a trace of an accent. Nos 2 [Pons] & 3 speak broken English.

'Nos 1 & 2 visited Germany in April, 1939 and July, 1940 respectively. The passport of No. 3 shows that he has drawn money from the German Bank. All three men claim to be fleeing from the oppression of Nazi rule in Holland.

'Four empty boats have been found between Lydd and Dymchurch (on the beach) which indicates that a fourth man has landed, but of whom there was, at present, no trace. The other men claim that they do not know his name.'[11]

At 5.30 pm, Lance Corporal Reginald Goody of 'D' Company, 6th Battalion, Somerset Light Infantry, was searching for the missing fcourth man with another soldier, Private McDonnell. Hidden in a corner of a field that adjoined a road away from the sea, they found a black thick leather case also wrapped in a khaki cover and tucked away under some long grass. It was about 70–75 yards from where Private McDonnell found his case. Goody unwrapped the cover, opened the case and found it contained a wireless (a valve, plug and two aerials). He handed the case over to Sergeant Thomas of Kent County Police in Hythe. Both cases belonged to Kieboom and Pons.

Waldberg had waited the whole day for Meier's return. At 8.30 pm, he decided to send out a wireless message, using an emergency code he had written in his notebook. He reported their safe landing and position, Meier's absence and the jettisoning of some of their papers. Translated from French, the message read:

'ARRIVED SAFELY. DOCUMENT DESTROYED. ENGLISH PATROL TWO HUNDRED METRES FROM COAST. BEACH WITH BROWN NETS AND RAILWAY SLEEPERS AT A DISTANCE OF FIFTY METRES. NO MINES. FEW SOLDIERS. UNFINISHED BLOCKHOUSE. NEW ROAD. WALDBERG.'[12]

At 8.45 pm, Captain Johnston in the Police Duty Room at the Home Office, received the following message[13] from Special Branch via Kent Constabulary in Maidstone:

'At about 4 am, some men landed in rowing boats between Dymchurch and Lydd. Three of these men who are Dutch have been arrested and they said there was one other man. He has not been traced. They claim to be refugees from oppression of Nazi rule in Holland and were found to be in possession of a considerable amount of English money. They stated that they intended making their way to a port to embark to Canada, travelling by night, and hiding during the day.

'Their description of the missing man was –

'Age 19, 5ft 7in.

'Fair, wavy hair.

'Loose build.

'Grey suit.

'Collar and tie.

'Believed carrying a dark-blue mackintosh.

'Speaks French only.

'Since the arrest of these men, Morse key, batteries of German make, connecting wires for Morse code signalling and a small wireless receiving set have been found on the beach near the spot where one of the boats came ashore at Dymchurch. Also a number of steel rods, similar to stair-rods, had been found erected inland near a telegraph pole.

'According to statements from the prisoners, only four men landed, but as two boats had been found – one capable of holding many men – it was possible that the number may be much greater. It was strongly suspected that these men are enemy agents.

'Special observation and enquiries were taking place, especially with the Home Guard and Coastguards.

'It is thought that the description furnished by arrested men is doubtless false.

'Extent of circulation

'Counties of Kent, East and West Sussex and Special Branch New Scotland Yard.'

As might be expected, this message instigated a flurry of activity.

The Home Office received the same message ten minutes later, and they advised Kent County Constabulary to notify the Immigration Officer at Folkestone. By 9 pm, Special Branch was concerned that Kent County Police had only advised the adjoining County Police, not the military. MI5 was contacted, but they had already received the message.

At 9.10 pm, Radio Security Services (RSS) were advised and they requested a copy of the report. Captain Grassby, the Army's Kent Regional Officer at

Tunbridge Wells, was telephoned at 9.20 pm to inform him about the landing, but he was unable to be contacted.

By 9.30 pm, Special Branch had informed various agencies that the prisoners were being interrogated by regional MI5 officers. Kent County Police had advised all police forces and the Home Guard, while Special Branch had notified the London Home Guard and the Port of London Authority. By 10.10 pm, the Home Office had spoken to various agencies, including the War Office and Director of Home Defence, giving them the gist of the earlier Special Branch message.

Wednesday, 4 September 1940:

After German boasts that Berlin is too well protected to be bombed, there is shock when the RAF hit the German capital for the first time on 25 August. Hitler is incandescent with rage over the attacks and today delivers his most aggressive speech yet to the German nation: 'When the British air force drops 200, 300 or 400 kilograms of bombs, then we will, in one night, drop 150,000, 230,000, 300,000 or 400,000 kilograms. When they declare that they will increase their attacks on our cities, then we will raze their cities to the ground. We will stop the handiwork of those night air pirates, so help us God.'[14]

At 2.40 am the following morning, the Police Duty Room at the Home Office received a message from the RPSO, Tunbridge Wells, which stated that Seymour Bingham, a Dutch-speaking civil assistant attached to the General Staff of the War Office, but who worked in B1d, Special Examiners, had gone to Seabrook Police Station to question the prisoners.

One of the prisoners admitted that he was sent by the enemy and gave information to enable the man still missing to be traced. The prisoner also stated that two more men were to follow them across the Channel.

MI5 and, in preparation for the captured men's incarceration, Mr G.F. Clayton, the governor of Brixton Prison, were informed.

The capture of the four men had initiated doubt and alarm. Was this it? Were they the only ones, or were more on their way? The Army, and in particular Captain Grassby, were concerned that this would be the start of something bigger. Grassby noted in his report, a copy of which was sent to MI5:[15]

'The Police at Seabrook received the message from the Sergeant at Dymchurch at 9.30 am on 3 September that the military had just brought the Dutchmen Kieboom and Pons to his house. It was apparent, therefore, that there was considerable delay between the time of these men being apprehended and their being handed over to the Police. This matter should perhaps be brought to the notice of the appropriate military authority, since it is plain that in a case of this kind any delay may be a serious matter.'

He continued:

'In view of the possibility of further landings of this kind, this aspect of the case should be brought to the notice of those responsible for the defence of the region in order that they may satisfy themselves that all the necessary precautions are taken.

'Arrangements have been made for taking charge of the two boats, and Commander Evan Thomas, SO1, Dover, has such particulars as will enable him to study the Naval aspect of the case.'

By 5 am, Waldberg was on his own, waiting, but had no doubt as to what had happened to his companion. He sent a further message:

'MEYER [*sic*] PRISONER. ENGLISH POLICE SEARCHING FOR ME. AM CORNERED. SITUATION DIFFICULT. I CAN RESIST THIRST UNTIL SATURDAY. IF I AM TO RESIST SEND AEROPLANES WEDNESDAY EVENING ELEVEN O'CLOCK. AM THREE KM NORTH [of point of] ARRIVAL. LONG LIVE GERMANY. WALDBERG'[16]

A third message in Waldberg's notebook was ready and waiting to be sent.

At 5.30 am, it was just about daylight, and as a consequence of a telephone message, Police Sergeant Tye, in company with Inspector Hadlow, Detective Sergeant England, Detective Constable Lyndsey, two MI5 officials and a number of soldiers of the Somerset Light Infantry (with loaded rifles and fixed bayonets) searched an inland area of about three-quarters of a mile between the Coastguard Station at Lade, which was halfway between Dungeness and Littlestone, and the Littlestone Pumping Station. They were looking for a man whose description they had already been furnished with, and whom they believed to have landed at Lydd from France.

About half a mile from the shore, Sergeant Tye spotted a man approximately 400 yards away, walking across the shingle towards the beach. As Tye approached him, he recognized the man from the description he had been given. It was Waldberg. Tye shouted to him, and he came toward the policeman. He had been on his way back to the boat to fetch the bag that contained the food.

So certain was Waldberg that the German invasion of Britain had begun that he demanded, in French, for Tye to take him to the nearest German Staff Officer.[17] Undeterred, Tye asked, 'Where are you going?' Waldberg, maybe now realizing the reality of the situation, changed tack, and now demanded, again in French, 'I want to speak to an English officer.'[18]

Fortunately, Tye had some knowledge of the French language and asked him for his passport, When Waldberg declined, stating 'No, no, no', Tye searched him for a firearm; he did not find one, nor a passport, but did come across a compass in Waldberg's outside jacket pocket.

Tye then said to him, '*Coucher*', asking him where he'd slept, and Waldberg pointed to the shingle towards Lydd, making a sign that he would show him.

At the time of Waldberg's arrest, it would have been almost impossible for any local resident – let alone a stranger – to move even 20 yards at night in this area without being challenged. The 'Brussels Four' had now all been apprehended, but the authorities were not taking any chances; as far as they were concerned, there could be others.

At about 6 am, Waldberg, Sergeant Tye and the other members of the search party proceeded to a spot near Littlestone Pumping Station, towards a large tree surrounded by bushes. The tree was situated about 450 yards from the Lydd–Dungeness road, and the boughs of the tree reached to the ground, creating a sheltered spot. In the fork of the tree, Tye found two black leather cases, both covered and fastened shut. Upon examination, one case was found to contain a wireless set, while the other had five Pertinax dry batteries and a Morse key on a lead. Also in the fork of the tree were two suitcases and a raincoat, but Tye did not examine the contents of the suitcases. There was also an erect aerial, which ran from a tree to a bush about 15 yards away. Waldberg dismantled the aerial and handed it to Tye. The police officer then escorted Waldberg and the recovered property to Lydd Police Station.

Also at Lydd Police Station at this time, around 8 am, was Seymour Bingham, the Dutch-speaker from the War Office. Bingham was there to ask Waldberg questions in French and German. Waldberg handed Bingham a green notebook. In it were two codes: one was fairly simple, in which letters were substituted for others, while the other was a grid code, with a stencil laid over a message to reveal its vital meaning.

Also in the notebook was a record of three messages. There were fixed times for sending any messages, presumably to prevent any jamming through the Pons–Kieboom pair transmitting at the same time. The notebook was subsequently handed over to Lieutenant Colonel William Edward Hinchley Cooke, of the General Staff Directorate of Military Intelligence at the War Office. Waldberg was also relieved of a brown leather wallet containing four £5 Bank of England notes.

At the Home Office, Captain Johnston in the Police Duty Room took a telephone call from Colonel Hill-Dillon of GHQ, who asked what the Home Office knew of the 'Dutchmen' who had just landed. Hill-Dillon was informed what had happened, and that the Regional Officers were 'in action'. Hill-

Dillon then asked whether Hinchley Cooke would be dealing with the case, and requested that he should ring him upon his arrival.

At 9.55 am, the Police Duty Room at the Home Office received the following message from the Regional Police Staff Officer, Tunbridge Wells:

'A fourth man was captured at Lydd at 04:00 hours to-day. Name Walter Walbeck [*sic*], age 22, address not known. Stated to be French but believed German. He was in possession of a wireless transmitting set and he is now in custody of police.

'Some of the four men captured admit being trained and sent over by Germans. It is thought that all the men who arrived in England have now been captured. Two others are believed to have been trained and are expected.[19]

Copies of this message were sent to MI5, Brixton Prison governor G.F. Clayton and others.

There was confusion at this early stage, as the above message reported Waldberg being captured at 4 am, whereas Sergeant Tye recorded the arrest as after 5.30 am.

Notwithstanding this, all four were interrogated at Seabrook Police Station. Pons was the last to be questioned, but the first of the spies who gave straightforward answers. He claimed that it had always been his intention to report everything to the police.

Kieboom, when questioned, was asked about his background, training, leaving France and his arrival in England. He stated not to know anything about a code which was given to the men, but later admitted that he had put the code down the lavatory while under military guard.

The conclusion of the unnamed interrogator was that Kieboom had made a very bad impression whilst being questioned and in the view of the officer who had asked the questions, would have carried out his instructions if he had been able to. Furthermore, Kieboom was absolutely convinced that the Germans would come to England, and was therefore afraid to admit any misdemeanour, fearing retribution when his masters arrived.

Major G. Lennox, of the General Staff at the War Office, telephoned Section B2 (Agents) to say that that Lord Swinton, Chairman of the Security Executive, had informed the War Office and the Admiralty of the men's capture and that they would be delivered to Latchmere House, the military internment camp at Ham Common, south-west London (also known as Camp 020). Lennox tactfully suggested to the Director(ate) Military Intelligence (DMI) that there was no cause to exaggerate the importance of these men, and that nothing could as yet be settled as to their significance.

DMI agreed entirely: the cases were civilian, and any interest in them was entirely the concern of MI5. MI9, which supported European Resistance networks, were also interested in the case, but only from the point of view of interrogation as to conditions on the other side of the Channel, and agreed that MI5 handle the matter.

At 10 am, Dick Goldsmith White, a counter-intelligence officer, communicated with MI5's Section B13 (Special Investigations) and stated that Mr Wood, from Section B24 (Domestic Security), had rung to inform them that four aliens – three Dutch and one either Belgian or French – had been picked up on the Kent coast, each having arrived there in a single open boat. They were being held by the police at Seabrook Police Station, Hythe. B2 reported that Mr Wood wanted to know what should be done with these four people. B2 consulted the Defence Security Service (DSS), and suggested that the men should be sent to Ham Common for interrogation. The DSS instructed B2 to contact the Home Office and arrange this.

B2 contacted the Chief Immigration Officer (CIO), a Mr Ralfe, to tell him to make a formal refusal to land the aliens and to instruct that the four men be lodged for detention at Camp 020.

Goldsmith White instructed Lieutenant Colonel Robin Stephens, Commandant at Ham Common, to arrange accommodation for the four, and said they would be delivered during the course of the day. Until he received further instruction from B13, the men were to be kept entirely separate to prevent any communication between them. Stephens said that listening rooms were available, should B13 decide to use them.

Having done this, B2 again contacted Mr Wood to ask him to telephone Seabrook and also make it quite clear that the four should be kept apart and not, under any circumstances, be allowed contact with one another. B2 was informed that Seymour Bingham had already succeeded in extracting from at least one of the prisoners that he was a German agent. B2 reported this to the DSS, who decided that B13 should be in charge of this case.

Bingham now returned to London and reported, with full statements, what had already been secured through interrogation of the prisoners. Goldsmith White asked Mr Wood that immediately Bingham arrived, he should report to B13.

During the course of the morning, several people had telephoned Goldsmith White asking what was being done about the case. When MI14 (specialists regarding intelligence about Germany) enquired, B2 replied that the matter was in the hands of MI5, who regarded the men as civilian internees, and they would be interrogated in due course, very carefully, as part of their investigations. MI14 replied that this would be in order, and that they would be glad to hear anything of interest regarding these cases as soon as possible.

Captain Grassby, the Kent Regional Officer who first communicated the arrival of the four, would, as a matter of courtesy, be informed that the matter was now in the hands of the Headquarters staff, and that no further action was expected from him. All the information supplied by Captain Grassby had been handed to B13.

Goldsmith White again contacted B13. He said as the four men were regarded as civilians, there was now some concern over the legality of holding them at Ham Common instead of, for example, Pentonville Prison. The Home Office legal department came to the firm opinion that there was no objection whatsoever to a person who had received a formal refusal to land, being detained in one of the military internment camps, of which Ham Common was an authorized unit.

To be completely on the safe side, the CIO was consulted. He was of the same opinion, adding that it was not usual to direct, in writing, where a person may be detained. This question was merely a matter of convenience, and no objection would be raised to the four men being held at Ham Common for further investigation. Because Ham Common was an authorized unit, the police could now deliver the men there for detention.

The CIO telephoned Goldsmith White and said that the four were actually on their way to London, and that they would be taken to Scotland Yard first. This was for clearance, prior to being taken to Latchmere House. Goldsmith White presumed that B13 were aware of this.

L.R.J. Halcro, of the Immigration Department at Gravesend, had travelled down to Seabrook with the intention of interrogating the men and to take any appropriate action, under the Aliens Order, against the four who were detained at the local police station after illegally landing in the vicinity.

Halcro arrived at Seabrook at 3 pm, when he was immediately informed by the police that the MI5 representative, Captain Grassby, had just gone to lunch but left a request that any interrogation be delayed until his return. Halcro duly obliged and waited in the Charge Room, requesting to see any papers that were found on the men. The detective in charge apologetically explained that any papers in the men's possession had been mislaid. When Grassby eventually returned, the papers were found and Halcro was given access to them. Grassby was accompanied by two other individuals with foreign accents, whom Halcro took to be interpreters.

Halcro's arrival was too late. Grassby's investigation had concluded, and although the MI5 man was affable, Halcro could see by his manner that he was anxious that the immigration officer should not interrogate the men. To say that Halcro was not satisfied would be an understatement. He had endured, at a moment's notice, a long car journey in which he had to deal with two air raids. With the few bits of significant evidence that he had, he felt that he could have added a little more to the final story.

The immigration officer surmised that the reason for Grassby's attitude was that he, Halcro, arrived at Seabrook rather late upon the scene and his intentions were obvious. Halcro reluctantly waived his legal rights rather than cause embarrassment, and issued four formal 'refusal to land' notices, which were duly accepted by Grassby.

The scraps of information that Halcro did gather were, unavoidably, second-hand and were not necessarily accurate. He reported that:'The four men arrived in two rowing boats; they asserted that they came from Brest after a week at sea, but later, and more probably (in Halcro's eyes), from Boulogne. All were arrested ashore, Pons by the military at Grand Redoubt, Hythe and Kieboom, also by the military, at Dymchurch. The two men admitted arriving in the same boat but denied any knowledge of anyone else. Meier was arrested by two civilians at Lydd while walking in the direction of Dungeness.

'The police told Halcro that they all spoke good English "with an Oxford accent", and that Waldberg was particularly frank, even describing his occupation as "Student of Espionage".

Halcro 'was told that the men carried about £130 in £5 and £1 English bank notes – due to the method of their arrival, Halcro did not apply currency restrictions – and among their possessions were a pocket compass, adjustable spanner, jack knife and a note book with about a dozen names of people in the UK.'[20]

The cash found on the men was broken down thus:

Kieboom, £61.15/6 plus 1,000 Belgian Francs;
Meier, £44.16/7½;
Waldberg, £20-,

Waldberg was the only one without papers; the other three each possessed a Dutch passport. During the short period he had the passports in his possession, Halcro could find nothing to suggest that they were anything but genuine.

The immigration man thought that the men were of refined appearance. This opinion was gleaned from just a brief observation as they were ushered from their cells to the cars to whisk them to London – the only contact Halcro had with the men. He knew that they had been under examination for many hours prior to his arrival – firstly by the police, and later by MI5 – and for Halcro to have insisted on further questioning would have meant retracing the same ground with any attendant delay, which would have forced obvious objections from MI5 and, to a certain extent, the police.

Kent County Police contacted the Police Duty Room at the Home Office at 12.40 pm, and informed them that the four men had admitted to being enemy agents and that they were sent to England with the object of gaining information regarding coastal defences and the morale of the British people. So far as could be ascertained, no other persons had landed in Kent, but according to the arrested men, two others had been trained for similar work; a watch was therefore being kept. MI5 and the governor of Brixton Prison, amongst others, were informed.

At 6.40 pm, Captain Grassby at Tunbridge Wells telephoned the Home Office to say that the four men had left Seabrook at about 5 pm in a number of separate cars, and that they should arrive in London at around 7.15 pm. He wished Scotland Yard to be advised that, upon Lieutenant Colonel Hinchley Cooke's instructions, they must only be allowed to enter one at a time, and that the constable on the gate there should be warned. In one of the cars was a suitcase and in another a bundle of clothes, which must be kept aside for re-examination and should not be handed to the men before Hinchley Cooke had given his consent. Hinchley Cooke, by his own admission, was the man personally responsible for the investigation of espionage cases.[21]

Superintendent Foster of Scotland Yard was telephoned. He knew all about the case and he delivered the request exactly as detailed.

Captain Grassby added that two Home Office representatives had also just left in one of his cars, bringing certain effects with them, and would reach London at about 7.45 pm. Upon their arrival, they should wait for Hinchley Cooke.

Hinchley Cooke had satisfied himself that the four men were German espionage agents and he was acutely aware of the imminent threat of invasion. Therefore, from a purely counter-espionage point of view, the men would be sent to Camp 020 and would be interviewed by a board of officers from the Navy, Army and Air Force – one or two from each service – with a view to getting out of the prisoners all the information that they thought might have to do with an invasion.

Hinchley Cooke wanted any information that may become available to be accessible to the Armed Forces. Initially, and as a matter of some urgency, the officer wanted to know if the four spies could tell him about the disposition of the German troops who may be about to attack England. This was his first priority.

Superintendent Foster contacted Lieutenant Colonel Hinchley Cooke at 10.15 pm and advised him that, as requested, the prisoners were segregated and were lodged as follows:

Jose Waldberg at Bow Street Police Station;
Sjoerd Pons at Canon Row Police Station;
Carl Meier and van den Kieboom at Rochester Row Police Station, but
separated from one another.

This, however, was just a temporary arrangement, prior to going on to Ham.

At the request of Hinchley Cooke, Captain Grassby was informed that his
driver was spending the night at Special Branch and would leave as soon after
daylight as possible.

During the day, Grassby had written a report entitled 'DUTCHMEN
LANDING NEAR DYMCHURCH' for MI5, but specifically for Hinchley
Cooke. He recorded the arrival of the four 'Dutchmen' in the early hours of 3
September and their subsequent arrests. He wrote:

'Each party appeared to be self-supporting with a supply of food, £30 in
English Bank and Treasury notes, a wireless transmitter, a pair of field
glasses, a certain number of clothes, cigarettes and brandy. Each party was
in possession of a code; Waldberg threw his into the sea while Kieboom
admitted that his code was disposed of down the lavatory of a building
in which he was detained. All articles found with these men have been
sent to London for examination by experts except for the food which is
being kept by the police at Seabrook Police Station [and] which will be
examined by them.'[22]

Grassby noted with some concern that there was considerable delay from
the time the men were apprehended to their being handed over to the police.
He recommended that this should perhaps be brought to the notice of the
appropriate military authority, 'since it is plain that in a case of this kind any
delay may be a very serious matter'.[23]

The men were at large for times varying between one and twenty-four hours.
One of them was only arrested by a chance encounter with a civilian, and
another was caught after a search had been organized as a result of information
given by one of his companions. Grassby added that, in view of the possibility
of further landings of this kind, this aspect of the case should be divulged to
those responsible for the defence of the region in order that they may satisfy
themselves that all necessary precautions were taken.

Grassby ensured arrangements were made for taking charge of the two boats
that the men arrived in, and that Commander Thomas, SO1, Dover, would be
given such particulars that would enable him to study the naval aspect of the
case.

The equipment with which the four spies had been provided consisted of the following:

Waldberg and Meier:
1 W/T set.
Circular code No. 4 (recovered from the sea).
Reagent for developing writing in secret ink.
Recovered from the sea:
    2 maps:
    a). London–Margate–Littlehampton.
    b). Marshes behind Dymchurch and Dungeness.
    Black–edged envelope addressed to Inspector Hallow.
£60 in £5 notes.
Food for ten days (but no water bottles).
Revolver (thrown overboard by Waldberg).
Wireless operator's licence and passport belonging to Meier.

Pons and Kieboom:
    Thrown away by Kieboom:1 W/T set.
    Circular code No 5,
    Reagent for developing writing in secret ink.
    Map.
£60 in £5 notes and 1,000 Belgian Francs.
Food for ten days (but no water bottles).
Revolver (FN).
Pair of binoculars.
Two pocket compasses.
Passport for each man.
One suitcase containing clothes and miscellaneous articles.

As mentioned in Grassby's report, all articles that were found with the men, except for the food, had been sent to London for examination by the experts. The food was retained at Seabrook Police Station for the police to examine.

Thursday, 5 September 1940:
Daylight bombing raids into Britain increase. The main objectives of the German daylight attacks appear primarily to be the airfields of Kent and the Thames Estuary.

By 1.20 am, confusion reigned as PC Morris, of Special Branch, telephoned the night duty officer regarding six drivers in five cars from Dymchurch, bringing four prisoners, and wanted to know what their instructions were regarding their movements; apparently, they did not know what they were supposed to do. The drivers and prisoners were waiting at Canon Row Police Station.

PC Morris was asked to personally get in touch with the men, as it seemed strange that they would be left without any orders.

PC Morris telephoned back at 1.35 am, saying that the earlier message was due to a misunderstanding and should never have been put through. He expressed his apologies.

Lieutenant Colonel Hinchley Cooke questioned Kieboom, Pons, Waldberg and Meier at New Scotland Yard. The interviews were conducted separately, and in the presence of Detective Sergeant Stanley Buswell of Special Branch, who recorded the questions and answers in shorthand.

Kieboom was interrogated first. After being cautioned, he was asked a number of questions in English. In the opinion of Hinchley Cooke, Kieboom understood English perfectly. Being an intelligent man, Kieboom knew that if he was suspected of being a spy, he would have to appear before a tribunal (which would have consisted of a number of officers). Kieboom took it upon himself to state only the bare facts. For example, he knew that Pons had been arrested, so he offered the information that he had arrived with a companion. He also insisted that he had come from Brest.

Pons was next, and certain questions were put to him under caution. Buswell again recorded Hinchley Cooke's questions and Pons' answers. Meier was next and it was the same procedure.

Waldberg was the last to be interrogated. He claimed not to speak a word of English, only French or German. Hinchley Cooke therefore asked 20-year-old Detective Sergeant William Allchin of Special Branch, who was conversant in both French and German, to be in attendance to verify both questions and answers.

Hinchley Cooke questioned Waldberg, under caution, in French and German, and repeated each question aloud, in English. Hinchley Cooke translated into English Waldberg's replies, which, again, were given in either French or German. All questions and answers were taken down by DS Buswell.

When questioned about his compatriots, Waldberg's initial reaction was one of indifference. The experienced Hinchley Cooke, however, genuinely felt that Waldberg could remember the names of Meier and Pons but not that of Kieboom.

Waldberg added, 'I knew them from the journey across, and I knew them from the journey from Brussels. Otherwise I know nothing of them.'

DS Allchin was present throughout this interview to corroborate Hinchley Cooke's interpretations of questions and answers, before they were taken down in shorthand by DS Buswell. Buswell then made typewritten transcripts of the shorthand notes in respect of the four men, and later handed over several copies to Hinchley Cooke. Copies of the prisoners' statements were eventually sent to the Director of Public Prosecutions.

Hinchley Cooke concluded that Waldberg was 'very nervous; he is a very young man, and he is very nervous'.

Waldberg made another statement, in which it was recorded that:

'He landed with three others in the early hours of the 3 September and was found near where he had hidden the W/T and personal belongings. Born 15 July 1918 at Mainz, Waldberg was of German nationality although his mother was French. He spoke French fluently, German badly. Brought up as a Frenchman in Strasburg–Pontoise–Lille–Maubeuge–Sedan and other places; claimed to have served in the Arbeitsdienst; taken on as an office clerk in the German SS at Wiesbaden and later on trained as an agent for the Germans in France.'

Regarding Wiesbaden, Waldberg said that the SS there was divided into an unknown number of sections. He said the leader of the SS at Wiesbaden was a General Kuhn. He said that in the office at Hitlerstrasse, he was a member of Section II, the leader of which was Oberst Meyer, whose wife lived in Berlin. Also in Section II was a Major Seynsburg, who was privately residing in Westphalia, and Oberleutnant Weber, who spoke English and Dutch fluently and was nearly always travelling. The latter was in London in 1939 for some time. There was also an Oberleutnant Werner Uhln, who was sent to Norfolk as a parachutist. He remained there for some time, before being taken back by plane. Uhln had been in South Africa, Egypt and France collecting information, and spoke French, Italian, English and Esperanto fluently. Oberleutnant Koch had formerly lived in Java, San Sebastian and England. He had been working in a hotel in London, and knew London quite well. He now resided at Frankfurt. Waldberg said Koch was due to be dropped as a parachutist in Norfolk or Suffolk in the near future. Finally, there was Private Peter Schneider, who was living at St Vith in Belgium with his family. Schneider was due to come to England by boat in the company of an unknown non-commissioned officer; both were said to speak very good English.

Waldberg confirmed he had worked in France and Belgium before training in Brussels. He said that they landed on the south coast of England; Meier had gone to find something to drink but he never returned. While waiting for his companion, Waldberg had sent his first message; he thought that this was about 8.30 pm. It read:

'JE SUIS BIEN ARRIVE – DOCUMENT DETRUI – PATROULLE ANGLAIS A DEUXCENTMETRE COTE PLAGE AVEC RESEAU

BRUN ET POUTRE DE RAIL DISTANTE SENQUANT METRE PAUE MIN PE SOLDAT BLOKAUS INNACHEVE NOVELL ROUTE.'

('ARRIVED SAFELY. DOCUMENT DESTROYED. ENGLISH PATROL TWO HUNDRED METRES FROM COAST. BEACH WITH BROWN NETS AND RAILWAY SLEEPERS AT A DISTANCE OF FIFTY METRES. NO MINES. FEW SOLDIERS. UNFINISHED BLOCKHOUSE. NEW ROAD.')

He said that the following day, between 5 am and 6 am, he sent his second telegram:

'MEIJER [*sic*] PRISONER. POLICE ANGLAIS ME RECHERCHE. SITUATION DIFICILE. JE POURRAI REGISTER A LA SOIF JUSQUE SAMEDI SI JE DOIS REGISTER ENVOYEZ MERCREDI SOIR AVION. SUIS ALENDROIT D'ARRIVE A TROIS KILOMETRE COTE.'

('MEYER [*sic*] PRISONER. ENGLISH POLICE SEARCHING FOR ME. AM CORNERED. SITUATION DIFFICULT. I CAN RESIST THIRST UNTIL SATURDAY IF I AM TO RESIST SEND AEROPLANES WEDNESDAY EVENING. AM THREE KM NORTH [of point of] ARRIVAL.')

A third message was not transmitted because Waldberg was arrested. He claimed to have thrown his code and revolver into the sea, but remembered a code that he had used before. During interrogation, he wrote down this code, but noticed that certain numbers were placed wrongly so the Germans would not be able to understand it.

Waldberg, who was the only one of the prisoners not to have any papers on him when apprehended, claimed not to be able to remember every detail of the code given to him and the other group. However, he did say what he was instructed to report about:

Military objects in the district Dungeness–Romney–Rye.
Occupation and number of units.
Names of ships passing this part of the coast.
Economic information, such as food, etc.
Aerodromes and number of planes.
Morale in general, and especially during air-raids.

He added that he was ordered to stay in the district until the invasion, and then, if possible, mix with the people who were fleeing the area, taking the W/T with him.

The invasion itself, Waldberg believed, would take place between 3 and 15 September. He revealed that the Germans had told him that their intention was to attack:

East and south from Dungeness and [redacted].
North and east from Norfolk.

He added that they would use artillery on the coast in France, many speedy boats, bombers and parachutists.

Waldberg revealed that notwithstanding the fact that he had admitted to being sent to England for espionage purposes, he was under the impression that he would be treated as a prisoner of war, an idea that the Germans had given him before he was sent. He revealed that he was afraid that the Germans would find him in England, and that he would be shot when they learned that he gave everything away. He claimed that he had not wanted to go to England, as he did not speak English at all, but did not have the courage to refuse because he feared the Germans would then have shot him.

After the completion of their interrogation by Hinchley Cooke, the prisoners were sent on to Camp 020.

Chapter Five

Camp 020 and 'Tin Eye'

Camp 020

The first of the spies started to arrive, one by one, at Latchmere House at 7 pm. Britain's wartime spy prison, also known as Camp 020, was a large, sprawling and gloomy Victorian building, just around the corner from Richmond tube station. It had served as a military hospital during the First World War. It had been a 'home for neurasthenics' and had 'lunatic' cells, so was ready-made for a prison, and was now fortified and was MI5's prime centre for questioning captured enemy spies. The rooms at Latchmere were turned into prison cells, each with a hidden microphone.

The premises were well furnished, with Intelligence officers and secretaries engaged, while guard officers and troops also arrived, all within seventeen days of Camp 020 becoming an internment camp.

While other internment camps at this stage of the war may have had poor organization, untrained staff and slack discipline, with corrupt and often drunk guards, it was a different story at Camp 020.

If justification were needed for Camp 020, it came very early in its history. Britain faced imminent invasion, and the Germans could be expected to introduce agents immediately before the event. Timely and energetic action in the years before the war, and during its early months, meant Germany had no spies in situ in Britain by late summer 1940. The first attempt in landing spies came with the arrival of the 'Brussels Four'. Admissions to Latchmere House prior to these four included '20 British Fascists and 27 subversive or espionage characters'.[1]

Recruitment, however, did not start well at Camp 020. The British fighting soldier had little sympathy for the kind of work done at such establishments. A battalion's worst soldiers would be unloaded when called upon for officers and men. For Latchmere this was particularly true: there was a literal procession of malcontents, unreliables and the medically unfit. For example, they received a man reduced to the ranks, another under suspension of sentence and a third who was 'excused carrying a rifle'. None of these exuded confidence, but they were still sent to the camp. A solution was reached, however, when the Adjutant General ordered that the commandant could handpick his men, and, for that matter, discharge them at will. A trouble-free unit was the result. The men did a dull job well – so well that they never lost a spy.[2]

A powerful psychological tool at Camp 020 was a particular room known as 'Cell Fourteen'. It had mystique, a sinister reputation, and played on the prisoners' own worst fears, which they imagined would come to fruition in Cell Fourteen.[3] It was a padded cell in peacetime, 'so protected that raving maniacs could not bash out their brains against the wall. Some recovered. Some committed suicide. Some died from natural causes.'[4]

Cell Fourteen had been converted so it seemed a perfectly ordinary room, just like all the other rooms, but around which a story of death and madness had been created. Upon entering, the prisoner was told that the previous occupant had committed suicide in it. He would not be spoken to again, and would remain there until he confessed – or until he was taken away 'for the very last time'.[5] As if to reinforce Cell Fourteen's morbid reputation, the mortuary was conveniently situated just opposite it.

The effects of Cell Fourteen varied amongst nationalities:

'A German lost his arrogance. A Spaniard lost the glint of his dark and fiery eye. An Egyptian visibly wasted. An Italian gesticulated wildly for writing materials within the hour. A Frenchman lost his nerve and talked of the "*cellule des condamnés*" [condemned cell]. An Icelander remained unmoved; between Cell Fourteen and the land of desolation there was no contrast.'[6]

Used as a last resort, if being in Cell Fourteen failed and the prisoner didn't cave-in, 'then little hope remained of a break[through]'.[7]

Notwithstanding Cell Fourteen's particularly gruesome reputation, the harsh conditions generally at Latchmere House led to several suicides in its cellblocks.

Camp 020 came under the command of one of the many unusual characters who found their way into the Security Service on the eve of the war.

Lieutenant Colonel Robin 'Tin Eye' Stephens

Lieutenant Colonel Robin Stephens took over as Camp Commandant in July 1940, and straightaway he insisted on being addressed as 'Commandant'.

Born in Alexandria, Egypt, in 1900, Stephens was known as 'Tin Eye' because of the monocle fixed to his right eye – even, allegedly, when he slept. Stephens had close-cropped hair, a mastiff's chin and a ferocious temper.

He was educated at Alexandria's Lycée Francais before returning to England to attend Dulwich College, the Royal Military Academy and then Quetta

Cadet College in India. Besides English, he spoke – and swore in – seven other languages fluently: Urdu, Arabic, Somali, Amharic, French, German and Italian. Stephens spent many years as an officer and was a rising star with the Gurkhas, the elite regiment of the Nepalese troops in the British Army.

He had seen much of the world, but was by no means broad-minded. He acknowledged that he was xenophobic, expressed a dislike for 'weeping and romantic fat Belgians', 'unintelligent Icelanders' and 'shifty Polish Jews', and believed 'Italy is a country populated by undersized, posturing folk'.[8] In Stephens' view of the world, Spaniards were 'stubborn, immoral and immutable', Frenchmen 'volatile', and as for Southern Europeans, 'for all their confounded tantrums, the Latins are less detestable than the Hun'.[9] Germans, however, were at the top of his most-hated list, and as for enemy spies, he wrote that they were 'the rabble of the universe, their treachery not matched by their courage'.[10] He displayed little or no tolerance for homosexual behaviour.

Stephens' charges were not classed as prisoners of war, and had not at that stage been charged with any crime. However, no 'prisoner' was admitted to Camp 020 without a strong prima facie case against them.

Stephens would never allow physical violence to be used against his prisoners; this was a command issued by him from the very first day at the camp. He was not a supporter of physical torture and strong-arm tactics. But this was not the result of progressive thinking on Stephens' part; he simply understood that a confession gained by torture could rarely be trusted:

'Violence is taboo for not only does it produce answers to please, but it lowers the standard of information … Never strike a man. In the first place it is an act of cowardice. In the second place, it is not intelligent. A prisoner will lie to avoid further punishment and everything he says thereafter will be based on a false premise.'[11]

The resident psychiatrist at Latchmere House was Dr Harold Dearden, a man for whom 'Tin Eye' had little time. However, while Stephens eschewed physical violence, he and Dearden devised various psychological regimes of starvation, along with sleep and sensory deprivation, to break the will of the inmates.

Interrogations were very formal, conducted by a seated panel and usually chaired by the monocled, immaculate, multilingual Stephens, who also possessed a loud, commanding voice. A secretary would be present to record proceedings on a stenograph. Stephens had the tenacity to bring attention to the most mundane and precise detail. Questions were rapid, sometimes shouted, often not leaving time for answers, but again there was no physical violence. One officer who struck a prisoner was sacked immediately. Stephens believed a good interrogator sought truth, not humiliation.

Behind the bluster, Stephens was an instinctive and inspired amateur psychologist. He did a great deal of reading on the human psyche, including Freud and Jung. Stephens had a very specialized skill: he broke people. His interrogative abilities, he claimed, stemmed from years of studying the complex minds of the Gurkhas he had commanded. He believed, and told his staff, that their function of Camp 020 was to crush a spy psychologically. They were to crush his mind into small pieces, examine those pieces and then, if they revealed qualities useful to the war effort – for example, becoming double agents – then they must be mentally rebuilt. Those prisoners who did not have the qualities required would end up before a firing squad or with a visit to the gallows.

Stephens' role was interrogating his prisoners and deciding whether they could be used as double agents against their German masters. Before they could be 'turned', however, the spies had to be 'broken' and to admit that they were spies. Stephens used his own carefully concocted methods to break his guests. One method was known as 'Blow-hot/blow-cold'. Stephens would begin by behaving ferociously towards the prisoner. A calm officer would introduce himself, apparently trying to pacify Stephens. The 'kindly' officer would take the prisoner aside and explain gently that perhaps it would be better if he confessed, because Stephens could become a very angry man indeed.

A 'breaker', Stephens opined in a report, 'is born and not made. Pressure is attained by personality, tone and rapidity of questions, a driving attack in the nature of a blast which will scare a man out of his wits.'[12]

Some of his colleagues considered Stephens quite mad, but he was outstanding at his job: establishing the guilt of the enemy spy, breaking down his resistance, extracting vital information, scaring him witless and then handing him over for use as a double agent. 'No one could turn a spy like Tin Eye.'[13]

Arrival at Camp 020

'We are not bound by any rules or regulations. We do not care a damn whether you leave this place on a stretcher or in a hearse.'[14]

(British Intelligence Officer, Camp 020)

The 'Brussels Four' arrived at Camp 020 without papers of any kind, and the statements they had made at Scotland Yard were not available. Upon arrival, all personal property was confiscated and thoroughly checked for any hidden equipment, especially writing materials. The prisoners were stripped and given a body search, which now included, after the earlier discovery of secret writing materials concealed in a false tooth, a thorough dental inspection. Prison clothing was then issued, which consisted of flannel trousers, a coat and a 6in diamond shape of white cloth which was sewn onto a prominent part of the clothing. The prisoners were then escorted and initially put into a cell alone. At this stage, each prisoner at the camp was permitted daily exercise and fed the same rations as the guards. Their particulars would then be taken: name, date and place of birth, nationality, height, weight address etc. A physical examination would be carried out. Photographs, in civilian and prison clothing, were taken. The photograph in civilian clothing could be used without revealing the detainee was at Camp 020; these photographs would be used for recognition purposes in the event of an escape.

Kieboom was the first to arrive. Captain Stimson, the Admin Officer, issued a 'body' receipt to Detective A.E. Higgs of Special Branch for the prisoner. Stimson also issued a 'body' receipt to Detective Constable Arthur Jones of Special Branch upon Pons' arrival, and a similar procedure occurred for Meier. Waldberg was not due to arrive until 6 September.

Kieboom was first to be questioned by Lieutenant Colonel Hinchley Cooke, amongst other officers. Shorthand notes on the questions and answers were taken by Detective Sergeant Buswell.

The prisoner was cautioned after he had confirmed a few identification details, and then explained how he was recruited. At first, Kieboom was not prepared to give information of any value. He was insistent, however, that he had been taken to Brest, put up in an empty house near there and eventually came over to England from Brest.

The immediate and urgent problem the interrogators faced was to break the spies' wireless code in order to send false intelligence back to Germany. But Kieboom was obstructive and, under orders from Germany, lied. Such was his resistance to the truth that it was only after persistent pressure that the code was ultimately obtained from him.

He admitted that they had a radio set but said that he had not sent any messages, as he was arrested soon after landing. Kieboom also admitted to throwing a code down the toilet after he was apprehended. He lived in hope of imminent German liberation, and required less gentle persuasion to part with his version of the story. He was described by his companions as the enthusiast of the party, and Kieboom admitted to being a pre-war agent of Ast Wiesbaden, having been informed of the mission after attachment to Ast Belgium in Brussels. The other three, he said, were more hastily recruited a few weeks before they set out. Meier had been recruited at The Hague, Pons and van Den Kieboom in Amsterdam, and all had been trained in Brussels.

Pons was questioned next. He confirmed who he was and explained that he could understand English if it was spoken slowly. When asked if he had arrived in England 'irregularly', his response was, 'I want to ask this. Regularly would be to come into the harbour on a steamer? Irregularly would be to come in any other way – in a hidden way?' Pons was then informed that anything he said would be used in evidence. He was confused about the term 'evidence', and when told that evidence meant before a court of law, he replied, 'Judges? … Some people who says you are guilty or not guilty?' He struggled with the meaning of coming before a judge or court-martial, until the German word *Kriegsgericht* (military court) was mentioned to him. He continued to struggle understanding English; when told that he was found on the south-east coast of England, Pons replied, 'No. I must say I was going to give myself to the soldiers.'[15]

He told his interrogators that his plan was to give himself up, but he feared going straight to the police while he had in his possession a wireless set, as he thought it was incriminating. 'I could not prove that I was not coming here to tell all of the English people about the German people. They would not believe me – the English,' he said.[16] Pons explained that he had hidden the wireless before going up to a soldier, announcing his presence and explaining that he was from Holland. Then he claimed that he was going to go to the English soldier with nothing and was going to say, 'There is the apparatus'. He stated that what he had meant to say was that he was prepared, under his own volition, to point out the hiding place of the radio set. He said that he had put it in a drainage ditch and that everyone knew that it was not possible to use a wireless once it has been under water. He continued by claiming that coming to England was a way of escaping the Germans, and it was always his intention to report directly to the police upon arrival. 'It was my meaning to go to England and give all I had to the Englishmen. I have told you all I could do. I have told you the truth,'[17] he told his interrogators.

When Meier was asked whether he had arrived in England 'irregularly', he did not need clarification and answered, 'That is right sir.'[18] When asked how he had got involved with the German authorities, he replied that they looked for people in The Hague who were willing to take on rather risky jobs. The only things that Meier knew, he claimed, were that he was to go to England for sabotage and/or spying.

He said he had been put in touch with the authorities via his 'friend' at the Food Control department at The Hague. Meier was adamant that he did not want to be a spy, but wished to help England. He said that before he came ashore, he threw overboard the code pattern and made Waldberg do the same with his gun. When asked why he did that, he replied:

'Because I did not want them to be found on us. As a matter of fact I never wanted to go in for this spying business at all. I accepted because I saw a good way of getting to England, and I thought in that way be of service to you, to my own country, and then perhaps as a reward, you would help me to obtain what I have desired ever since I was in America … So perhaps you could help me … I behaved very foolishly when I got here. I did not create the impression of being honest because I thought of the possibility that the Germans might come over here and find out. So I was scared to carry out my original plan for I had signed up with them.'[19]

The belief that Waldberg was the weakest link invited him to be singled out for a particularly interrogational onslaught. When Waldberg was asked, 'Can you speak English?', and replied, 'I cannot speak a word of English', his interrogation was conducted in German and French. Waldberg's replies in those languages were translated into English by Hinchley Cooke and recorded by DS Buswell. He was informed on more than one occasion that, under English law, he had the right to refuse to answer any questions that were put to him, but each time he said that he would.

Waldberg claimed to be a German soldier – at least on paper – but said he had no military training. He referred to the Headquarters of a German Espionage Service at Wiesbaden, which Hinchley Cooke ascertained had until recently operated against Great Britain and France.

Unlike his co-conspirators, Waldberg did not try to defend his actions. He was open about his association with the Germans, and how he wore a German uniform while acting as secretary to the major of the espionage centre at a prisoner of war camp. He was acquiescent to his interrogators, willingly giving information that could eventually be used against the other three.

When asked how he came to be in England, Waldberg said he was sent by 'my Chief', a major in the German Espionage Service. He said that the major was his boss at Wiesbaden and admitted being a spy by profession, saying that he had been one for about two years. He went on to say that he answered a summons to Wiesbaden because 'I am a German. My father is a German; merely my mother is French.'[20]

The prisoner confessed to sending back two messages after he had arrived in England. He had given a copy of the messages to the arresting officer. Waldberg had no identity papers on him, and added that none of the Germans who would come to England would carry any documents. He admitted, 'There are three Germans who are coming – a lieutenant, a non-commissioned officer and a soldier. I had two secret codes, one [of] which I carried in my head and the other was a sheet of paper with holes in it.'[21] He conceded that he had dropped the secret code, maps and an automatic pistol into the sea.

He added that at 5 pm on 3 September, a German plane came over and signalled to him. Waldberg said that it dived down to where he was standing, and that he gave them a signal with his handkerchief, also placing his bathing towel on the ground, showing up as a square.

He said that after being caught, he had rolled in his aerial, packed it up and handed it to the person who arrested him. He added that he did not break anything, and he could make the radio work 'in five minutes'.[22]

Due to his claim that he could not speak English, Waldberg was not asked to sign his statement. The other three had theirs read to them, amended where necessary, and voluntarily signed them.

Kieboom, Pons and Meier were each shown their passport and asked to confirm its ownership; Waldberg was the only one of the four who did not have such a document.

The interrogation at Ham had revealed that the agents had been given a short-term operational mission: to report on troops, airfields and planes, anti-aircraft defences, ships under repair and civilian morale. Waldberg – allegedly the weakest link, but the only agent with previous experience – had been given instructions which he was ordered to withhold from his companions. After he arrived in England, he was to seize a motor-boat and make for Boulogne. Immediately upon arrival there, he was to report his return and the following day he was to return to the Dungeness area with one of his instructors, 'Werner UHL' alias@ 'WERNER'.[23]

Later that afternoon, the initial interrogation[24] of Kieboom by 'Tin Eye' Stephens (S) and other officers took place. The questions (Q) and answers (A) were recorded as follows:

Q. (S) You made statements to Scotland Yard, you realise the position?

A. Very precarious.

Q. (S) Precarious, you call it, do you! What do you mean by precarious?

A. Very dangerous for me, sir.

Q. (S) Dangerous – in fact you realise you are more likely to be shot! Is that quite understood? You come over here to spy in time of war. You come over to this country in order to help win the war for Germany. That's the situation.

A. I'd like to give myself up.

Q. (S) Don't lie to me. If you lie you will get into further trouble.

A. If you don't believe me …

Q. (S) Certainly I don't believe what you say at the moment. I am making you realise where you stand. You have information and I intend to use it. Do you understand that? If I don't get that information there is only one possible result – you will get shot. And because I know you are likely to lie I am going to check your statement with the statements made by three other spies who came with you. Do you realise the position?

A. Yes, sir.

Q. (S)   You are a man of intelligence and if your statement does not tally with statements given by the other three people there is no hope whatever for you. You understand?

A.   You can rely on me to give you …

Q. (S)   You have information and I intend to use it, do you see?

A.   Yes, sir.

Q. (S)   You are going to be asked a certain number of simple questions and my advice to you is to tell the truth, if you know what that word means! And I'm going to ask those questions of the other three people arrested with you; if they check out there may be some hope for you. I don't hold it out as a promise at all. There may be some hope. Do you understand that?

A.   Yes, sir.

Q. (S)   What was the frequency you sent your messages on?

A.   Five thousand and something.

Q. (S)   What do you mean 'five thousand and something'? You come here to answer a direct question. I want a proper answer without any of these 'somethings'. Do you understand?

A.   I understand perfectly, sir.

Q. (S)   Of course you understand perfectly well, and you know perfectly well what the Germans expected you to do.

A.   Yes, I know.

Q. (S)   If you think you can bring a lot of your damned nonsense here, saying 'five thousand and something' you are very much mistaken. Do you understand?

A.   Yes sir, I do.

Q. (S)   You are asked a direct question and I want a proper answer to that. You were given this instrument to work and you know how to work it, and we want to know how to work that machine, do you understand?

A.   Yes.

Q. (S)   Well, answer that question properly.

A.   This machine is only able to work on one frequency.

Q. (S)   What is the frequency?

A.   It is on the set – I do not know.

Q.   What is the frequency of the set you were given?

A.   Five thousand, sir, I think. I did not get it, really I didn't.

Q.   Then you must be very stupid.

Q.   What was your emergency frequency?

A.   I do not know.

Q.   And what messages were you supposed to send? Connected with what?

A.   Anything of military importance.

Q.   For what purpose?

A.   I don't know.

Q. (S) Don't lie; you make me sick. You had instructions and had to send out specific information. What had you to look for?

A.   Batteries.

Q.   What else?

A.   Obstacles on streets.

Q. (S) Whether there was any Air Force?

A.   No, airports, sir.

Q.   What else? Go on. What else? Don't waste my time.

A.   I am trying to think, sir. Whether the southern part of England was evacuated or not.

Q. (S) What else?

A.   What was the morale of the civilian population, and whether the price of food had gone up or not.

Q. (S) The object of this was in order to facilitate an invasion – is that right?

A.   I think so.

Q. (S) Well, why the hell didn't you say so before? And when is [an] invasion supposed to take place?

A.   I don't know, sir – I don't suppose they'd tell me.

Q.   How long have you been in the employ of the Germans?

A.   I have never been in the employ of the Germans, sir. Never.

Q. (S) You are now.

A.   Well … sir.

Q. (S) How long have they been in touch with you?

A.   A few days before the 26 July when we came over to Brussels.

Q. (S) That is a lie too, isn't it?

A.   It is not a lie, sir.

Q.   You have only been in touch with them since 26 July?

A.   A few days before that they came to fetch me, sir.

Q.   Why did they come to fetch you?

A.   I do not know, sir. I don't know why they came to fetch me.

Q. (S) They just picked on you out of several million people! It is rather an odd thing to do, isn't it?

A.   It is, sir.

Q.   You don't think that it's true?

A.   I do think it, sir …

[Interrogation ends]

Although the interrogation of spies was a deadly serious endeavour and presented a very difficult task to obtain the facts, the questioning in this instance was littered with elements of sardonicism and laced with, as to be expected, threats and anger in order to determine the veracity of the answers.

Kieboom was interrogated further by Stephens:[25]

Q. (S)   With regard to the transmissions, with regard to the messages, let's go over that business again. How do you start your message?

A.   I start by finding the chronometer sir.

Q. (S)   Go on, tell us what it is.

A.   ZNK sir. Then I have to give a dash ... then three points and a dash and then the cipher, the number of letters in the code (the message) then a dash and then the message itself.

Q. (S)   Nothing else?

A.   No sir.

Q. (S)   Are you lying about this, because either you are lying or other people are lying. I prefer to believe that <u>you</u> have lied about it. What have you omitted? What do you suppose you can gain by telling the half-truth?

A.   I don't know what I have omitted sir. I don't know what you mean sir.

Q. (S)   Do you ever use the letter P?

A.   [Inaudible]? Not yet.

Q. (S)   And how did you end this message? Did you ever hear of the letter T? Come on, come on, tell the truth.

A.   Yes sir; that's right.

Q. (S)   Where do you put that?

A.   At the very end of the message sir.

Q. (S)   Why didn't you say so before? ... You snivelling little swine, what do you stand to gain by lying like this? Do you think you are so clever that you can tell any lie you like and we have to accept it? Have you enough intelligence to realise that you are going to be shot, and that the only way of trying to save your neck is by trying to tell the truth, or have such faith in your Boche masters that you think that they will welcome you with open arms when they come into this country? How many more lies have you told?

A.   I think that is everything sir.

Q. (S)   That's just a couple of quick ones is it? Why did you say you had left Brest when it was Le Touquet? Answer the question. It's no good hesitating to think out another quick lie. Why did you say Brest instead of Le Touquet. You sailed from Le Touquet didn't you?

A. No sir, it was not Le Touquet, it was Paris Plage they called it.

Q. (S) Paris Plage. Why did you say then that you had left Brest?

A. Because they told us to say that we came from Brest.

Q. (S) I see. So you are still telling lies – you still believe in your masters, is that right?

A. It isn't that sir. When we had to go to …

Q. (S) Yes it is. You lying swine, you were under orders from the Germans to tell these lies. They said that you were to leave Brest … What were the lies about the area which you were supposed to cover in this country?

A. I told you that exactly sir.

Q. (S) Is that what the Germans told you to say?

A. No sir, the area was between Dungeness and Hythe … seaports that was the original, to work back in Ashford.

[Note: telephone conversation interrupts audibility]

Q. (S) But the Germans told you to say that your beat was between Dungeness and some other place and to work back to Ashford.

A. Yes sir.

Q. (S) They told you to say that.

A. No sir, that was our mission.

Q. (S) Well, how am I to believe that in the face of lie after lie?

A. Well sir you might find a map I threw away in the …

Q. (S) You think that's easy?

A. It is a chance.

Q.(S) You have lied within the last five minutes. How many more lies have you told tonight?

…

Q. (S) That was a lie, and your second lie was about this transmission and the third lie was about the secret ink. Who is your contact in this country?

A. Nobody sir.

Q. (S) Is that your fourth lie? How am I to tell whether you are speaking the truth or not?

A. It <u>is</u> the truth sir, absolutely.

[Interrogation ends]

This second interrogation followed shortly after the first one and was conducted in the same vein: cynical, with threats and anger in order for the interrogators to get the prisoner to reveal the truth. Sometimes during these interrogations, Kieboom's answers did not necessarily bear any resemblance to the questions asked.

In another interview conducted at Latchmere House, Pons was questioned. He was evasive and deliberately obtuse with some of his answers to the questions put to him. He denied recognizing names and any knowledge of his compatriots on the mission, save for his immediate partner. He did admit he knew how precarious the position was in which he had found himself. Pons also admitted that he came to England to work against the British; that he came over from Le Touquet, and that if his companion claimed they came from Brest, then Kieboom must be lying, insisting that he, Pons, was telling the truth.

When asked how many people were at the house in Le Touquet, Pons' response was: 'Civilized people?' When told not civilized people but people like him – a spy – he immediately denied being a spy.

He was initially evasive when questioned about having a map and denied knowing where he was supposed to land in England. Pons then muddied the waters by saying that he left from Boulogne. He then admitted using a map and that he was to land at Dungeness, eventually making his way to London.

Next, he was asked about codes and sending messages. Pons professed to leaving his code in the boat, but when questioned how he was to send messages in an emergency without that code, he said that there was another method, which he described.

Pons was then given a message to send by the interrogator and told to put it into code. He was warned, more than once, 'If you do this wrong you will lose your life, you understand?'[26] He tried to ask a question, but was rebuffed as the interrogators conversed with one another. Pons' reaction to all this was phlegmatic. He went on to explain the process of how he would send a message back to the Germans.

He denied loving Germany, but repeated that he thought that the Germans would soon arrive in England. He expected an invasion of England and thought that it would be 'this year', but did not know when. When asked why, he answered that most Germans thought the same. When pressed, he said he believed that they might have already arrived; he thought that they may have been in England since August.

Under further questioning, he changed his tune and said that he did originally think that the invasion would happen in August, but now did not believe that the Germans would come to England. He said that while he had heard artillery fire while he was at Le Touquet, he had not seen a lot of troops there.

It was suggested that he must have known about an invasion because of the amount of money he had upon him when arrested, enough for about two weeks. However, he claimed not to have the money; his accomplice had it. When asked what would happen if his partner had died and why he did not take half of the money himself, Pons' reply was nebulous: 'I have a daughter with money enough.'[27]

Pons said that his only reward from the Germans for working for them was that he would be free from their persecution. He was still afraid that the Germans would shoot him if they had already landed in England.

He was then threatened by the interrogators to be shot as a spy, 'Suppose we shoot you? Why shouldn't we shoot you? You are a spy.' Pons again denied being one, saying, 'Sir, you know I am not really a spy.'[28] He went on to say that his sole intention when he arrived in England was to give himself up to the authorities, with the hope that the English would eventually 'spirit' him and his wife away.

When asked about his role when he came to England, he replied that he was to find information on coastal mines, patrols and guns, but, to the incredulity of his interrogators, not aircraft.

When presented with a W/T machine, Pons could not verify whether or not it was his, 'It is all the same. There are many of the same kind … I have seen five or six … in Brussels … It was all wrapped up, I have only seen the ground sheets wrapped around it.'[29]

When asked what he was supposed to do when the batteries had run down on his transmitter, his response was, 'They said to me "they run not down".'[30] He had been told that they would last for months.

Leonard William Humphreys, an inspector from the Radio Branch of the Post Office Engineering Department, had examined the captured wireless sets, which were still in their thick leather black cases. He concluded that:

They were designed to transmit and receive Morse signals.

They had a range of up to 100 miles, easily capable of sending Morse messages from the south-east coast of England to the Continent.

It would have been impossible for the equipment to have been immersed in water and still have been in perfect working order.

The batteries would have lasted about a fortnight if run continuously.

The sets were, in the opinion of Humphreys, 'in perfect working order'.[31]

Meier was questioned again. After three-and-a-half hours of interrogation, he showed willingness to provide information. He was the first to admit that he came to England with another intention, and also mentioned where his companion, Waldberg, could be found, saying that he was in possession of a W/T transmitter.

As well as being questioned, Meier wrote,[32] amongst many other things, about going to America and his love for the country, and his medical studies in Germany, financed by money he inherited. He also wrote about his fiancée, Margaret Moseley, and his views on the Germans:

'When she went to continue her studies in Berlin I went there too and I stayed till summer 1938 when I applied for an immigration visa to the US. Being sure I'd get on the Dutch quota I arranged everything for my departure, bought a ticket for the passage and everything. In Rotterdam I found out that I couldn't get on the Dutch quota as I was born in Germany.

'Up till my fifth year I've had German nationality. I became a Dutchman, because my mother, who was originally Dutch, went back to Holland and got re-naturalised after my father had died. As I had my education up till seventeen years of age in Holland, you'll understand that by that time I had become a thoroughbred Dutchman and didn't feel German in the least. As a matter of fact the German disregard for other nations' achievements, the boorish manner in which they give expression to their contempt for other people, [meant] Germans have irked me always and from time to time I've downright hated them. Their disregard of every moral code if it suits their plans is maybe very interesting as a practical conception of Nietzsche's philosophy, but there can be no peace in this world as long as it is not based on trust and the way things are at the moment is a direct result of the Nazi-policy, which has destroyed this possibility and now nobody seems to trust nobody.'

Meier said that he had met NSNAP member Koos Vorrink, who persuaded him to work for Germany. He was told this would involve going to England by plane, landing by parachute and sending radio messages. Meier's story, as he attempted to save his life, seemed all too predictable to his interrogators:

'I was all for it, because here I saw my chance to get away. My first intention was to fool the Germans, walk to the nearest police-station as soon as I had landed, turn over the radio and everything, tell the secret service as much as I could, expecting as a reward full support from the English Government to get me an immigration visa to Canada. I came to change those plans and built myself a miserable net of lies in which I got tangled up hopelessly, because I happen to be about the worst liar ever born.'

Meier said he was told by Vorrink that he'd have to join the NSNAP party:

'... so I did and showed the most possible enthusiasm, joined the SA and all that sort of stuff. Mind you, please [believe] that all this was part of the game I had to play and that for me it will always be America forever. It has been that way ever since I went there the first time. If you'd ask me, what I like most about it, I'd say: "It's the wonderful feeling of freedom, space and wealth you get there." To use a phrase, "The wide open spaces got me." To me there is just nothing that can compare with the Midwestern corn fields when they're ripe. America is my country as it has my heart and I'd never allow anyone to slight it. By the end of June 1939, when the tension around Danzig was growing rapidly, I went to the army offices in Chicago and asked them whether I could enlist in the American army as a volunteer. I went together with a Chicago friend of mine, a Mr De Roover, a Belgian and although the office may not know it anymore, they refused, they don't take foreigners. He will tell you that I'm speaking the truth. I'm sure you can find plenty of good references about him.

'The man who worked together with the German officials in Holland in order to recruit people for this job was a Mr Lensing from Utrecht. The one who did his job in The Hague was Group Leader Goyvaerts, a Belgian of origin, living [at] Paramariborstraat, 2a, The Hague. The German talent scout's name is Kurt Mirow, a cavalry captain; he had with him at that time a certain Dr Erfurt, a gefreiter, who helped him because of his knowledge of the Dutch language. With me were recruited, Mr Heidenrich, working for a garage in Amsterdam, Mr de Vreede from New York, Mr Klein Nagelvoort from The Hague …

'I was the only one who knew beforehand what was expected of me, at least from my group. Vorrink had told me. They had asked him for a rather dangerous job, the particulars of which he'd hear in Brussels, and which required ability to work with the Morse code and knowledge of the English language. He asked, point blank, "Why don't you call a spade a spade, why don't you say you want me to jump out of an aeroplane and send messages from England?" They admitted it. He told me about it and warned me not to accept. For the foretold reason [to escape the Germans], I accepted eagerly, that was exactly what I had wanted the minute he had told me before about a possible job of this kind, only less danger involved, not in prohibited areas, quite openly playing refugee and sabotaging. I knew very well what I wanted at that moment, I felt I was outwitting the Germans very nicely and all that. On the 30th of July we left The Hague, de Vreede and I, for Brussels together with Mr Mirow. In the next two days, they got the other fellows. They had to do it that way, because they couldn't get hold of a bigger car. They used a small 1938 Opel type with a licence plate from the province of Hanover bearing the number I5 … (I don't know the cipher) … The first week de Vreede and I were in Brussels we stayed at the Hotel Metropole at the Place de Brouckère. I have noticed many very High German officers, like generals, etc there. I don't think the staff is there because there seems to be no telephone connection with the hotel, except of course the house telephone. The Germans have opened a telephone centre in the Plaza Hotel on the Rue de Malines, and another hotel I know where quite a number of officers live is the hotel Gallia et Britannia on the corner of the Avenue des Arts and Rue Joseph II. After that week we were put in the Hotel Les Ambassadeurs, Avenue de l'Astronomie 2, whose proprietor is a man called de Block, originally from Kortrijk Kourtray, correspondent and salesman of the Rheinisch-Westfälische Zeitung. Exceedingly pro-German, and married to a French wife, who was also moderately pro-German. The house is always filled with subaltern German officers and soldiers. The man told me how he turned over somebody to the Gestapo. It is a fact that the house could stay open all night and that contrary to all Belgian laws, he sold liquors to his customers per glass. He claimed he could do so because nobody would harm him. After about a fortnight of rather lavish entertainment, including expensive nightclubs like Maxim (Place de Brouckère), Atlanta, a new joint underneath the Atlanta Hotel, the Gatzy (in [the] hands of a German), etc., we were taken to a red brick house on the Rue Stevin 4, and asked by Mr Morow and Mr Kohler (his alias was Dr Kuhn) whether we wanted to go through with this plan. We had been told earlier about the plan, after about a week in Brussels they asked us to sign a paper that we were going through with it. The others refused, I signed. Here's the plan. We were to be landed in England either by plane or with a fish cutter and to send radio messages about the impression the German bombardments and so on made on the people. Of course no military information, that would be too dangerous. I bet you notice the technique as well as I did.'

Meier also spoke of visiting Rue Stevin and Rue Joseph II in Brussels for Morse training, instruction regarding the British Army, the areas in England the Germans were interested in, where the Germans ate and who he came to Brussels with:

'We got trained in two different houses, one on Rue Stevin No 4, the other one Rue Joseph II 48. We had to learn something about the British Army and also how to Morse, not more than 40 letters a minute was required.

'Here are the places the Germans said they were interested in: the space included by a line London, Reading, Oxford, Northampton, King's Lynn, Ipswich, Colchester, and London. Furthermore, the troops standing on the line Croydon, Bristol. I don't know whether they just said it in order not to scare us too much because they said "You don't need to go near the coast, because we know there are troops there, we want to know where the reserves stand though."

'Here are two places I know where lots of Germans eat: Plazer (mainly higher officers), Metropole Chausse de Louvain, St. Josse (mainly soldiers), the latter place has a very peculiar thing, no rationing – tickets of any sort are required. To me this is very suspicious, because the rationing must have been going on ever since the Germans came.

'While I was in Brussels, I was allowed to take a trip to Maastricht. Mr Mirow took care of that. I stayed there for two days and told the family I had a job in Brussels as an interpreter. This was very shortly after we had arrived in Brussels.

'I forgot to tell you that from the fellows I came to Brussels with, two were very eager to do at least something, Klein Nagelvoort (KN) and de Vreede. KN wanted to go as a refugee and sabotage [*sic*]. Last I've heard of his plan was that it's definitely off. But he may do harm some other way. De Vreede is going to work in the US and Canada. He's following a course in Berlin now, and will go there by way of Siberia and Japan. Please warn the American Embassy about him. He may be swindling the Germans, however, as he has no Nazi ideals at all and is a Theosophist, which is a line of thought not very much appreciated in Germany.'

Meier continued:

'We went through Boulogne in which port I saw several small German warships. I believe they were mine-sweepers; the port is guarded by balloons and anti-aircraft guns. I did not see the exact places where they stood, I can only describe about the position of one big anti-aircraft gun. It stands on a big hill quite near the chateau of Mr de Liepvre ... there is a built-in coastal gun (I don't know which size) on the cliff on the sea side of the main road between Boulogne and Wimereux, shortly before this road begins to turn downward to Wimereux. The big white hotel by the beach is used by the Germans. I know ... that they have an officers' and a soldiers' mess there.

'We were put in the chateau of M de Liepvre, this is important; it's a communication radio-station. It communicates with Brussels. I think the station in Brussels is in the Ministere de Ravitaillement or in the Ministry of Economics in the Rue de la Loi. I know for more [*sic*] it must be around there, besides I saw that official Ministry stationery was used. I want to tell you again, I'm not sure about the exact spot or Ministry; I'm only sure of the location it must have [been] about.

'The hill with the heavy anti-aircraft gun they said, is east of the chateau at least so a German soldier told me. Two days before our final start for England we went to row [at] La Canche near Etaples. Going downstream [at] La Canche, before you reach the bridge in the east block of houses is the harbour-police station. There we got into our clothes each time we went to row.'

Meier attempted to justify his actions and why he didn't give himself up to the authorities:

'They also told us that since we had signed we couldn't go back on them anymore and if we were to squeal, they'd get us as soon as they were in England. Besides, the English would just make use of the information given to them and shoot us for safety's sake. It seemed probable to me, I hadn't thought of it that way and there seemed no other way out than to leave the radio and anything behind and play [at being a] refugee. On the other hand I thought it possible that the Germans might succeed in getting across. There would undoubtedly be records and so on left, of when and how we arrived and what we said and so on. So we, or at least I, because I didn't know how Waldberg thought about the matter, could not very well walk up to the police on the very first day, as the Germans were going to put us ashore somewhere between Rye and Dungeness in what they think they told us was a rather deserted region and would not be guarded very well. It might seem suspicious to them, besides, what was Waldberg going to do, would he squeal? So, I'd better go through with it, get [the] radio and sack hidden ashore, beat it and tell the police my refugee story, which would be the best thing.

'As you see I had got myself into a mess and didn't know how to get out again. One thing was clear with me; I was going to get rid of this spying business somehow. I didn't want to go through with it. But how could I give this scheme up without raising Waldberg's suspicion. I hardly knew what to do.

'While we were in the dinghy I wanted to throw the radio overboard and the sack but didn't dare because of Waldberg. I could convince him though to throw the gun he had overboard, and I threw the code pattern away.'

Meier concluded his statement with a certain resignation:

'I don't want to write anymore, I'd rather have you question me. I'll be glad to give any information that can be of service to you.

'I realise I've made a mess of it whereas perhaps if I had told you everything from start and done as I first intended to, if I hadn't been such a coward, we might to-day shake hands, whereas now you see every word I write only as a self-defence and not a word of truth.

'If you think it absolutely necessary to kill me, please do so quickly, but tell me and give me time to write a farewell letter to my mother and fiancée.'

It was early evening by the time Stephens and other MI5 officers interviewed Meier. He knew he was out of his depth and his tone was conciliatory. He tried to ingratiate himself by saying things like America was really his country and that England and his beloved America worked together in tandem. He was compliant, telling them:

> 'I'm going to tell the truth, because I always wanted to go to America. That is really my country and I know that England and America, they work together … I will give you any information you want, and true information. You can check up on it … I assure you of my loyalty.'

Stephens was unsurprisingly belligerent:

> 'You don't know the meaning of the word "loyalty". People like you are the scum of the earth. You fiddle about in everything and you talk about loyalty. Damned impertinence, that. I want the truth out of you, and the price of it is your neck. That's the business, do you understand?'[33]

Meier was in no doubt. He understood. He had given exhaustive information regarding codes, and named his fellow spies. He described his journey to England and how he trained in Brussels. He was quite happy to do whatever was necessary to placate his captors.

He claimed to want to go to England alone and 'spill the beans' to the English authorities as soon as possible regarding the nefarious deeds he was ordered to undertake. He was very cooperative, and repeated statements like, 'I will give you any information you want, and true information. You can check up on it … I assure you of my loyalty.'

He was happy to admit that should his fellow spies' accounts not tally with his then it would be them lying, not him. He denied all knowledge of any messages having been sent back to the Germans.

Meanwhile, Captain Grassby's department sent a 'Secret' letter to Lieutenant Colonel Hinchley Cooke which answered the latter's request by sending him a sketch map based on a 1in Ordnance Survey map which showed the approximate positions where the four men had landed on the morning of 3 September. The letter also informed Hinchley Cooke that the Chief Constable of Kent had arranged for photographs of the boats, and of the landing places where they were originally found, to be taken and forwarded to the security services. Furthermore, any food that was found there was sent to Hinchley Cooke.

As a result of the treatment received by Mr Halcro when he tried to interview the suspects at Seabrook, an officer from the Immigration Office at Gravesend swiftly fired off a complaint to HM Chief Inspector. He maintained that a legally authorised Immigration Officer should have dealt with the aliens first and foremost, and not have his role and function reduced to a formality by the intervention of a representative from another department. He continued by saying that it was an unfortunate instance of overlapping. The immigration authorities recognized that the military authorities had certain powers under the Defence regulations for taking part in the examination of people whose activities were open to suspicion, but that an Immigration Officer experienced in interrogation and with possibly linguistic qualifications was the proper person to examine all aliens. If the Security Service wished to interrogate such persons, it should have been in conjunction with the Immigration Officer, or if this was not possible, after the Immigration Officer; certainly not before.

He added that it was unfortunate that there were long stretches of coast with ports at which there was no Home Office representative. If it were otherwise, he added, it would have been possible to ensure that any aliens were dealt with by an Immigration Officer appointed by the Secretary of State under the Aliens Order. He concluded that in this case it was conceivable that these men were all Germans who just happened to be furnished with Dutch passports, but that without personal examination it was obviously impossible for an Immigration Officer to ascertain this or any other valuable information.

Chapter Six

Spies in Surrey

Friday, 6 September 1940:
A Messerschmitt crashes near Old Romney, Kent. Troops are quickly on the scene. The pilot is still in the blazing cockpit. There is no way that they can pull him clear. Instead, they shoot him as an act of humanity so as to stop any undue suffering.[1]

The last of the 'Brussels Four' had arrived and all four spies were now ensconced at Camp 020, but the statements the men had made at Scotland Yard were still not available.

Lieutenant Colonel Stephens called a conference and discussed the new intake with the respective case officers. Policy and tactics were agreed upon. In such a group investigation, it was essential to concentrate at the outset on the weakest link. The indication, from the Orderly Officer's report on the men's demeanour in the course of his last inspection and from previous interrogations, identified Waldberg as that weakest link.

In a memo marked 'Secret' and 'Urgent', Stephens reported that he had interrogated three of the German spies (Kieboom, Meier and Pons) between 7 pm on 5 September and 0.45 am on 6 September. Three officers from W (Wireless) Branch and one MI5 officer were also present at these interviews. The main object of the interrogations was to obtain technical information to enable W Section to transmit false intelligence, using the captured transmitter, back to Germany.

During the interrogations, strategic questions were put by Stephens, and a consensus from the three prisoners was finally obtained. Stephens reported[2] that the following five points resulted from the interrogation:

(a) The spies were under instructions to report on British defensive measures on the coast near Dungeness, and the Army reserve formations in depth from Dungeness to Ashford and then on to London.

(b) German concentration for invasion centres on Le Touquet and Paris Plage. The spies had been instructed by the 'Doctor' from Brussels, if caught by the British authorities, to mention falsely concentrations at Brest. (This point was treated with extreme suspicion).

(c) The spies' version tallied in respect to considerable concentrations of mountain troops, equipped with mules, in Le Touquet.

(d) The demeanour of the spies was such that they were convinced the invasion of England would take place before the middle of September. Spies were to work in pairs; food for seven days had been provided and £60 per pair in English currency for expenses calculated to last fourteen days.

(e) No German contact in England had been given as it was deemed unnecessary since the German armies would themselves be in England within fourteen days. Each spy had special instructions in regard to signalling by handkerchief to the approaching German forces and each was in possession of a formula to make himself recognized by the German Intelligence Officers.

Stephens' report was telephoned to the Defence Security Service at 9 am.

Stephens concluded that the most intelligent of the men was Kieboom, who had excellent language skills. The other two, Pons and Meier, spoke English well, and all three had been instructed to represent themselves as refugees from Nazi oppression.

It was noted that during his internment, Pons particularly expressed anti-Semitic views, as well as admiration for German efficiency.

A 'Secret' report, destined for the Joint Intelligence Committee, was also issued as a result of the four men being interrogated by MI5 officers in London shortly after their arrest and detention.

Their stories in each case tallied: Pons and Kieboom arrived in one open boat, Meier and Waldberg in the other, before daylight on 3 September. They had come from Boulogne, and had been towed by two minesweepers, towing two fishing smacks with two rowing boats attached. They were cast off somewhere south of Dungeness, and one boat, carrying Meier and Waldberg, was beached at Lydd-on-Sea, with the other, carrying Pons and Kieboom, near Dymchurch Redoubt. Each party appeared to have been self-supporting, and carried a supply of food for about fourteen days, £30 in English bank and Treasury notes, wireless transmitters, a pair of binoculars, a certain number of clothes, cigarettes and a bottle of brandy, but no water. Each party had possession of a code.

The report[3] also stated that the four men were sent to London and interrogated by officers of MI5, who elicited certain information:

1. The spies were under instructions to report on British defence measures on the coast near Dungeness, and on Army reserve formations from Dungeness to Ashford and thence to London.

2. By reason of the fact that they had been given provisions for only fourteen days, and from everything they gleaned from their contacts on the other side,

the spies were convinced that invasion would take place before the middle of September.

3. All the accounts agree that there were considerable concentrations of mountain troops, equipped with mules, at Le Touquet.
4. The spies were given no German contacts in England. They explained this by saying it was unnecessary as the German armies would be here within two weeks. They gave accounts of making themselves known to German army officers after the arrival. The method seems to have been no more than the waving of a handkerchief, and the impression has been gained by our interrogations that the German SS directors are entirely indifferent as to the fate of these men, once they have accomplished the task allotted to them during the next few days.

At 5.45 pm on 6 September, a telephone message from Lieutenant Colonel Stephens was received, which read:[4]

'Between 11.30 am and 1.50 pm on 6 September, Waldberg – the most experienced German agent of the four – was interrogated by Stephens at Latchmere House. Also present were officers from RSS, B24 and W Branch.

'The object of the interrogation was primarily to corroborate technical information already obtained with a view to transmitting false intelligence to Germany by wireless. Stephens understood that the interrogation had been successful in this respect and Captain T.A. 'Tar' Robertson, Head of MI5's B1 (a), (Special Agents), would be sending messages in the near future.'

It said that during the interrogation Waldberg had revealed:

- He had to report to the Nazis on the coastal defences Rye – Dungeness – Hythe and the interior bounded by the old Royal Military Canal.
- Reporting 'weak coastal dispositions' would constitute a false message that would induce the Germans to invade in this area. Strong forces in the Royal Military Canal would not affect matters. On the other hand, a report that the coast was strongly held would result in abandonment of an attack in that area, but would not prevent a landing on the East Coast of England from Aldeburgh as far as, but not including, the Wash, as German Intelligence knows the Wash to be heavily mined.
- The general German plan is to attack London simultaneously from Rye/ Hythe and Aldborough/The Wash.

- Waldberg, as did his compatriots, confirmed the presence of troops 'with mules' in the Le Touquet area. The inference drawn by Stephens is that the troops with mule transport are to be used:
  I.   to reduce sea transport of heavy motor vehicles;
  II. to cope with the nature of marsh country near the S.E. coast.
- Waldberg admits he was a Fifth Column spy in the invasions of Belgium and -France and he further asserts that he is the first of the spies to be landed in connection with the invasion of Britain. He denies others have been sent before him but he claims that he knows of an Oberlieutenant [*sic*] and two German soldiers who may follow the original party of four 'civilian spies'. He gives the impression of not fearing anything as he considers himself to be a 'prisoner of war' and is not liable to be shot as a spy. He then volunteers to work for England 'loyally' giving his '*parole d'honneur*' (word of honour) until the Germans arrive. He is quite convinced the invasion will succeed before the middle of September.
- Finally, Waldberg states that he can send a message to Germany, which would result in his contacting a Messerschmitt by sheet and handkerchief signal, to which the aircraft would reply by a burst of machine-gun fire. Thereafter other instructions would follow.

The agents were already partially broken, but it was vitally important and urgent to extract from them the full details of their recruitment, training and mission, and to learn whether any further agents might be expected from the same source. Another immediate and urgent problem the interrogators faced was to break the spies' wireless code in order to send false intelligence to Germany.

The information from Waldberg was telephoned to the PA to the Defence Security Service at 5 pm.

As a direct result of the four German spies landing in England, there was a real belief that similar tactics may well be adopted by others attempting to infiltrate England by land or air. The Home Office therefore reacted by issuing a set of instructions, under the direction of the Secretary of State, for various police forces and other agencies. The Home Office was conscious of the fact that other spies may be arriving in England to take refuge, masquerading as men escaping from the clutches of the Germans on the Continent.

The authorities were trying to learn from what had happened just three days earlier, as shown by this summary of a Home Office circular:[5]

'Immediately review your existing arrangements for detecting surreptitious landings both from the sea and the air, and warn all members of your force to exercise the utmost vigilance in this direction. Any person found in suspicious circumstances who cannot give a satisfactory account of themselves should be detained for enquiries.

'If any person thought to have landed surreptitiously is arrested or detained the procedure set out [in a memo enclosed with Home Office circular (700,170/116)] is subject to the following modifications:

'(i)   The Duty Officer, W Section, MI5 should be informed immediately by telephone, and ask for directions as to further action, including the disposal of the prisoner. The regional representative of MI5 should be informed by telephone as soon as possible afterwards.

'(ii)   All articles in the possession of each prisoner should be carefully preserved and kept separate; any articles found in the neighbourhood which are likely to be connected to the case but cannot be assigned to a particular prisoner should also be kept separate.

'(iii) Special care should be taken to search the immediate neighbourhood of the arrest, and of the place where the prisoner is thought to have landed, for any wireless apparatus, or object likely to be such apparatus, and batteries, and for blank paper. (Wireless apparatus may be quite small – possibly no larger than a hand camera – and may be concealed.)

'(iv)   Special care should be taken to see that the prisoner does not make away with any article in his possession while relieving, or feigning to relieve, the calls of nature [as Kieboom claimed to have done].

'(v)   A thorough search should be made in the vicinity of the arrest both for suspicious persons and suspicious articles, and in the case of landings from the sea the Coast Watchers in the police district should be asked to give special attention to the possibility of other landings being attempted.

'A description of any missing person thought to be connected with a prisoner should be circulated to neighbouring forces as quickly as possible, e.g. by Express Message, but the message should be confined to essential information and should not give more details of the case than are necessary to enable the missing person to be identified.'

Clearly, lessons had been learned following the arrest and interrogation of the Brussels Four.

A Mr Frost (quite possibly Malcolm Frost, Head of (B3) Communications, and (B3a) Censorship) produced a report[6] of his interrogation with Kieboom, Pons and Meier. The interview was primarily for wireless purposes. Frost concluded that:

1. None of the three had sent a message.
2. Pons and Meier did not know their frequency. Kieboom ultimately said his was 5929 or 5939 (the frequencies of the captured sets were 5939 and 5986). Frost recommended little reliance should be put on Kieboom's statement.
3. Kieboom and Pons denied knowledge of which was their set. Meier said his was No. 4 and that sets Nos 4 and 5 came to England.
4. All three agreed that the working times were 5 am to 8 am and 10 pm to 2 am MEZ [Central European Time]. Pons and Meier asserted that a daily call should be made and if they had nothing of importance to send then they should send weather reports. Kieboom, on the other hand, said a call should only be made if there was anything to send.
5. Calls from Kieboom were prefixed with 'ZNK' [ZINKBADEWANNE] whilst Meier's had 'RGB' [RANGIERBAHNHOF]. These calls must be sent 3 to 5 minutes [*sic*] and messages to be sent twice.
6. All three asserted they had no receiving sets and no other method of receiving instructions. All say that wireless was their only method of sending information. All three tell the same story that the invisible ink apparatus was for their own use so that they could make invisible notes during the day to transmit at night.
7. Meier gave the full preamble of a message – the others confirmed portions of it. It was: RGB RGB RGB – KA – ... – P – – – No of letters and figures; – ... – text AR . – . SK.
8. All agreed they had two ciphers and that the first had been destroyed – one being thrown overboard and the other, by Kieboom, down a drain. The destroyed documents were the frame with blanks. The other cipher, the emergency cipher, was a simple transposition with key work, for Kieboom ZINK BADE WANNE; for Meier RAN GIE RBA HN HOF (calls are linked with these words). The letter 'P' in the preamble above indicates that the emergency code was being used. The messages were to be signed with the letter 'T', part of the encipher, a full stop was XX; a semi-colon X; and an X was to be put before and after figures.
9. Kieboom said the aerial was to be put north and south, being directed for Brussels, where they all pretended the receiving station was.
10. The three agreed that there was no scheme of replacement for the batteries, and they all thought the batteries would last till the Germans had invaded England.
11. Their general instructions seem to be to report on troop concentrations; obstacles; civilian morale, etc, on the sea from in the Dungeness, Hythe, Folkestone area, and possibly inland as far as Ashford.

Other miscellaneous information was also gleaned by Frost:[7]

1. Their spy names were:
   a) KIRCHE (Kieboom)
   b) PLEITE (Pons)
   c) MILCH (Meier)
2. The agent school is in Brussels, and Dr Kohler paid them, and instructed them on the organisation of the British Army. The Dr also went to Le Touquet, where he gave them a cheery good-bye, and [told] them about the difficulties of landing.
3. Capt Mirow appeared to tout around concentration camps enlisting spies.
4. A man by the name of Kuhrit had a set near Boulogne, which he worked at Brussels, and said he might be dropped by parachute, but this was doubtful as it was voluntary. This particular set is both a receiver and a transmitter.
5. Peter Schroeder came with Meier from Brussels to Boulogne, and appeared to be an agent expert in W/T.
6. There was an agreement that there were a large number of 'Mountain Troops', with mules, stationed along the coast of Northern France.
7. The Dr had given instructions that if captured they were to say they came from Brest.

Captain Grassby sent a 'Secret' memo to Hinchley Cooke, which informed him that the two sacks of food and drink which belonged to the four suspected enemy agents had been sent to him. Grassby also requested an acknowledgement. In another 'Secret' memo to Hinchley Cooke, Grassby sent photographs of the landing boats and landing places of the four men. A key to the photographs was also sent.

Saturday, 7 September 1940:
'The Blitz' hits London. Following Hitler's promise of retaliation on 4 September, German bombers raid London in earnest with the first coordinated attack on the city in an effort to break the resolve of the British people.

George Frederick Bunston, a fisherman, was walking along the seashore at Lydd-on-Sea towards Lydd Coastguard Station at 7.30 am when, opposite a cottage named *Sea Close*, he spotted a brown paper parcel secured by an elastic band. He undid the parcel, which, because it was wet, caused the wrapping to fall to pieces and reveal a stone with a piece of white paper wrapped around it. Around this were wrapped two maps; one was a map of Kent, Sussex and Essex, while the other was of the Romney Marsh district of Kent and was printed on the back of a map of Valenciennes, Cambria, Le Cateau area. There was also a code (which Meier claimed he had thrown overboard). Round the stone, paper and maps were wrapped two sheets of brown linen material, one of which bore type in German, while the other had a series of holes punched into it. There was also a strip of white paper with letters and figures typed on it. This was connected with the code and appeared to give times that the agents may transmit, using the twenty-four-hour system, and certain code letters. The brown material was a code for transmission of service information. The perforated material appeared to be a grid used for enciphering messages.

About forty minutes passed before Bunston handed his find to Sergeant Tye at Lydd Police Station.

Lieutenant Colonel Stephens interrogated Waldberg from 11 am to 1.30 pm. Beyond members of MI5 staff, there were no other officers present. Stephens felt that there was some possibility of obtaining a cohesive narrative from this prisoner without interruption, with not having too many people interrogating him at the same time.

Waldberg, because of his membership of the German Secret Service and his holding the relative rank of second lieutenant, regarded the other three spies – Kieboom, Meier and Pons – as amateurs of only some three weeks' service. Stephens felt that Waldberg had the arrogance of a German officer and spoke with some authority. He also thought that if double-crossing was the present objective of the British Secret Service, then the Germans would pay more attention to Waldberg than the others.

Waldberg was prepared to double-cross his operators. He made an offer to return to France and bring back Werner with him, together with an album containing photographs and finger-prints of some thirty German agents. This offer, not surprisingly, was declined. Stephens was put on his guard as Waldberg's scheme was to obtain papers of importance from the headquarters of the Second Section of the German Secret Service at Chateau de Wimille. Stephens considered the chances of success to be no better than 1,000–1, and that should Waldberg's departure be countenanced, then it was likely he would never be seen again. Stephens was searching his mind assiduously for any motive other than escape, so questioned Waldberg whether his immediate superiors, Kohle (the name was recorded as Kohle but it was most probably Dr Kohler) and Werner, were homosexuals who had attempted to force their attentions upon him, but this line of questioning drew a blank.

It did transpire, however, that considerable animus existed between 'Kohle' and the rest of his staff. Waldberg was outraged that 'Kohle' tried to break off a relationship between him and a young Belgian woman, denouncing her to the Gestapo as being of Jewish origin. Waldberg was also livid that two of his boon companions who refused to land in England, pleading that they knew no English, were summarily shot. Finally, Waldberg was labouring under the greatest of all injustices, namely that the German Secret Service had deliberately deceived him, without any knowledge of English at all, to visit south-east England and land upon soil which was described to him as deserted and in ruins. The reality was different: he was in deadly peril and abandoned in a country, contrary to what he had been told, displaying strength and having plenty.

> Stephens concluded that Waldberg's bitterness knew no bounds. Vengeance, therefore, may be the reason for his *volte-face*, but Stephens found it difficult to place any trust in what he considered a strange character. Waldberg was asked whether he was prepared to send a message to Germany saying Pons had been shot, that the rest of the party had been in hiding for three days and that he was in great danger, and calling for an aircraft to land on the south coast. A successful outcome would mean Waldberg's importance could be assessed and they would get a German aircraft for nothing.

Waldberg appeared enthusiastic and Stephens considered the idea worthy of examination. Waldberg also agreed to send a message for a '*Schnellboot*' (quickboat) to fetch him from the coast, and once again Stephens thought that they may thus gain something for nothing.

Waldberg asserted that he did not know the frequency of his radio set. The important thing in sending a message was the letter 'T', which was to say that the message was coming, from whom it should have been sent and that it was not a false message. If the message did not contain that letter, then it would be considered false and destroyed. Consequently, containing the letter 'T' would give the message credence; it would be considered genuine and held to be correct. Moreover, the call-sign remained the same each day.

Waldberg confided that if there was any danger, they were ordered to destroy the code at once and his code and maps were to be thrown over the side of the boat. When they had spotted a patrol boat upon approaching the coast, just before they landed, this, he claimed, was what he had done.

Waldberg was questioned about the invasion. He thought he had landed with sufficient funds for about ten days, because the Germans thought they would be in England before that amount of money was exhausted. Waldberg was certain this would be the case, as he had discussed it with the 'Chief' before he left. The 'Chief', he explained to his interrogator, was Major Seynsburg of the 'Grand Section' at Wiesbaden. Seynsburg told Waldberg that if the local population started to evacuate, he was to remain where he was.

He said that three other agents were also to come over: Oberleutnant Koch, an NCO and a private. The officer would be dressed entirely in brown leather, with brown boots and trousers. Waldberg did not think it would be necessary for the military men to join them now.

He said the invasion force was to arrive from the French coast – from Boulogne, Calais and Le Touquet. There were a large number of soldiers on the coast, including 'special' soldiers – elite troops trained for 'special' tasks, who had with them a variety of instruments to detect and destroy mines in the ground, as well as wireless experts and troops for rapid bridge construction.

Waldberg said he knew of a number of small, fast, armed boats that could transport about fifteen men each. These boats were littered all along the coast, held in small pockets in places that were forbidden to the general population and were well guarded. The boats were protected by guns which, themselves, were protected by barage balloons. The balloons were hoisted very high up in the sky at night when the moon went down. Painted black, they encircled the whole district where the little boats were.

There were also mechanized columns and mules, but as the soldiers dressed alike – save for the 'special' ones – Waldberg could not confirm if there were any mountain troops present.

He was asked, 'Do they send spies over every day? Are there many agents like you here?' Waldberg replied:

'Four came over before; it would be, perhaps, three weeks ago. There was too rough a sea for them to disembark. Two others were stopped by an English patrol boat; they said they were officers and they were asked their route; they were warned of mines in a certain part along the coast. They subsequently turned round and returned to France, reporting the mines.'

When asked how many others there were, Waldberg replied, 'They said that they were sending me ten days or so before they would attack – not too long beforehand because of the danger; that is all the 'Chief' told me. They are going to attack … I was to have come by parachute and not by boat.'[8]

As for communication with aircraft: Waldberg admitted sending a second message saying that he was in trouble and asking whether he should surrender or resist. He asked that an aircraft be sent on Wednesday evening, 4 September. On the previous Tuesday he received a message at 6 pm, stating, 'If you cannot recognize the ground you have only to spread your ground-sheet on the grass.'[9] When he could see or hear a Messerschmitt in the distance, he was to look through his binoculars and was to signal with a handkerchief and the ground-sheet. This could be seen quite clearly from the aircraft, and as the aircraft passed the pilot would fire a volley from his machine gun to show that his position had been recognized.

Because his German masters wanted to know exactly where he was, Waldberg had prepared a third message to be sent: that he was approximately 1¼ miles from Dungeness, almost 700ft south of the water reservoir. He never sent the message because he did not have the time.

Waldberg explained what he was to do when the Germans arrived in England. When he saw a German soldier, he was to remain stationary, take out his handkerchief and signal. As the soldier approached, Waldberg was to say, in German, 'Where is your officer? I want to speak to your officer.' When the officer arrived, Waldberg was to say the codeword 'Elizabeth'. After that he didn't know whether he would have stayed with the troops or be sent away.

When asked what he would have done had the Germans not arrived, he said he would have given himself up – once his provisions had run out.

Waldberg vehemently denied taking a spy name. He claimed that he kept his own name as he could see no advantage in taking another. He denied, 'on my word of honour', that he ever took the spy name of Dubois – his mother's name.

When asked whether he was prepared to send a dictated message, Waldberg replied, 'Yes, on my word of honour. I am ready to do what you want.' For the Germans to attack in an area, the message was to have said that there were no troops or anti-tank defences in a certain region; if that criteria was not satisfied, then another place would be targeted.

When asked if he had been paid or asked for money, he replied, 'No. Because I will tell you one thing, if I had said "no" [to a request to carry out spying activities] then the same thing would have happened to me as happened to two of my comrades. They took them into the woods, and they never returned.'[10]

Waldberg wrote a letter, in French, to Lieutenant Colonel Stephens requesting a verbal interview. He did not want to write down everything as he had a lot to say. He was not happy being told by his German masters that before his departure, the whole coast had been bombed, with London and all the factories destroyed. He felt the National Socialist leaders had lied and spread propaganda, but which he initially believed to be sincere. He now talked about getting revenge on the Germans.

Stephens released a 'Secret' report that reiterated certain information. He said that the four spies had arrived at Latchmere House without papers of any kind, and that the statements they had made at Scotland Yard were not available. The urgent problem, Stephens added, was to break the spies' wireless code in order to send false intelligence to Germany, and that had indeed been done.

From an academic interrogation point of view, he continued, various points required elucidation before a satisfactory report could be drawn. Stephens pointed out the sequence which had to be followed in these cases:[11]

1. Kieboom: The first to arrive, the first to come to the attention of Stephens. He was not prepared to give any information of value and it was only after persistent pressure that the code was obtained. After midnight, Stephens

re-interrogated Kieboom, and many 'of the lies that he told during his first interview were rectified'. When reading the verbatim report on the case, Stephens stated it would be seen that the first part consisted of stubborn obstructionism and lies, as they were under orders from Germany.

2. The remaining spies gave information in varying degrees of accuracy. In addition to Kieboom, two others were interrogated on 5 September while the fourth arrived on 6 September and was interrogated during the day.

3. Stephens said that regarding the code there was complete agreement from the four spies. As for the German invasion requirements, the separate versions of the spies were much the same.

4. Finally, in regard to the contacts and background, Stephens ascertained that certain routine work remained to be done. From Waldberg there was a description of 'The Doctor' – a tall thin man with a gold tooth and a curious twist to his mouth.

5. SIS proposed to visit on 9 September and Stephens hoped to have a complete picture before then.

Kieboom was now instructed to send a message to Germany, reporting that Pons had been shot and the rest of the party had been in hiding for three days.

Captain Grassby sent a 'Secret' memo to Hinchley Cooke and enclosed the codes and maps found by the fisherman off the coast near where the four 'Dutchmen' landed. Grassby added that there also appeared to be 'a wrist-watch strap, and some kind of stone'.

Sunday, 8 September 1940:
A direct hit is made on a shelter: during an air raid, Block K of the Peabody Estate, Whitechapel, East London, receives a direct hit. Almost eighty people are killed.

Robin Stephens interrogated Waldberg again at Latchmere House at 10.40 am. Stephens initially reported that the prisoner had shown, in writing, his willingness to give his interrogators all the information in his possession, as he felt he had been grossly deceived by his superiors. He had fully expected to find very visible and widespread signs of destruction caused by the Luftwaffe, especially in London. He was disgusted not to see any such trace, at least when he landed on the Kent coast.

Waldberg stated that his mission was to arrive at the coast between Dungeness and Rye, noting down in an area allotted to him any gun emplacements, anti-aircraft dispersals, aerodromes, any other military information, the state of bridges etc., all the time making small sketches to fix their situation. He had been told that on the coast he would be able to find a suitable motor-boat, which he was to commandeer and cross the Channel back to Boulogne. He was to stay one day in Boulogne and return the following night in the company of Werner. Before crossing, he was to have marked down a characteristic landmark which they could spot from a considerable distance out at sea to facilitate landing back at the correct place. Immediately before departure, Werner was to wireless his English contact, who would send a car to pick him up at a place indicated by Waldberg on a map: a stretch of secondary road between Pen Bars and an inn to the south of it, quite close to Dungeness.

Werner had previously landed at night by aeroplane near the Norfolk coast, and had walked some distance to a prearranged rendezvous where a car picked him up and took him to London; Waldberg did not know whether it was central London or the suburbs. He stayed there for two or three days before being driven back to Norfolk, to the place where he had landed, and an aeroplane whisked him away. Werner's contact in London was an Englishman, and there appeared to be several others, also English, about whom Waldberg knew no detail. When Werner was picked up again, he was to go to London and communicate directly with Wiesbaden.

Waldberg spoke in detail about Chateau Wimille, its location, constitution of troops etc., as well as some of its inhabitants: the latter included Oberleutnant Werner Uhln, Oberleutnant Weber and Dr Kohler, who were all personnel from the German SS centre in Brussels.

The following were reported by the four spies:

Peter Schneider/Schroeder: 21-year-old NCO in a special assault company, trained in mines and pontoon work. Black hair, dark brown eyes. Present at Brussels and at a lecture given by Kohler at Wimille. Spoke French. It was understood he was to land on the south coast of England.

Franz Schneider: Cousin of Peter, age approximately 26, thin, with black hair, sported a gold tooth and wore horn-rimmed glasses.

Paul Schneider: Another cousin of Peter, possibly brother of Franz. Age about 26, very small and fat, with brown hair and blue-green eyes.

Walter Pfeiffer: Age 20, short, fat, scar on left cheek running from corner of his mouth to his neck, fair hair and a slight sunburn. A soldier destined for the UK.

Kuhert: NCO, W/T operator.

As well as the above, Waldberg claimed that there were two Dutchmen, a sailor (on guard duty in plain clothes), an NCO who specialized in wireless transmission, three chauffeurs, and another NCO who spoke English and was scheduled to go to England.

Waldberg said that he had been a soldier for about two years, but had no military training; a soldier merely on paper, he was granted the rank of second lieutenant just before France declared war but had never been in uniform. His pay was: in Germany, 400 Marks per month; in Belgium, 80 Marks per week, in France, 60 Marks per week.

As a 'guarantee of his good faith' and willingness to give good information, Waldberg gave his interrogators details about the military aerodrome at Le Touquet, using a sketch. He said that it was well-camouflaged, contained three squadrons of Messerschmitt 109 fighters, three troop-transport aeroplanes – several three-engine Junkers – and, he thought, two or three small Storch liaison aircraft, although Waldberg used the French word *Cigogne* (stork). He admitted that he was not certain about the latter.

He went on to give details of German Intelligence personnel. The officer in charge of this section was said to be a general, aged about 41 and virtually bald – his remaining hair having grey streaks and described as being 'pepper and salt'. Waldberg did not know his name and claimed to have only seen this officer once or twice.

Due to secrecy and prohibitive communication, Waldberg knew practically nothing about the Intelligence organization, save for his own section. For example, he didn't know how many sections there were. The chief of the second section was Colonel Meyer, aged about 50, of medium height, bald, who wore a monocle in his left eye and had a scar on his right cheek, probably caused by a student duel. He wore a number of rings on each hand, usually one with a large square blue stone, and on the little finger of his left hand he had a wedding ring. He took over the section two or three weeks before the Belgian invasion. His predecessor was Major Seynsburg.

As if to reinforce his new-found 'loyalty', Waldberg suggested further military objectives to attack, besides the aerodrome at Le Touquet:

1. A petrol dump situated some 15km from Boulogne. It was situated at a brickyard, which could be identified by a very high chimney, together with a number of low buildings with dark wooden roofs. The petrol was stored in 100-litre drums under these roofs. The place was not camouflaged but was guarded by AA guns. He reiterated that at the port of Boulogne there was a very high barrage balloon, much higher than those in London. The balloons were put up every night, and were guarded. There were between seven and nine fast motor torpedo boats moored in the port.

2. He further described the strongest AA battery located in Brussels. This consisted of three guns of 'the greatest calibre'. This battery was functioning fourteen days ago and had not been bombed; it was simply too well guarded.

It was 2½ miles from the aviation field of Evre and Haren. The battery was situated near the railway station of Etterbeek, a commune of Brussels, and consisted of three very large barracks at the top of a parade ground, from which they were separated by a wide avenue with trees on the side furthest from the barracks. The middle building was used by airmen, and the other two by anti-aircraft forces and the air force medical corps. About a mile away was a hospital, marked with a red cross.

3. Waldberg also referred to a state chemical factory near Frankfurt am Main, which he claimed was the largest in Germany. His description, however, was too vague to be of any use.

Not content with offering additional military targets, Waldberg offered up some suggestions to satisfy his desire for vengeance.

Waldberg had been assured by his superiors that it would be easy to steal a boat to return to Boulogne, as the sentries on the English coast would have grown slack in their long wait for the invasion; and anyway, the country would have been laid to waste as a result of German air attacks. Having seen that not to be the case, he was anxious to avenge himself on Kohler – whom he described as one of England's most dangerous enemies. Waldberg despised Kohler, so he said that if supplied with poison, he would do away with him. He would also bring back Werner, together with the album containing the photographs and fingerprints of some thirty agents.

The album was kept at Wimille under the mattress in an NCO's office bed. Waldberg would have used no violence toward the NCO, but would have removed the album while secretly substituting some other package, the nature of which would not be discovered until he and Werner were in England. The album was taken out and inspected at irregular intervals, whenever required by any member of the section.

The plan for himself and Werner, assuming their return to England was successful, would have been to fall back with the population as they evacuated northwards.

Asked what guarantee he could offer for his good faith, Waldberg generously suggested that ten German officers should be put to death in the event of his failure to return!

Waldberg then turned his attention to communication: He said all German agents were supplied with two codes. Those of the different agents were not, however, identical; the dates were the same on all, but the number of holes varied slightly. The agents were instructed to destroy this code if there was any danger of capture.

Waldberg said he had no means of conveying messages to aircraft other than to spread a sheet on the ground, which would indicate his presence. When asked why he was not to be taken back by plane, he said that this option was considered too dangerous. He was prepared to send a message asking that a plane be sent to pick him up if he was in great danger, and in hiding, though he was uncertain of the probable response. He could not himself suggest any suitable landing place.

When asked whether he thought the scheme of returning to Boulogne by sea and then returning with Werner was feasible, Waldberg replied that he had already carried out more difficult enterprises. A boat would be waiting for him before he had sailed 6 miles from the English coast. For the return journey, a *Schnellboot* would be used as soon as it was dark. Such boats were always placed at the disposal of the section. Arrangements were made for scuttling these boats if necessary.

Waldberg claimed that he had no accomplices waiting for him in England. He did not know the name of a single German spy in England, he said, otherwise he would readily disclose it.

He then spoke about relations with Kohler, although again some information was repeated.

Asked whether Werner or Kohler were homosexuals, Waldberg replied that he was perfectly certain that Werner was not, as he showed a marked taste 'for the female society' and could be found in nightclubs. As for Kohler, Waldberg was less sure; he disappeared from time-to-time, but for what purpose was not known.

Waldberg confessed to detesting Kohler on account of the latter's victimization of a Brussels girl with whom Waldberg had been in love. Her name was thought to be Helene Koepens. Kohler had fabricated a dossier against her in which, amongst other things, she was alleged to be of partly Jewish origin, with a view to preventing her further association with Waldberg. Kohler was commonly supposed to be a member of the Gestapo and was frequently seen in the company of one of its leading members. Waldberg expressed the opinion that the Gestapo was all-powerful, even over officers of the highest rank.

Kohler was in charge of the instruction of agents to be sent to spy in England, and had been responsible for doing away with two of Waldberg's friends who had refused to be sent to England; these two men disappeared within 48 hours of their refusal.

Waldberg next told of his antecedents. His father had been a German courier between Berlin and Paris from the end of the First World War until 1935, when he was killed in an accident. The family had been very well-to-do. Waldberg himself had been in Mainz in 1918, and the family had moved to Strasbourg in 1926. Since that time, he had lived mostly in France, which explained his fluent French. He could not speak *Hochdeutsch* (high German), but only Alsatian *Plattdeutsch*. His mother was Alsatian (from the Alsace region of France).

It was noted that Waldberg used terms of phrase common in Belgium and Switzerland, but not in France. His general conversational style was quite incompatible with his apparent well-to-do upbringing in France.[12]

Monday, 9 September 1940:

The bombers return for a second time to bomb London in what is becoming known as 'The Battle of London'. These air raids are having a detrimental effect on public morale. Working-class people in cities like London have no alternative but to remain and seek refuge in shelters, provision for which is often inadequate.

Kieboom was interrogated by Stephens and Seymour Bingham, of B1d, Special Examiners, between 2 pm and 3 pm. He was cross-examined on various points arising out of previous interrogations. His attitude belied the fact that he knew a lot more than he was prepared to say: he feigned ignorance of various names and circumstances which would have been extremely unlikely to have escaped him.

Kieboom regurgitated information regarding his past. He said he learnt French when he lived in Belgium, during which time he acquired knowledge of German and Dutch. He maintained that he only spoke a few words of Dutch occasionally with his father. Despite having lived the first thirteen years of his life in Japan, Kieboom also asserted that he only spoke a few words of Japanese. He explained that he only spoke English at school and with his father and friends. He added that what little Japanese he knew he had mostly forgotten.

Kieboom continued by saying that, in 1935, he started work at the Hotel Victoria, where the manager was an Austrian named Zax. When questioned about the name, he clarified that he did not mean Sachs, insisting that Zax was the spelling that he knew. He repeatedly claimed during the interrogation that he had no knowledge whatever that the Hotel Victoria was a German spy centre, but admitted that a certain amount of shady business and curious goings-on occurred there.

He explained why he was sacked from the Victoria. A man called Bach, who said that he was a Polish Jew, tricked Kieboom into advancing him 300 Guilders, which he did from hotel funds. Bach disappeared, and Kieboom joined the army and agreed to pay back 10 Guilders per month out of the 90 Guilders he got from his army pay.

He claimed to have paid back 170 Guilders, but when Bach was arrested, no evidence of the money supposedly paid back was found.

While Bach spoke German, Kieboom insisted that he was Polish. Although Kieboom gave Bach as a reason for his dismissal from Hotel Victoria, he added that the main reason was that the new manager, named Cadalla, did not like him. He said he knew Cadalla well because he was formerly the book-keeper at the hotel.

He denied knowing a man called Herbert Luft, and when questioned about mail for guests at this hotel he claimed never to have seen any as it was distributed by the post clerk or the telephone attendant.

Kieboom said he had a master key to the safe where guests deposited valuables, but this was not sufficient to open it. It could only be opened when guests produced another key.

The prisoner was questioned about other contacts. He remembered a Mr Holzmann (Michael) as staying for a long period at the hotel, apparently spending large sums of money on cars, expensive clothes etc. Holzmann gave some trouble about paying his hotel bills, which were very large. Upon being pressed, Kieboom mentioned one of Holzmann's 'shady' friends, a Frenchman named Letellier, aged 45, very thin with greyish hair.

Holzmann was said to be interested in gun-running in Spain. The centre of this traffic appeared to be in Paris, but controlled from Amsterdam. Kieboom claimed not to remember the name of Holzmann's (male) secretary, although he saw him a number of times during Holzmann's stay, which consisted of several months. Holzmann's secretary spoke several languages, but Kieboom claimed to have noticed him so little that that he could not describe him. Kieboom also disclaimed any knowledge of the following people: Oliver Hoare, Zetland and a Karl Flesche. He stated that he remembered 'Potato' Jones, who stayed at the Victoria. When questioned about Handelskammer (board of trade/chamber of commerce), Kieboom claimed that he knew nothing about it or the various Germans at the hotel connected therewith. The spy did remember a Miss Petersen. He described her as being rather slight, about 5ft 4in tall, with a rather pointed nose and fair hair. When questioned further about her, he said that he was aware of her being attached as a hairdresser to the hotel, but did not think it strange that she was frequently absent from the place and claimed not to know the names of any of the people who visited her regularly.

Kieboom asserted, in his defence, that it was only when he had reported in Brussels and asked for an explanation of the need for training, that he and Pons were given the option of undertaking a mission to England on behalf of Germany or being sent to a concentration camp for smuggling Devisen (foreign exchange) Marks. Kieboom tried desperately to convince his interrogators that he accepted the first alternative in the belief that it offered him a chance of surrendering to the British authorities.

Further interrogation of Kieboom revealed the following salient points:[13]

1. The list of names in Kieboom's notebook was given to him by Meyer, while in Brussels. Meyer was then supposed to have sent off to Amsterdam to get the addresses behind the names.

2. If the team ran short of provisions, they would report this by wireless, and a plane would drop new supplies near to the place where they had originally landed.

3. Descriptions were obtained of Meyer; Schrie (or Schree) and Schnacke (or Schnake), Morse instructors at Rue Stevin, Brussels; Dr Kohler (or Dr Kuehn), instructor in general knowledge at Brussels and Wimille; and Oberleutnant Weber (alias Rosy or Duvreuil).

4. Chateau Wimille had a transceiver (a radio device that could both transmit and receive communications) set up in the garden. It transmitted during daylight hours, at irregular times, but not before 8.30 am.

5. At Amsterdam, the following hotels were taken over by the Germans: Victoria, Carlton, L'Europe and Amstel Centraal; also street-car and tram fares were as before the invasion. Almost everybody carried their ration card, which served as identification. Kieboom claimed, however, that nobody ever had to identify themselves, and there were no restrictions on travelling between towns.

6. At Chateau Wimille, Peter Schroeder and the NCO W/T operator, Kuhert, waited for orders of passage to England.

MI5's Section B2 referred to their records and issued a report regarding Kieboom's contacts:[14]

1. Engineering Artificer Apprentice Robert George Wade, who in January 1939 lived at 35 Priory Road, Exeter. This man was suspected of Communist tendencies, but apparently was cleared of these suspicions. There was nothing to connect him with the Purley address that Kapitan Meyer had issued to Kieboom, but as he was a sailor, he would probably have moved around a good bit.

   There was also a Robert Wade, who in June 1936 was living at 75 Deansbrook Road, Edgware, whose motorcycle was found outside a meeting of the British Union of Fascists.

2. A certain Dr Peter H. Schroeder, a Dutchman from Rotterdam, who was connected with the German shipping company of Van Ommeren of Hanburg.

   There was also a Mr Schroeder of La Madeleine (Lille), Boite (box) Postale No 72. He was apparently a sub-agent of the Gestapo Kriminal Kommissar von Knappen, at Aix La Chapelle. There was a Peter Schroeder, whose name, together with the address Albrechtstrasse 32, Neufahrwasser, was included in Communist cover addresses. This information was dated from 26 October 1933.

3. Captain Mirow. There was no trace of this name, but there was a Fregattenkapitan (Frigate captain) Mirow of Tirpitzufer 72–76, Berlin W35, which was the German SS Headquarters. It was possible that this was Kapitan Meyer, also known as Kurt Mirow, part of German SS in Brussels.

4. Leonhardt. A man of this name, without the 't', appeared in correspondence between Rantzau (Major Nikolaus Ritter?) and Snow (Peter Walter Snow?). Meyer had issued Kieboom with contact names and addresses in England, one of whom was Peter Snow.

5. There was a Rittmeister (cavalry captain) Haupt, who, in about 1936, was head of the German SS in Denmark. There was also a Polizei, Oberst Haupt.

Tuesday, 10 September 1940:
Buckingham Palace is hit by a German bomb.

As a result of the interrogation of Kieboom, Captain Grassby was instructed by the head of B1 (a), Captain Robertson, to see that a sheet or towel was laid out in the Dymchurch area (map reference 563501/504380) as a possible recognition signal for German aircraft so that they could see that at least one of the four men was still alive. Should this ruse work, and if any message was dropped by an enemy aircraft, this would be seen and picked up immediately.

The interrogators, except for DS Allchin, returned to read the transcripts and the answers to each prisoner, and were invited to make corrections, should they wish. Each prisoner initialled their changes and signed each page of their transcript, acknowledging that the changes were correct.

Waldberg was not asked to read over the English interpretation of the questions and answers that were put to and given by him, because he claimed not to understand English. His document was therefore not corrected.

Three days after Stephens' report, Herbert Hooper of MI5's Section B24 requested information on David Bankes-Price, one of the contact names found on Kieboom. Detective Inspector Pendleton of Coventry Police investigated and filed a message stating that Bankes-Prices' address, 128 Cuthill [*sic*, Churchill] Avenue, Coventry, did not exist. Enquiries at the Employment Exchange, Food Control Office and the National Registration Office were made without success. There was, however, a David Bankes-Price who lived at Keresley, near Coventry. He was aged 27, 6ft tall, of good build with dark brown hair. He was a service engineer employed by Alfred Herbert Ltd, Toolmakers, of Coventry. In the course of his employment he had travelled extensively in various parts of the world, especially Norway, the Low Countries and France before the invasion.

Lieutenant Colonel Hinchley Cooke was contacted in a 'Secret' memo, on behalf of Captain Grassby, which enclosed a police report on the discovery of the packet containing the code, concluding 'one more link in the prosecution story'.[15]

A report was received from Sergeant Tye of Kent County Constabulary, describing how George Frederick Bunston found the map of Kent and Romney Marsh and the code on the seashore at Lydd-on-Sea, which was subsequently taken to Lydd Police Station.

Wednesday, 11 September 1940:

Spitfire versus Dornier: Geoffrey Wellum, the youngest Spitfire pilot to fly in the Battle of Britain, is just over 18 years old when he goes into combat with No. 92 Squadron for the first time.

He describes[16] how ten Spitfires are outnumbered by Me 109s and Dorniers, the nervousness and the chaos with so many aircraft crowding the same piece of sky. There is urgency, not panic, as Wellum's training takes over. The fear is palpable: 'Please, dear God, like me more than you do the Germans.'

Between 11 am and 12:30 pm, further interrogation of Meier took place at Latchmere House. He gave information regarding training in Brussels, the information wanted by the Germans after landing in England, the instruction given at Wimille and what he knew about Waldberg.

During the afternoon, a conversation[17] between Meier and Waldberg was monitored. Meier said he didn't believe that they were set up to fail, while the importance of Kohler in relation to an invasion was discussed, as was Waldberg's dislike of Kohler.

Summary of conversation between WALDBEG and MEIER
Time: 2.30 to 4 pm
Date: 11.9.40

'The first part of the conversation was an account by Meier of the way he was arrested. After an exchange of general remarks about their present plight, during which each one pointed out various shortcomings of the organization of the trip, Meier threw out the suggestion that perhaps the Germans wanted them to be caught to plant on us faulty information which would lead us into believing that the German attack was coming from a different quarter. He suggested that it was on purpose that they were sent over without proper registration cards or other convincing proof of their bona fides. Waldberg apparently listened to this with interest, because he remained silent until Meier, who spoke French haltingly, had completely finished before he intervened. He did not immediately pass any remark on the suggestion, but later in the conversation gave voice with considerable emphasis to his criticism of the organization.

'An interesting point was that, when discussing the other "boatmen", Waldberg said he had been under the impression that the name of the "Japanese" was Pons. Waldberg appeared to be convinced that the Germans will land. Werner was to come here by aeroplane in order to contact various influential people, and according to Waldberg, Werner's report would have considerable influence on the choice of the actual day for the attack. Meier, at this point, asked Waldberg what his real name was, to which Waldberg replied, "That is my real name."

'Waldberg then spoke with conviction and considerable vehemence in his condemnation of Kohler, who, he said, had given them an entirely false idea of the ease with which their job could be carried out, describing at some length Kohler's word-picture of the devastation that the German Air Force had wrought in the South of England and London. Both men were struck straightaway by the absence of evidence of bombing.

'Waldberg repeatedly threw out violent threats about what he would like to do to Kohler if he could lay his hands on him. He also blamed Kohler for the fact that he (Waldberg) was obliged to break his engagement with a girl because she was half Jewish, and also because Kohler, or his agent, endeavoured, so he said, to entice him into a liaison with a girl of Kohler's choice. At that moment, Meier mentioned Peter Schneider and said he thought the name was Schroeder. Meier said, "They wanted us to mislead the British, don't you think?" To this Waldberg countered with the opinion that German spies, owing to the activities of the British Secret Service, were unable to correspond with Germany, so the Germans have to send people over to contact them, and he spoke in this strain later on when he referred to Werner's proposed visit by aeroplane.

'Meier opined that the Germans would save him and his companions, but by the same token, they would no doubt get rid of them as of course, they would assume that they would have "split". Waldberg thought that German Agents were already in touch with very highly placed people here. He thought that Werner would get into touch with them during his visit and that these interviews will have an effect on the decisions as to the day and the time of the coming attack. There followed a certain amount of description of Werner's past activities in France, Egypt, etc. Waldberg evidently had a high opinion of Werner's importance.

'This trip appeared to have been stage-managed by Kohler, or at least the actual departure, and Waldberg expressed the opinion that if arrangements had been made by Werner instead, the whole thing would have run smoothly. "Kohler is a bungler." The English speakers should have been provided with an identity card, and Waldberg appeared to have suggested this, but his suggestion was pooh-poohed by his superiors. Waldberg did a lot of grumbling about Kohler's last-minute decisions, and he instanced one or two cases of red tape. One of which got him into trouble. He said something like this, "Those swine misled us; damn the Gestapo, that business cost me eight days CB (confined to barracks) in Brussels." It would appear that Kohler was Waldberg's pet aversion; he referred to him repeatedly and at length with strong expletives and expressed the desire to put a knife into him. In this connection he several times spoke of his disgust at the way he was hoodwinked into believing that the aerial bombardment of this country would make his job an easy one. He described his adventures as a badly organized show, but of course could not dare to refuse to come over here. One could not, however, escape the impression that had the "show" been better organized, Waldberg, apparently, would have gone in to it with zest.

Kohler & Co, were referred to again, Waldberg said "they have not been loyal to us", but he did not entirely agree with Meier's denunciation of German duplicity. There followed some talk about their instructions to reach the coast on the 12th inst. and to commandeer a small motor-boat for the purpose of making their way back to the French coast. Meier pointed out that, according to the newspapers, all private boats in Britain are chained up and drained of petrol and had been so for over a month.

'There was some discussion about their ultimate fate; they were not quite sure whether they would be shot by their British captors, and they were not quite happy as to what would happen to them when the Germans "deliver" them, especially Waldberg, who said he gave an account of what he had been doing here, confining himself, however, to facts. They seemed equally convinced that it was quite futile to attempt an escape, and that the Germans will eventually release them from here. There followed a long discussion which proved that neither of these men was sure either of the date or day. Waldberg seemed to think that the invasion would start with the landing of troop-carrying aeroplanes at night, "probably between ten and midnight on a misty night". He also seemed to think that [due to] the Germans' connection with certain high quarters, invasion would be facilitated to some extent from the inside.

'According to Waldberg, Werner spoke French with sufficient fluency to pass himself off as a Belgian; he also spoke English very fluently, Dutch and Italian with some fluency and can make himself understood in Chinese. On his forthcoming aeroplane trip, he would be clad in brown clothes, and carrying two silent automatic pistols.

'Two points added by Meier to the list of discrepancies in the organization of the men's landing were: (1) the Bank Notes which were handed to them are of no practical value, as no doubt the British Police would know by the serial numbers that they came from the Continent, and (2), in the bag of rations which they carried with them, full water bottles were omitted.

'Extracts of importance: In general, the conversation confirmed previous statements of both men. It may be worthy of note that Waldberg was convinced of the imminence of the invasion, that the hour and place would be decided by Werner, after the receipt of plans brought back by Waldberg, and consultation with 3 important personages in London. Waldberg said that three-quarters of the German agents in England were unable to communicate directly with German authorities and also considered that the second section at Vimille [*sic*] was in the habit of sending out spies without proper preparation or any definite idea of what they were to do.'

Matter Recorded: full record taken of conversation.

Taken by: A.D. Meurig Evans

Waldberg was interrogated at Latchmere House at 5 pm by Albert Dan Meurig Evans and Sampson, with the intention of obtaining further particulars of Weber and Werner.[18]

Waldberg stated that Weber was a first lieutenant, who was also known as Rosy and Duvreuil. He was described as aged 35, fairly tall – 5ft 9in to 5ft 11in – and thin, always holding himself upright. He had fair hair cropped very short with a small parting on the left side, grey-green eyes, a stern expression, reddish face, was clean-shaven and had one gold tooth.

The prisoner had known Weber for approximately two years, having first met him at Wiesbaden, where he was often with the 'Grand Chief' (Major Seynsburg). Weber was sometimes in uniform, sometimes in civilian clothes. During the first year, Weber had been travelling a great deal. He had seen him at Mainz in the second year, when Waldberg was secretary to Major Schmidt in a camp for prisoners of war.

He said Weber had come on one occasion to bring Dutch dossiers containing plans of fortifications near the Dutch–German frontier. These plans had been supplied by a Dutch captain.

Waldberg said that he had arrived at Mainz in the middle of March 1940, and Weber visited Mainz at the end of March. He had seen him again in Brussels, where Waldberg arrived ten or twelve days after the Belgian armistice. Waldberg had been at the Rue de la Loi until 26 August. During the period from March to August, Weber was frequently in the office, though he had no room of his own there. He made many journeys, on three occasions for eight days each, and once he went to Paris for four days in the first half of July. He always travelled in a private car.

Waldberg also said that Weber was in touch with English people in the diplomatic and military world in London, and that he spoke English, Dutch and a little French.

While the other subject of this interrogation was normally known as Werner, Waldberg said this was his Christian name, his surname being Uhln.

The description given tallied with that in the interrogation by Stephens on 8 September, but not regarding languages, with Malay substituted for Esperanto. Asked how Waldberg knew Werner spoke Malay, he said he had been in Java and spoke Malay sometimes to Koch.

Waldberg had never seen him in uniform, but thought he was in the 14th Artillery Regiment, to which Schmidt also belonged. Werner had done service as an agent in Austria, South Africa, Algeria and Menton (France). Waldberg described him as a very important person who had travelled a great deal; he had everything at his disposal.

Seynsburg had said of him that he was the most powerful man in Germany. Like Weber, he was one of Seynsburg's principal assistants in Brussels. Waldberg had first seen him in Wiesbaden, and again in Paris when he was there on holiday in August 1939. Werner had been at Rue Joseph II in Brussels nearly every day and had given instructions to Waldberg.

Waldberg stated that Werner had been to England during the war, but had returned to Brussels. He had landed in an aeroplane and had been fetched by English people who came from London. Four days later, he was picked up at the same place by aeroplane.

Waldberg said that he, Waldberg, was a sous-lieutenant (second lieutenant). Upon being questioned about this, he said he had the rank but not the grade of a sous-lieutenant. He explained that this meant that his commission had not been gazetted. When in camp, he dressed as a simple soldier but wore a badge on his arm representing a sword. This, apparently, was a sign that he belonged to the Secret Service, which enabled him to pass freely.

Thursday, 12 September 1940:

The code breakers at Bletchley Park, working on the highly secret German Enigma traffic, are having difficulty breaking into the German Naval signals. It is suggested that directly obtaining German Naval code tables would be the fastest method of making progress. A plot had been hatching since the end of August to capture a German Enigma-cipher codebook. Earlier projects have vaguely and verbally been discussed but the first concrete proposal is made by a Lieutenant Commander Ian Lancaster Fleming (future author of the *James Bond* novels). Fleming is working in British Naval

Intelligence and he proposes Operation *Ruthless*. The operational plan is proposed by Fleming to the Director of Naval Intelligence, Rear Admiral John Godfrey:

'TOP SECRET. For Your Eyes Only.
12 September 1940.
To: Director Naval Intelligence
From: Ian Fleming
Operation Ruthless

I suggest we obtain the loot by the following means:

1. Obtain from the Air Ministry an air-worthy German bomber.
2. Pick a tough crew of five, including a pilot, W/T operator and word-perfect German speaker. Dress them in German Air Force Uniform; add blood and bandages to suit.
3. Crash Plane in the Channel after making SOS to rescue service.
4. Once aboard rescue boat, shoot German crew, dump overboard, bring rescue boat back to English port.

In order to increase the chances of capturing an R or M [*Räumboot* – a small minesweeper; *Minensuchboot* – a large minesweeper] with its richer booty, the crash might be staged in mid-Channel. The Germans would presumably employ one of this type for the longer and more hazardous journey.

Fleming draws up a detailed list of material and personnel required. The pilot was to be 'tough, bachelor, able to swim'; the German speaker was to be 'as for the pilot' and was further earmarked, with a touch of autobiographical genius, as 'Fleming'".

He later adds other details to the plan:

'NB Since attackers will be wearing enemy uniforms, they will be liable to be shot as franc-tireurs if captured, an incident that might be fruitful field for propaganda. Attackers' story will therefore be that it was done for a lark by a group of young hot-heads who thought the war was too tame and wanted to have a go at the Germans. They had stolen the plane and equipment and had expected to get into trouble when they got back. This will prevent suspicions that party was after more valuable booty than a rescue boat.'[19]

Captain Stimson received three bags – one green, one brown and one beige – along with overcoats, blankets etc., which, he presumed, all belonged to Meier, Kieboom, Pons and Waldberg.

Meier was interrogated by Lieutenant Short and Meurig Evans at Latchmere House. Short was a specialist in interrogating agents who had knowledge of codes and cyphers.

Meier told of his first contact with the Germans. In July 1940, he met Goyvaerts, NSNAP Group leader at The Hague, and was told that the Germans needed men with knowledge of English for work involving a certain amount of risk. Meier also met Vorrink, who said that he had refused such work. He went to Goyvaerts' flat, where, apart from Goyvaerts' wife, were de Vreede and Klein Nagelvoort. Goyvaerts then renewed his proposal to Meier.

Meier also gave a description of Gerfreiter Erfurt.

Lieutenant Colonel Stephens noted from this interrogation Meier's first contact with the German Secret Service. Furthermore, he felt that Goyvaerts now came into the picture and acted in a liaison capacity for the German Secret Service.

Stevens submitted what he described as a report of an 'audition' between van den Kieboom and Meier:[20]

CONVERSATION BETWEEN Van den KIEBOOM and MEIER on 12.9.40.

'Meier gave the impression that he did not think very much of the Germans, as he considered that he had been let down. It was ridiculous that they had been sent over without any water, and what were they to do with a pocket book full of messages. Naturally, the English would not believe them. The numbers of the bank notes which they had been given had been noted by the police, and therefore the money was now of no use to them. Van den Kieboom criticized the fact that they were not given identity cards. A general discussion followed concerning their treatment here, which was much gentler than might have been expected, had the situation been reversed. Both men agreed that the whole business was a hoax. Meier stated that after landing in this country, he expressed a desire to return, but Waldberg insisted on going through with the business. Meier then described what he and Waldberg did on landing. Meier also described his meeting with an Air Raid Warden at a "little Inn", with whom he had drinks, and of whom he asked questions regarding the number of military in the district. While there he was asked whether he had registered, and whether he had an identity card. On replying that he had not, that he was a refugee, and had arrived the night before, he was taken to the police and arrested. Kieboom gave an account on how he was arrested, being observed by a couple of officers who were passing in a car, and who challenged him. They took charge of him and handed him over to the police. He did not know how Pons fared after he left him, and it is remarkable to note that at this point of the conversation he did not say anything about Pons' fate. In a phrase that is not clear, van den Kieboom seemed to imply that he gave misleading information. They are both agreed that, under the circumstances, it was best to tell the truth when questioned as they have practically a 100% chance of being shot.

'There was a long comparison of notes about their interrogations without any particular point of interest being raised.'

Taken by L King, and Lieut Macintosh

In part of a 'Secret' report from Stephens, he stated that although they had taken certain facts from Meier, Kieboom and Pons, he did not think Waldberg would be as forthcoming: 'with two years service in the German Secret Service he has much to hide. We will, however, try.'[21]

Two notes from Section B24 appertained to three of Kieboom's contacts. There was Arthur Butterworth at 11 Leadenhall Street, and Herbert Barfoot at Lloyds Building, Leadenhall Street. Both addresses were the same – Lloyds Buildings. Neither man, the report claimed, was known in Lloyds but may have worked in one of the numerous insurance offices working for Lloyds. It concluded that a man called S.W. Butterworth was struck off the list of Lloyds members as he was going abroad.

The third contact was Robert Wade of 8 Warren Road. The property was a detached cottage with a large garden overlooking Purley Railway Station, and it was up for sale. The estate agents, Slade and Church of Purley, were approached in order to obtain a permit to visit. Information from the police and the Food Office showed that Wade had moved from there on 8 July 1940 to 43 The Mall, Surbiton.

Later information revealed that Wade's new address in Surbiton was a small house near the River Thames on Portsmouth Road. He lived there with his wife and son, was not known to his neighbours, and no wireless aerial could be seen from the outside.

Chapter Seven

Velvet Glove?

Friday, 13 September 1940:
SS *City of Benares*, with 197 passengers, including ninety evacuee children, leaves
Liverpool in a convoy bound for Canada.
The Italians invade Egypt.
Buckingham Palace is damaged by German bombs.

Meier was questioned by Meurig Evans, an interrogator at Camp
020. He was trying to elicit information on two spies Meier met in
Brussels: Robert Heidenreich and Hoogeboom. All Meurig Evans
managed to extract about the men were general details, such as appearance,
background and languages spoken. He reported that Heidenreich had been
living in the Dutch East Indies, in an unknown capacity.

Further questioning[1] by another officer was able to elicit specific information:

1. Were Kapitan Meyer and Kurt Mirow the same person?
Kieboom and Meier were interrogated separately regarding this matter as they
had previously referred to these names. The interrogator was quite satisfied
and stated definitively that Meyer and Mirow were one and the same. The main
characteristics of this man varied: according to Kieboom, his major impression
was that of a stocky man with a small round head. Meier, on the other hand,
remembered him because of his objectionable habit of constantly clearing his
throat. Furthermore, Kieboom remembered the two names Meyer and Mirow
being used on various occasions.

2. Information on the man described by Kieboom as Schnake, and by Meier
   as Schnacke.
Meier and Kieboom's descriptions led to the conclusion that the names
Schnake and Schnacke undoubtedly referred to the same man, the German
Morse instructor at rue Stevin, 4, Brussels. Both men agreed that Schnake was
definitely a German who spoke French extremely well. Meier considered that
he may have been born in Lorraine, but this was obviously a guess; he also
considered him to be artisan class.

3. Clarification from Kieboom regarding the names Tabrush and Kruger.

When questioned, Kieboom stated that he had no knowledge whatsoever of Tabrush. To his knowledge, the six people only concerned with visiting England were Kieboom, Pons, Meier, Waldberg, Werner and Schroeder. Kieboom admitted to having been in a very nervous condition during his interrogation and consequently had no memory of this part.

Regarding Kruger, Kieboom was emphatic that the man referred to was Kurhert, the man at Chateau Wimille who operated the portable transmitter in the garden. This transmitter was in a brown leather case and was both a transmitting and receiving set, and was a similar type to that supplied to the four spies prior to arriving in England.

When questioned in detail, and at considerable length and with the greatest pressure, the only information regarding the call sign was that it was one of three letters. In Kieboom's opinion, the main function of this station was to keep in touch with Brussels, and he was definite that whilst he was staying at the chateau, Brussels was the only other station in which they were in communication. The interrogators thought it was interesting to note that the soldier Hasselbrink could also use the transmitter. Kieboom drew a plan of the villa, as he called it.

4. Peter Schneider and Peter Schroeder.

Both Kieboom and Meier stated that Schneider or Schroeder were the same person, and did not transmit from Brussels.

5. Three addresses in Brussels – rue de la Loi, rue Stevin, 4, and rue de Joseph
   – and their functions.

Rue de la Loi was the headquarters of the German Secret Service in Brussels and was in the charge of Kapitan Meyer. Kieboom and Meier certainly were not allowed to visit this address.

Rue Stevin, 4 was where the men were instructed in Morse by Schnacke, being required to reach a standard of receiving forty words per minute and transmitting sixty words. All four men reached that state of proficiency.

Rue de Joseph was the office of Kohler, where the spies received instruction regarding the constitution of the British Army. This seemed to have been repeated many times, and as far as could be gathered, mainly consisted of gathering details of the regular Army, Territorial Army and the military and how they were all fused together. The interrogators noted the Home Guard was not considered of sufficient importance to receive any serious attention. The four men received their pay from Kohler at rue de Joseph. Furthermore, Werner was more often than not seen at this address.

6. The circumstances of the departure from Le Touquet.

The four explained, without any dramatic revelations, their departure from Le Touquet and that they were escorted part of the way by diesel-driven minesweepers until the two steam trawlers carrying the men continued on their own. Then the two pairs each got into their respective rowing boats and rowed to the Kent coast. Each pair was told that if they left their rowing boats after landing, the tide would take them back out to sea; this didn't happen.

Two points came out of the interrogation which the interrogating officers did not think had been covered before:

1. The officer in charge of Chateau Wimille was a Korvettenkapitan and the other regular at the chateau was a seaman called Siegmann. They concluded, therefore, that the chateau was run not by the Gestapo but exclusively by the German Secret Service.
2. Whilst they were studying at rue Stevin, 4, they were visited by Oberleutnant Weber, who gave them materials and instructions in the use of invisible inks.

A letter, designated 'Secret', was sent from the Borough Police Office, Halifax, by Chief Constable Richardson to Major Geoffrey Peter Wethered, MI5 Regional Security Liaison Officer, regarding another of Kieboom's contacts, Alfred Doleman, of 143 Huddersfield Road, Halifax.

The letter stated that for the past 14 years, Doleman had been the Continental and Scandinavian representative for Messrs Patons and Baldwins Ltd, worsted and woollen spinners of Halifax. About the beginning of August 1940, he went to Toronto with his family to take up duties with his firm. The police reported that Doleman was a British–born subject, well-known in Halifax as 'a person of excellent character, and one who has at all times been anxious for the welfare of this country'.[2]

Chief Constable Richardson concluded that his address may well have come into the possession of the suspect, Kieboom, through Doleman's business travels to various countries. This lead did not, on the face of it, open up new possibilities.

Saturday, 14 September 1940:

A 'Secret' report from the War Cabinet considers the damage of the air raids on supplies in and around the London area. It provides a fascinating insight of the problems with which the powers-that-be have to wrestle:

Electricity, Water and Gas.

Electricity: Serious damage has been done to particular installations ... As regards both water and gas, the damage to the mains has been more serious than the damage to central installations, water mains in particular having proved more vulnerable than was expected ... the damage can be repaired or the service reinstated ... rather quickly unless further and more serious damage is sustained in the meantime.

Drainage.

The damage done is more serious and will take longer to repair ... sewage is discharging into the River Lea instead of the Thames. The pumping machinery has also been damaged, and it ... will take several months to repair. The Minister of Health is endeavouring to arrange that the repairs shall be expedited ...

Docks.

Major damage has been done in all the London dock areas ... The great diminution in traffic coming into the port of London [is] making this damage of less consequence than would otherwise be the case. Unless the ports on the West, and North-East Coast, or the inland transport system, are also extensively damaged, the situation should continue manageable.

Railways.

Attacks have mainly been directed to terminals ... A large number of vital points have been hit, particularly south of the River [Thames]. The trouble lies ... in the number of places hit, and in the time-lag caused by unexploded bombs ... The War Cabinet has already had under consideration the question of ensuring that a due proportion of Bomb Disposal Units is available ... We regard the railway position with some anxiety ... if the rate of damage was to increase the position might well lead ... to serious traffic congestion ... the supply of coal to the South of England ... is bound to be aggravated ... the position on the railways is one which should be closely watched.

Food Stocks.

Damage to food stocks varies from negligible quantities of bacon, meat and coffee, to half a week's consumption of sugar, 13,600 tons. Two days' consumption of wheat and tea has been lost. These losses are less important than the destruction of flour-mills, cold storage plants, margarine factories, and oil and cake mills, situated in the London dock areas. As regards the milling industry, reserve capacity will be brought into use and longer hours worked in order to increase the proportion of stocks held in the form of flour, which is more readily dispersed than wheat. The loss of cold storage capacity will create some difficulties in regard to meat.

Material Stocks.

The main known loss is 20,000 standards of sawn timber in the Surrey Commercial Docks. Before the intensification of air raids, steps had been taken to effect a considerable dispersion of stocks throughout the country. The Minister of Supply has considered whether this process can be carried further. He intends to arrange for releases of pit props to Colliery Companies on an increased scale. The Companies would be warned against depleting the stocks so released by consumption at an abnormal rate, since they could probably not be replaced. The possibility is also being examined of dispersing, e.g. to the West Riding, some of the stocks of wool in London, which amount to 300,000 bales. The position of stocks of rubber and cotton is also being examined.

Assistance for Homeless Persons.

An extensive scheme of Emergency Rest Centres is being operated by the London County Council. But the scale of attacks in the last few days, and the wide use of time bombs, have made it necessary to increase the scale of the scheme ... The arrangements for evacuating homeless people to other areas are now working satisfactorily, but are being impeded ... by the reluctance of those concerned to move to other areas ... the food provided at the Emergency Rest Centres consisted mainly of bread and tea ...

Communal Feeding.

... provision must also be made for those who are unable to cook in their own homes owing to failure of the gas supply; while any system of communal feeding will also take into account the population of very poor districts, although the needs of this class are not in any way the result of enemy bomb attacks.[3]

Waldberg was interrogated by two officers from SIS, Mr Sampson and Mr Meurig Evans. The prisoner explained about his experience at Wiesbaden, its staff and its head – a general whom he barely saw and could not describe. The general code letter for Wiesbaden was 'Z', and the members were referred by Z plus a letter or number, e.g. Za. During his short stay at Wiesbaden, Waldberg revealed he was Z22; when he left on missions, he was Zh8. At Wiesbaden, Waldberg's duties included the delivery of incoming telegrams.

Some of the members and agents Waldberg revealed were as follows:[4]

Major Schmitt.   Age about 50, tall, powerfully built, spectacles for reading, white hair but receding, heavy gait, clean shaven.

Wichmann.   Waldberg never saw him at Wiesbaden, but was aware of his name; he may have been at Wimille.

Walter Pfeiffer.	Ex-soldier recruited about June 1940 for work in England, but in August he refused to go.
Peter Schroeder.	He was with Waldberg at least until Wimille, and was expected to be in the party to go to England, but his taking part was countermanded at the last moment.
Koch.	A lieutenant who learned cooking in London; lived, from June 1940, in requisitioned accommodation at Avenue Cribeaumont, Brussels. Waldberg claimed that he was intimate with the general who was head of the SS. Koch had been to England, Java, China and the Cameroons, always as a spy. He was professedly anxious for special missions. He was expecting to go to England (Norfolk) by plane and parachute; if in trouble he would hide in London's Chinatown. Koch was about 49 years of age, small in stature, with very small eyes, fat and had a heavy gait. He had in his possession three sets of papers, two in a name other than Koch, which he concealed from Waldberg. Koch may well have been a sobriquet.

Waldberg explained his time in France, from July 1937 until 4 April 1938, as an industrial spy. He arrived at the SS Centre at Wiesbaden on or about 4 April 1938. He told of his time in Brussels, between 9 September 1939 and 28 March 1940, where he reported on the state of public opinion. There he lived at the house of the German Commercial Attaché at Place d'Arrego, but did not remember his name. He described the attaché as tall, about 50 years old, and his wife was from the Alsace region of France, aged only about 20.

Waldberg said he reported to the embassy in Brussels to an unknown man, who was short, aged about 40, with white hair. He drove a small Mercedes-Benz which sported a CD (Corps Diplomatique) plate. Alternatively, Waldberg reported to his female secretary, whom he described as medium height, very dark and plump. Waldberg was paid 80 Marks per week and his lodgings were free. Whilst in Belgium, he visited Namur, Charleroi and Wetteren.

Waldberg went on to explain that between March and June 1940, he was in Mainz at an internment camp used for prisoners of war, acting as Schmidt's secretary in interrogating captured French officers.

On 14/15 June he had arrived back in Brussels from Mainz. Initially he stayed in two guesthouses, and then with Koch in Avenue Cribeaumont.

Lieutenant Colonel Stephens thought some of Waldberg's information to be correct, but commented, 'he is having recourse to his imagination in the hope of pleasing us.'[5]

Stephens sent a 'Secret' memo from Latchmere House to MI5, in which was a sketch plan of the Villa Wimille. He requested that 'it be sent forthwith to the Air Ministry for the favour of bombardment'.[6]

Section B24 sent a note regarding one of Kieboom's contacts in England, Percy Walter Snow, of Hillcrest Road, London, SE26. Snow had lived at that address, number 14, for up to a year, but according to the current tenant, he had previously moved out for the North of England and did not leave a forwarding address.

A 'Secret' memo sent on behalf of Stephens to Lieutenant Colonel Hinchley Cooke stated that, in accordance with Hinchley Cooke's wishes, they had kept the code which was fished out of the sea for prosecution purposes. The memo also stated that the code was being returned to Hinchley Cooke that afternoon as Colonel J.P.G. Worlledge, CO (RSS), was going to approach Hinchley Cooke with a view to its transmission to the Government Code and Cypher School at Bletchley Park.

Sunday, 15 September 1940:
German air raids extend to Southampton, Bristol, Cardiff and Manchester. During the day, Germany sends 1,700 planes against Britain. Eighty are shot down, with British losses of thirty-five fighters. Adolf Hitler is convinced an invasion of Britain is impossible at this time, due to the lack of air superiority.

Following Meurig Evans' interrogation about Heidenreich and Hoogeboom, Meier made a statement after remembering further details regarding Hoogeboom. He now referred to a man with a double-barrelled name – Sinclair de Rochement. Hoogeboom's brother supplied information – the subject of which was unknown – to Sinclair, who seemed to be working with several men of 'Hoogeboom's type'. Meier added that it was long supposed that Sinclair was working for the Germans. There were rumours that he worked for both sides at the same time. He went on to note that one of the other men working with Sinclair was a member of the NSNAP. He was also caught, and Meier was firmly convinced that the man had been working for Germany all the time. Meier finished by saying that he got this information from Goyvaerts – The Hague Group leader of the NSNAP – who, incidentally, did not mention a name.

Monday, 16 September 1940:
On the night of 15/16 September, Sergeant Hannah, who serves with 83 Squadron based at RAF Scampton, is the Wireless Operator/Air Gunner on an aircraft detailed to carry out operations on enemy barge concentrations at Antwerp.

After completing a successful attack on the target, his aircraft is subjected to intense anti-aircraft fire, during the course of which the bomb compartment receives a direct hit. A fire starts and quickly envelops the Wireless Operator/Air Gunner's and Rear Gunner's cockpits. Both the port and starboard petrol tanks are also pierced, causing grave risk of fire spreading still further.

Sergeant Hannah succeeds in forcing his way through the fire in order to grab two extinguishers. He then discovers that the Rear Gunner is missing. Quite undaunted, he fights the fire for ten minutes, and when the fire extinguishers are exhausted he beats the flames with his log book. During this time, ammunition from the gunner's magazines is exploding in all directions. In spite of this and the fact that he is almost blinded by the intense heat and fumes, he succeeds in controlling and eventually putting out the fire. During the process of fighting the flames, he turns on his oxygen to assist him in his efforts.

On instructions from his pilot, Sergeant Hannah then crawls forward to ascertain if the navigator is alright, only to find that he also is missing. He informs his pilot and passes up the navigator's log and maps, stating that he is quite alright himself, in spite of burns and exhaustion from the heat and fumes.

An inspection of the aircraft reveals the conditions under which Sergeant Hannah was working. The sides of the fuselage are ripped away by enemy action and exploding bullets. Metal is distorted and the framework scorched by the intense heat. The two carrier pigeons are completely roasted. His own parachute is burned out.

During this operation, in which he received second degree burns to his face and eyes, Sergeant Hannah displayed outstanding coolness, courage and devotion to duty of the very highest order. By his action he not only saved the life of his pilot, but enabled his aircraft to be flown back safely to its base without any further damage.

At this stage of the war, Sergeant Hannah has completed a total of 74 hours flying as a Wireless Operator/Air Gunner on eleven operational flights against the enemy.[7]

The German Luftwaffe redirects its bombing campaign to now cover night-bombing of British cities. A night raid on London causes extensive damage to Oxford Street underground station, and twenty people are killed when a high-explosive bomb rips through the roof of Marble Arch station and explodes in the tunnel.

Despite his predicament, Waldberg – if anything, one of the more impertinent of the spies –brazenly requested a private cipher telegram be sent on the German wireless transmitter to Brussels. It would appear that Waldberg had made a rather odd arrangement before he left, suggesting that some sort of floral tribute be sent to a young Belgian woman, his fiancée Helene Ceuppens, in Brussels, for her birthday on 19 September.

To this end, 'Tin Eye' Stephens approached MI5 first, telephoning Malcolm Frost (who was not available). He then spoke to 'Tar' Robertson, explained to him why it was not possible to carry out Waldberg's request: it appeared there was no useful purpose in this matter. Stephens noted that a point-blank refusal appeared to be indicated, but he felt that there were possibilities if a telegram was sent, as it would indicate 'beyond a shadow of doubt' that Waldberg was still alive and capable of sending messages. Thereafter, a further series of telegrams containing false information could usefully be sent.

Tuesday, 17 September 1940:

Approximately seventy-seven children are lost with the SS *City of Benares*. The liner left Liverpool on 13 September with 197 passengers, including ninety children who were being evacuated from wartime Britain to Canada. At about 11.30 pm, she is torpedoed and sinks. The latest report states that almost eighty children are among the 134 passengers killed, as well as 131 of the 200 crew.

The British Government announces conscription of males between the ages of 21 and 35.

The formal decision taken by Hitler to indefinitely postpone Operation *Sealion*, 'although "preparations will be continued" to ensure that the British had to maintain their vigilance'.[8]

The following is a summary of information elicited from Waldberg and Meier after being in Mainz:

Training for England
Waldberg's account of his training in military espionage differed from that of Meier in three important particulars:

1. Waldberg understood that he was to reconnoitre the coast from Aldeburgh, and not the inland East Anglian district.
2. He had never heard of the Croydon–Salisbury railway line.
3. He understood the Margate–Folkestone line mentioned at Wimille was as an example only.

It was again noted that Waldberg bitterly resented having been sent to England, and would go to almost any lengths to avenge himself on Kohler, whom he took to be responsible for his predicament.

Wimille
Waldberg's account tallied with that of Meier, except that Waldberg mentioned a secret album of photographs and fingerprints of Section II agents which were kept under the mattress of an NCO's bed.

Le Touquet

Waldberg's account fell in with that of Meier, except that Waldberg was instructed (unknown to the others) to return to Boulogne as soon as he had collected sufficient information. He was then to return to England with Werner, who would be picked up by an English contact in a car. Waldberg was to send a wireless message announcing his departure, steal a boat and put out to sea. He would then be picked up from some fast craft sent to meet him.

Landing in England

Waldberg admitted sending two wireless messages: On 3 September he announced his arrival, giving information and the jettisoning of the grid code. Then, on the morning of 4 September, he told of Meier's arrest, complained of thirst and asked for a plane to be sent.

Communication with aircraft

If he lost his bearings, Waldberg was to spread a sheet on the ground which was to be seen by aircraft (these instructions were given in a wireless message on Tuesday, 3 September).

Other persons who may be sent as spies to England:

There could be up to six others prepared to be sent to England as spies: Werner, Koch, Peter Schneider, Franz Schneider, Paul Schneider and Walter Pfeiffer.

German plans and troop movements

Waldberg believed the following:

1. The invasion was likely between 3 and 15 September.
2. He thought, with some certainty, that the invasion would be on the coast between Cromer and Aldeburgh. A simultaneous landing would be made in the Dungeness area, unless strongly defended between the coast and military canal.
3. Like Meier, he mentioned concentrations of troops with mule transport near Le Touquet and specialized engineer units, along with many *Schnellboot*, each capable of carrying about fifteen men, moored along the coast.
4. The Kommandantur of the invasion troops was next door to Seynsburg's villa at Paris Plage.

Thursday, 19 September 1940:

12 noon: At a meeting of the War Cabinet in the Prime Minister's Room, House of Commons, the Chief of the Air Staff, Air Chief Marshal Sir Cyril Newall, says that enemy air casualties during the twenty-four hours ending 7 am that morning had been as follows:

	Destroyed	Probable	Damaged
Bombers	36	5	7
Fighters	10	11	12
Total	46	16	19

British losses during this period were twelve aircraft, but nine pilots were safe.

Nearly 200 British aircraft had carried out bombing operations on the previous night, mainly against the invasion ports. Except for attacks on Berlin, which would be resumed as soon as the weather was favourable, it was intended that Britain's bombing effort should be concentrated almost entirely against these ports.

An order from General Wilhelm Keitel, Chief of the Armed Forces High Command, outlined the first practical steps of the abandonment of Operation *Sealion*. It stipulated that 'movements for the strategic concentration of shipping, as far as have not yet been completed, will be discontinued and that concentrations in assembly harbours will be dispersed so that losses of shipping tonnage owing to enemy air attack will be kept to a minimum'.[9] The Kriegsmarine was only too aware of the apparent omnipotence of the Royal Navy and the Royal Air Force. The Kriegsmarine cited the 'use of [RAF] aircraft for attacks and reconnaissance over the German operational harbours, frequent appearance of destroyers on the south coast of England, in the Straits of Dover ... stationing his patrol vessels off the north coast of France'.[10]

Friday, 20 September 1940:
Hundreds of people are being killed every week, even if the exact figures are somewhat elusive. Just three days ago, on 17 September, a bomb killed twenty people sheltering in Marble Arch station in Central London. When people are crammed together, the toll of injuries and deaths are magnified. One solution to this problem comes when Alfred E. Moss (whose son Stirling would become a Formula One racing driver) submits his patent design for an indoor air raid shelter, a modified design of which becomes the Morrison shelter.

Two 'Confidential' memos from the Investigation Branch (Special Section) of the General Post Office (GPO) were sent to MI5 counter-intelligence's Dick Goldsmith White regarding two of Kieboom's contacts.

One stated that they were informed that a Percy Walter White used to reside at 14 Hillcrest Road, London, SE 26, but had left that address over a year ago. His current address was not known. The check had been suspended pending further instructions from MI5.

The second memo informed Goldsmith White that, as a result of the check on Robert W. Wade of 8 Warren Road, Purley, a redirection notice to 25 Eastcheap, London, EC, was received and that the check had been transferred accordingly.

Friday, 27 September 1940:

The US Ambassador to Britain, Joseph Kennedy, sends a report to his President, Franklin D. Roosevelt, in which he portrays Britain's predicament in extremely disparaging terms.

He describes how the air raids are affecting production, despite what may be publicly proclaimed, and with transportation 'smashed up', he predicts that production will continue to fall.

Kennedy feels that the British are in a bad way, with the Germans conducting daylight bombing almost with impunity.

Kennedy goes on to convey his complete lack of confidence in the British and their conduct in the war thus far. He also expresses his delight that Roosevelt has so far chosen not to enter the war, adding, rather scathingly, that the British have nothing to offer the United States, not in leadership nor a productive industry that would be of any value to Roosevelt or the US.

A 'Secret' report by Lieutenant Colonel Stephens made reference to a written statement by Waldberg in which he referred to a woman whom he thought to be Italian. She was very tall with an oval, sunburnt face, brown or black hair, beauty spot on the left above her upper lip and very fine teeth. She wore, on her left wrist, a gold bracelet. She drove a blue limousine and the number plate contained a double 'R'. She left Antwerp, via Berlin, to report on a mission to the 'Grand Chief'. She actually came from Burgos in Spain, but lived in New York.

Stephens stated that immediate identification of the woman would be of great value to him before he questioned Waldberg further. Stephens also noted that Waldberg was doubtful as to his future, and was willing to give information. He warned that Waldberg was inclined to romance, and said that he, Stephens, did not want to be 'party to a wild goose chase'.[11]

Certain items found on the four men were sent by Dick Goldsmith White for scientific analysis to H.L. Smith at the GPO. The items were split into two groups:

In the first group, Goldsmith White was looking for what was thought to be an oil or liquid which, when rubbed over paper which had previously been written upon by a pointed implement with water, revealed any writing. Wads of cotton that 'appear to be impregnated with chemicals'[12] were included for analysis.

A curious feature was that each agent was in possession of one white tablet and one green tablet of soap. 'This no doubt reflects the methodical procedure for equipping agents,'[13] said Goldsmith White, who sent Smith specimen tablets for analysis.

The second group contained a tin marked 'Capacetyl', which contained an ingredient that cannot be identified because the name was redacted from the report. There were also ordinary Aspro tablets. The spy on whom these were found claimed that, if dissolved in alcohol – common gin would be satisfactory – an adequate secret ink would be produced. Goldsmith White was sure that the 'boffins' were well acquainted with this fact, but he sent Smith the tablets for analysis anyway.

There was also a small piece of paper on which was written a name, which was also sent to be tested for secret writing. Also included was a small cotton bag, said to contain stomach powders. While Goldsmith White believed this to be true, he erred on the side of caution, and this was also sent in case they were more sinister than first appeared.

Goldsmith White politely reminded Smith that, as far as the analysis was concerned, time was of the essence.

Saturday, 28 September 1940:
Yesterday, Germany, Italy and Japan signed a tripartite pact in Berlin. The pact provided for mutual assistance should any of the signatories on the pact be attacked by another nation.

There was growing concern about an article in a Portuguese newspaper (dated 15 September 1940), purporting to come from a United Press (UP) correspondent in Amsterdam. Captain Felix Cowgill of SIS rang 'Tar' Robertson to say that his attention had been drawn to the article. The exposé was to the effect that seven Dutchmen had been arrested in England for espionage and that cipher documents and a transmitter had been found on them. Robertson was anxious to know whether any UP correspondent had recently left England, bound for either Lisbon, Northern Ireland, Eire or the USA.

Monday, 30 September 1940:
At 4.40 pm, Sherborne in Dorset is heavily raided by a force of some 150 German bombers which, having been turned away from Yeovil (Somerset) by fighters, drop several hundred bombs (about 60 tons) in a straight line from Lenthay to Crackmore.

About eighty-six buildings are destroyed, seventeen civilians, including six children, died as a result of the bombings and thirty-one casualties are taken to hospital, one of whom died from his wounds (six years later).[14]

Forty-seven German aircraft are shot down over England.

In a handwritten reply to 'Tar' Robertson after discreet inquiries were made via their London office, UP denied any of their correspondents had recently been to Lisbon. Furthermore, they refuted that the message could have gone by cable from Amsterdam to Lisbon. The news of the arrests, however, was widely known in Kent, and it was suggested that the information may have been leaked by some other channel.

A reply for Goldsmith White arrived from H.L. Smith, which addressed the issues raised regarding the two groups of items that were sent for analysis. Among the liquids in the first group were Vedette and Oeillet Fringe, which would have enabled writing when used with water, using a pointed implement. These two small bottles contained a preparation of iodine which resembled that stated to be used by the Germans. The British, however, had a similar formula.

In the second group, the tin labelled 'Capacetyl' contained one tablet (name redacted) and several unmarked tablets. The redacted tablet was known to be used as a secret ink, and the British had received statements that it was being used by the Germans for secret writing: 'Every German appears to carry it and we have reported on it many times.'[15]

The other tablets were not Aspro but a derivative of Antipyrine, which can be used for secret writing. It was considered that simple Antipyrine was better as a derivative. Smith reported that, so far, they had not discovered amongst the material any substance which could be the specific developer for either of the substances.

Also, there were tablets labelled Dextro Sport, which essentially consisted of dextrose – a sugar useful for increasing one's energy during exertion – otherwise it was of no interest. The work was not completed, however, but had focussed on the material to which attention was drawn on the 27 September. A further report would follow as soon as anything interesting was found, or when the examination was completed.

Tuesday, 1 October 1940:

Start of German BF 110 twin-engine night-fighters taking advantage of the new Lichtenstein radar systems to track, target and engage RAF bombers.

Naval Intelligence monitors Kapitanleutnant Gunther Prien, the German U-boat 'ace'.

H.L. Smith and the Scientific Section responded with another report to Goldsmith White, which stated that they had finished the examination of the material sent to them on 27 September.

Smith said that apart from the two bottles which contained an iodine solution (that would develop a simple form of secret writing), the other bottles contained scent and toilet preparations as indicated on their labels. Although some of them were unpleasant, they had no application in secret writing.

The report continued that almost anything could be used for secret writing, provided the conditions could be controlled. Dr Will's Brilliantine, for example – which was part of a sample in the first group – could be used for writing, and could be developed by means of graphite. 'It is not particularly good,' the report remarked.

The soaps were normal and of no interest. As far as the tablets were concerned, no material had been found which could be used to develop the tablets, although they may, of course, be used for outward correspondence only, the contents to be 'exposed' by the Germans.

The box of white cotton wool contained nothing but that. The cotton wool, which was stained mauve, was impregnated with a considerable quantity of calcium chloride, which took up moisture from the atmosphere; this accounted for its moist feeling. The colour changed and disappeared when wetted. An extract of the wool behaved like a very dilute blood. Writing in this extract could be developed in the same way as blood. It made a good secret ink. Annotated by hand on the report was, 'We found no substances to develop this among the material.'[16]

Finally, no secret writing was found on the small piece of paper in the second group.

Smith indicated that he would like to retain the remainder of the mauve-coloured wool as there were some curious features about it, and he asked whether he should return the remainder of the material to Goldsmith White.

Thursday, 3 October 1940:
Sir Kingsley Wood is made Chancellor of the Exchequer, with Ernest Bevin appointed Minister of Labour & National Service and Sir John Anderson Lord President of the Council. All are members of the War Cabinet.

Wednesday, 9 October 1940:
The Luftwaffe launches a heavy night-time air raid on London and the dome of St Paul's Cathedral takes a direct hit from a bomb.

Goldsmith White wrote again to H.L. Smith and apologized for the delay in acknowledging his letters of 30 September and 1 October. He said he was 'very interested' in Smith's analysis and requested any further information that he may have on the impregnated cotton wool. He also asked Smith's section to return the rest of the material.

Thursday, 10 October 1940:

At a meeting of the War Cabinet in the Prime Minister's Room, House of Commons, at 11.30 am, the Chief of the Air Staff reports that on the previous day there had been three main enemy attacks, of which two had penetrated to London and one had crossed over Kent and the Thames Estuary. It is believed that these attacks had been made by Messerschmitt 109s.

Casualties had been: one British aircraft (pilot safe); four enemy certain, with another four probable and five damaged.

On the previous night the enemy air activity had been rather heavier than usual, and amongst places hit was St Paul's Cathedral, where the altar had been badly damaged. Discussion ensues as to whether publicity should be given to the damage to St Paul's. It is felt important not to give the enemy information of operational value by publishing reports of damage caused. It is noted that the enemy has ceased to give particulars of the damage which British raids cause in Germany.

Kieboom, Pons and Meier were held temporarily at Richmond Police Station. Lieutenant Colonel Hinchley Cook, along with Detective Sergeant Buswell, arrived there to interview the prisoners. They were seen separately.

Kieboom was the first to be seen by Hinchley Cook. The MI5 man said to him:

> 'You will no doubt remember that I saw you some time ago at New Scotland Yard, when I asked you a number of questions to which you gave replies and which were taken down in shorthand by Detective Sergeant Buswell. I want to read the transcript of the shorthand notes over to you so as to make quite certain there is no misunderstanding. Will you please stop me if there is anything with which you disagree? Do you understand what I say?'

'Yes, I understand, Sir,' the prisoner replied.

Hinchley Cook then handed Kieboom a copy of the typewritten transcript of the shorthand notes taken by DS Buswell, which was perused by the prisoner, whilst Hinchley Cook read aloud the transcript from another copy.

During the reading of the transcript, Kieboom asked that several of the replies that were made by him on 5 September be amended. These alterations were duly made on the typewritten transcript, in ink, by Hinchley Cook, and Kieboom initialled the lines amended to show that he agreed with them. He was then asked by Hinchley Cook if he would care to sign the amended transcript, although there was no obligation on his part to do so. Kieboom said he would, and proceeded to sign each page, with his initials witnessed by Hinchley Cook and DS Buswell.

Pons was next to be seen. Hinchley Cook reminded him of their previous interview and asked him to read the transcript of DS Buswell's shorthand notes to see whether they were correct.

A copy of the transcript was duly handed to Pons for him to read, whilst Hinchley Cook read aloud from another copy. Pons asked that some of his replies be amended. Hinchley Cook made the necessary alterations in ink, and Pons initialled the lines to indicate his agreement. Hinchley Cook then asked Pons if he had any objection to signing the amended document, although he was not obliged to do so. Pons replied, 'I will sign it willingly.' He then signed each page, and his signatures were witnessed by Hinchley Cook and Buswell.

Finally, it was Meier's turn to be seen. Hinchley Cook said to him, 'You remember seeing me a little time ago?' Meier simply replied, 'Yes.' Hinchley Cook, as with the other two prisoners, indicated the transcript from their previous interview and explained that he wanted him to check it for any errors. Hinchley Cook handed Meier a copy of the transcript whilst he himself read aloud from another copy. At Meier's request, Hinchley Cook made several written alterations in the transcript, one being that the Germans approached Meier first instead of his seeking them out. The alterations were initialled by Meier to show his agreement, and he too agreed to sign each page of the amended transcript, with his signature duly witnessed by the two officials.

All the signed transcripts were retained by Hinchley Cooke.[17]

During this encounter, Meier, eager to please, made three small sketch plans, which showed where he had landed in the Dungeness area, as well as the Hastings to Sheerness area and a general plan of Kent, parts of Sussex, Essex and London, indeed pretty much the whole of south-east England

Friday, 11 October 1940:
As part of Operation *Medium*, HMS *Revenge* bombards Cherbourg. *Medium* is a joint Royal Navy and RAF Bomber Command operation. Joining HMS *Revenge* were cruisers, destroyers and motor torpedo boats.

As the cells at Camp 020 were bugged, it followed that conversations between the spies would be monitored. Meier and a fellow internee named Goose, alias Karl Grosse,[18] indulged in, for men in their predicament, a series of eclectic and even prosaic conversations:[19]

Conversation between Goose and Meier. (Verbatim extracts)
Time: 10.30–11 am. DATE: 11.10.40
M. [Meier] There was a wireless message someone said on the corridor,
    I think it was this Polish man in the next room, No. 4 and he said

something about Germany and then about Russia and then I heard 'diplomatic relations' being broken off.

G. [Goose] Shucks! When the triple alliance was closed they had the same talk and then a few days later the Russian papers came out saying it wasn't true.

M. Well anyhow, this I definitely heard and it was said over the wireless. Later on I thought maybe the reverse had happened, that 'diplomatic relations' between England and Russia had been broken off but they seem quite confident, the soldiers. But this Pole says Russia is terribly strong and has 25,000 aeroplanes and all that.

G. It doesn't sound as though diplomatic relations between Germany and Russia are broken off.

M. That's why I think it is the opposite. I just wanted to make sure if you had heard too.

…

M. The Germans say that when the English want anything they put on the velvet glove so that it is more pleasantly carried out. When the chap says he will, of course, speak favourably to him, that means he has got all he wants and you and everything else can go into the wastepaper basket.

…

G. Do you know this name?

M. Oh, yes.

G. Do you know who he is?

M. Oh yes. I mean …

G. QUIET!

M. The trouble is that long ago …

G. Oh No!

M. You may be right with one person, but you may not be right with another one, that's the trouble. They say it is alright – but they promise things they can't really promise.

G. They don't promise anything. Don't you see what it means? They say things are going favourably – favourably to whom? He thinks we are questionable foreigners, but he says, 'Your case is proceeding favourably' – that means his case is fine, he has got a lot out of us. It's favourable to him.

M. That's right.

G. Oh. Hell. It doesn't mean anything. He says, 'We will see what we can do about you.' They say 'for you', and they mean 'about you'.

…

M. I made a mistake to say 'we' when I should have said 'I'. I mean when they arrested me, so they knew there must be somebody else. I said 'we arrived here last night'.

G. They caught you first?

M. Yes, they caught me first so they know there is somebody else. I said there is a Frenchman but they put him off the fish-cutter earlier. Later on this man said to me I think you had better tell us where this Frenchman has gone if you know, because you say he doesn't speak any English and as you know he might get into all sorts of trouble that way.

...

G. How the hell did they get all these names – Kohler, [inaudible], and so on.

M. Gosh, I don't know them. They got them from us, it was terrible, all four of us were brought and they knew we were not telling the truth when we came out with our refugee story. They knew about the whole thing already. Each one of us had another story. It didn't tally at all and after a while you got scared in case someone had told more than you had and they really knew quite a lot. That's the way the whole thing came out. They used the revelations of another always, and they bluff saying there was nothing to do about it. I decided the best policy to follow ...

G. I wonder how they got hold of the news about me. They said, 'we have been expecting you.' It was a bluff but they told me lots of things about ...

M. That's a bluff too as that happened to me several times, they said, 'She knows you' and all that. I said, 'That's very funny, I don't know her.'

G. Are there women here then?

M. No, not here but they caught a woman too, they said, 'She knows you.' I said, 'That's funny, I have never met any women in this.'

...

M. Were you in Berkeley (USA?)

G. Yes.

M. Have you been at the International House by any chance?

G. Yes, in Chicago.

M. I know the International House all right. I never lived there ...

G. Those people are known as the most terrific Nazi agents [laughter].

...

M. I know a man from Vienna and one from Munster (presumably connected to the International House).

G. The Munster one – was he the son of the minister?

M. I don't know, I don't think so, but what is his name? Perhaps if you say
     …
G. I don't know – but he is the son of the Protestant minister.
M. It is possible, he was not very pro-German.
G. Red-head?
M. Yes.
G. That is the same.

Whilst there were no German contacts in England, there was concern over Kieboom's English contacts. As a consequence, a 'Secret' memo[20] was despatched:

'To The POSTMASTER-GENERAL, and all others whom it may concern thereby authorise and require you to detain, open and produce for my inspection all postal packets and telegrams address to:

'David Bankes-Price   128 Churchill Avenue, Coventry.
'Herbert Reynolds Barfoot   Lloyds Buildings, London.
'Arthur Butterworth   11 Leadenhall Street, London.
'Alfred Doleman   143 Huddersfield Road, Halifax.
'Robert W. Wade   8 Warren Road, Purley, Surrey.
'Percy Walter Snow   Hillcrest Road, London, SE 26.

'or to any name at that or any other address if there is reasonable ground to believe that they are intended for the said individual and for so doing this shall be your sufficient Warrant.
'*One of His Majesty's Principal Secretaries of State.*
'These men are suspected of being in contact with an enemy agent.'

While in Stephens' custody, Waldberg repeated certain facts, including to being a willing German spy – but the others all vehemently denied being such. Waldberg also admitted that he was not new to the work, and had been a professional spy for about two or three years, and claimed to have effectively transmitted from behind the French lines during the Blitzkreig that led to the capitulation of the country.

Sjoerd Pons claimed that he had intended to give himself up as soon as he arrived. 'I want to take it all to you,' he said, 'I want to tell the police and take him my apparatus under my arm.'[21] Pons was asked whether he would be willing to become a double agent. His dilemma was clear as he stumbled over an answer. Believing that the Germans would invade Britain in the coming days, he didn't know what to say. After all, if he refused to cooperate, the British might

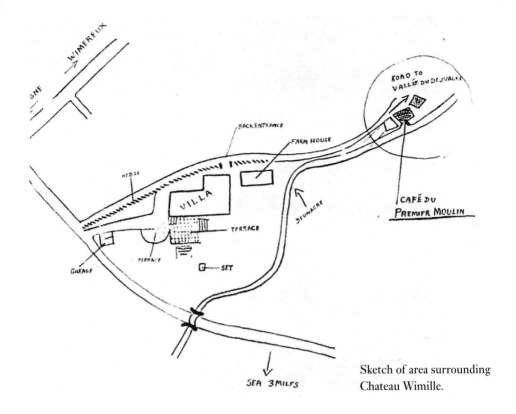

Sketch of area surrounding Chateau Wimille.

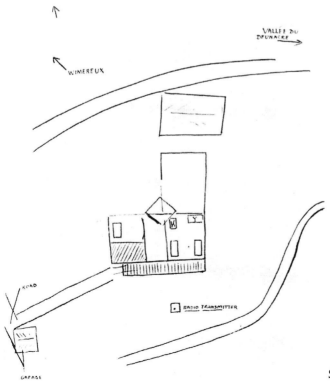

Sketch plan of Chateau Wimille.

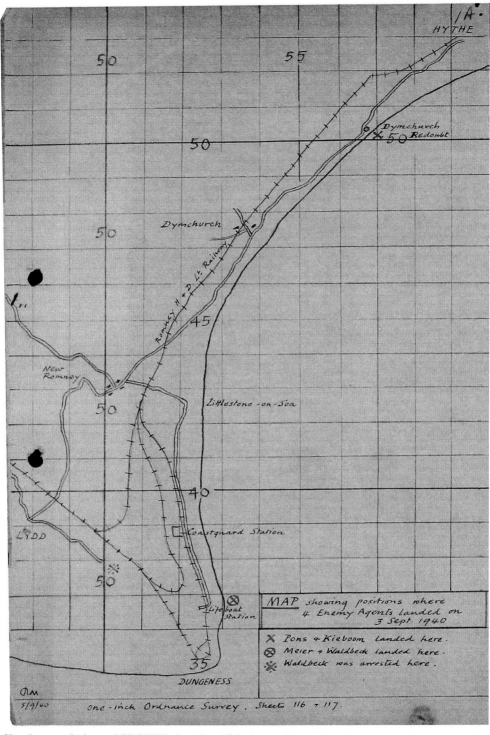

Sketch map – designated SECRET – based on 1″ Ordnance Survey showing the approximate positions where the four landed as sent to Hinchley Cooke, 5th September, 1940.

Transmitting set.

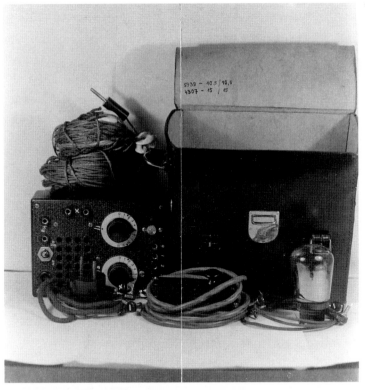

View of boat No 1 used by Pons and Kieboom.

View of No 1 boat (as identified by Kieboom) taken from sea-wall, by Grand Redoubt, West Hythe.

Scene of landing of boat No 1. Note the barbed wire on the sea-wall.

View of dyke where the bull rushes are growing, this being the hidout of party No 1. This is immediately behind the sea-wall and was known as Beach Holiday Camp, Dymchurch.

View of boat No 2, used by Meier and Waldberg.

Scene of landing for boat No 2. View of beach with an old boat on the left. Meier and Waldberg utilised this old boat.

View of subsequent hideout of Waldberg. The tree on the right is spacious underneath and he slept there. The wireless was erected in a clearing in the middle of the bushes on the left and an aerial was flung across the bushes.

Transmitting set.

Transmitting set with
Pertrix battery.

Charles Albert van den Kieboom.

Jose Waldberg.

Carl Meier.

Sjoerd Pons.

execute him summarily as a spy; but if he agreed, the Germans might execute him upon their arrival. So Pons chose a different option: instead of answering the question, he asked his interrogator whether he could possibly be sent to America, where he had wanted to go all along. The answer, not surprisingly, was 'No!'

Stephens concluded that the men could not be used as double agents. He gave three reasons. Firstly, Waldberg had already made contact with his handler. Secondly, their arrests had been widely observed. Thirdly, three of them denied being spies at all. Therefore, they were all committed for trial at the Old Bailey – except for Waldberg, the only one who had pleaded guilty.

Stephens had found significant leverage in a provision of the law under which, in wartime, captured spies who refused to cooperate could face execution.

Monday, 14 October 1940:

The Blitz moves even closer to the heart of the British Government: Winston and Clementine Churchill were being served dinner in the Garden Rooms at 10 Downing Street, when several heavy detonations are heard close by. Churchill orders his butler and parlour maid into the garden shelter and returns to his dinner table. Several minutes later a high explosive bomb hits the Treasury Gardens, yards from No. 10. Three civil servants on Home Guard duty in the Treasury Green shelter are killed, and Treasury Building offices are destroyed. The blast rocks Downing Street. Although the Churchills are unharmed, No. 10's upstairs kitchen and pantry are wrecked, a large plate glass window is shattered and the State Drawing Rooms, Pillared Drawing Room and some dining rooms are damaged.[22]

The scientists wrote again to Goldsmith White, reporting further on the materials they had previously sent. The report[23] started by summarizing from previous communications:

1. 'Two small bottles of a special iodine solution which can only be intended to develop a simple form of secret writing.'
2. 'Some tablets, one of which was Pyramidon, made a good secret ink which had been reported several times as a substance used by the enemy for secret writing.'

The report documented more fully on the white and coloured 'wools'. The white one yielded nothing to solvents. The coloured one yielded a considerable quantity of substance. This substance was largely calcium chloride. An extract diluted so as to contain only 1 per cent of calcium chloride, when used for writing on paper, reacted as blood and made an ink which developed legibly and strongly. As other substances react giving much the same colour as blood, the scientists felt that it was necessary to examine this further, but no such substance was found. It was concluded that the colour was due to blood or a product from blood, such as haemoglobin.

The report specified that it was doubtful that the impregnated 'wool' should be considered a good and subtle method of carrying secret ink; it was thought very crude. The 'wool' appeared abnormal; the calcium chloride was easily detected and, if used as a secret ink, could be readily developed, apart from the small amount of blood. On the other hand, it had made it very difficult to prove the presence of blood. What was definitive was that the 'wool' contained two substances, and when an extract was used for secret writing, either substance could be developed independently. No other explanation could be brought forward for the use of the impregnated 'wool', except for the purpose of secret writing.

The report concluded that the coloured 'wool' was dealt with more fully than usual as it was felt certain that the substances that this was impregnated with were definitely intended for the use of secret writing and not for innocent purposes.

Tuesday, 22 October 1940:

At 3.30 pm in the Cabinet War Rooms, a meeting of the War Cabinet Defence Committee (Operations) is in progress. The discussion is primarily about West Africa and operations conducted by General de Gaulle. Vice Admiral T.S.V. Phillips (Vice Chief of Naval Staff) refers to local signals that had been intercepted in which it appeared that Vice Admiral Cunningham was not satisfied that the operation he is involved in 'was being carefully planned'. A concern was that unless success is certain it is most undesirable that naval forces should be committed to operations in West Africa when they are badly needed elsewhere.

General de Gaulle had asked for two further Blenheims from Takoradi (Ghana). The advice was strongly against diverting any aircraft from the Middle East reinforcement programme. Besides, de Gaulle already had six Blenheims and eight Lysanders.[24]

A raid on Chateau Wimille, most likely by the RAF, had been mooted. Waldberg had drawn a plan of the chateau and Captain Felix Cowgill of SIS, along with MI5 (B2), had discussed this. A representative from SIS had been invited to MI5 to inspect Waldberg's plan and discuss the feasibility of a raid.

Wednesday, 23 October 1940:

Adolf Hitler and Spain's Francisco Franco meet in Spain. Hitler tries to get Spain committed to the war, or allow German troops to assault Gibraltar. Franco reluctantly agrees to eventually enter the war, in return for military, agricultural and territorial demands, and only at a time of Spain's choosing.

The Brussels Four were still in Camp 020 and were due to appear before the Chief Magistrate (sitting in camera) at Bow Street for the purpose of being remanded in custody. Any necessary steps would be taken to ensure that no reference whatsoever was made in the press regarding any legal proceedings.

A handwritten note[25] emanated from MI5's Section B13, detailing security measures regarding handing the men over to the civil powers:

1. Case taken over by Inspector Bridges, Special Branch.
2. Had spoken with Mr Waddams (Prison Commission). Complete isolation at Brixton Prison was agreed. All correspondence in and out (if any) to be seen by the note's author [name unknown].
3. Spoke to Wood. A Mr Mackee would act as interpreter.

Chapter Eight

Home for Incurables

Thursday, 24 October 1940:
A meeting of the War Cabinet is held in the Prime Minister's Room, House of Commons, at 12 noon. The Chief of the Air Staff reports that enemy activity on the previous day had been on a reduced scale, only thirty-five aircraft being involved. One enemy aircraft had been damaged by British fighters, without loss themselves.

The previous night only 100 German machines had been over the country, twenty-five having been over London. Many of these had flown from Norway, probably on account of the weather being better in the North than in the South.

On the previous night, ninety-five RAF bombers had been despatched to attack enemy targets, which included ports, shipping, industrial plant and Berlin. Three of these bombers were missing. One, which had come down in the sea, was being searched for.

The Chief of the Air Staff undertakes to enquire what progress has been made with experiments to enable British aircraft to give a better indication of their whereabouts when they come down on the sea.

Two enemy merchant ships (of 4,000 tons and 2,000 tons) had been torpedoed by RAF aircraft off the Dutch coast.

The four spies left Camp 020 at 10.30 am to be charged at Bow Street Police Court, but just before their departure, they were handed over by the military authorities to the Civil Power, specifically Detective Inspector Frank Bridges, for their later trial at the Old Bailey. DI Bridges explained to them that he was a police inspector and asked whether they could speak English. All except for Waldberg replied 'Yes', and Bridges explained to them that he would take them into custody, and that later they would be charged with an offence that would be explained to them. The three men were cautioned, and none made any reply. Also present was 28-year-old Detective Sergeant William Allchin, also from Special Branch, who asked Waldberg whether he could speak German; he said he could. Allchin explained to Waldberg, in German, that he was a police officer and would take him into custody, and that he would be charged with an offence, details of which would be explained later. Subsequently, Waldberg was charged. When Allchin read the charge to Waldberg, he cautioned him. Waldberg also made no reply.

At 11.40 am, at the rear of the court in Bow Street, all four prisoners were charged with an offence against section 1 of the Treachery Act, 1940. The men were before the Chief Magistrate, Sir Robert E. Dummett, who granted the application of Vincent Evans, of the Director of Public Prosecutions, for proceedings to be held in camera.

After the charge had been read to them, they were cautioned, and asked if they understood. Meier replied, 'Yes, sir', while both Pons and Kieboom replied, 'I understand'. Waldberg was read the charge by DS Allchin and again he was cautioned, but he made no reply. DI Bridges and DS Allchin both gave evidence, and the prisoners were remanded. Depositions were taken.

There was great concern regarding the secrecy of the trial. Sir Joseph Ball, an MI5 intelligence officer, had sent a 'Secret' and 'Urgent' note to C.J. Radcliffe, KC, Director General of the Ministry of Information, regarding a telephone conversation that Radcliffe had with a man called Duffy concerning the four men who appeared at Bow Street Police Court. Ball was concerned that if, by 'any mischance', the names of the four spies appeared in the press, the future work of an important branch of the Military Intelligence Service 'would be gravely prejudiced'.[1] Ball requested that every possible precaution be taken to prevent this from happening. Ball also pointed out that while Radcliffe was of the opinion that an existing D–Notice (Defence Notice, requesting the press not to publish information for reasons of national security) covered this point, he (Ball) recommended that Radcliffe issue a special reminder to the press because as the D–Notice stood, the press could contend that the mere mention of the spies' names would be permissible. Due to the urgency of the matter, Ball sent the note by hand in the hope that, a reminder having already been issued, the evening papers would comply before they appeared on the streets.

Thursday, 31 October 1940:

At a meeting of the War Cabinet in the Cabinet War Rooms at 11 am, the Prime Minister expresses his displeasure in that he is not satisfied that Commanders-in-Chief are at present being kept sufficiently in touch with the general political and strategical situation. As part of the measures to remedy the situation, it is proposed to invite Commanders-in-Chief to meetings in London about once a month. There is much discussion about the form and scale of an invasion during the winter months. It is agreed that the most likely areas for invasion are those that the German fighters can afford protection. Because the Germans have plenty of troops and are prepared to incur heavy losses, it is felt that it should be considered that landings elsewhere, maybe as diversionary tactics, are entirely possible.[2]

For an invasion to be successful, it is said, Germany needed control of the skies. This did not happen, So as a consequence, the Battle of Britain has ended.

DS Allchin, in the company of Detective Sergeant G. Smith, visited Waldberg in HM Brixton Prison, London, at 12.30 pm and said to him, in German, 'It is my duty to hand you copies of statements made by Carl Heinrich Meier, Charles Albert van den Kieboom and Sjoerd Pons, the other persons charged with you.' He handed over to Waldberg the statements, which had been translated into French, and also gave him identical copies typed in English. Waldberg made no reply. Next, DS Allchin went to see Meier, Kieboom and finally Pons, on each occasion handing them statements made by the other three. Like Waldberg, none of them made any reply.[3]

In a memo addressed to a Captain Stringer, MI5 officer John Marriott expressed concern about the necessity of collecting all the property with which the four spies landed, mainly Waldberg's notebook. Marriott stated that Waldberg alleged that he had sent two messages, and had been ready to send a third. He further claimed that all three messages were written down by him in a notebook and handed to an officer. This notebook was, as Marriott understood, an ordinary grey exercise book with squared paper and was certainly, at one time, in Marriott's office. Marriott continued by saying that it occurred to him that it may have been handed to Major Gill (communications), and Marriott would be very grateful if Stringer could have a 'pretty thorough search made for it'. The memo concluded, 'I hardly [need] say that it is a most important piece of evidence and simply must be found.'[4]

Friday, 1 November 1940:

A meeting of the War Cabinet is held at 10 Downing Street at 12 noon. The Chief of the Air Staff says that enemy air activity over this country has been on a reduced scale both by day and night. During the earlier part of the previous day, some sixty-five enemy aircraft had been over the country, chiefly on reconnaissance. In the afternoon, a number of aerodromes had been visited, but little damage had been done. Several towns had been machine-gunned. One hundred and forty-five RAF fighters had been up, but owing to cloud conditions had made no interceptions.

During the night, about 100 enemy aircraft had been over the country, of which about thirty had London as their main objective.

Nine RAF fighters had been up, but no interceptions had been made. Three had crashed on landing.

A reconnaissance from Malta had shown that the Italian Fleet was still in Taranto and Brindisi.

Six Wellingtons had now reached Malta and had been despatched the previous night to bomb Naples. Five had reached their targets and dropped about 5 tons of bombs on the central railway station and the oil tanks. The anti-aircraft fire had been heavy but inaccurate. The aircraft had all returned safely. A communiqué was to be issued but would not indicate the source of the raiders.

At 10.30 am, the four men appeared on remand at Bow Street before magistrates Sir Robert Dummett and Mr T.W. Fry. Vincent Evans appeared for the Director of Public Prosecutions. The following gave evidence for the Crown:

Dennis Henry Hayles, labourer.

George Frederick Bunstone, fisherman.

Horace R. Mansfield, aircraft inspector.

Leonard William Humphreys, wireless engineer.

2nd Lieutenant Batten, Lance Corporal Goody and Privates Tollervey, Chappell and McDonnell, Somerset Light Infantry.

Lance Corporal North, Royal Engineers.

Lieutenant Colonel Hinchley Cooke, MI5.

Police Sergeants Tye and Robertson and Police Constable Pearman, Kent County Constabulary.

Inspector Bridges and Sergeants Buswell and Allchin, Special Branch.

Depositions were taken from those mentioned above in the presence of the accused.

The Police Court proceedings took place in camera. For secrecy, it was requested that the necessary steps be taken to ensure that the press were not informed of any proceedings. The defendants reserved their defence and were committed for trial at the Central Criminal Court Sessions, commencing 12 November 1940.

Saturday, 2 November 1940:

Greek Air Force pilot Marinos Mitralexis, after running out of ammunition, rams an Italian bomber using his propeller to clip the tail of his enemy. It smashes the bomber's rudder, sending the plane out of control and crashing into the Greek countryside below.

Though Mitralexis' aircraft is severely damaged, he manages to execute an emergency landing near the downed bomber. He promptly captures the surviving four Italian bomber crew using only his service pistol.

Inspector Bridges, via an internal memo, responded to a note sent from the governor of Brixton Prison asking, on behalf of Sjoerd Pons, for permission to receive money and also the property taken from the prisoner at Seabrook Police Station. Bridges replied that certain money and property that belonged to Pons was in the hands of the Metropolitan Police, and under no circumstances could it be returned. The actual location of the remaining property was unknown, but it was made clear that Pons could receive none of it until after his trial.

Tuesday, 5 November 1940:

Winston Churchill addresses Parliament: 'Herr Hitler declared war on 4th September that as we would not bend to his will, he would wipe out our cities. I have no doubt that when he gave the order he sincerely believed that it was in his power to carry out his will into effect. However, the cities of Britain are still standing. They are quite distinctive objects in the landscape, and our people are going about their tasks with the utmost activity. Fourteen thousand civilians have been killed and 20,000 seriously wounded, nearly four fifths of them in London. That has been the loss of life and limb. Against this, scarcely 300 soldiers have been killed and 500 wounded. So much for attack on military objectives. A great deal of house property has been destroyed or damaged, but nothing that cannot be covered by our insurance scheme. Very little damage has been done to our munitions and aircraft production, though a certain amount of time has been lost through frequent air-raid warnings.' (*Hansard*)

Franklin D. Roosevelt is re-elected to a third term as President of the United States.

Pons was informed by Brixton Prison's governor of Inspector Bridges' decision not to return his personal property.

Tuesday, 12 November 1940:

Hitler issues Directive No. 18 on the German seizure of Gibraltar. Codenamed *Felix*, the operation is subject to the co-operation of Franco.

Thursday, 14 November 1940:

The Luftwaffe targets Coventry in a massive raid; among the devastation is the destruction of the city's ancient cathedral.

The four accused men appeared at the Central Criminal Court to face the charges levied against them prior to the beginning of formal court proceedings.

Tuesday, 19 November 1940 (Day 1 of the trial):

At 9.30 pm, a meeting of the War Cabinet Defence Committee (Operations) convenes. The Air Ministry had received a telegram from the Air Officer Commanding-in-Chief (AOC in C), Middle East, requesting further aircraft to support British Army Forces in the Western Desert. The AOC is left in no doubt regarding the committee's decision:

I.   With the knowledge that 34 Hurricanes would be arriving in Egypt early in December, the Air Officer Commanding-in-Chief should be able to make full use in the front line of the 58 Hurricanes which he had available, and which were the equivalent of three squadrons.

II. Everything possible should be done to expedite the arrival of HMS *Furious* at Takoradi, and the onward passage of the 34 Hurricanes carried in her ... the AOC in C should also be pressed to make arrangements to bring them rapidly into action upon arrival.[5]

In the first major German air raid on Birmingham, approximately 440 bombers kill 450 people and badly injure 54 others.

Coventry is bombed to destruction. The Luftwaffe, in a massive raid which lasts more than ten hours, leaves much of the city devastated.

Leicester is also hit by the Blitz. Until now, Leicester has always been considered a relatively safe location, even suitable for the reception of evacuees. Now that it has been bombed, there seems to be no part of Britain that is safe from the danger of the Blitz.

The four spies appeared before Mr Justice Wrottesley at Court Number One of the Central Criminal Court, the Old Bailey.

Appearing for the prosecution was the Solicitor General, Sir William Jowitt, KC, MP, leading Counsel for the Crown, assisted by Mr Lawrence A. Byrne. Appearing for the defence was Mr Travers Christmas Humphreys for Kieboom and Pons, Mr Stephen Gerald Howard, KC, for Meier, and Mr R.H. Blundell for Waldberg. George Walpole & Co were appointed shorthand writers at the Central Criminal Court.

The men were charged under a brand-new law – the Treachery Act – which had just been introduced to fill a legal loophole, and only received the King's Assent on 23 May, just thirteen days after Winston Churchill entered Downing Street. Historically, this was the first case that there had ever been under the Act.

The Solicitor General, Sir William Jowitt, made an application under the Emergency Powers Act, Section 6, that the whole proceedings, to the very end, be in camera, and a request to the judge to make an order under that section with a prohibition against the disclosure of any information with regard to any part of the proceedings. The Solicitor General added that he thought there were obvious security reasons which would make this necessary. The judge made an exception which stated that information must be disclosed to higher authorities. Mr Humphreys, acting for Kieboom and Pons, requested that the judge's order cover the parts of the building below ground, not just the courtroom. This would have enabled the prisoners involved in the case not to be identified.

The judge agreed, and made an order directing that, 'all persons be excluded from the court other than the officers of the court, the police in attendance in the ordinary way in court, the jury sworn, all counsel engaged in the case and their clerks, the Director of Public Prosecutions and persons attending on his behalf or on his instructions including Colonel Hinchley Cooke, the witnesses, the shorthand writer, prison officers, sheriffs, aldermen on duty and Sheriff's chaplain.'[6] He forbade the publication of proceedings except under any authority granted by or on behalf of His Majesty.

The trial was thus held in secret, behind locked and guarded doors.

The interpreter for Waldberg was sworn in before the Clerk of the Court read the charges:

'Carl Heinrich Meier, Jose Waldberg, Charles Albert van den Kieboom and Sjoerd Pons: you are charged that you, between the 28th day of July 1940 and the 4th September 1940 with intent to help the enemy, conspired together and with other persons whose names are unknown, to transmit to the enemy information with regard to naval, military or air operations of His Majesty's forces. There is a second count which charges you all that you, on 3 September, 1940, with intent to help the enemy, did an act designed or likely to give assistance to the naval, military or air operations of the enemy, or to impede such operations of His Majesty's forces, that is to say, landed in the United Kingdom.'[7]

Individually, they were asked to plea; three pleaded not guilty, but Waldberg, through his interpreter, pleaded guilty.

The jury was duly sworn in with twelve citizens, all drawn out of the usual ballot. None were specially picked. All were sworn to secrecy.

The Clerk of the Court read the indictments to members of the jury. The judge informed them that disclosure of any information would result in punishment and imprisonment, while emphasizing that it was not the punishment that would interest the jury, but the fact that it was thought to be very much in the nation's interest and that 'you should let no word whatever escape you of the proceedings in which you are now to take part'.[8]

Sir William Jowitt added that the form of the order would be that the proceedings were not to be disclosed except by authority or permission granted by or on behalf of the King.

Sir William opened the case for the prosecution by trying to persuade the jury of the guilt of the three men who had pleaded not guilty. He started by reminding the jury that they were assembled in court to do their duty and to perform a task,

'which is perhaps as solemn and as grave as any citizens of this country or any other country can be called upon to perform. These men stand accused of crimes of such gravity as render them if they are guilty liable to the penalty of death. I need not say more as to how serious is the task you have to perform.'[9]

He mentioned facts that the jury should bear in mind, namely that the men were working for the German Secret Service and that they landed in small boats off the south coast of England early in September. It was a matter, the Solicitor General stated, that could not be disputed. The only possible defence, he added, was what he called the 'classic defence' under the circumstances, in which a man may say, 'Well, although I was under German instructions, really Germans are very hard taskmasters; they gave me a nasty task that I had to face, and consequently I came to this country really intending as soon as I got here to give myself up to the English authorities; I never intended to do anything against your country at all.'[10]

He told the jury they must ask themselves, after listening to the evidence, whether the 'classic defence', in any sense, squared with the facts?

Sir William then explained the charges in the indictment. In particular he said, 'Conspiracy is an act of the mind, but it is an act of the mind which is proved by what we call overt acts … You not infrequently get conspiracies, odd though that may seem, where the conspirators never know each other at all.' He continued,

'It matters not the least bit in the world, it is a mere coincidence that those people met together and had a farewell luncheon. The case would be exactly the same if these two parties, each of two, had been on completely separate expeditions, having never seen or heard of one another, and had set off from France to do acts in this country. Always provided that, if they are foreigners and not British subjects, I cannot try them for a conspiracy, which is a mental state unless I can show that that conspiracy is to be carried out in part of this country. If I find the overt act in this country then I can indict them all for this conspiracy.'[11]

During his explanation, Sir William quoted the case of Rex v Meyrick and Ribuffi.[12]

He said the men were charged under the Treachery Act 1940 – with various sections and sub-sections being utilized – and because the defendants were foreigners and held no allegiance to the King, Section 4 of the Act made it quite plain, 'to anything done by any person in the United Kingdom, no matter what nationality he may be – anything done in the United Kingdom'.[13] More specifically, Section 4(c) of the Act read, 'This Act shall apply to anything done by any person in the United Kingdom or in any British ship or aircraft not being a Dominion ship or aircraft.'[14]

Jowitt went on to say that Section 1 of the Act stated, 'If, with intent to help the enemy, any person does or attempts or conspires with any other person to do any act which is designed or likely to give assistance to the naval, military or air operations of the enemy, to impede such operations of His Majesty's forces or to endanger life, he shall be guilty of felony and shall on conviction suffer death.'[15]

He said that foreigners conspiring together in a foreign country did not render them to British Law, but directly that they arrived in Britain to carry out activities in 'furtherance of the conspiracy they had entered into then of course they are amenable to our laws in respect of the acts done in this country'.[16]

Evidence was given in turn by the deponents Private Tollervey, 2nd Lieutenant Batten, Private Chappell, Private McDonnell, Lance Corporal Goody, Lance Corporal North, Horace Mansfield, Police Sergeant Tye, Dennis Hayles, George Bunstone, Police Sergeant Robertson, PC Pearman, Leonard Humphreys and, for additional evidence, Seymour Bingham.

Before proceedings were adjourned for the day, Mr Justice Wrottesley turned to the jury and advised them:

'Members of the Jury remember what I said to you. Two things I want to say to you: Keep an open mind, of course, and do not discuss this case with anybody. Make up some story if you are asked what you have been trying, and do not make up your minds until you have heard both sides. Do not let there be any question of discussing it with anybody else.'[17]

Wednesday, 20 November 1940 (Day 2 of the trial):

At a meeting of the War Cabinet held in the Prime Minister's Room, House of Commons, at 11.30 am, the Chief of the Air Staff, Air Chief Marshal Sir Charles Portal, reports that on the previous day about 150 enemy aircraft had been over this country, but little damage had been done. During the night about 400 German aircraft had been over, of which some twenty or thirty had attacked London; sixty had attacked Birmingham, where considerable damage had been done; and the rest had attacked various areas in the Midlands and East Anglia. One interception had been made, a four-engine Condor having been hit but not brought down. The enemy lost five aircraft, with one by balloon barrage and four from causes unknown.

Sixty-three British bombers had been despatched to attack targets in Germany and the occupied countries, including Berlin, Lorient and the Skoda Works at Pilsen. Three of these aircraft were missing.

The Prime Minister stresses the importance of conserving bomber resources in the present circumstances. The right course is, he thinks, to combine heavy blows at particular objectives with attacks on a number of targets, thus interfering with production over widespread areas of Germany.

As the case resumed at 11 am, evidence was given, separately, by Lieutenant Colonel Hinchley Cooke, DS Buswell, DS Allchin and DI Bridges.

Meier, Kieboom and Pons now began to give evidence on their own behalf, with each man initially cross-examined by the Solicitor General.

Meier entered the witness box first. He admitted knowing that coming to England would involve either spying or sabotage and that he would be well paid. He went against his initial statement when he said that he had pressure put upon him to go to England. He said he omitted to tell Hinchley Cooke that he had taken money out of Germany to go to America, and now claimed that he had been afraid that the Germans would delve further into his past.

Meier admitted that he had felt that any invasion would be a success, and that the Germans would be in command of this country in a short period of time, before his rations were exhausted. So convinced was he that the Germans were to successfully invade, that the reason he gave for not going to the police and telling them his story was the threat of what the Germans would do to him after he was convinced that his companion, Waldberg, had reported that Meier had let him down.

Kieboom was then sworn in. He claimed not to believe the Germans would invade. He said that he and Pons had agreed that should they be caught, they would tell everything, the truth. In Pons' statement, however, he stated that it was his intention to go to the police directly and report himself. Kieboom agreed that this also applied to him, except that they would first try to find a boat to America. The port of Liverpool was chosen, despite the fact that they did not know where Liverpool was, even after consulting a map. They planned to get to Liverpool by walking along a railway track that was heading in a north-westerly direction. This was their plan despite the fact that they knew that due to being blockaded, there were pretty well no ships available, and should they have reached America, they would have needed a visa.

When asked if he had hidden a wireless set, Kieboom said that he hadn't, that he just laid it in grass and brushed the grass on top of it, thereby effectively admitting that he had indeed hidden it.

Before being challenged by the soldiers, Kieboom claimed that he threw himself to the ground to avoid being seen and shot. He admitted putting a code down the toilet, which was said to be inconsistent with his resolve to tell the truth, as was when he initially said that they came from Brest and not Boulogne, and not telling 2nd Lieutenant Batten that there was a companion with him. Furthermore, he admitted telling Hinchley Cooke only the bare facts, despite the fact that he recognized him as a senior officer. He only mentioned Pons once he knew that Pons had been arrested. Kieboom never once mentioned him in his statement to Hinchley Cooke.

Kieboom's questioning was interrupted. when the Solicitor General informed the Judge that he had a Mr Robert Churchill from E.J. Churchill, gun makers, at the court and made a request, 'Would it be convenient to interpose him?'

'Yes. You can cross-examine this man tomorrow,' ordered the Judge.

Kieboom left the stand to be replaced by Mr Churchill, who gave evidence that a firearm found in the possession of Kieboom was not in working order. Churchill had made an attempt to fire it, but found that the point of the striker was broken through ordinary wear and tear, and therefore it was impossible to fire it in its present condition.

Following Churchill's evidence, proceedings were adjourned for the day.

Thursday, 21 November 1940 (Day 3 of the trial):

A meeting of the War Cabinet is held in the House of Commons (Annexe) at 3 pm. The Chief of the Air Staff, Sir Charles Portal, reports that sixty enemy aircraft had been over the country on the previous day. The RAF had destroyed one and damaged another without loss. On the previous night, 230 enemy bombers had been over, with 180 dropping bombs over a widespread area in the Midlands, including Birmingham and Coventry. One interception had been made, without any decisive result. On the previous night, sixty-four RAF bombers had been despatched and one had failed to return. Duisburg had been the main target.

In security patrols, one enemy twin-engine fighter was shot down, and one British aircraft was lost.

The Secretary of State for the Home Department and Minister of Home Security, The Right Hon Herbert Morrison, MP, reports that little damage had been done the previous day. The casualties had been as follows: London: no casualties. Elsewhere: none killed, two injured.

On the previous night, the Midlands had been attacked, Birmingham being the principal objective. The casualties had been: London: eleven killed, forty-five injured. Elsewhere: twenty-five killed, 220 injured.

The figures for the casualties in the Birmingham area for the raid on the night of the 19th/20th had been: 211 killed, 596 seriously injured.

Back in court at 11 am, Kieboom was immediately recalled to the stand and was cross-examined further.

Pons was then the third of the accused to enter the witness box. He adhered to what he had said in his statement to Lieutenant Colonel Hinchley Cooke, and Mr Christmas Humphreys, on his behalf, said that his whole conduct was consistent with a man acting under duress. Pons' counsel said that his client, under pressure from the Nazis, landed at the Dymchurch Redoubt, a place which he must have expected to find bristling with soldiers. The whole area was a prohibited one, Mr Humphreys said, and Pons could not have expected to get far without being challenged. His first act upon reaching shore, the counsel continued, was to immerse the radio set in water, and then he approached one of the witnesses, Lance Corporal North. This, he claimed, was in accordance with his client's original intention.

However, evidence had been given that the ditch in which Pons placed his radio set was dry; that neither the case nor the radio set (which was in working order) showed any sign of having been immersed in water; and that Lance Corporal North had walked towards Pons and challenged him – the soldier himself denied, under cross examination, that he was approached by Pons. The judge reminded the jury of all these points and asked them whether it was likely, as Pons had said in the witness box, that he did not know that his companion, Kieboom, had a code in his possession.

Leonard Humphreys, an inspector in the radio branch of the Post Office's Engineering Department, had already written a report which stated that he had examined both wireless sets and found them to be in perfect working order, and capable of being used for transmitting Morse signals from England to the Continent. Neither set showed any traces of having been submerged in water

Sir William Jowitt, in his cross-examination, threw some doubt on Pons' evidence that the Gestapo had a hold over him because he had been engaged in smuggling jewellery from Germany to Holland. The Solicitor General also asked why, if it had been his intention to give himself up on arrival in England, had he not rowed his boat more slowly so as to arrive in daylight, and why didn't he strike a match to announce his arrival after stepping ashore?

Mr Howard started a lengthy address to the jury on behalf of Meier:

'There is no dispute here that he landed in this country; there is no dispute here that he came over with Waldberg and agreed to come with Waldberg and land in this country. The question is with what intention did he do that thing and agree to come. You might think that this trial taking place here is a great tribute to the stability and balance of this country, a trial in its whole form and proceedings just as fair as the trial of any Englishman standing charged with any offence, and I know that this is the spirit in which each one of you will come to consider this matter – a matter … as solemn and grave as any you are ever likely to be called upon to consider. I know the spirit in which you approach that task will be just as fair as the form and the letter of the proceedings. Gentlemen of the jury, it is not an easy task as you well know in the middle of a war this country is fighting for its life against a formidable and ferocious enemy, at a time, as the sirens have twice reminded you this morning, when you and indeed all of us are in daily danger at the hands of that enemy, when you are asked to pass judgment upon a man who, upon the evidence, has worked for that enemy, and upon the evidence came to this country in the company of a self confessed agent of that enemy it is not an easy task to judge of that man in these times coolly and calmly, but gentlemen, because you are Englishmen, because you have been born and brought up in a tradition of fair play, I know when the time comes that you will accord to the Dutchman in that dock just the same scrupulous fairness that you would give one of your own countrymen who was standing in the same place.'[18]

Howard made the plea that the prosecution had not proved, beyond reasonable doubt, that Meier arrived in England with the intention of serving Germany or indeed to harm England.

Mr Christmas Humphreys then spoke for Pons and Kieboom. In their defence, he said to the jury:

'You are not trying a man for acts, you are trying these two men for the state of their minds in the dark in the early hours of the 3 September as they approached the English shore and when they landed. What was in a man's mind can only be known by what he does or says, and there again when you are considering what they say remember that they are both foreigners, speaking a foreign language, and although they speak it well I know you will not try to trip them up upon the exact phraseology or the words they have used, or the under-tones or over-tones of any particular phrase which they used. You have to decide what was in their minds, the intent, to the extent that any was formed, with which they came to this country or conspired in the way alleged in the Indictment.'

For the prosecution, before trying to convince the jury of the men's guilt based on the evidence, Sir William, in his opening speech, addressed the jury's sense of fair play and patriotism, while at the same time reminding them of their collective responsibility before arriving at a decision:

'Although the Germans may bomb this building brick by brick they will never succeed in destroying the heritage we have handed down to us and will hand on of British justice and British fairness. I entirely agree that you will not let your prejudice against these men sway you. I entirely agree that if there is any reasonable doubt that you will give them the benefit of that doubt. My plain task is this. War is a grim business, it is a stern business; my business is a stern business today.

'All I ask you to do is what I know you will do, to carry out your duty without fear or favour, without prejudice, but do not shrink from your duty because it is an unpleasant duty. Many of us today and many of our young men today have to do duties, from which they might shrink, but thank God they do not shrink, and you will not shrink to do your duty as you see it.'[19]

The men's respective counsel pleaded that there was no dispute as to fact, but held that the prosecution had not proved, beyond reasonable doubt, that the 'intention' of their clients was to assist the enemy. Proceedings were then adjourned for the day.

Friday, 22 November 1940 (Day 4 of the trial: summing up):
At a meeting of the War Cabinet held in the Cabinet War Rooms at 12 noon, the Chief of the Air Staff makes the following report:-

Day, 21 November – Activity had been on a very small scale, consisting almost entirely of reconnaissance flights and visits to convoys. About eighty enemy aircraft had been over the country.

Weather conditions had been cloudy, with bad visibility.

Night, 21–22 November – There had been no change in weather conditions. In all, 120 German aircraft had been over the country. RAF fighters had been unable to make any interceptions. Attacks had been on a small scale after the first hour of darkness. Raids had been plotted chiefly to the Midlands and East Anglia, with no particular town as a target.

The air casualties for the previous twenty-four hours had been:British, one aircraft lost (one pilot killed). Enemy: one aircraft destroyed, one aircraft damaged.

RAF bombing operations over Germany had been cancelled. Hudson aircraft had, however, carried out a successful attack on an aerodrome near Stavanger in Norway.

Back in Court Number One, at 11 am, Mr Justice Wrottesley addressed the jury:

'Members of the jury, the case is now going to pass into your hands for a decision. As to whether any one of these men is guilty is for you; all I am proposing to do is try to give you a little assistance … I do not think it necessary for an English Judge to say to an English Jury that you must keep anything like prejudice out of this trial; of course you will, and of course you will demand exactly the same standard of proof before you find a man guilty as you would in any other case. I shall not insult you by lecturing you on that point … If you have any doubt in the case of any of these three men your duty is quite clear. You must say not guilty. Of course if you have no doubt and are satisfied of their guilt your duty is not less plain and you will do it in the same way as you would do your duty in any other case.'

'Would you like to retire, members of the jury?' asked the Clerk of the Court. 'Yes,' replied the foreman.[20] Thus, at 11.57 am, the jury retired to consider their verdict.

While deciding the fate of the accused, the jurors had other matters that weighed heavily on their minds. The judge had told them to keep 'an open mind', but this was a period when spies were feared and hated, when an invasion was an ever-constant threat, when the Blitz was raging, when Britain and its dominions were fighting without help from Russia or America, and when enemy agents and fifth columnists, people believed, were everywhere and anyone could fall under suspicion. Recent instances of suspicious behaviour had included the following:

- A woman who made notes on the Woolwich ferry was accused of spying.
- A man who smoked a cigar in Kensington was accused of making signals to enemy bombers. He had puffed 'particularly hard' to ensure a good light, and then had seemed to point the cigar skywards. He was arrested and formally charged.
- A woman who failed to draw her blackout curtains was also charged. She had allowed a beacon of light to spill out across Hampstead Heath and was accused of being an enemy agent. She was fined £2 at the local magistrates' court for the blackout offence, and was subsequently shunned by her neighbours. Wherever she went, she was followed by whispers of 'Fifth Columnist'.

Hundreds of reports on suspected Fifth Columnists came pouring into the office of the Director General of MI5: accounts of strange marks daubed on telegraph poles, of nuns with hairy arms and Hitler tattoos, of municipal flower beds planted with white flowers in order to direct planes towards munitions factories.[21] It might sound hysterical, but the fear was palpable and very real.

At 1.20 pm, the jury returned to the court. The clerk addressed the foreman and said, 'Members of the jury, I understand there is some suggestion you want to put to the judge; would you mind mentioning it now, Mr Foreman?' The foreman did not ask a question as such, but instead said, 'My Lord, we are not quite clear as to one of the prisoners, that on arrival in England he intended to carry out his contract with the enemy; we rather felt by our deliberations together that he intended only to save himself and not to help the enemy.'[22]

'You mean he decided not to help the enemy?' enquired the Judge. 'Yes,' replied the foreman.

Mr Justice Wrottesley: 'If that is your view then you must give a verdict of not guilty.'

The foreman: 'Thank you, my Lord. May I ask whether we can, in that case, find the man guilty on the first but not the second indictment?'

Mr Justice Wrottesley: 'You mean can you say you think he was guilty of conspiracy in the case you are thinking of?'

The foreman: 'Yes.'

Mr Justice Wrottesley: 'That he conspired?'

The foreman: 'Yes, but when he arrived in England he decided that he would not do anything to help the enemy but he would make a clean breast of it here.'

Mr Justice Wrottesley: 'You mean at no time while he was in the United Kingdom did he intend to spy?'

The foreman: 'That is right.'[23]

Turning to Sir William Jowitt, the judge said interrogatively, 'That means a verdict of not guilty.'[24]

Sir William concurred, 'I think that would be a verdict of not guilty.'[25]

The judge then so directed the jury.

The Clerk of the Court then asked the jury whether they were agreed on a verdict. They were, and subsequently returned a verdict of 'not guilty' against Pons and 'guilty' against Meier and Kieboom. Pons was asked to stand back.

Mr Humphreys requested that his client, Pons, be discharged, subject to other powers.

Waldberg was instructed to return to the dock to join Meier and Kieboom. The clerk asked the prisoners whether they had anything to say why the court should not give them judgment of death according to the law; this was interpreted for Waldberg. Waldberg's interpreter handed a translated statement made by Waldberg, and it was read to the court by Mr Blundell.

Sentence of death was subsequently passed upon Meier, Waldberg and Kieboom. None of the prisoners made any reply as the death sentence was passed.

The counsel's plea for Pons must have carried some weight with the jury, who, although they could safely have found a verdict of 'guilty' following Mr Justice Wrottesley's summing up, no doubt were impressed by his reminding them that Pons was the only one of the four who, when arrested, had volunteered the fact that he had a companion.

In the eyes of many, Pons was as guilty as his three comrades. The jury, however, believed his evidence, given on oath, that he had been blackmailed by the Gestapo, that he feigned agreement to act as an espionage agent and that he had come to England with the intention of giving himself up immediately on landing.

After consultation with the Solicitor General, the judge discharged Pons. It had been arranged that Pons should immediately be rearrested, pending the issue of a Home Office Detention Order under Article 12(5)A of the Aliens Order, 1920. Pons was rearrested at the Old Bailey and detained initially at Canon Row Police Station.

Detective Inspector Bridges was in no doubt that Pons was guilty. He stated after the verdict, 'From my enquiries and from the evidence I am satisfied that Pons was as culpable as his three confederates but that he owes his life to the scrupulous fairness of an English jury.' He considered Pons to be a dangerous man who 'obviously should be kept in custody until the cessation of hostilities'.[26]

It was indeed intended that Pons would remain in detention for the duration of the war.

There was considerable concern regarding leakage of information during court proceedings. It transpired that, because of instructions which emanated from the Cabinet, extraordinary precautions had been taken as soon as the proceedings had commenced to prevent any details becoming known to the press or elsewhere. Furthermore, at the beginning of the trial, Mr Justice Wrottesley had made the order forbidding the publication of any of the proceedings. It was recommended by DI Bridges that the court 'papers should be taken under cover by hand to the Home Office and handed to some responsible official of the Aliens Department'.[27]

What would certainly not have helped Meier, nor Kieboom for that matter, escape the scaffold was that when he was asked why he did not go straight to the police upon landing and make a clean breast of it all, he replied that, having seen the downfall of Holland, Belgium and France, he was convinced that Germany would successfully invade Britain and overrun it just as she had conquered other European countries. If he 'ratted' on the Germans and fell into their hands when they arrived in England, he believed his fate would have been sealed. He was certain that at the end of the ten days' rations, he and his companions would be out in the open and attached to a victorious German army.

Saturday, 23 November 1940:

Prime Minister Winston Churchill informs the First Lord of the Admiralty and the First Sea Lord that British policy in the Far East will be strictly defensive, accepting the consequences.[28]

Special Branch, and in particular DI Bridges, wasted little time in making Pons the subject of a Detention Order, applying to the Home Office for one. Home Secretary Herbert Morrison duly issued the Detention Order. He felt that the deportation of Pons would be 'Prejudicial to the efficient prosecution of the war ... I am of the opinion that the detention of the said alien is necessary or expedient for securing the defence of the realm.'[29]

Inspector Bridges called to say that Pons was due to arrive at Pentonville Prison. Hinchley Cooke was informed of this by Major Langdon (B1b, Espionage, Special Sources) in a handwritten note. He added that long-term internees were normally sent to Walton Gaol in Liverpool. Should Hinchley

Cooke desire that Pons be kept at Pentonville, then he was advised to write to the Prison Commissioners to that effect. Bridges said he had to leave his copy of Hinchley Cooke's interrogation of the prisoners with the jury, and if possible would like another copy for his Special Branch file.

Pons was duly detained at Pentonville Prison.

L.C. Ball, the governor of Pentonville Prison, contacted the Prison Commission to inform them that he had received Meier and Waldberg into his prison under sentence of death. There was no recommendation for mercy by the jury. Newspaper reports of the trial were not yet available, and it was not known at present whether Meier or Waldberg had any previous convictions.

Ball requested from the Prison Commissioners, in the cases of Waldberg and Meier, to be furnished with a list of candidates reported to be competent for the office of executioner, together with copies of records as to the conduct and efficiency of each of them. He concluded, 'I beg also to apply for a copy of the memorandum of instructions for carrying out the details of an execution.'[30] Also, and somewhat morbidly but entirely necessarily, a copy of the table of drops (a manual issued by the Home Office which was used to calculate the appropriate length of rope for long-drop hangings) was requested.

Tuesday, 26 November 1940:

Swordfish aircraft from 815 and 819 Squadrons leave HMS *Illustrious* and raid the Italian seaplane base in Port Laki, Leros, Dodecanese Islands, to distract Italian forces while Allied convoys of Operation *Collar* traverse the Mediterranean.[31]

The Prison Commissioners contacted Pentonville's governor, Mr Ball, to remind him that the Medical Officer should report on the mental and physical condition of the prisoners while under his observation, 'calling attention to anything which may have been brought forward at the trial bearing on the prisoners' condition'.[32]

The services of Albert Pierrepoint were recommended for employment as Assistant Executioner for Meier, and Mr Henry Critchell as Assistant Executioner for Waldberg. As the execution was a double one, Grimsby-born Harry Kirk was recommended as the third assistant.

When engaging the Assistant Executioners, Ball was requested to forward each one a railway warrant for a return third-class ticket at the cheapest possible rate. Care should also be taken to see that the Assistant Executioners returned the warrants, should their services not be required.

As alluded to previously, there was some regard by the authorities as to the prisoners' mental well-being in what would be the final moments of their lives. The Prison Commission issued a minute which stated that in the case of Meier and Waldberg, in the event of a double execution taking place, various instructions would be observed. First of all, three assistant executioners should be employed. The executioner should put the cap on and arrange the noose of one man, and an assistant should carry this out simultaneously with the other man. The other assistants should carry out the strapping of the legs simultaneously. This would mean that one culprit did not stand by while the other was attended to.

Herbert Hooper of Section B24, in an internal MI5 enquiry to Major Langdon, noted that Pons, having been acquitted, was 'lodging' at Pentonville Prison. He added that there was a great number of politically undesirable aliens who passed through the prison. Hooper continued that the evidence against those individuals was not always strong enough to warrant continued detention, and that there was a chance that some of them would be released after some time.

He added that the detainees had every opportunity of associating with one other, and it had been found that messages were being passed out of the prison. Hooper was adamant, however, that this practice had now stopped.

It was recommended to Major Langdon that, in view of this, it would be rather dangerous to keep Pons in Pentonville in case he should start talking to his fellow prisoners. Hooper stated that there was a man in the prison who may have belonged to the same organization as Pons, but against whom apparently no definite evidence had been obtained. For this reason, Hooper recommended that Pons be removed from Pentonville to a prison where 'discipline is more severe'.

He concluded by saying that, despite there being a 'stoolpigeon'[33] in Pentonville who would be able to report on Pons' conversations, it did not appear to weigh up against the dangers mentioned previously, i.e., messages being passed out of prison.

The Chief Constable of Kent, Jock Davison, wrote a 'Secret' and personal letter, titled 'Four Men in a Boat', to Brigadier Oswald Allen 'Jasper' Harker, Acting Director General of MI5, expressing concern about Scotland Yard's involvement. Davison said that Captain Grassby had told him that Lieutenant Colonel Hinchley Cooke and a 'representative of the Department of the Director of Public Prosecutions' were coming round to check up on the statements of witnesses. Davison said that he was 'astonished' to find that Hinchley Cooke was accompanied by Inspector Bridges of the Metropolitan Police.

Davison continued that Hinchley Cooke professed no knowledge of the position beyond an assurance that Inspector Bridges was not seconded to MI5 to deal with such cases. Davison also said that had this been the case, he would have gladly accepted the situation. Davison spoke to Sir Norman Kendal of Special Branch, who knew nothing of the arrangement, and neither did Sefton Cohen of the Director of Public Prosecutions Department. Davison asked Brigadier

Harker what the position was: had Scotland Yard been ordered to take over the inquiries without the Chief Constable's knowledge and consent? Davison thought that the brigadier would agree that the ancient traditions should not be overridden without consultation. He also said that the whole Police Service should pull together, and he would be only too delighted for Scotland Yard, if necessary, to work in his area. He added that in his first murder case in Kent, he called in the Yard within a quarter of an hour of being informed of the facts. However, he had his own team of police officers to consider, and in this case, Davison was concerned for the feelings of his superintendent at Ashford, who was not told of the arrival of the Metropolitan Police officer. Whereas Davison found that Hinchley Cooke was getting all the attention and assistance that he wanted, he was not able to tell his own officers what the position was.

Davison said that when he raised the point at a Chief Constables' Conference, certain older and more distinguished officers than him were 'strangely surprised' to hear of this case.

Finally, Davison apologized for bothering Harker personally on this matter, but said that having spent eleven-and-a-half 'very happy' years in close co-operation with Harker's department, he was 'very anxious' that the co-operation 'shall be whole-hearted and happy as in the past'.

Wednesday, 27 November 1940:
The Royal Navy and the Italian Navy clash off Sardinia in the Battle of Cape Spartivento, an inconclusive battle.

Governor Ball sent two memos to the Prison Commission reporting that he had received a letter from the Under Sherriff of London which informed him, subject to appeal, that the High Sherriff for the County of London had fixed Tuesday, 10 December at 9 am as the day and hour for the executions of Meier and Waldberg. Ball was also informed that the High Sherriff proposed to employ London-born Stanley Cross as executioner. The governor concluded by saying that he had acknowledged the Under Sherriff's letter and that the usual accommodation for the executioner would be provided.

G.F. Clayton, the governor of Brixton Prison, sent a memo to Hinchley Cooke, stating that he was confident that Pons had not had a conversation with anyone concerning his case, 'and through methods I had better not disclose, I feel certain he will not do so in the future'. Annotated in pen, Clayton added, 'I succeeded in putting the wind up him and am quite satisfied and am pretty certain he was telling the truth. I thought this might relieve you of anxiety.'[34]

Sir Norman Kendal, of Special Branch, wrote to Sir Alexander Maxwell at the Home Office, bemoaning the fact that he regarded the case as a 'hopeless mess when we were dragged into it at the last moment to retake most of the statements, find out who got hold of the various things which had been taken by these men from their various interrogators and generally try to put the case in apple-pie order for the Director and Counsel for the Prosecution'.[35]

He added that as Pons was acquitted, the only option was to keep him in Pentonville, where he now resided. He thought that Pons was very fortunate to be acquitted, and that it would be ridiculous to allow him to remain in England as a free man.

A representative of the Defence Security Service (DSS) contacted B Branch (Espionage) at MI5 regarding Pons. The DSS representative had been in contact with Lord Swinton of the Security Executive, who told them that he thought that Pons was acquitted because the jury did not feel keen on his execution. Had there been the possibility of a lesser penalty, the Solicitor General thought he would have been convicted.

As a result of this case, the DSS spokesman thought that it would probably have been better if these cases had been tried by a tribunal of three judges, without a jury. He thought that the Director of Public Prosecutions was of the same view. This arrangement would have suited a number of the Secret Service sections and, should the technical difficulties be overcome, then the political ones would need to be addressed. Howsever, the question arose whether it would have been a dangerous precedent to establish?

In the meantime, another question was being asked: what was to be done about Pons' permanent home? He was still in separate confinement at Pentonville Prison

Thursday, 28 November 1940:
After surviving a sea battle, Malta's latest supply convoy is attacked by enemy aircraft as it nears its final destination, the Grand Harbour, at about 2 pm. Ten bombers, escorted by ten fighters, approach the convoy and unleash two payloads of twelve high explosive bombs over the ships. No damage is caused.[36]

Kieboom was now in a condemned cell at Wandsworth, Meier and Waldberg were in condemned cells at Pentonville and Pons was now in (temporary) isolation at Brixton Prison. The executions had been fixed provisionally for 10 and 11 December. Vincent Evans of the Department of the Director of Public Prosecutions stated that the three condemned men did not intend to appeal, but petitions for clemency would be submitted to the Home Secretary, Herbert Morrison, by counsel on behalf of their clients.

There was a question of publicity regarding the executions. Under the Criminal Punishment Act, 1868, there was an obligation to affix a notice to the prison doors of an intended execution. Under this Act, the Home Secretary was empowered to make amendments (as was done so in 1902), to the effect that 'a notice must be affixed to the doors of the prison not less than twelve hours before any execution takes place, and that such notice must remain in such position until the inquest on the executed person has been completed.' It was considered that although the Home Secretary could pass another rule with regard to the Act, it would be thought to be 'extremely doubtful whether he would do so unless the matter was of vital importance'.[37]

Section B13 decided that there would appear to be no further need for secrecy from an Intelligence point of view, and suggested that the execution notices be displayed in the normal way, but that the press be warned not to publish the names of the executed persons and that a carefully worded press notice be issued for publication on both days.

Brixton Prison's prisoner 3334 Pons S had written a letter, in English, to his wife, who in fact did not read a word of the language! Notwithstanding, he told her that it was possible that she would not receive many letters from him, and not to worry about it, that he was in good health and was being kept momentarily in prison as an internee. Seeking to reassure her, he explained that he had been in other prisons but that Brixton was 'the best of all'. He said that the food was good, the prison was clean, he had access to books and was able to study, and had two hours' association as well as two hours' exercise. He said that he could work and earn money, and as an internee he was allowed to buy cigarettes and tobacco. Pons went on to say, 'I understand that you can't read a word English [*sic*]. But father will translate this letter for you.'

Pons was being optimistic; trying to be confident and set his wife's mind at rest the best he could. He told her that he was still alive, in good health, and not to worry if she did not hear from him in the future because, as an internee, he thought that by being in prison he was in the safest place. He continued, 'I can assure you that my thoughtlessness [*sic*] will be many times with you in the future.' He ended by saying, 'And now I can feel me already happy thinking on the moment that we will meet us again [*sic*] after the war is over. So dear again I say don't trouble about me. I will finish now and don't forget keep your sunny side up.'[38]

The governor of Pentonville Prison, L.C. Ball, had written to Brigadier Harker at MI5 on behalf of Meier. Ball requested the return of the prisoner's wallet and photos of his mother and fiancée, which Meier claimed were taken from him by the police at Lydd in Kent. Ball asked whether Harker had any objections to this request, and enquired as to their whereabouts.

Ball issued minutes to the Prison Commission in which he stated that Meier had been visited by Hinchley Cooke, who was in charge of Meier's case and told Ball that it was 'very necessary' to keep Meier's conviction as secret as possible. Ball noted that steps had been taken to warn all members of staff of the necessity for secrecy. Furthermore, Ball wanted to know whether the posting on the gate of the usual notices could be dispensed with.

Similar minutes had been forwarded to the Prison Commission in respect of Waldberg.

Meanwhile, Major Benjamin Dixon Grew, governor of HMP Wandsworth, informed the Secretary of State that condemned prisoner 7969 Kieboom had his execution provisionally fixed for Wednesday, 11 December at 9 am, as directed by the High Sheriff, County of London.

Friday, 29 November 1940:

Liverpool endured nearly eight hours of bombing which killed 165 people and left 2,000 people homeless.

An estimated 300 people were sheltering in the basement of the three-storey Ernest Brown Junior Instructional College when it was struck in the early hours. Among those sheltering were workers from nearby factories and passengers who had left trams during the air-raid, in addition to local residents. It was described by Prime Minister Winston Churchill as, 'the single worst civilian incident of the war.'[39]

The Aliens Department at the Home Office issued a memo to the Commissioner of Police of the Metropolis, for the attention of Inspector Bridges, which stated that they were directed by the Secretary of State to 'transmit' a Detention Order (along with two copies), which was made under Article 12 (5A) of the Aliens Order, 1920, directing the detention of Sjoerd Pons. Bridges was requested to enforce the Order by serving it on the alien in Brixton Prison.

One copy of the Detention Order, the memo added, should be handed over to the alien and the other to the Prison governor. The original Order should be returned, in due course, to the Home Office, endorsed as to the date and fact of service.

A day after being given a date for Kieboom's execution, the governor of Wandsworth Prison formally issued a notice stating that Kieboom had officially lodged an application for leave of appeal against his conviction and the sentence of death. Kieboom also wanted legal aid and permission to be present during the proceedings of the appeal.

Saturday, 30 November 1940:

The German cruiser, Admiral *Hipper*, sails from Germany.

Pons was still around and still posing the problem of what to do with him. In an exchange of correspondence between MI5 and Sir Alexander Maxwell *et. al.*, it became clear that they were searching for answers as to what to do with spies held in internment. An extract from a letter to Sir Alexander revealed one possible solution:

'It is suggested that a *Home for Incurables* be opened for those agents who for some reason or other show signs of divulging the confidential information with which they have become acquainted in the course of their work or training …

'We have yet another case of a somewhat similar kind, namely, that of Pons, one of the four boatmen who have been on trial at the Old Bailey. Pons was acquitted on the grounds that he had been coerced into acting as a spy, had intended to give himself up on arrival but not had either the time or the opportunity to do so … Arrangements have been made to keep him apart from other prisoners, but such arrangements are difficult since they very much interfere with the routine of prison life. Pons might possibly be a suitable candidate for the *Home for Incurables.* On the other hand it might be felt that he was rather in a category by himself.'[40]

Chapter Nine

My Name is Henri Lassudry

Monday, 2 December 1940:

At a meeting of the War Cabinet held in the Cabinet War Rooms at 5 pm, the Chief of the Air Staff, Air Chief Marshal Sir Charles Portal, reports on the air operations from Thursday, 28 November, to Sunday, 1 December.

The enemy had carried out fighter sweeps and reconnaissances over the country, sending over an average of 280 aircraft a day. To counter these operations, the RAF had sent up an average of 500 fighters a day. The casualties for the four days had been: Enemy: twenty-three aircraft destroyed, six probable and seven damaged. RAF: seventeen destroyed (eight pilots lost).

On the nights of 28/29 and 29/30 November, the enemy had sent some 250 bombers and fifteen to twenty minelayers over the country. On the two following nights, they had sent over 120 and eighty aircraft respectively, the reduction being on account of fog.

RAF night-bombing attacks on Germany and German-occupied countries had been as follows:

	Number of British bombers sent out	Number of British Bombers missing
28 November	77	2
29 November	45	1
30 November (no attacks made)		
1 December	10	0

On 29 November, a Coastal Command aircraft had sighted a convoy off Terschelling, and had successfully attacked an 8,000-ton merchant vessel.

On the Greek Front, RAF Gladiators had brought down eight Italian aircraft on 28 November for the loss of just one Gladiator.

The Under Sheriff for the County of London, P. Kynaston Metcalfe, wrote to the Under Secretary of State to inform him that he had received notification from the governor of Wandsworth Prison that Kieboom had lodged notice of application for leave against his conviction and sentence. The Under Secretary of State noted that, in the event of the appeal being dismissed, the High Sheriff should appoint a further date for carrying out the sentence, and confirmed that he would give due notice.

Tuesday, 3 December 1940:
The Greeks capture Sarandë in Albania from the Italians.

The Home Office replied to the letter from the Under Sheriff. The latter was informed that the Home Office acknowledged that the provisional date for the execution of Kieboom, now lying under sentence of death in Wandsworth Prison, had been cancelled in view of the prisoner's application to the Court of Criminal Appeal.

Under a blanket of security, there was excessive secrecy fuelled by a concerted effort by the Security Services to keep the public unaware that a trial had even taken place, but there was some soul-searching. Sir Alexander Maxwell from the Home Office had written a 'Most Secret' letter[1] to Viscount Swinton, GBE, MC:

'I wonder if you could assist the Home Secretary by letting him have a letter giving a reasoned statement of the purposes for which, in the view of the Security Services, it is necessary to keep the public and the Press entirely unaware of the trial of the German spies who were recently caught on the coast of Kent. As a result of a verbal request from Brigadier Harker and of the reasons which he gave me for that request, I arranged with the Clerk of the Central Criminal Court that the most unusual steps should be taken with regard to this trial. One of the prisoners has now appealed and I have written to the Registrar of the Court of Criminal Appeal asking that similar exceptional measures shall be taken to prevent any knowledge reaching the Press or the public that such a case is before the Court of Criminal Appeal.

'The Home Secretary, however, may at any time be asked by his colleagues or perhaps by the Lord Chief Justice whether he is satisfied that these unusual steps are really necessary in the interests of the defence of the realm, and I think he ought to have on the Home Office records a letter from you on the subject.

'From the judge's notes and from the transcript of the interrogation by Colonel Hinchley Cooke it appears that before Waldberg was arrested he had sent out a message stating that Meier was a prisoner and that the English police were searching for him, Waldberg. It is therefore arguable that the enemy must know that some at any rate of this party were captured.

'In addition, numerous members of the public know, including many people in the Kent area. We may, therefore, have to answer the argument that we are taking great pains to conceal something which the enemy must be presumed to know.

'In addition there are important considerations in favour of publicity: (1) it would be advantageous to the morale of the people of this country to know that some spies have been caught and brought to justice; (2) the deterrent effect of the sentences will be lost if the trial and the sentences are kept secret – it will be said that publicity ought to be given to these sentences as a warning to any other persons who may be induced by enemy threats or promises to follow the example of the men who have been caught; (3) it is of course as a general proposition wrong that a sentence of death should be passed and executed without the public knowing anything about it. Such sentences, it will be said, are of great importance, and the Government and the Courts ought to know what the public opinion thereon is. Public opinion and public criticism is the most important safeguard for the proper administration of justice, and to carry out sentences of this kind in secrecy is contrary to all our traditions.

'I do not of course for a moment suggest that there may not be very good reasons for departing from these general principles in an exceptional case, but I feel that the Home Secretary should be safeguarded by a full statement from the Security Service of these reasons.'

There was almost a palpable sense of fear for security regarding the arrest, conviction and sentence of death on three of the spies. An official from the Home Office, who simply went by the initials 'M.D.P.', issued a handwritten notice on the matter:

'It is necessary for military reasons to keep secret the fact that three German spies have been arrested, convicted and sentenced to death.

'It is unavoidable that a large number of officials at the Old Bailey, Home Office, and the Prison Service should be in possession of the facts of the case but we may hope that none of these will be guilty of divulging what they have learnt. There remains however a very serious possibility of leakage by means of the Coroner's Jury.

'Had the Germans been members of the Armed Forces of the enemy they could have been dealt with under the Army Act ... and all questions of an inquisition, etc would not have arisen, but I understand that at any rate two of them were civilians. The best method of keeping the execution secret would be, of course, that it should not be carried out.

'As the purpose of the death penalty is that it shall act as a deterrent, there seems much to be said for not carrying it out; if it is carried out in secret it cannot act as a deterrent to other spies or potential spies. All but a few persons of those who are aware of the conviction and sentence will assume that it has been carried out and the men will still be available to Military Intelligence should occasion arise.

'If the executions are to be carried out it seems impossible to dispense with a Coroner's inquisition. The inquisition can, however, and should be held in camera … and special care should be taken in the selection of the jury who should be informed by the Coroner of the importance of secrecy.'[2]

The thinking of the time was that this was the way forward, and special care was to be taken in the selection of the Coroner's jury, 'socially responsible individuals', who would be informed by the Coroner of the paramount need, in the national interest, for secrecy. Hinchley Cooke said that he would have been glad to interview the Coroner and/or the jury if it would help.

Referencing minutes to the Prison Commission by L.C. Ball, governor of Pentonville Prison, on 28 November, M.D.P. suggested that normal protocol be dispensed with in the name of National Security. In a handwritten annotation of minutes sent from Pentonville on 28 November, and seen by M.H. Whitelegge, he was pessimistic, when he wrote:

'I am afraid that the secret of these men's convictions and sentence will be in a great many hands …

'Printed copies of the surgeon's certificate of death, the declaration of execution and of the Coroner's inquisition are required by Section 10 of the Capital Punishment Amendment Act, 1868, to be exhibited as soon as possible after the execution on the principal entrance of the prison and to remain so exhibited for at least 24 hours.

'The legal obligation is quite clear but the safety of the State in this instance requires that it should be ignored.'

With a degree of uncertainty, he concluded:

'The Prison Commissioners to instruct the Governors of Pentonville and Wandsworth [to] not display the certificates, etc on the prison gate, to impress on all concerned, eg Under Sheriff, etc, the importance of secrecy and to endeavour to obtain the Coroner's concurrence to the inquest being held in camera and to his selecting beforehand a jury of specially responsible individuals.'[3]

Wednesday, 4 December 1940:

The War Cabinet Defence Committee (Operations) meets in the Cabinet War Rooms at 9.30 pm, with discussions dominated by a debate of the strength and efficiency of Coastal Command.

Lord Beaverbrook (Minister of Aircraft Production) suggests that Coastal Command should be taken over by the Admiralty, including the training of all pilots from the beginning. He says that the condition of Coastal Command is a grave reflection on the Air Ministry, which has starved it of equipment and not given it the right type of aircraft. Although the Air Ministry is now promising reform, Lord Beaverbrook adds that there is no satisfactory solution unless the Admiralty takes over all flying over the sea. The Admiralty cannot assume full responsibility for the protection of convoys unless it has control of the operations, equipment and training of these air squadrons employed on this work. Sir Archibald Sinclair, Secretary of State for Air, denies that the Air Ministry has starved Coastal Command or that they are trying to make a last minute reform. It is eventually agreed that Coastal Command shall remain an integral part of the Royal Air Force, but that for all operational purposes it will come under the control of the Admiralty.[4]

Brigadier Harker sent a reply, issued on his behalf and designated 'Secret', to Pentonville governor L.C. Ball that referenced his letter of 28 November. With the reply he enclosed five photographs that were found in Meier's wallet, and said that as far as his department was concerned, there was no objection to them being issued.

Whitelegge responded to M.D.P.'s minute from 3 December which suggested managing what was becoming a very difficult and delicate situation:

'I agree that the exhibition of the notices required by Section 10 of the Act of 1868 may be dispensed with; and but for the fact that ... the "secret" is already, or will be, in so many hands,* I should have been inclined to suggest going one step further and disposing of the executions without bringing in the Coroner at all.

'I think it would be of distinct advantage to arrange for the executions to take place in one prison, so as to bring in one coroner (and jury) only – preferably Pentonville and Mr Bentley Purchase who, I understand, is particularly likely to fall in with any official requests.

'I have spoken to Colonel Hinchley Cooke of MI5 who will apparently be more than content with the non-posting of the notices. He said he would be glad to interview the Coroner (and/or the jury) if it would help. He asked that a note might be sent to him (c/o Room 055, War Office) as soon as possible, of the steps which we are taking in this matter.

'The prisoner in Wandsworth [Kieboom] has now appealed (encouraged I gather by the fact that a fourth man, who was working with him, was acquitted at the Old Bailey).

'(I understand moreover that one of the men concerned, who was the last to be apprehended, stated that he had succeeded in passing a message to Germany about the arrest of the others).'

With more than a degree of uncertainty, the memo concluded, 'Proceed as proposed.'[5]

Two memos, designated 'Secret', were sent on behalf of Brigadier Harker to the governors of Pentonville and Wandsworth Prisons. One referred to Meier and Waldberg, who both resided at Pentonville awaiting execution, and the other to Kieboom, who was at Wandsworth. Both memos asked permission for Major Lennox from the War Office to have access to the prisoners, adding that the major would identify himself by his official pass. It was stressed that in both cases, 'It is essential, in the interest of complete secrecy, that the interview should take place within sight but NOT within hearing of the prison staff and I trust that this will be possible under existing regulations.'[6]

The same day, the governor of Pentonville Prison sent a memo to Hinchley Cooke that explained that neither prisoner 8601 Carl Heinrich Meier nor prisoner 8602 Jose Waldberg had appealed, written any more letters or received any visitors.

Major Grew, at Wandsworth Prison, issued a notification to the effect that Kieboom had initiated a Notice of Abandonment of all proceedings.

Throughout the period of his detention and trial, Waldberg affirmed that he was Jose Waldberg, but in his petition to the Home Secretary for clemency he stated that he was, in reality, one Henri Lassudry, a dairyman of Belgian origin, born on 13 June 1918 at Beaumont, of a Belgian father and French mother, and that he had accepted service with the German Nachrichtendienst solely for the purpose of saving his father's life.

In what can only be suspected as a last-ditch attempt to escape the gallows and the '9 o'clock walk', Waldberg, who was still under sentence of death at Pentonville Prison – and the only one of the four who pleaded guilty – made a confession to Special Branch; a translation, requested by the Home Office, was made by Detective Sergeant William Allchin. Throughout the period of his detention and trial, he affirmed his identity to be Waldberg, but now he gave an entirely different story of his life:

'It is with remorse that I take this opportunity of informing you that I am not the spy Jose Waldberg, but actually Henri Lassudry, born 13 June 1918, at Beaumont, of a Belgian father and French mother.

'Accordingly I entreat you to have the goodness to consider my petition, for I am going to speak with an open heart, as my role is finished, and if I have lied I had a very great and noble reason. Here is the story from the beginning when I was at the mercy of the Germans. I am a dairyman by occupation and was in business with a friend of my father at Brussels, where my family live at 22 Rue des Colonies. He is the president of the Society of Retail Dairymen. Among our clientele were the German Ambassador and the German Commercial Attaché, Mr Barenzt, who had been our customers for about six months. He learned that I was going to Denmark to study the making of butter which is the unsurpassed speciality of that country. He spoke to me often on business matters. Our society was going to buy a dairy to make the butter it needed. On the morning of 28 March 1940, Mr Barenzt asked me if I wished to accompany him on a journey to Denmark, where he would arrange visits to dairies for me, and I accepted this proposal with pleasure. He advised me not to say with whom I was going, as it concerned nobody else, so I told my parents that I was leaving on a journey with a client and would be back in three days' time. We crossed the Belgian frontier at Moresnet, and stopped at a restaurant at Aix-la-Chapelle. Mr Barenzt left me for a moment, and then two men wearing tunics with a death's head on their caps asked me for my passport, but as I only had my Belgian papers on me they took me to the police station, where an interpreter spoke to me. I was taken to Dusseldorf where I stayed for five days, and from there I was conveyed to the large camp at the citadel of Mayence. I was treated very well, but I asked them for the reason of my detention. They told me I had been arrested because I was in a fortified zone. I explained to Commandant Schmitt who I had come with and where I was bound for. I was asked some questions about my country, and the morale and opinions of the nobility and the lower classes. I remained for three weeks without seeing anybody apart from prisoners from my window. Then Commandant Schmitt came and told me that a safe-conduct pass was due from Berlin to take me back to Brussels. In the meantime I made the acquaintance of two young Germans who spoke French. I was there six weeks, when suddenly I was told that Belgium was at war with Germany and that consequently I had to remain there. At the beginning of June, the Commandants Seynsburg and Schmitt told me that my father had been arrested for striking a soldier and that the Gestapo were concerned in the matter, which was very serious for my family. For eight days I was mad with anxiety as to what was to become of my mother and my two sisters, if my father should disappear. Then I was told by agreeing to work for Germany I should be assisting to obtain my father's freedom. I did not hesitate for a second and accepted without knowing what it was about, for I had one thing in mind, to save my father and my family. They made me sign a paper to the effect that I should take on a secret mission and not question the instructions that I should receive. On 13 June 1940 the Commander Schmitt informed me that I was leaving for Brussels, but that I should not have the right to see my parents. I accepted, in spite of the disappointment which I felt, and the anxiety for my family who had had no news from me. They put me with a lieutenant of the German "2me bureau", and I was always in his company. I knew that they were watching me to see if I respected my parole, and by the month of July, they had a great confidence in me. I gained the complete confidence of the chief of the second section by the enthusiasm I showed in my studies all of which I had to expound from beginning to end, and by remaining faithful to my undertaking, for in England they would be informed of my conduct. I passed my Morse examination at Brussels at the same time as Pons, Meier and Kieboom. The account which I have given is exact, except of my conduct. You will say to me why did I not give myself up on arrival? Impossible, sir, because there was life which was dear to me and dependent on me, thus in the second and last message I said that the English police were looking for me, but I did not know that, for the task important to me was that I had proved my sincerity to the Germans and at the same time save the lives of my family. I should have told the truth to the judge, but I did not have the opportunity to do so, because I had been three minutes in front him when they interpreted to me that I had been sentenced to death. I accepted the sentence with courage, for if I have undertaken this low profession it was not to come to spy on you as I confessed, but was indeed a work of self-sacrifice to rescue the life of a man who fought through four years of war and lost his health for the defence of his country and his family. It was only just that I should give my life for him. Hoping that you will consider my petition, and thanking you in advance, I beg you to believe in my sincerity.'[7]

This story gave no explanation of the extensive information that he supplied about the German Secret Service Centre at Wiesbaden. Waldberg produced another variation of his story for the benefit of his companion, Meier, in which he claimed Swiss nationality, but this again did not tally with the information that he had given under interrogation.

MI5 gave no credence to Waldberg's assertion, which was considered to be merely an afterthought in the hope that a reprieve would be forthcoming.

The Home Office questioned why this was not the story Waldberg told Lieutenant Colonel Hinchley Cooke or his own counsel. If his confession was correct, why did he persist with the other story? If what he said was true, the authorities believed that it should not affect the question of his sentence. They were not concerned with the reasons the spies put forward as having been induced to take service with the enemy, whether it was duress, blackmail or if they claimed that they came to Britain with no intention of spying at all. These stories only surfaced once they were caught. If things had gone right for these men – as improbable as that seemed – then they would conceivably have done useful work for their employers.

Thursday, 5 December 1940:

At 9.30 pm, in the War Room Cabinet, Operation *Workshop* (the plan to occupy the Italian island of Pantelleria, south-west of Sicily) is being discussed. Admiral of the Fleet, Sir Dudley Pound, says that the Chiefs of Staff have studied the plan for the Operation this afternoon, in consultation with the Director of Combined Operations. There are two main questions involved:-

(a) The problem of getting the assaulting force to the beaches;
(b) The adequacy of the assaulting force to capture the island once they had established themselves ashore.

The Chiefs of Staff fully appreciated the need for seizing every opportunity to take the offensive against Italy, and the loss of prestige which the Italians would suffer if the island was captured. It was, however, their duty to report frankly their opinion as to the likelihood of the success of the operation.

Sir Dudley Pound explains that the Italians could not fail to spot the ships en-route but would of course not suspect Operation *Workshop*. He adds, 'Without crediting the Italians with exceptional initiative it would be reasonable to expect that they would dispose their light craft with the object of intercepting the convoy.' Surprise in this operation, therefore, is thought doubtful.

The Commander in Chief, Mediterranean, meanwhile, considered *Workshop* as being an insufficient prize.

It is decided that the present plan for *Workshop* cannot be accepted, but if the plan can be improved then further consideration will be given.[8]

Regarding bombing attacks across Britain, The Home Security Situation Report for the week ending today reports that due to bombing over the week, approximately 775 people have been killed, which includes 277 in London and 264 in Liverpool.

A memo arrived from Whitelegge of the Home Office to MI5's Hinchley Cooke, informing him that the governor of Pentonville Prison had been authorized to dispense with the usual notices of execution regarding Meier and Waldberg, and also that the Coroner should be approached so that the 'preservation of secrecy in connection with the inquest'[9] can be assured. Whitelegge understood that Lord Swinton had been in correspondence with the Home Secretary on the subject.

Whitelegge wrote to the governor of Pentonville Prison to tell him that the Prison Commissioners had referred the governor's notes of 28 November to the Home Office. Whitelegge had written at the behest of Sir Alexander Maxwell at the Home Office to say that the posting of the usual notices of execution regarding Meier and Waldberg may, as governor Ball suggested, be dispensed with due to the special circumstances of these cases.

Ball was asked to arrange to see the Coroner and to explain the importance that was attached by the military authorities regarding the preservation of secrecy about the executions. The Coroner was to be told that the Home Secretary would appreciate any steps which he could take to this end in connection with the inquisitions, for example, by keeping the proceedings as private as possible and by impressing on the members of the jury the paramount need, in the national interest, of refraining from any mention of the matter outside.

Whitelegge spoke to Hinchley Cooke, who offered to help in interviewing the Coroner, but Whitelegge thought that this was not necessary.

Ball was reminded that a third prisoner, Kieboom, was in Wandsworth Prison awaiting execution, and had made an appeal. If his appeal failed, it was proposed, in the circumstances, to transfer him to Pentonville for the purpose of execution.

The Secretary of the Prison Commission was sent a copy of the letter. However, before the letter was sent, Whitelegge annotated, in pen, 'I have just heard that he has abandoned his appeal.'[10]

Lord Swinton gave a very informative reply,[11] designated 'Most Secret', to Maxwell's letter of 3 December. He thought that it was possible to publish the conviction of the three men, but any information that was released must be very selective to maintain the integrity of the Security Services:

'I am much obliged for your letter of the 3rd December.

'In the particular case of the three men, we have come to the conclusion that it will be possible to publish the conviction; and we propose that this should be done in a carefully prepared statement, to be issued to the press on the day the execution is carried out.

'The fact that a conviction and sentence can be published does not affect the importance of the trial being conducted in secret. It is very difficult in a genuine spy case to select any part of the proceedings which can be conducted in public.

'Something may slip out which it is most desirable to keep hidden; and even in passing sentence a judge may inadvertently err, from a security point of view, if he makes any observations.

'I fully share your view that the fact of conviction and the execution of sentence should be published wherever possible; and also that this should be accompanied by such statement of the case as can be made public. What can be given in such a statement requires very careful consideration in each case.

'As you know, the policy which is being followed is that when an agent is caught, he is thoroughly examined. The first and overriding consideration is what information we can get to build up our knowledge of enemy plans and organization. On this the Secret and Security Services and the Directorate of Intelligence work in close co-operation; and the examination often takes a considerable time.

'In some cases it is both possible and necessary to use the man and his equipment. In other cases, the man can ultimately be brought to trial. Even where a man is tried and convicted, it may be absolutely essential to keep the fact secret; it may be necessary to the whole chain of counter-espionage that the enemy should believe him to be still at large. But even where this is not so and the conviction can be made public, many of the facts disclosed at the trial must be kept secret.

'I want to make it plain that there is much more in this than keeping the enemy in doubt as to the fate of his agents, as in the case of the submarines. The combined work of all the services has built up, and is continually adding to, a great structure of intelligence and counter-espionage; and a single disclosure, affecting one individual, might send the whole building toppling. I have no love for unnecessary secrecy; but in this matter we cannot afford to take any avoidable risk.'

In a letter[12] to Captain Felix Cowgill of SIS, Dick Goldsmith White expressed several points regarding Waldberg's 'after-thoughts' (4 December), which had been translated:

1. If Waldberg was only recruited by the German SS sometime in March 1940, his story that he was two years at Wiesbaden Stelle could not be true. On the other hand, he was very specific in his descriptions of the personnel and activities of the Wiesbaden Stelle, and if he was not there, then he must have been very well informed, perhaps by Seynsburg, about its work, which, according to Goldsmith White, seemed to be unlikely.
2. Goldsmith White said that at the back of his mind was the memory of the reactions of the other three who came with Waldberg to his claims that he had been for two years in the German SS. They never really swallowed this, and thought that their compatriot was simply boasting.

3. Goldsmith White asked, 'Which story is correct?' He thought that it seemed to matter very little, as existing information confirmed that Wiesbaden was an important Stelle which used to direct activities against France and the Low Countries.

Goldsmith White reflected that in light of Waldberg's turnaround, there were now uncertainties regarding the information that he had given, especially about Chateau Wimille. Goldsmith White felt that somehow a warning should be given to the people conducting the enterprise against Wimille, and that they could not now be quite so certain of the facts, especially from Waldberg. Goldsmith White presumed the motive was to make his case similar to that of Pons by representing that he was coerced, thus avoiding the worst consequence of his crime, i.e. the death penalty.

It was sufficiently concerning to Goldsmith White that Hinchley Cooke was on this day going to the Director of Public Prosecutions with Waldberg's after-thought to assess whether the legal position was altered in any way. Goldsmith White was of the opinion that it did not.

Goldsmith White also sent Waldberg's after-thought to Robin Stephens at Latchmere House, whom he had rather strangely referred to as 'Robert', but said that it hardly altered anything that had gone before. If it were true, he added, the information about Wiesbaden which Waldberg supplied was either obtained by him through hearsay or else was entirely fictitious. Goldsmith White doubted the latter because information from other sources had highlighted Wiesbaden as an important SS station working against France and the Low Countries.

Goldsmith White recommended Stephens not to 'puzzle your head much over it', as it was unlikely to alter Waldberg's (or Lassudry's) ultimate fate. He concluded by saying that Stephens may like to have the document 'as an interesting round-off to your file'.[13]

Major Grew, governor at Wandsworth Prison, was very concerned regarding the delays in the postal arrangements, and said he would be very grateful if he could receive any communication from the Under Secretary of State regarding Kieboom 'in good time'. Kieboom's date of execution was still scheduled for Wednesday, 11 December, at 9 am.

Friday, 6 December 1940:
At 12 noon, a meeting of the War Cabinet is held at 10 Downing Street. The Chiefs of Staff report on operations, the main points of which are as follows:

On the night of 4/5 December, the enemy had sent over some 155 bombers, the main attack being against Birmingham. The RAF had despatched eighty-seven bombers to attack targets in the Ruhr and Turin. One RAF aircraft had been lost.

On 5 December, daytime casualties had been as follows: RAF, two machines (one pilot safe); enemy, fourteen aircraft certainly destroyed (one by AA fire), plus three probable and two damaged.

On the night of 5/6 December, the enemy had attacked Portsmouth and Southampton.

On 4 December, RAF Gladiators in Greece shot down eight Italian machines for certain, plus seven probables, without loss.

Very bad weather had been experienced in the North-West Approaches. Seven merchant ships were adrift, but there was no reason to think that they would not make port.

L.C. Ball responded to Whitelegge's letter of 5 December, and noted the fact that the usual notices were to be dispensed with. Ball stated that appropriate action had been taken and the Under Sheriff had been informed, and added that the notices would be signed by all concerned, with the usual copies sent to the Under Secretary of State and the remainder being filed at Pentonville Prison for reference.

Ball said that he had seen the Coroner, 'who is agreeable that the proceedings shall be kept as quiet as possible'.[14] He added that no press representatives would be admitted, and that the Coroner had undertaken to impress upon the jury the need for secrecy.

The governor noted that Kieboom may be transferred to his prison for execution and assumed that, as Kieboom had appealed, the sentence could not be carried out until fourteen to eighteen days had elapsed from the date of abandonment.

The Director of Public Prosecutions telephoned and left a message for Hinchley Cooke, asking whether he wanted the speeches of counsel included in the shorthand notes? They wanted to know by the following Monday.

At Wandsworth, Major Grew made it known that, acting on the advice of his counsel Mr Christmas Humphries, Kieboom had now withdrawn his appeal. He was thus scheduled to hang on 11 December at 9 am. In accordance with Hinchley Cooke's instructions, no notices informing of the hanging or that it has been carried out would be posted on the prison door.

Grew pointed out that the actual authority for this should be the High Sheriff, and in effect it would be P. Kynaston Metcalfe, Under Sheriff for the County of London, who would normally be able to authorize this. Grew thought that it was essential for an inquest with a jury to be held.

Grew also contacted the Coroner, R.B. Hervey-Wyatt to inform him that the proceedings were to be held in camera, and suggested that the Coroner should waive his right to bring a press representative to the inquest. Grew also suggested that the Home Office might be approached to give the Coroner definite instructions on this point.

The governor pointed out that both Waldberg and Meier were to be hanged at Pentonville at 9 am on Tuesday, 10 December, and said his remarks regarding the Coroner applied equally to their cases. The Coroner, however, would be a different one, as Pentonville was in another Metropolitan Division. Arrangements were under way, therefore, to transfer Kieboom to Pentonville.

The Registrar of the Court of Criminal Appeal issued a notice for His Majesty's Principal Secretary of State, and said that on 4 December, they received from Kieboom a notice of abandonment of all proceedings regarding his appeal to the Court of Criminal Appeal. Subsequently, the appeal was now deemed to have been dismissed by the Court of Appeal.

Kynaston Metcalfe had written to the Under Secretary of State to inform him that he had just received notice from the governor of Wandsworth Prison informing him of Kieboom's abandonment of appeal. He also reminded the Under Secretary that, having been informed by him that, in these circumstances, the execution should take place on Tuesday or Wednesday of the week commencing Monday, 16 December, the High Sheriff had nominated 17 December for Kieboom's execution.

Whitelegge informed W.H. Waddams, from the Prison Commission, of the decision that authorized the governor of Pentonville to dispense with the posting of the usual notices of execution, and that he had been asked to approach the Coroner. He added that it was proposed to transfer the third prisoner, Kieboom, from Wandsworth to Pentonville for execution.

Whitelegge annotated in pen at the foot of his note that he assumed that the governor of Wandsworth was equally aware of the need for secrecy and to arrange for him to be reminded.

Section B13 at MI5 received a message from the Defence Security Service which stated that, at 4.15 pm, the deputy governor of Wandsworth Prison rang to say that he had received a letter dated 4 December, which contained an illegible signature, but was signed on behalf of MI5's Brigadier Harker, asking that Major Lennox be allowed to visit the condemned men. The name of S.G.P. Corin had been added to this letter. The deputy governor wanted to check that this was correct, and was subsequently told that if Major Lennox had taken Corin, or introduced him, it would be alright. The telephone call was made from a call box, as the telephone system at Wandsworth was out of action.

A handwritten annotation at the bottom of the message stated that Lennox had previously telephoned about this, but it was not possible to inform the governor because the lines were out of order. Lennox said that he would take Corin anyway.

Sir Alexander Maxwell, at the Home Office, issued a 'Secret' memo to the Secretary of the Prison Commission which stated that the Home Secretary, having considered the cases of Carl Heinrich Meier and Jose Waldberg – who were currently lying under sentence of death in Pentonville Prison – had failed to discover sufficient grounds to justify him in advising His Majesty to interfere with the due course of law.

The fate of these men, at least, was now pretty well sealed.

Saturday, 7 December 1940:
The RAF carry out a heavy attack on Dusseldorf and smaller attacks on Antwerp, Dunkirk, Calais, Boulogne, Lorient, Brest and various German airfields.[15]

Whitelegge referred to Meier and Waldberg when he wrote to Ball at Pentonville Prison, and said that, as he had explained on the telephone, there had been some changes since he last wrote to the governor.

It was still desired that the names of the prisoners should not be divulged, but it had been decided to issue a Press Notice in some form immediately after the executions, and that the three notices which were required to be exhibited after the execution (surgeon's certificate, Sheriff's declaration and certificate of Coroner's inquisition) should be posted as usual, except that those responsible for them should be asked to draw them in terms of 'Prisoner A' and 'Prisoner B'. The preliminary notice required by No. 3 of the Secretary of State's rules of 5 June 1902 should not, however, be posted.

Now that Kieboom had abandoned his appeal, attention turned to secrecy in his case. Major Grew at Wandsworth Prison was reminded by W.H. Waddams at the Prison Commission that, with Kieboom's execution looming, there were important reasons why the matter should be kept as secret as possible. Waddams was in no doubt that Hinchley Cooke had already warned him of this, and that the governor had also been informed that all members of staff should be concerned of the necessity for secrecy in the matter.

Waddams went on to say that with the object of confining knowledge concerning the matter within the narrowest possible limits, it had been decided by the Home Office that the execution of Kieboom should be carried out at Pentonville Prison. The inquest would then be held by the same Coroner, and possibly the same jury, as would have functioned at Pentonville when the other two men convicted in the same case, Meier and Waldberg, were executed.

It was understood that the Sheriff had been informed by the Home Office of the change of venue, and Grew was asked to contact him confidentially. The governor had been in contact with his Coroner, as it would be necessary to let him know that the execution would not now be carried out at his prison.

Grew accordingly arranged for Kieboom to be transferred to Pentonville on 16 December, the day before the planned execution, with the officers who had charge of him at Wandsworth to accompany him to Pentonville. Grew was advised to inform the governor of Pentonville of any matters of importance which he ought to be aware of. It would also be necessary to arrange for the executioner and his assistant to attend Pentonville and not Wandsworth.

It was suggested to Grew, as a precautionary measure, to have the usual tests of the execution apparatus at Wandsworth to be carried out, in case there was a last-minute hitch or a change of decision for the execution to take place there. It was emphasized, once again, that secrecy was paramount.

Waddams wrote to Whitelegge and enclosed a copy of the letter he sent to the governor of Wandsworth Prison; the governor of Pentonville had also been sent a copy for his information.

Whitelegge spoke to Waddams on the telephone and, as promised, sent him a note of the latest decisions about procedure in connection with the executions of Meier and Waldberg – he also included a copy of the Treachery Act, 1940 – which explained the position.

Whitelegge issued a notice – regarding Meier and Waldberg – as to the question of the inquest, notices etc., and, after having been in contact with Sir Alexander Maxwell (who already had been in communication with Lord Swinton), and the Coroner, Mr Bentley Purchase, who visited Whitelegge, the following was the result:

A press notice was to be issued immediately after the executions. At this time the terms of notice were still under consideration.

The posting of the preliminary notice required by No. 3 of the Secretary of State's Regulations (5 June 1902) was to be dispensed with, but the other notices (surgeon's certificate, declaration of Sheriff and certificate of Coroner's inquisition) were to be exhibited after the execution.

The names of the prisoners were to be suppressed so far as possible. In the three notices to be posted after the execution, they should be referred to as 'Prisoner A' and 'Prisoner B' respectively. Mr Bentley Purchase was quite agreeable so far as his inquisition and certificate were concerned. He was satisfied that sufficient evidence of identity could be given at the inquisition without any mention of names.

Whitelegge explained matters to the governor of Pentonville over the telephone and had also written to him. The same steps were being taken regarding the Under Sheriff, but Whitelegge did not think it likely that he would raise any difficulty.

The same procedure would have applied in the case of the execution of van den Kieboom.

Bentley Purchase told Whitelegge that he would do all that he could to 'pick a jury of reliable persons'.[16]

Whitelegge had spoken to Waddams and explained the present position. They had sent the necessary instructions to Wandsworth.

Sunday, 8 December 1940:

Churchill seeks support from Roosevelt, informing the President what he thinks 1941 will bring. Churchill says most Americans realize safety depends on the survival of Britain and its Empire. Control of the oceans is essential for security and to stop the war spreading to the US, he adds. Gloomily, he says that soon Britain won't be able to pay for shipping and supplies.[17]

A report[18] was issued regarding the interrogation of the three condemned spies – Waldberg, Meier and Kieboom – by Section B8 (L) of MI5, when they elicited details of the position, and other details, of Chateau Wimille. The interrogations were carried out at Wandsworth and Pentonville Prisons in the presence of Captain Edward John Ronald Corin of MI5, who acted as interpreter for Waldberg and as an assistant interrogator. Arrangements were made for the interrogations to be in secret, within view, but not within earshot of the prison authorities.

Regarding Waldberg, the report stated that he maintained that his correct name was Henri Lassudry. At the beginning of questioning:

'He appeared to be in a very nervous and highly strung condition; it took some time for him to calm down and regain his composure. He was very willing to talk and appeared anxious to give all the information he could. The interrogator was impressed with Waldberg telling the truth to the best of ability, but not being completely trustworthy as a witness as a result of his mental condition because, as the events happened some time ago, some of the details he gave the authorities may have slipped his memory, for example, distances and times.

'Waldberg claimed that he had gone on foot to the Chateau from the village of Wimille. He later said that he had visited Wimille on foot from the Chateau, but it was thought that this visit to the village may well have been without permission. He also said that the Chateau was situated at the back of Wimille village as shown on the line drawn by Waldberg (unfortunately he gave no indication of compass directions):

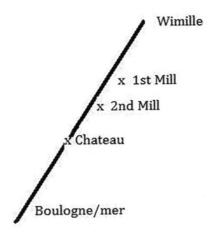

'Waldberg said that the path followed a stream. The path was rough and flinty. The Chateau was near the 2nd water-mill. These mills were not used as mills but had been converted into restaurants frequented by the Boulonnaise. From the second mill the path widened to become a poor road that allowed cars to park at the mill.

'It should be noted that at this juncture, Waldberg was talking of the mills as if they were approached from the village of Wimille, so that when he talked of the 1st mill he undoubtedly meant the mill furthest from the Chateau, and when he spoke of the 2nd mill, he meant the one nearest the Chateau which was in fact known as Cafe du Premier Moulin. That information should be born in mind throughout this statement.

'Waldberg was asked to describe the route from the church in the village of Wimille to the Chateau. He said that as you left the church on a local road [you] followed it until you joined the Route Nationale. He thought that there were houses on either side at the beginning of the Route Nationale. Almost at once, the Route Nationale took a left-hand curve. After a few metres, a path led off the Route Nationale to the left. This path skirted a wood.

'Waldberg said that after the wood there was a meadow on the left in the distance. Also after the wood there was a farm about 3,500 yards from the wood. On arrival at the farm there were two ways to go, and it was the one on the left that should be followed. At this point the Denacre stream was lost to view. The path then dropped downhill to the 1st Mill, [and] this and the stream would come into view again about 150 yards to the left where there was a "thin wood". In the middle of this wood there was a plank bridge over the river before you arrived at the 2nd Mill. The river ran through the grounds of the 2nd Mill, and there was a small cascade and an old water-wheel. A rough car road now started toward the Chateau.

It was a narrow road, flinty and full of pot-holes. The path then passed a farm before arriving at the Chateau.

'Waldberg claimed that it took him about ten minutes to walk from the village of Wimille to the Chateau. Evidence suggested that the Cafe du Premier Moulin was in or very close to the village of Denacre, and as the Chateau was beyond this, the estimate of a ten minute walk to the Chateau from the village of Wimille was underestimated by Waldberg.

'In the opinion of the interrogator, the journey from the Chateau to the village of Wimille would take at least twenty-five minutes, but there was no surprise that Waldberg was wrong over this considering the lapse of time since he did the journey. Indeed, it was only on this point that his evidence differed from that of Meier and Kieboom.

'Waldberg was asked for details about life at the Chateau. He said that at night there was an NCO and a Naval Rating on duty, but that they were probably asleep. He said that rooms were available for officers, but as far as he knew, they were empty. The Chateau had doors on all sides. There was a garden with flower beds. The ground rose from Denacre Stream behind the Chateau to a "butte" (a hill with steep sides and a flat top). There were no woods near the Chateau, the nearest being the "thin wood", closest to the 1st Mill on the way from Wimille village. There was no sentry at the Chateau, but five or six sentries were posted on the road towards Boulogne. There were no sentries on the side toward Wimille village, but he thought that there might be "some sort of man" on duty in Wimille village, because, after 9 pm, all civilians were stopped for examination of their papers. He added that after this time, a special permit was necessary to avoid being arrested. Waldberg thought that the sentries on the road were relieved every hour.

'He said that near the Chateau there was a large outhouse with a military guard on duty, day and night, but he seemed somewhat vague over this.

'Waldberg went on to say that there was a gate-keeper who had a dog; he thought that this was the only dog on the premises. There was no barbed wire round the Chateau. No cooking was done there, and meals were taken at the restaurant, "at the Mill". He said that many of the officers, however, used to go into Boulogne for their meals.

'As for work at the Chateau, all that Waldberg was able to tell the interrogators was that one NCO was nearly always on duty "for communicating with Brussels".

'Regarding cars on the premises, Waldberg said that there was one Mercedes, one Ford, one Studebaker and one Auto-Union. Two were saloons and two were touring cars. They were probably the cars that took the officers to the Chateau, and possibly that they were not actually stationed there.

'Finally, Waldberg said that he was taken to Etaples for rowing exercise. He described the road to Etaples from the Chateau fairly accurately. He stated that he went to Le Touquet only for embarkation, and surprisingly enough he maintained that he did not cross the river to get to town, but embarked on the far side of the harbour. This was in complete variance with other evidence available and merely went to show that Waldberg's description about routes and places was not altogether reliable.'

The report then moved on to Meier's interrogation:

'He appeared to be very calm and collected, and while he was quite willing to talk, he was not as anxious to please as his predecessor, Waldberg.

'Meier stated that he went to the Chateau by car from Cassel through Boulogne. He noticed a monument on a hill at just the point where the side road which led to the Chateau turned off from the main road. He said that upon arrival at the Chateau, it appeared as if the side road went straight into the grounds, but in actual fact the road bent just before the entrance. The Chateau was approached by a drive.

'He said that meals were taken at the restaurant in the old mill near to the Chateau. He thought it was two or three minutes' walk from the Chateau to the mill. He explained that at the mill the stream was higher than the path, with steps that led up to the first floor of the mill, and that there was a system of locks near the mill. He had never walked into the village of Wimille from the Chateau, however, he stated that there was another empty chateau near Chateau Wimille, but when cross-questioned about this, he became rather nebulous.

'Regarding life and the work at the Chateau, Meier said that an NCO, a sailor and "the other wireless operator" slept at the Chateau. He thought that the officers probably slept at a hotel in Wimereux (north of Boulogne). He mentioned "The Grand Hotel". He said that officers frequently arrived by car. The only car he had seen which remained at the Chateau was an abandoned one in the garage.

'Meier told his interrogators that the Chateau was divided into two parts, one part for military and the other for what he simply described as "a woman". It was thought that this was a Frenchwoman, and that only half of the Chateau had been taken over. Meier said that there was a flower-garden with a front lawn and a few trees around the house.

'As to any guards, he thought there were only two, presumably the NCO and a sailor, and he did not know of any concierge. He said there was always one man in the house and that work began at 9 am and ran in two shifts using a replacement, but was very irregular and depended on the requirements of Brussels. The time of finishing work was not fixed.

'Meier stated that they embarked at Le Touquet after receiving instructions from Major Seynsburg and Dr Kohn (spelling uncertain by the interrogators). Meier claimed that they lived in a large house which was some distance from the sea front at Le Touquet, and that it was surrounded by pine trees. The point of embarkation was inside the mouth of the river, and in order to get out to the sea it was necessary to round a long sandbank.

'Finally, when shown a photostat sketch map of Chateau Wimille, Meier agreed that it was fairly accurate.'

Finally, Kieboom's interrogation was reported:

'He too was very calm and collected, and very willing to talk. He was considered by his interrogators to appear, in some ways, the most intelligent of the three men.

'Kieboom stated that he went to Chateau Wimille by car from Boulogne and that the journey took about fifteen minutes. He said that they left the Route Nationale by an abrupt turn to the right along a side road. At this point a monument on a hill (as stated by Meier) was visible to the left. The side road led through a high embankment or cutting and then across "a short moor". There was a bend to the right downhill. It next passed a few houses and then there was another bend at a point where the lane led off to the left to the village of Denacre (south of the village of Wimille). The Chateau was situated at this point where the lane leads off. The Chateau was before the village of Denacre, and in Kieboom's opinion, about one minute's walk from the village. The side road, after passing the entrance to the Chateau, crossed a bridge over the Denacre stream. It was possible to see the bridge from the Chateau. Kieboom had never walked to the village of Wimille, but he had been to Wimereux by car from the Chateau, and as far as he remembered, the journey took about fifteen minutes.

'He had meals at a hotel in Boulogne and at Wimereux, and also at the cafe in the old mill; he explained that this cafe was the first house in the village of Denacre going to the village by the lane past the Chateau. He added that as one went from the Chateau to the cafe, Denacre Stream was flowing in the same direction. He referred to the cafe as the Cafe des Deux Moulins and not as the Cafe du Premier Moulin.

'Regarding the course of Denacre Stream, he said that after it had passed under the bridge carrying the side road, it flowed through the

Chateau garden, and then behind the Cafe des Deux Moulins. He agreed that there were two cafes in the old mills, and he said that there was a cascade at each cafe. When shown a photostat sketch of the Chateau, he agreed that it was substantially correct, and pointed out that the village of Denacre began where the Cafe du Premier Moulin was shown on the sketch. He pointed out the direction of the sea was wrong, that it ought to be West or North-West instead of to the South.

'As far as life and work at the Chateau was concerned, Kieboom claimed that the spies slept four in a room. He said that in the Chateau there was one sergeant, one corporal (a marine) and a civilian. The officers did not sleep in the Chateau. Work was irregular and at no fixed hours.

'There was a radio station in the garden. He said that there were no guards at the Chateau, and as far as he knew, there was no concierge, and no dog. He thought there might have been someone on duty guarding the garage, but he was not sure. A German in civilian clothes, presumably the civilian already mentioned, was at times in charge of the radio where calls were occasionally made to and received from Brussels. On one occasion he heard the word "mascot" in connection with one of those radio messages. There were no typewriters in the Chateau and no clerical work seemed to be done. Indeed, he said that there was no office and that nearly all the rooms were empty. In the room in which the spies slept, there was, of all things, a piano as well as beds. Half the Chateau was occupied by "French civilians". In the garden of the Chateau an English tin helmet was found and when Kieboom himself was wandering through some of the empty rooms in the building he found in a cupboard a "British Army Field Manual".

'The prisoner said that a "Captain Lieutenant", who he thought was an Austrian major, was sometimes in charge of the Chateau, and gave the spies lectures and showed them photographs, but that he never stayed there long and came at no fixed times.

'Kieboom stated that they went to Le Touquet by car from the Chateau to a villa on the outskirts of Le Touquet, and then on to the coast to embark. He also said that the embarkation was made from the estuary. He did not remember seeing a lighthouse, although it was believed by the interrogators there were in fact two. He described the villa as a semi-detached house, standing among pine trees at some distance from the sea, and not very far away from an aerodrome.'

As a result of the interrogation of the three condemned men, the authorities were convinced that they, the authorities, now knew the position of the Chateau Wimille. The only doubt that remained was that the distances and some of the descriptions supplied by Waldberg did not quite agree with the information supplied by the other two.

According to Waldberg, the Chateau was much closer to the village of Wimille than shown on the map, but that was in direct variance to the statements of the other two. From them, and especially Kieboom, it was clear that the Chateau was very close to the village of Denacre, but further up the stream than the village. On the map, a chateau was shown on the north side of the village; the interrogators, however, thought that this was very unlikely.

As far as Major Seynsburg's house in Le Touquet was concerned, from the evidence it was impossible to pinpoint this, but it seemed that it was most probably in the pine trees at the back, to the west of town, where it was understood there were housing estates and fairly large houses amongst the pines. Unfortunately, none of the spies could give precise information as to the whereabouts of this place, but it seemed that it was probably of more importance than Chateau Wimille with regard to any contemplated raid. It was stated that, despite this observation, should a raid on Chateau Wimille be seriously contemplated, it would be an extremely difficult project to carry out and aerial reconnaissance would be strongly advised. With aerial photographs, the pin-pointing of the Chateau ought to be a simple matter, despite the attendant difficulties in reading such images. Even as the crow flies, the Chateau was at least 2 miles from the coast. There were cliffs on the coast, except for a small area close to Boulogne, and there was high ground between the coast and the valley of Denacre in which the Chateau was situated.

There was not the slightest reason to suppose that the Chateau was anything other than a billet, a place where the spies were housed before being sent to England, and there was nothing at all to indicate that it was a secret headquarters where important documents were kept and important people stayed. Consequently, should a raid on the Chateau occur, it was felt nothing of any importance would be found. The interrogators were aware that the information about the Chateau would cause some disappointment to Felix Cowgill *et al.* at SIS, but after lengthy questioning, the interrogators had come to the same conclusion independently.

One of the difficulties that Captain Corin and his colleague had faced was the fact there were no maps of the area available on a larger scale than the 1:50,000. Enquiries had been made from all possible sources but failed to get anything larger than this. Indeed, they were informed that a map on a larger scale did not exist. In the hope that that it might be of some help to them, the interrogators obtained Michelin motoring maps because, while they were not necessarily as accurate as an ordinary map, they showed more road details.

While the interrogation of the three spies was in no way hurried, Corin and his colleagues were convinced that no further useful information on the issue of Chateau Wimille could be obtained from them.

Pentonville's governor, meanwhile, wrote to the Under Secretary of State and enclosed Waldberg's petition. Waldberg had written the statement for the governor's perusal.

Time was rapidly running out for Waldberg. In Pentonville Prison, and resigned to his fate, he decided to write three letters, all in French: one to his parents, Monsieur and Madame Lassudry Hestor, in Brussels; one to his Aunt Raymonde and Uncle Pierre, in Paris; and one to his fiancée, Helene Ceuppens, in Ixelles, a commune of Brussels. The letter to his fiancée[19] was translated from the original, and read as follows (included are any of the original grammatical and spelling errors):

'To my darling Helene,

'Since I left you, my darling, you have probably suffered greatly from my prolonged silence, you must have thought that I had forgotten you, that I no longer thought of you; no, dear Helen, do not think that, for I too have suffered, and in exile, a prisoner, far from the one I loved with all the strength of my heart. Alas, my darling, our sweet and lovely dream cannot come true, to my great despair. I beg you to forgive me with all your heart, for now I can no longer keep that promise, so you know the vow I made you! That I would be yours for ever or die. Do not be frightened, little Helen of my heart, at this great word, so terrible to pronounce. Take courage and strength, as I do; you will go on to a future happiness, for you deserve it, you are a brave girl; I for my part to on [*sic*] towards my tragic and terrible destiny, death. But, my darling, this will perhaps be a heavy blow for you, but you should only think that my last thoughts will be of you and of my mother. I do not fear their sentence of death, which the tribunal passed on 22nd November 1940, to be executed on the 10th December at 9 o'clock. You know how sincere and true I was, and you can say that it was that which was my downfall. One thing is certain – that my judgment was a great mystery to me, but still it does not matter, as the great error that English justice is committing will be avenged later. You know my courage, and with that proud and noble courage I shall give my soul to God. How heartless I am! Darling Helene, I have not even asked how you are, are you still well? And your dear mother? Your sister? Your father and brother-in-law? Henriette and Julienne? My dearest Helene, as you see, I have been taken prisoner, then condemned, but do not mourn for me, I have got what I deserved since it was the will of God. I have been sacrificed on one side and on the other, through vengeance ... In spite of the great grief and sorrow in my heart, I keep a good spirit, for, darling, I am even now reading the whole life of Louis XVI and of his death on the scaffold.

'Where are the happy days, little Helene? The happy evenings we passed together, indeed, all our pleasures, in spite of the war. Our great and beautiful love has been destroyed too by this catastrophe, so dreadful for us both. My darling Helene, forgive me with all your heart for the cruel words that follow. I give you back your word of the 26th August, because I cannot keep my engagement to you, you are free, forget me; do not think me heartless to speak so to you, no my dearest, I ask one thing only, my greatest wish before going to the other world, a little place in your sweet, gentle heart. All that you have of mine keep in memory. You will get my letter, God knows how long, how many years after my death. As you see, Helene, I have remained the same as when I left, you have not only the same place in my heart, but even greater, even deeper than before. Be happy, dear Helene, forget me, my greatest wish that I desire with all my heart is that you may be happy and always well, that is my dearest thought, darling Helene; the one you loved tenderly is soon leaving for ever, without having seen once more your dear smile nor heard again the sound of your gentle voice. Say goodbye for me to Henriette and Julienne, and I end this terrible news, little Helene of my heart, sending you my last, my sweetest and most loving thoughts and most fervent kisses. Goodbye my darling, we shall meet again one day.
The one who loves you to distraction.
JOSE.

Waldberg had put on a brave face to his fiancée, even though he thought that his sentence was harsh and unjust. He was pragmatic; his predicament could not realistically dictate otherwise.

In the letter[20] to his parents, he apologized for not having been in contact sooner, 'for this long and cruel silence' – he had not been in contact with them for at least nine months – and also for not visiting them when he was in Brussels that June because he was continually watched and was always in the company of a German officer. Waldberg said he had been forbidden from seeing them until he had finished the job the Germans had set for him.

He explained that the he was sent to England 'to save you [his father] from the vengeance of the Gestapo and I couldn't back out of it … I was tricked. The Germans made me learn a whole romance and a false name and I had promised them to keep my word on condition that before the judge I might say the whole truth.'

Waldberg opined that although he had been well treated and lacked nothing during his captivity, he considered British justice had committed a 'great mistake':

'Well, I was true in all respects to the English, except as regards my person as I pretended to be a German – so they gave me a lawyer who spoke no French, and I had to deal with an interpreter who said that my lawyer advised me to plead guilty ... but I didn't have a trial as you may think, far from it, only three minutes to hear the sentence through the interpreter and [then it] was over.'

Although Waldberg was sentenced to death, he asked his parents to forgive British justice 'with all your heart', that it has made a great mistake. He added, 'You know, father, how brave little Belgians are when it comes to a fight, and you will be able to say of your poor son Henri that he died with the same noble courage.' He pointed out that he was sent to England without being able to speak or understand English. He asked his father that when the war was over – whenever that may be – to have his coffin brought back to Brussels.

He ended the letter, one of his last, with:

'... never again to see the son you loved and who loved you with all his heart. God knows when you will get this letter, maybe in a year or even two; anyhow I ask your forgiveness with all my heart for all the great sorrows and troubles I have caused you. That is my greatest wish before going to the next world, to be forgiven by you, as here they did not deign to judge me nor even to reward the loyal and sincere information I gave them ... you can be proud of your son, for he will die like a brave Belgian ... Goodbye forever, from your son who loves you. HENRI.

'I shall die on Tuesday December 10th at 9 o'clock. Your loving HENRI.'

A handwritten note arrived at the Police Duty Room that highlighted Waldberg's grievances. The receiver, in the knowledge that Waldberg's sentence was not going to be carried out immediately, decided that it could be dealt with the day before his execution. The gist of Waldberg's main points in the note were as follows:[21]

His interpreter was a Belgian: could Waldberg divulge secrets to his own countryman? (This was the 'best sense' the duty officer made of it).

The advocate was English but didn't speak French.

Waldberg was only allowed two hours with the advocate before the trial.

The advocate advised him to plead guilty; if he had understood, then he would not have pleaded guilty.

It was a very brief hearing; no-one asked him any questions, save the judge.

There was no jury.

Waldberg's letter[22] to his Uncle Pierre and Aunt Raymonde, addressed to 'Monsieur et Madame Lassudry Pierre' in Paris, was his first to them in almost a year.

He tried to explain his predicament and why he was in it. 'Yes uncle, your adopted son, as you used to call me, will be dead when this little letter reaches you, but bravely, because I shall have faced it voluntarily to save father from the hands of the Gestapo.' He said his father had allegedly struck a German soldier, and Waldberg claimed that he was forced to work for the Germans in order for his father to be set free. Waldberg clearly wasn't surprised about the predicament his father found himself in: 'I don't doubt it; you know too how he is when he has finished at his card–club and drunk a bit, it goes to his head. Yes, but it was serious, you understand, to strike the occupying force in Belgium, especially the SS.'

He explained that he was true and sincere to the English, but not to himself, as he had a false name. Waldberg claimed that 'English justice is most odd'. He reiterated to his aunt and uncle what he had told his parents, that he was given a lawyer who could not speak French, that an interpreter told him to plead guilty on the advice of his lawyer, and that after only three minutes (including translation) in front of the judge, he was sentenced to death. He said that he was told that the Secretary of State would revoke the sentence. 'The whole thing has been a great mystery,' he continued. He was generous about his captors, but he was also pragmatic and unrepentant: 'The Governor is very kind, in fact every one, so you know I have nothing to reproach in that way ... in 48 hours I shall be in the other world, but death does not frighten me. A little Belgian knows how to die bravely, especially when it is for a noble cause that I sacrifice my life, I do not regret it.'

Waldberg clearly had a close relationship with his relatives, and he reminded them that they often referred to him as their adopted son, ending by asking his aunt and uncle to forgive those who had sentenced him, as he says that he had forgiven them for 'their great error ... I shall die peacefully with only the regret that I did not see you again, not my father, nor my dear sweetheart.' He concluded with: 'Anyhow, I have one resolve – my heart remains and will remain very brave to the end. I will show them that a Belgian knows how to die. Your nephew who loves you, HENRI. Goodbye.'

In Pentonville Prison, Meier also busied himself by writing letters: one to his fiancée, Margaret Moseley, in English; and one to his mother, Mrs J. van Waltmeyer-Tamson, who lived in Maastricht, Holland. The latter was written in Dutch.

In the letter[23] to his fiancée, Meier began starkly when he said, 'This is going to be the hardest letter I've written to anybody.' He explained that as he was writing from England, she would guess why he was there. He said that he could not detail everything in the letter, as he knew it would not get past the censor. He planned to write a far more detailed letter and give it to the Prison Chaplain, 'who really is a very nice fellow and who will forward it to you after the war is over. Even then it might not be allowed to pass through.' He said that in all probability it would be the last letter that she would receive from him, as he had been informed that the Home Secretary has failed to see any reason why the sentence should not be carried out. However, he was given hope by the prison officers that there might be the possibility of a last-minute reprieve, in which case the letter would not be sent. He did not, however, want to give her false hope, and stated, 'Tuesday, 10 December at 9 am would be the date of odious finality to all the optimistic hopes we cherished together in regards to our future life.'

He went on to say that maybe he was only meant to live until he had conquered his cowardice, and that she, despite her love for him, must have known: 'For the first time in my life I've been able to set my jaws and clench my fists and say: "Life or death, I will live up to my ideal, so help me God!"' He believed that this he had now done, and was prepared to look death in the face. He felt that this was his destiny. He admitted that he went into this venture with his eyes wide open, and told himself, 'That a man who has an ideal must be willing to sacrifice everything for it or else the ideal isn't an ideal at all, or the man is no man at all, but a man-like creature who deserves only pity.'

He said that from the few letters that he had sent to Margaret from Holland, which had come at a crucial point in the shaping of his life, he thought that she knew which way he was going, and if he had lived, he would have been just as headstrong about his ideas. He asked her for posthumous forgiveness for his 'philandering' and the pain that it inflicted upon her.

He reminded her that she still had her whole life ahead, and that there would be much happiness in store for her if she kept her mind open to that fact. Meier added, 'somehow I feel that we shall meet again sometime, somewhere else.'

He asked her not to necessarily forget about him, but not to attach too much importance to the fact that he ever lived, that his death should not ruin her life, and to get as much happiness out of her life as she possibly could.

Meier had planned for his debts to be paid, and he wished that any of his monies in Freiburg should be put at the disposal of the German Red Cross. He wanted Margaret and his mother to take what they wished from his belongings, and the rest to be sold and the money also given to the German Red Cross. He ended his last letter to his fiancée with, 'Darling, keep your chin up! Say good-bye to all our friends from me and here's all the love that my last thoughts will convey. I'm not going to say goodbye, because there might be something after this. Darling xxxx … so long!'

In a (translated) letter to his mother,[24] Meier asked her – despite the fact that she was a spiritualist – to bear the fact bravely that when she received his letter, her son would be dead. He again spoke of his ideals, the belief that his mother would understand, and it was better for him to die for his ideals:

'I intended in one way and another to do my duty as a soldier for our greater Fatherland … Actually I've never possessed the strength to live according to my ideals. My last act, however, has broken this tie; and for the first time I feel free to believe that the object of my life was to conquer myself in this respect. As far as I'm concerned, there is nothing awful in the reward which God has given me for this self-conquest. What hurts me most is that it will irrecovably [*sic*] be a blow for you.'

Making reference to his mother's spiritualism, he confirmed to her that he was condemned to death on 19 November and that, 'I will of course try as soon as the opportunity arises, to get in contact with you, probably very shortly, as I feel myself very well-prepared for the great event.'

He included the mundane detail that he had sold his bicycle, and he did not give it to Vorrink, as he had told her. He continued by saying that Rittmeister Mirow had impressed upon him that no-one should know of his plans, but he felt that it was clear to his mother the kind of task he had taken upon himself, and she would have become suspicious. He added that Rittmeister Mirow would confirm that any money he may have earned would be an entirely secondary consideration. Basically, he had acted for his ideals and not for money.

He ended this letter to his mother by writing, 'little mother – keep your head up. I shall be all the more proud of you. Receive a last kiss from your son, Carl.'

In neither letter was Meier repentant. He was not a man innocently mixed up in a sordid episode. He accepted his fate and his ideals were everything.

Regarding the press notices prior to the executions, Sir Alexander Maxwell rang MI5's Section B13 and said that as Meier and Waldberg were to be executed at Pentonville the following Tuesday, 10 December, the notices should go out on the Monday evening.

Maxwell appeared anxious that the names of the prisoners should be published, together with a statement that they had been caught immediately after landing; this was for morale purposes, to reassure the public that that they had not been operating in the UK for any length of time before being apprehended.

Maxwell was told that B13 was not in a position to give any decision, and that the matter would be referred to the DSS, which no doubt would wish to consult Lord Swinton, especially in view of certain correspondence which had passed between Lord Swinton and Maxwell (on 3 and 5 December).

Maxwell added that the third guilty prisoner, Kieboom, would probably be executed a week later, but this was not certain.

Before the press notice was drafted, it was thought that certain points should be taken into careful consideration:

Should the names of the prisoners be given? Non–disclosure might create doubt in the minds of the German SS regarding other matters.

In view of the fact that Meier and Kieboom were Dutch subjects, and in the event of it being decided to publish their names, the Foreign Office should be consulted as some odium would undoubtedly be directed towards the Dutch. A Mr Hopkinson at the Foreign Office was contacted.

Should reference be made to Pons' acquittal? If no mention was made, then the German SS would be kept guessing and they would wonder what had become of this prisoner.

Should the method of arrival be mentioned? Should it merely be given out that the spies arrived 'surreptitiously'?

Should the fact that they were equipped with wireless sets be published? It was emphasized that 'for important reasons', on no account should it be given out that their equipment was for 'one-way' traffic only.

The press should be especially warned not to attempt to elaborate on the official statement or to send out reporters for the purposes of interviewing witnesses.

Maxwell was telephoned and was asked to allow the matter to stand over until Monday, so as to give the DSS the opportunity of discussing the whole question with Lord Swinton and the Foreign Office. Maxwell agreed, and went on to add that in the official execution notices for Meier and Waldberg, the Coroner would refer to the executed men as 'Prisoner A' and 'Prisoner B'.

Monday, 9 December 1940:

At 9.30 pm, a War Cabinet meeting is in progress. The Chiefs of Staff, in their examination of Operation *Workshop*, an attack on Pantelleria, consider two possibilities: the first, a raid, where the forces are subsequently withdrawn; the second, that the island is permanently occupied after capture. The conclusion is that a raid would not be worthwhile, and they therefore concentrate on the second alternative. Until quite recently, it appeared that there was insufficient strategical justification for capturing and holding the island. Now, the Fleet Air Arm fighters had gained greater domination over the Italian Air Force, and the Commander-in-Chief, Mediterranean, was veering round to the idea of taking convoys through the narrows by day and not by night.

The Committee approve Operation *Workshop*, that preparations for its execution should be completed in all respects and that the forces taking part should sail with the December convoy. Furthermore, the operation should be carried out provided that weather conditions are favourable and surprise is obtained. The Defence Committee had the option to cancel this decision at any time before the operation took place, if the situation rendered this liable.[25]

The British attack the Italians in the Western Desert. The British 7th Armoured Division launches attacks on the Italian camps positioned near Sofafi and Rabia, and makes its way toward the critical ocean-side road near Buqbug.[26]

Waldberg wrote[27] to his aunt in Luxembourg, putting a brave face on his predicament. He explained that it had been a long time since they had been in contact and she would be 'astonished' to learn that his letter not only came from England, but it brought sad news, 'those words that strike a family so cruelly – Death. Yes, my dear aunt, your little nephew that you loved and who loved you, will have returned his soul to God. But, dear aunt, if this tragedy has come to the family, if I am dead, it is in a noble cause, and your little nephew will have gone bravely to his death.'

He clarified how his plight had materialized, and explained that, 'one fine day', 28 March 1940, he was taken on by someone he trusted in Germany. He was arrested and taken to a prisoners' camp until 12 June. He was told that his father had been arrested, and that for him to be freed, Waldberg had to do the Germans' bidding; he didn't hesitate and accepted without question. He said he was given a new name and a cover story. He put his heart into it, which he declared surprised his German chiefs, and thus won their confidence.

Again, Waldberg explained how he felt that English justice was not meted out fairly to him:

'When the English took me prisoner, I gave them every information except with regard to myself, as once before the judge I was going to reveal my true name. For you know Aunt that one cannot speak perjury before God and the judge; but unfortunately I did not get the chance as my lawyer – through an interpreter as I could not speak their language – told me to sign some papers and said I should plead guilty; so that the judge did not even give me a trial and I was condemned to death by English justice on the 10th December 1940 at 9 o'clock in the morning. So dear Aunt, I have been rottenly tricked, because they didn't even explain to me why I should plead guilty. Well it doesn't matter – I shall show them up to the last moment of my life that a little Belgian knows how to die for a proud and noble cause.'

He continued by saying that it was useless for him to ask her to pray for him as he knew that she prayed for his mother, father and for the whole family every day. He also said that if she wanted a 'souvenir' of him, to ask his father and mother for 'a fine portrait of Marshal Foch which I drew some days before my fatal departure. This letter, dear aunt, occupies the last hours of my life ... I have told all the family of my situation; I shall die with the sacraments of the Church ... HENRI.'

It was interesting to note that in the letters to his family he ended with 'HENRI', but the one to his fiancée, he signed off as 'JOSE'. Did she know him as Jose Waldberg and not by his 'real' name, Henri Lassudry?

Waldberg must have known all letters would be censored. Although he was the only one who pleaded guilty and according to him it wasn't explained to him why he should do so, maybe he tried to persuade the authorities, via these communications to his family, that he was innocent and was, in fact, a victim of injustice. Were the letters the last throes of a desperate man?

Sir Alexander Maxwell at the Home Office wrote to the governor of Pentonville Prison, stating that he had been directed by the Secretary of State that the governor should inform Waldberg that, after careful consideration had been given to his letter, the Secretary of State regretted that he must adhere to the original decision and 'he can find no sufficient grounds to justify in him interfering with the due course of law'.[28] The governor immediately ensured that Waldberg was informed of the Secretary of State's decision.

A memo to the Foreign Office's Mr Hopkinson from Major Lennox stated that the Foreign Office had been given the full facts, and that there was no objection to their communicating with the Dutch Minister in strict confidence, with the exception of any reference to the case of Pons. The authorities were anxious to keep the Germans guessing about Pons, and the concern was that if the Dutch were told anything about him it may well have leaked back to the Germans.

Regarding Waldberg, the memo stated that after his conviction he had concocted a story about being a Belgian subject. It was recommended that this should be disregarded and that he be treated as a German. Consequently, there was little point in the Belgian Minister being informed.

As for Meier, publishing that this man was of German origin would ease the situation vis-à-vis the Dutch.

Finally, there was a communiqué which it was proposed should be issued to the Press, subject to the approval of Lord Swinton and the Home Secretary.

Arrangements had been made that instructions be sent to Pentonville Prison to the effect that as soon as the execution had taken place, a telephone message should be sent to the Press Room at the Home Office saying that it had happened. Furthermore, no notice should be posted on the prison gates until one hour after that message had been sent.

Arrangements were to be made with the Ministry of Information for the circulation of the Press Notice, and that the Foreign Office had no objection to the publication of the proposed notice to the Press.

Major Grew wrote to Waddams at the Prison Commission, thanking him for his letter of 7 December, in which Grew was advised of the change of venue for Kieboom's execution and that the need for secrecy had been deemed at the highest level. The contents had been duly noted and the appropriate action taken. He reinforced one of the key tenets of the original letter when he concluded, 'The utmost secrecy has been the keynote throughout.'[29]

MI5 had made it known throughout that they were in no doubt that Pons was as guilty as his three companions. In their opinion, Pons succeeded in persuading the jury by his evidence, given on oath, that he had been blackmailed by the Gestapo and had feigned agreement to act as an espionage agent, intending to give himself up immediately upon landing. Pons would now remain in detention for the remainder of the war under Article 12 (5A) of the Aliens Order, 1920.

Tuesday, 10 December 1940:
During the British counter-offensive in Libya at Sidi Barrani, the Italian camps at Tummar East fall to the Allies. Selby Force (consisting mainly of the 3rd Bn, Coldstream Guards) forces the Italian 1st Libyan Division out of Maktila. The Italian XXI Corps is in full retreat and some 38,000 Italian soldiers are taken prisoner by the Allies.

The Home Office's M.H. Whitelegge, when he referred to Meier and Waldberg, stated that he acted under directions from Sir Alexander Maxwell when he rang Ball at Pentonville Prison and told him of the following modifications to previously issued instructions:

A telephone message would be sent to the Home Office press room immediately after the execution which would inform them that it had taken place, and it would be clear that the message came from Pentonville Prison.

No notice would be exhibited on the prison gates after the execution until the expiration of an hour after the message to the Press Room.

The names of the two men (but no aliases) to be included in the notices to be posted after the execution.

As previously indicated, the preliminary notice under No. 3 of the Regulations of 1902 should not be posted.

Whitelegge asked the governor in writing to take down these instructions, and to explain the position to the Under Sheriff (with whom Whitelegge has been unable to get in touch). Whitelegge then informed the Press Room to expect to receive a message shortly after 9 am.

He also explained matters to Bentley Purchase, the Coroner, who rang Whitelegge and enquired whether or not the Press should be admitted to the inquisition. 'No,' Whitelegge answered; information to the Press was meant to be limited to the terms of the notice which was to be issued after the execution.

Whitelegge had received a telephone query from assistant executioner Harry Kirk about some additional material which the *Evening Standard* had in its possession, and the question of instructions to the Coroner. In view of the urgency, he was advised to contact Sir Alexander Maxwell direct.

In a handwritten annotation, Whitelegge noted that Bentley Purchase did not understand why 'felony' was included in the charge and was minded to ring up the Old Bailey about it. Whitelegge referred him to Section 1 of the Treachery Act.

Meanwhile, at 9 am, Meier and Waldberg had taken the '9 o'clock walk' and were executed at Pentonville Prison. Theirs were the first spy hangings at the prison since Sir Roger Casement was executed for treason on 3 August 1916 for his participation in the Easter Rising rebellion in Ireland that year.

Governor Ball notified the Under Secretary of State of matters via two separate statements, each regarding Meier and Waldberg separately, and in each case ended with, 'I have the honour to inform you that the above named was executed at this prison at 9 am today the 10th instant. The execution was carried out without a hitch.'

James Liddell, the surgeon at Pentonville Prison, formally issued two notices which stated that he had examined the bodies of Meier and Waldberg, and in each instance had pronounced them dead.

Two notices were then posted outside Pentonville Prison, stating that two spies – Waldberg and Meier – had been hung.

William Bentley Purchase issued two declarations, each signed by the jurors, which stated that he was satisfied that the death sentences of Carl Heinrich Meier and Jose Waldberg had been lawfully carried out, and that he was also satisfied that the bodies he had examined were identical to those of the offenders. The followiong press release was also issued:

Announcement to the Press.

<u>For immediate release.</u>

Two enemy agents, acting on behalf of Germany, were executed at Pentonville Prison today, following their conviction under the Treachery Act, 1940, at the Central Criminal Court on 22nd November. Their names are Jose Waldberg, a German born on 15.7.1915 [*sic*] at Mainz, and

Karl [*sic*] Meier, a Dutch subject of German origin born at Koblenz on 19.10.1916.

These agents were apprehended shortly after their surreptitious landing in this country. They were in possession of a wireless transmitting set which they were to erect in the fields at night, and of considerable sums of money in £1 notes. They had instructions to pose as refugees from enemy occupied territory and to move about amongst the population obtaining as much information of a military kind as possible. They had been made to believe that they would shortly be relieved by German invading forces.

Note to Editors

Editors are asked not to press for any additional facts or to institute enquiries.

Editorial comment might profitably take the form of drawing public attention to loose talk of all kinds, particularly in the presence of strangers.[30]

Kynaston Metcalfe, Under Sheriff for the County of London, now issued two declarations which stated that both Meier and Waldberg had been executed at Pentonville Prison, witnessed by the Prison governor and the Prison chaplain, and signed by said witnesses.

Kynaston Metcalfe seemed somewhat perturbed with the dealings regarding Kieboom. He sent to the Under Secretary of State what only can be interpreted as a curt memo: 'It will be a great convenience to me, if it is possible for you, to let me know, before 4 o'clock on Friday next, if this execution is to take place or not at Wandsworth, on the 17th inst.'[31]

Kynaston Metcalfe heard from Wandsworth Prison that Kieboom was to be executed at Pentonville. He then informed the Under Secretary of State that he was making the necessary arrangements on behalf of the High Sherriff for the execution at that prison, which was to take place at 9 am on 17 December.

Two separate but identical memos were issued to the Prison Commissioners and signed by governor Ball, which stated that at 9 am, Meier and Waldberg were executed, the inquest had been held later and the jury returned a verdict of 'Death by Judicial Hanging'.[32]

After the executions of Meier and Waldberg, in its 6 pm news programme, the BBC broadcast a talk containing additional facts which were not available in the official release to the press. The person responsible, ironically, was, 'an officer intimately concerned with preventing the leakage of information to the enemy'. The broadcast ran as follows:

'Two enemy spies this morning paid the extreme penalty in Pentonville Gaol.

'One of them was a German subject, and he, we may hope, embarked on his final and perilous adventure in the belief that he was rendering a service to his fellow-countrymen.

'The other, although of German origin, was the subject of a country which has already been ravaged by the legions of Hitler. This man offered his services to the enemies of his country from no other motive than that of the reward he would receive. He was not only a spy but a traitor, and he has now gained a reward different from that which he expected, but none the less deserved.

'These two men landed surreptitiously in this country some weeks ago. They posed as refugees from occupied territory, and brought with them iron rations and considerable sums of English money. They also carried a wireless transmitter, with which they could communicate direct with the headquarters of the German Secret Service.

'Fortunately their activities were short-lived, and they were arrested by the authorities. Once captured, they confessed and told of the instructions which they had received from their German masters.

'They had been promised that they would be quickly rescued by the German invasion forces: more evidence that in September Hitler did not reckon with the striking power of the Royal Air Force. They planned to spend the nights hiding in the woods, in quarries, or in uninhabited buildings. At dusk, they would have erected their wireless aerials and transmitted to the enemy valuable information, which they had obtained during the day. In the morning, they would have emerged from their hiding, leaving their equipment concealed in some convenient spot, to which they could return.

'They were to observe and report on all important military objectives, such as aerodromes, concentration of troops, gun emplacements and ammunition dumps. In particular they were to mix among the civilian population; in trains, buses and public houses, listening carefully to all careless talk broadcast by indiscreet citizens. This brings me to the main object of my broadcast tonight – careless talk.

'However successful our intelligence services and police may be in detecting enemy agents, we must never rely on the dangerous assumption that this menace has been completely eradicated from our midst. Modern methods of transport – the aeroplane, the submarine and the speed boat – and modern methods of communication, such as wireless, all facilitate the work of the spy. While we have been glad to welcome to our country many thousands of genuine refugees from Nazi oppression, the presence of so many foreign subjects in our midst can only make the detection of the spy more difficult. Whereas an English accent, heard in the streets of Berlin, might immediately betray the presence of a British agent, a foreign tongue spoken in Britain today does not even call for comment. It is therefore a most important duty for all of us to make the work of the enemy spy, who may be present in this country, as difficult as possible. We can do this quite easily if we make an absolute rule never to discuss any subject, likely to be of interest to the enemy, in a public place.

'Do you discuss such subjects in the bus, in your club, or on your way home in the train? You may look round quickly, and say to yourself – oh, it's alright, we're all friends here. Or you may say – well, there's no harm in talking about that here, because everybody here knows about it.

'But are you quite sure there is no stranger present? Are you sure that [in] all of the people round you, there is not one man who might be an enemy agent and ignorant of the things you are discussing? In a few hours, he may be sending this information back to the enemy, causing inestimable damage, and maybe the loss of valuable lives and property. Do you think for a moment that the enemy is only interested in what appears to you to be highly secret and important information. The main work of all intelligence services is piecing together scraps of information – perhaps from hundreds of sources – the net result of which may be the disclosure of operational information. Just one final word of advice. Many of us in the Fighting Services, in Government Departments and in the factories, have in our keeping information of the greatest value to the enemy. Remember this. The more people who know a secret, the greater the chance of it becoming known to the enemy. Don't pass on secret information to others, even though you may have every confidence in their integrity and though they may be working in privileged positions like yourself, unless it is absolutely essential in the interests of the work that they should be told.

'War calls for many sacrifices. And one which we must all make, men and women, young and old, is of the occupation – often pleasing and harmless in peacetime, but highly dangerous in war – Gossiping.
'Ministry of Information.'[33]

Following the broadcast, George Watson, Chief Officer in charge at Brixton Prison, wrote to Lieutenant Colonel Hinchley Cooke and asked that as the BBC had made the execution of Waldberg and Meier public, whether Pons should be kept in solitary confinement. With the exception of exercising for one hour per day, he had been kept in solitary since his acquittal.

It was stated in a communication from the Defence Security Services, by Brigadier 'Jasper' Harker, to B Branch (Espionage), 'How do you propose that we should continue to deal with Pons as I feel, the Home Office would begin to get a bit querulous about this and we must decide exactly what we want done.'[34]

Meanwhile, the governor of Pentonville Prison sent an internal memo to the Prison Commission and enclosed two letters written by Meier and four letters, in French, from Waldberg. The letters were written in the last day or two prior to their executions. Hinchley Cooke wished to see all letters, both in and out, for and from these men in case they contained anything of importance to MI5.

Chapter Ten

Epitaph for a Spy

Wednesday, 11 December 1940:
Bombers begin attacking Italian-held Sollum. The Italian Catanzaro Division is captured, delivering another 30,000 Italian prisoners of war.
Russian general Georgy Zhukov warns of a German assault.

The Under Sheriff for the County of London had written to the Under Secretary of State and informed him that he had just heard from Wandsworth Prison that Kieboom was now to be executed at Pentonville Prison. He was making the necessary arrangements on behalf of the High Sheriff for the execution to take place at Pentonville at 9 am on 17 December.

Brigadier 'Jasper' Harker was briefed by Sir Alexander Maxwell that the Home Secretary had been informed that, despite their agreement with Harker, no information should be given about the case of Waldberg and Meier beyond that given in the official press notice, and that the officer who gave a BBC talk was allowed to mention particulars which were not included in the agreed Press notice. The Press was naturally very angry that the BBC should have been allowed to disseminate information which was refused to the Press.

Harker was asked to look into the matter and let the Home Secretary know how it came about that the man who gave the broadcast talk was allowed to mention such particulars.

He added that as the Home Secretary was responsible for the Press notice and for telling the Press that no further information could be given to them, he would be forced to bear the blame for allowing the man who gave the talk to add certain particulars.

The Times newspaper had published a Home Office announcement under the heading 'TWO ENEMY SPIES EXECUTED' and the sub-heading 'WIRELESS TRANSMITTER FOR USE IN FIELDS', reporting on the arrest, trial and execution of Waldberg and Meier. Nearly half of the report paid attention to the wireless transmitter, accompanied by a photograph on another page. The conclusion of the article reflected that there was a lot of nervousness and consternation regarding 'Careless Talk', stating, 'In official quarters it is suggested that the capture of these two enemy agents emphasizes still more the need that the public exercise the greatest care when talking among strangers.'[1]

The *Daily Express* ran the headline 'Epitaph for a Spy', and printed one of the two notices posted outside Pentonville Prison. It said of Meier, 'Carl Heinrich Meier now here lying dead at His Majesty's Prison Pentonville ... was a prisoner in the said prison, indicted and convicted for felony-treachery and sentenced to death for the said offences ... judgment of death was duly executed and carried into effect.'[2]

In the wake of the executions, the important day-to-day intelligence work continued. Section B8L – the Counter Intelligence branch of B branch at MI5, responsible for security of camps in the war – produced a report on the Abwehrstelle at Brest, where the following was declared:

'Major Klug arrived in Brest on 20th August and insisted upon taking Unteroffizier Kokoschka and Holm to Le Touquet, to meet Major Seynsburg for a special enterprise. This was undoubtedly connected to the departure of the trawler *Mascotte* and the four spies, Waldberg, Kieboom, Meier and Pons, and it is found interesting to note that Klug confirms the fact that Major Seynsburg attached special importance to this expedition, and that he wished to be assured on the best advice possible that the trawlers were in good condition.'

After dates were checked, it was felt quite certain that the 'special enterprise' referred to in intercepts was none other than the departure of the four spies to England. The report continued that 'Krag' (presumably Klug) stated that he heard afterwards that the expedition had been entirely satisfactory, in direct contrast to his own abortive attempt, a few days later, with the *Anni Braz-Bihen*.[3]

This was not a 'little local difficulty' but an international one, as illustrated by the following memo, signed by an 'I.P.I.':[4]

11th December, 1940.

Mr Curry.

We wish to send to the DIB (Director of the Intelligence Bureau, India) particulars of wireless transmitting sets of the type likely to be used by enemy agents, to show the police in India what to look for.

We should therefore be very grateful if you could provide us with one or more reasonably sized photographs of the type of transmitting set used by German spies in England. An example was mentioned in the Home Office announcement published in to-day's papers about the spies executed at Pentonville.

Some members of the public were not at all thrilled with the executions. A Mrs A. McGrowther, from Glasgow, was one such person. Her letter,[5] dated the day after Meier and Waldberg's execution, read:

'Sir,

'I wish to protest to you against the execution of the two men who were trying to wireless information to Germany. It was a quite cruel and needless punishment [and] they could have been kept as prisoners till the war was over. The worst bit about it too was that we the British nation were art and pert in [i.e., in some way responsible for] their crime providing pubs and drink to loosen mens [*sic*] tongues to give away news. Actions like that will not help Britain nor the Labour Party who will soon be kicked out of office by their sometime friends the Tories.'

Thursday, 12 December 1940:
The 'Steel City' of Sheffield is subjected to a heavy bombardment.

The fallout from the BBC talk that was given continued to rumble on. Brigadier Harker regretted what happened, and explained that the intention was to release to the Press a copy of the talk given on the BBC some hours before the broadcast was made, so that any item of information given in that talk would be known to the Press before being disseminated over the airwaves. As it turned out, something went wrong with the timing and the 'advanced' copies of the talk did not reach the Press until the talk had taken place. For this, Brigadier Harker expressed his regret.

Harker was reminded that even if the timetable had worked properly, the position would not have been satisfactory because it would have still been open to the Press to complain that the Home Office, having stated that 'Editors are instructed not to press for any additional facts',[6] had nevertheless authorized a broadcast speaker to give certain additional facts.

Although the additions contained in the broadcast talk may have been seen as very meagre, every crumb of news of this kind was highly valued by the Press, and Harker felt that MI5 ought not to have added one crumb to what was previously announced as the maximum ration.

Two days after the execution of Meier and Waldberg, W.H. Waddams of the Prison Commission forwarded to Whitelegge at the Home Office the four letters from Waldberg and the two from Meier. The letters had been forwarded to the Commissioners by the governor of Pentonville Prison. Waddams wished Whitelegge to pass them to MI5.

A particular concern was raised to Meier's reference in his letter to Margaret Moseley wanting to hand detailed letters to Pentonville Prison's chaplain.

Reassurance was given to the Commission by the prison's governor that Meier had not handed over any letters to the chaplain of the prison.

Kynaston Metcalfe sent a note to the Under Secretary of State at the Home Office, which informed him of the deaths of Meier and Waldberg on 10 December, and enclosed the following documents: declaration of the Sheriff and others, one applicable to each case; certificates of the surgeon; and Coroner's inquisitions.

A telephone message to Hinchley Cooke from a Miss J. Williams at the Home Office pretty much ratified the date and place of Kieboom's execution: 'To confirm Tuesday at Pentonville.'[7]

As a result of this telephone message, Section B13 contacted B2, and informed them that Kieboom's execution would take place on 17 December at Pentonville Prison. B13 said that the DSS would possibly wish to consider the drafting of the Press announcement before he left for his usual weekend visit to the country office. There was some doubt as to whether the fact that Kieboom was half-Japanese should be mentioned.

A minute was sent to the Head Office of the Prison Commission on behalf of L.C. Ball, in which he submitted three newspaper reports on events surrounding the execution of Meier and Waldberg.

One newspaper, the *London Evening News*, which was printed on 10 December, led with the following headlines:[8]

TWO GERMAN SPIES EXECUTED
Bogus Refugees With One-Pound Radio For Use In Fields
APPARATUS FOR
NIGHT MORSE IN
TWO SMALL SATCHELS
One-Valve set to Send
Information to Germany
SPIES TOLD INVADING
ARMY WOULD FOLLOW

Friday, 13 December 1940:
Adolf Hitler issues Directive No. 20, undertaking Operation *Marita*, to prevent the English establishment of an air base in the Balkans, which would threaten Italy and Romania. To achieve this, the forces in Romania must be increased, to be moved across Bulgaria to the north coast of the Aegean when the weather permits.[9]

Brigadier 'Jasper' Harker at MI5, in a 'Secret' and personal letter, replied to Chief Constable 'Jock' Davison's original letter of 26 November, which had been headed 'Four Men in a Boat'. He apologized for not replying sooner, but said he was waiting until the question of any possible reprieve was finally decided. Harker, however, had instructed Hinchley Cook to keep Davison informed by telephone from time to time, generally through a Major Surtees, and he felt Davison must now be aware that the execution of the third man, Kieboom, had been fixed for 17 December.

Harker further explained that the reason for any delay was the fact that Kieboom first gave notice of appeal, and claimed that he was forced to spy because of vengeance that would befall his relatives. He later withdrew this appeal, relying entirely on his counsel's appeal to the Home Secretary for clemency.

Harker enclosed a copy of MI5's report – originally submitted on 9 December – to the Foreign Office for information of the Secretary of State. The report detailed the arrival of the four men, their being almost immediately apprehended, their stories as to why they were in England and their (lack of) documents. The report also gave details of their trial and the subsequent outcome.

Transcript copies of the whole of the proceedings at the Central Criminal Court were in the process of being typed, and Harker said he would send to Davison a complete copy, together with photostat copies of the principal exhibits, namely the prisoners' signed statements, as soon as they were available.

Regarding the question Davison raised in the original letter concerning Scotland Yard's involvement, Harker explained that both Hinchley Cooke and himself were more than sorry that there should have been any misunderstanding between the Chief Constable's department and Harker's office.

Harker reminded Davison that the four prisoners had been kept in military custody within the Metropolitan Police District for nearly two months when it was suddenly decided by a higher authority that they should be prosecuted, with as little further delay as possible. The Director of Public Prosecutions had decided (with the approval and consent of the Attorney General) that the case should be tried at the Central Criminal Court, availing himself for this purpose of Section 3 (3) of the Treachery Act, 1940 (nicknamed the 'Carted Stag' Section).[10]

In view of this decision, Harker said the case became one for a section run by a Mr Wallace (as against Mr Sefton-Cohen's section), and the former, through Vincent Evans, had instructed that Albert Canning, the Deputy Assistant Commissioner in charge of Special Branch, should provide an officer to take the prisoners over from the military into civil custody. This accounted for the fact that neither Mr Sefton-Cohen nor Sir Norman Kendal of Special Branch were aware of the matter at the time Davison asked them.

Inspector Bridges had subsequently been instructed by the Director of Public Prosecutions to take the prisoners into police custody and to charge them before a Metropolitan magistrate. Bridges was also instructed to get in touch with the officer in charge of Seabrook Police Station, to which the prisoners had been brought by various people as a result of them being arrested, for the purposes of ascertaining whether the various witnesses, especially the military ones, were still available, and linking up their statements with the different exhibits which had been handled by a good many people in the moment of first excitement and had subsequently been brought to London and handed over to Hinchley Cooke.

Hinchley Cooke was instructed to accompany Inspector Bridges so that the different witnesses could formally hand over to him the various exhibits, thus overcoming a break in the chain of evidence.

Harker explained to Davison that he appreciated that Inspector Bridges telephoned the Divisional Superintendent at Ashford and advised him that he was coming, and that Hinchley Cooke instructed Major Grassby, Harker's normal link with Davison, to inform him that he was accompanying Bridges.

Harker added that he understood that Hinchley Cooke had called on Davison at his Headquarters the day after he had seen him at Seabrook, and explained the case to him and his detective superintendent.

Harker repeated that Hinchley Cooke had endeavoured to keep Davison personally informed of every phase of the proceedings, and ensured Davison that he would have been admitted, without delay, to the Police Court proceedings, and the trial at the Central Criminal Court, had he wished to attend.

Harker ended the letter by saying that he hoped he had made the position quite clear, as he was anxious that there should be no room for misunderstanding in such delicate matters.

In May 1940, Winston Churchill had appointed the Canadian, William Maxwell Aitkin, a.k.a. Lord Beaverbrook, as the Minister for Aircraft Production (MAP). Major Turner from the War Office (public relations) now rang Desmond Orr at MI5 to say that Lord Beaverbrook wanted to borrow the wireless apparatus found in the possession of the German agents recently executed, for his Spitfire Exhibition that was being held in Leeds until 28 December.

Orr spoke with Captain Guy Liddell, MI5's Director of Counter-Espionage, who had no objection to the apparatus being lent for this purpose. Lieutenant Colonel Hinchley Cooke arranged with Special Branch to deliver the apparatus to Room 055 (MI5's room in at the War Office), and when it was delivered, Orr issued a receipt.

Orr then contacted the MAP's Public Relations Branch and spoke to someone called Nash, who sent a colleague, W. Robin Douglas, in a taxi to Room 055, to take delivery of the wireless equipment; he subsequently issued a receipt and thanked everyone for their prompt handling of the request. Robin Douglas acknowledged the receipt, from Room 055, of two leather cases that contained wireless apparatus for the Leeds Spitfire Exhibition, and that they were returned as soon as possible after 28 December.

Meanwhile, Major Turner rang Orr's office to say that Paramount News wanted to take a film of the apparatus. Other newsreel concerns had been granted permission by Scotland Yard, but he could not say what the concerns were, or on whose authority they had acted.

In the absence of confirmation, Orr had explained to Major Turner that the apparatus was already at Leeds, and that if Paramount wanted to film they needed to obtain permission from the Home Office and/or Ministry of Information and/or whatever authority was concerned, after which Lord Beaverbrook would gladly have allowed the film to be taken at the exhibition itself. Nash had previously agreed to this, on the suggestion that the film would have helped rather than hindered the financial success of the exhibition.

A deciphered telegram was received by MI5 from the Royal Canadian Mounted Police (RCMP) in Ottawa:

> 'We are anxious to secure details of the wireless sets discovered in the possession of the two German spies, executed at Pentonville on Dec. 10th. Diagrams of the sets are essential and also your means of discovering them. We have strong suspicions that similar equipment is in use in Canada. Our information has been received through the press.'[11]

Saturday, 14 December 1940:
Extracts from a report from the Chiefs of Staff Committee:

French.
Officers and Men in the Royal Navy.

There are now 567 Frenchmen in the Royal Navy. The majority of them are now at sea, mostly in French ships taken over by us.

Morale is generally very good. Discipline is improving, though still somewhat below our standards.

There is no change in the feeling of contempt for the Vichy Government.

Slight interest is taken in General de Gaulle's operations; the general himself appears to be regarded with respect. The RN French are whole-heartedly loyal to us and confident of victory; they regard themselves as British in every way.

Army.
Strength: Camberley –

	Officers	Other Ranks.
Foreign Legion	5	43
Remainder	61	721

Equipment issued during month:

Rifles,	300	1,000
Bayonets	–	1,000
Motor cycles, solo	–	7

Employment – normal training has taken place, including route marches.
Tank units have been given instruction in the driving of all vehicles.
Welfare – the provision of an institute, to be ready by Christmas, has had a very good effect.

Air Force.
The RAF Franco–Belgian Air Training School at RAF Odiham is now in full operation, with a full establishment of pupils. In the first week of flying training, in spite of bad weather conditions, 180 hours were flown.

Fifteen Free French pilots are serving in RAF fighter squadrons, and the destruction of two enemy aircraft has been credited to them during the month.

A telegram message had been swiftly dispatched by B2 to the RCMP in response to their telegram:

'Reference your telegram of 13th December. Detection was by Police methods, not by W/T interception.
'Particulars of W/T sets are following by mail.'[12]

The reply to Brixton Prison's Chief Officer George Watson's letter of 10 December stated that Pons should remain in solitary, at least until the execution of Kieboom, when the situation would be reviewed.

The Home Office responded to Kynaston Metcalfe's letter of 12 December, acknowledging, under direction from the Secretary of State, receipt of his letter and the following statutory documents relating to the executions of Meier and Waldberg: declaration of Sheriff and others; certificate of surgeon; and Coroner's inquisition.

Monday, 16 December 1940:
At 9.30 pm, a War Cabinet Defence Committee (Operations) meeting is in progress. It is pointed out that in the event of a German move into Spain, it would be advantageous to have in hand a small force, such as that prepared for Operation *Workshop*, which could go at once to the assistance of the Spaniards, or to act as the advanced guard of a larger force for operations in North Africa. There would be no great disadvantage arising from a postponement of Operation *Workshop*, and it is therefore agreed that it would be better to keep the forces for the present in this country, where they could continue their training.[13]

The Home Office was in a dilemma regarding Mrs McGrowthers's letter of 11 December, which berated the decision to execute Meier and Waldberg. An internal minute asked the question, in response to Mrs McGrowther's letter and her protestations, 'Lay this by?'

M.H. Whitelegge recorded that the governor of Pentonville Prison rang and enquired about instructions regarding Kieboom's execution. After consultation with George Griffiths at the Home Office Press Department, who had received an approval notice for the Press and had been in communication with the governor, Whitelegge rang the governor and informed him that the 'drill' in connection with Kieboom's execution was to be exactly the same as in the cases of Meier and Waldberg.

A memo was sent to Lieutenant Colonel A.M. Heape, Chief Military Advisor to the Censorship at the Ministry of Information, in which was enclosed a copy of the press announcement to be issued on 17 December to the News Department of the Ministry of Information:

<u>Draft Announcement to the Press (for 17.12.40).</u>
A third enemy agent acting on behalf of Germany was executed at Pentonville Prison to-day, following his conviction at the Central Criminal Court on 22nd November.

His name is Charles Albert van den KIEBOOM, a Dutch subject, born at Takarumuka [*sic*], Japan, on 6.9.1914.

This agent was tried at the same time as the other two, who were executed last week and with whom he was associated. He was similarly equipped with a portable wireless transmitting set.

The date of execution was postponed in KIEBOOM'S case because he gave notice of appeal to the Court of Criminal Appeal, but he subsequently withdrew this application.

<u>Note to Editors</u>
Editors are again asked not to press for any additional facts or to institute enquiries.

Editorial comment might profitably take the form of drawing public attention to loose talk of all kinds, particularly in the presence of strangers.[14]

The problem as to what to do with Pons was still not resolved. Further to the note from 'Jasper' Harker on 10 December, a hand-written annotation on the note read, 'Home Office are trying to arrange for a Home for Incurables on the Isle of Man in which Pons might suitably be placed.' Harker annotated, after that last comment, 'Let me know what is settled.'[15]

Tuesday, 17 December 1940:

On 8 December, Prime Minister Churchill wrote to President Roosevelt informing him that the British would very soon not to be able to pay for materials supplied by the United States.

Today, the President gives a Press Conference, delivered at the White House in Washington, in which he proposes a Lend–Lease programme providing for military aid to any country (more than thirty over the course of the war) whose defence is vital to the security of the United States. Recognizing that it is in America's best interests to help Britain, the plan gives Roosevelt the power to provide – or 'lend' – the supplies that Great Britain needs to continue its fight against Germany. The USA additionally does not insist upon immediate payment, but there is the understanding that, after the war, America will be paid back in kind.

Kieboom took the '9 o'clock walk' and was executed. Curiously, Kieboom came from the same country as Mata Hari (Margaretha Geertruida 'Margreet' MacLeod), the notorious female spy, exotic dancer and allegedly a lover of Admiral Canaris. She was executed in France during the First World War for being a German spy.

The press release regarding Kieboom's execution was issued to the Press Bureau for general Press and broadcast release.

The governor of Pentonville Prison also issued the following statement[16] to the Under Secretary of State Office:

CAPITAL CASE.
8748. Charles Albert Van Den Kieboom.
Sir,
    I have the honour to inform you that the above named was executed at this prison at 9 am today the 17th instant.
    The execution was carried out without a hitch.

Kynaston Metcalfe also issued a declaration which stated that Kieboom had been executed, and it was witnessed by the prison governor and prison chaplain, and signed by said witnesses.

James Liddell, the surgeon at Pentonville, issued a certificate which stated that he had examined the body of Charles Albert van den Kieboom and confirmed that the man was dead. William Bentley Purchase issued a declaration, signed by the jurors, that he was satisfied that the body he had examined was indeed that of Charles Albert van den Kieboom and that the death sentence was lawfully carried out.

Whitelegge wrote to Hinchley Cooke, and forwarded the two letters written by Meier along with those written by Waldberg, all composed on 9 December, the day before they were executed. Meier's letters, the ones written in English, did not give concern, but Whitelegge could not fathom the one written in Dutch, so he had requested a copy of the translation from Hinchley Cooke.

Waldberg's letters, on the other hand, did cause a little concern. While in one of them he conceded he had received good treatment while in prison, he complained that English justice had failed him. He alleged that *inter alia*, he was deceived into pleading guilty and that his trial took just three minutes. Whitelegge noted that his records showed that Waldberg made passionate complaints on the same matters to the Home Office, which reflected unfavourably on the British justice system.

Whitelegge's concern was that such statements from Waldberg may well have been prejudicial from the Home Office's point of view, if there were any question of forwarding them to their destinations. Whitelegge considered the possibility of discussing the matter when Hinchley Cooke had time to consider the letters.

Wednesday, 18 December 1940:
Adolf Hitler issues Directive No. 21, *Case Barbarossa*, an order for the invasion of the Soviet Union.

Kynaston Metcalfe had written a note for the Under Secretary of State at the Home Office, which informed him of the death of Kieboom and enclosed the declaration of the Sheriff and others, the certificate of the surgeon and the Coroner's inquisition.

Brigadier Harker issued a note to accounts that requested B13 were to be given a cheque for £51.13.-, payable to 'The Director of Public Prosecutions' in respect of the transcript of shorthand notes in the Rex v. Kieboom (and others) trial.

The public were by now informed that three men had been convicted and executed. A photograph of Waldberg's radio transmitter had even appeared in *The Times*. An important consideration in favour of publicity was that it would be advantageous for the morale of the people of Britain to know that some spies had been caught and brought to justice.

The letters written by Meier and Waldberg, which were submitted to the Home Office by the Prison Commission for disposal, had been studied by Whitelegge, and he issued a Home Office minute. He observed that of Meier's two letters, one was in very good English and the other in Dutch. From the point of view of the Home Office, they did not appear to contain anything that was objectionable.

Waldberg's letters were all written in French, and while he appreciated that he was treated well in prison, he again complained that the counsel assigned to him could not speak French, that he was 'deceived' into pleading guilty and that the trial lasted just three minutes.

Whitelegge declared that he could hardly imagine any question of these letters being despatched to their overseas destinations; but if they should, then Waldberg's letters, in particular, would hardly pass as they stood. The letters were sent on to MI5's Hinchley Cooke.

Thursday, 19 December 1940:

Meeting at 4.30 pm, the War Cabinet has before it a Memorandum by the Secretary of State for Air, the Right Hon. Sir Archibald Sinclair, Bt, MP, proposing improved and extended arrangements for pre-entry training for the Royal Air Force.

The Secretary of State for Air explains the arrangements under his scheme at the universities, public schools, secondary schools and other schools. In addition to these, his scheme will provide pre-entry training for young men who have already entered industry. This part of the scheme will be drawn up in consultation with the Minister of Labour. Broadly speaking, the object of the pre-entry scheme is to prepare for Air Force service boys and young men from the age of 15 upwards, who are not at present up to the educational requirements.

In view of the prospect of heavy casualties in the 1941 and 1942 campaigns, it is inevitable that a long waiting list for entry into the Royal Air Force should be maintained.

MI5, or more specifically Brigadier 'Jasper' Harker and Dick Goldsmith White, sent Commissioner S.T. Wood of the RCMP in Ottawa details and photograph of the wireless set as requested by his telegram of 13 December.

Saturday, 21 December 1940:

The Liverpool Blitz continues with an intense raid on the city.

Chief Constable 'Jock' Davison, of Kent Police, responded to Brigadier Harker's letter of 13 December, and thanked him for satisfactorily explaining the whole and very difficult matter of the 'Four Men in a Boat' case. He said that Hinchley Cooke had been to see him and filled in the bits and pieces of the case, although it had not really been necessary.

The Chief Constable was perfectly happy regarding future cases under the Treachery Act, and wished to forget any little differences that there may have been in the past between the Kent Police and MI5.

Davison thanked Harker for letting him have the transcript of the notes of the case, which, he said, would forever be a document of very historical interest to members of his force, notwithstanding the fact that they only played a 'small and humble part'. He was particularly glad to receive it as he thought that such a document would, in the far and distant future, tend to emphasize upon the young entry to the force the 'Chapter and Verse' tradition of which they were so jealous, and which he hoped would continue to stand so high.

Davison concluded by saying that Harker may rest assured that the document would be kept under lock and key 'until the happier times of peace return', and gave the brigadier his best wishes for Christmas and the New Year.

Whitelegge responded to Kynaston Metcalfe's letter of 18 December, reporting that he was directed by the Secretary of State to acknowledge receipt of the Under Sheriff's letter and the documents from the Sheriff, surgeon and Coroner relating to the sentence of death and execution of Kieboom.

Monday, 23 December 1940:

German bombers sink the SS *Breda* in a convoy off the coast of Scotland. The ship is not directly hit, but a nearby bomb blast causes it to sink.

The editor of *Practical and Amateur Wireless* wrote a short letter to the Home Secretary, asking for permission to take photographs of the miniature transmitting sets found on the spies who were recently executed, and to publish circuit details of the equipment. He said he would be glad if such facilities could be placed at his disposal.

Friday, 27 December 1940:

The continuing heavy storms, strong winds and exceptional cold are beginning to affect troop morale in Malta. After thirty-six hours of non-stop rain, military chiefs order a rum ration to be issued to troops to help cope with cold desert nights.[17]

Pentonville governor L.C. Ball forwarded a letter, written in Dutch by Kieboom on the morning of his execution, to the Prison Commissioners for information and disposal.

Monday, 30 December 1940:

London digs out from the Second Great London Fire caused by the Luftwaffe raid on the previous night. Royal Engineers and other troops are brought in to bring order to ravaged streets and dynamite destroyed buildings in the City of London.[18]

Kieboom's letter that was sent to the Prison Commission on 27 December was now forwarded to the Home Office ('C' Division).

Tuesday, 31 December 1940:

During December, 3,793 civilians are killed and 5,244 injured in bombing raids.[19]

A cheque was eventually dispatched to L.N. Vincent Evans, of the Department of the Director of Public Prosecutions, for the sum of £51.13.0 in respect of the trial transcripts for the account of Messrs Geo. Walpole & Co. A formal receipt was requested.

Thursday, 2 January 1941:

A meeting of the War Cabinet is held at 10 Downing Street at 11.30 am. It hears that the attack on Bremen the previous night, in which 133 heavy and fifteen medium bombers had been engaged, appeared from preliminary reports to have been highly successful. No British aircraft had been lost during the operation, but three Wellingtons manned by Polish crews had crashed on landing. Two of the crews were killed.

An interesting report is received from General Heywood on conditions on the Greek Front. Notwithstanding the very rigorous conditions, which caused some frostbite, the Greek Army were in very good heart.

The Minister of Food, the Right Hon. Lord Woolton, says that a reduction in the ration is necessary, first, because home farmers have not recently offered as much meat as they had been doing and, secondly, because of the decline in imports. He had taken soundings as to what effect the reduction in ration would have on labour, and had been assured that it would cause no trouble. The Minister says that it is necessary to ration pork and offals in order that poor people might be able to obtain them. He is fully aware of the importance of cheese in the diet of manual workers, and is already distributing cheese in larger quantities to industrial areas and taking the risk of other areas going short.

It is suggested that when the reduction of the ration is announced, attention should be called to the Press to the fact that even the reduced meat ration is considerably above the 1918 ration. Emphasis might also be laid on the success that had attended the rationing system during the war, and to the complete absence of food queues.

The War Cabinet agrees that the meat ration should be reduced to 1s 6d a week as from 6 January, pork and offals included.

The War Cabinet has before it a memorandum by the Minister of Labour and National Service, The Right Hon. Ernest Bevin, MP, asking authority to submit to His Majesty the draft of a new Proclamation to register and call up further age-classes under the National Services (Armed Forces) Act.

For the second time, German bombs fall on Ireland.

The letter from the editor of *Practical and Amateur Wireless* of 23 December 1940, asking permission 'to take photographs of the miniature transmitting sets found on the spies recently executed, and to publish circuit details', was forwarded by M.H. Whitelegge at the Home Office to Lieutenant Colonel Hinchley Cooke.[20]

Whitelegge felt that this was not his 'pigeon', but it seemed to be a matter for Hinchley Cooke and his department at MI5 rather than the Home Office. If he agreed, he was asked to arrange for a reply to be sent direct to the editor.

Whitelegge sent Hinchley Cooke a further letter written in Dutch by Kieboom on the morning of his execution, which was originally forwarded by the Prison Commissioners for disposal.

Vincent Evans at the Director of Public Prosecutions sent a receipt to Hinchley Cooke for £51.13.0 in respect of the trial transcript. Instructions had been given for payment to Messrs Geo. Walpole & Co.

Friday, 3 January 1941:

As part of Operation *Compass*, the first British military operation of the Western Desert Campaign, British forces assault the Italian army at Bardia, inside the Libyan frontier. They capture 45,000 troops, 129 tanks, 400 guns and 706 trucks.

G.F. Clayton, governor at Brixton Prison, had written to Hinchley Cooke asking whether, as the third 'confederate' (Kieboom) had now been executed, Pons should still be kept in solitary confinement?

Monday, 13 January 1941:

At 11.20 am, a brand new Handley Page Halifax MK1, from 35 Squadron, takes off from Linton-on-Ouse in North Yorkshire for a fuel consumption test. About 30 minutes later, the aircraft is seen at about 3,000ft, with the port undercarriage down and a trail of vapour behind the port side of the aircraft. One of the port engines is also seen not to be working.

A large fire erupts on the port side of the aircraft, after which it enters into a steep dive before crashing at 11.35 am. All six men on board are killed. The crew were prepared to bail out but when the aircraft entered its spiralling dive, they were unable to. This is the first Halifax incident in Yorkshire.

Pons arrived at Camp 006 in Lingfield, Surrey, the Racecourse Aliens Camp.

Tuesday, 14 January 1941:

The Government announces new price controls to try to prevent food profiteering. Price freezes are announced for more than twenty food items, including coffee, rice, biscuits and jelly.

In a 'Secret' memo[21] to Air Vice Marshal Sir Philip Game, GCVO, GBE, KCB, KCMG and DSO, the Commissioner of Police of the 'Metropolis', New Scotland Yard, Brigadier 'Jasper' Harker congratulated the police on their involvement in the capture of the four spies:

'My dear Commissioner,

'Now that the case of Rex v. KIEBOOM and others has been brought to a satisfactory conclusion, I should like to express to you my very great appreciation to the excellent work done by Detective Inspector F Bridges and Detective Sergeants F Coveney, G Smith, S Buswell and D Allchin.

'Lt Colonel Hinchley Cooke, who, as you are aware, was handling the case at this end, informs me that he has nothing but admiration for the way in which all these officers put their very best into this case, which goes down to history as the first one under the new Treachery Act, and for the very happy relationship existing between Special Branch and himself.'

Wednesday, 15 January 1941:

The British Air Ministry issues a directive to Bomber Command regarding the importance of German oil targets.

Whitelegge at the Home Office contacted Hinchley Cooke. Making reference to his letters of 17 December 1940 and 2 January 1941, he requested from the MI5 man – if only for his records – translations of the letters Kieboom had written in Dutch. He added that he would also like to know, from a military point of view, the fate of the letters.

Thursday, 16 January 1941:

At a meeting of the War Cabinet at 10 Downing Street at 11.45 am, the Minister of Home Security, the Right Hon. Herbert Morrison MP, says that on the previous night raiding had been sporadic, but widespread, mainly over the North Midlands and London. Damage of national importance was slight, apart from interruption of the LNER mainline at two points north of Peterborough. As many as 100 people might be trapped as a result of a bomb in Lambeth.

Apart from this incident, the casualties of the previous night are:

	Killed	Injured
London	18	50
Elsewhere	22	38

Attention is drawn to several recent telegrams suggesting that the Germans are considering the use of gas against the country. The general public had grown slack in anti-gas preparations; and very few people now carried gas masks. The Minister says he is considering steps to secure that anti-gas preparations are in a state of readiness.

Tuesday, 21 January 1941:
Australian infantry with sixteen Matilda tanks attack Tobruk in Libya, forcing the surrender of 25,000–30,000 Italians and capturing eighty-seven tanks.

R.L. Hughes, Radio Security Services Liaison, W6B, sent an internal memo, addressed to Major Robertson but which was seen by Hinchley Cooke, in which he attached a page from the *Picture Post* of 28 December. The cutting carried pictures from the *Daily Express*, *Daily Telegraph*, *Daily Mirror*, *Daily Herald*, *News Chronicle* and *Daily Sketch*. The pictures showed different people with the captured spies' radio set, and the *Picture Post* asked,

> 'You remember those German spies they caught? You remember their radio set? It seems to have changed hands a lot. All the papers show it in the hands of someone different ... But what happened to the little radio set? Almost every London daily paper photographed it. We reproduce their photographs ... Each one shows the set in possession of someone different. What we want to know is who did have the radio set, anyway?'[22]

Hughes pointed out that the valve shown in the *Daily Express* was different to that shown by the *Daily Telegraph*, and that the cases in the *Herald* picture did not appear to have buckles and straps attached to the covers. Hughes ended the memo with the missive, 'We will hope that all these photographs are of the same set!'[23]

Friday, 24 January 1941:
The United States of America denies a Vichy French request to welcome German Jewish refugees to America.

Pons had remained at Camp 006. Here, Pons remarked that even he could not understand how he had escaped the death sentence. His captors were under the impression that he could not speak German, but it was reported that he was actually teaching another prisoner the language.

Monday, 10 February 1941:
The British War Cabinet elects to offer Greece military assistance.
    The largest aerial raid over Germany sees more than 222 British aircraft bomb Hanover, causing enormous damage. Seven bombers are shot down.
    The British four-engine Short Stirling bomber debuts in active service. Its target is the oil tanks at Rotterdam.

Pons was returned to Camp 020 at Ham Common, where he remained in internment.

Tuesday, 18 February 1941:

Thousands of Australian troops arrive in Singapore to prepare the region for a possible attack by the Japanese.

The German troops fighting in North Africa officially receive the name Deutsches Afrikakorps (German Africa Corps).

In an extract from a letter from Lord Swinton to 'Jasper' Harker regarding the transfer of internees from Latchmere to a special 'Black Sheep Pen', Swinton stated:

'I confirm that I have arranged with Sir Alexander Maxwell that the three Cuban spies ... shall be transferred from Lingfield back to Latchmere House, as also Pons, if he has not already been transferred.

'These men should not be kept in solitary confinement. As far as is practicable at Latchmere and without interfering with its investigation work, men who are held there, instead of being held in an internment camp, should be allowed to associate as they would in the segregated house we hope to establish in the Isle of Man.'[24]

Wednesday, 19 February 1941:

First day of the Allied authorities meeting in Cairo, Egypt, to review the situation in Greece. It is agreed to commit some 100,000 British soldiers to the fighting.

Exactly two months since Brigadier Harker sent Commissioner Wood of the RCMP details and photographs of the wireless set found in possession of Waldberg and Meier, the Commissioner replied to Harker, saying that having carefully examined the information, 'we are at a loss to understand the use of the chart shown ... therefore we would appreciate if you could supply us with a circuit diagram of the set in question, which it is presumed, would explain the use of the chart'.[25]

Saturday, 22 February 1941:

Arthur 'Bomber' Harris becomes British Air Marshal.
Nazi SS begins rounding up Jews in Amsterdam.

Between 4 pm and 4.45 pm, an interrogation of Pons was conducted at Latchmere House by Lieutenants Goodacre and MacIntosh. The summary[26] of this interrogation simply regurgitated what was already known, with no new information forthcoming:

1. The object of the interrogation was to remove the obscurity enveloping the circumstances of Pons' departure from Le Touquet and thereby obtain a clearer picture of the way in which the Brussels Four was linked with the activities around Brest-Stelle and the subsidiary organization at Le Touquet/Paris Plage.

2. At the end of August, Pons was taken by car from Brussels to Chateau Wimille; about 15 minutes drive from Boulogne.

3. No officers lived there but the Chateau was visited daily by a naval Kapitan who went by the name of Klapps. Klapps instructed on the geography of the English coast. Notwithstanding, although he appeared fairly conversant with the English coast, Pons considered that the officer had never been to England but only observed the coast frequently from the sea. He was a Naval Reserve officer who, in peace time, had been in the Merchant Service.

4. 8 am, 2 September, and Pons and his party were taken to Paris Plage in two cars, a journey of about 1½ hours. Shortly before reaching Le Touquet they crossed a bridge over a river (the Canche at Etaples) and while crossing, Pons saw two aeroplanes landing on the Le Touquet side. The aerodrome was hidden from view and Pons wouldn't of [sic] known it existed had the two aircraft not landed there.

5. Ten minutes after crossing the bridge they stopped in front of a villa; Pons thought that it may had been a residence as a woman was cooking. There was no guard at the front, but there were a number of soldiers at the back.

6. At the villa, Pons and his party were handed over to a Major who was in a room with seven or eight other officers, including naval officers, all of whom, he thought, were captains. One or two of the army officers wore the Iron Cross, but none of the naval officers. The officer spent a few minutes with the men separately, indicating to them on a map where they were to land on the English coast, and their operating area.

7. After lunch the men were taken by car to a small jetty where a motor boat took Pons, Kieboom and Klapps to board one of five moored fishing smacks. Klapps returned to the jetty and took Meier and Waldberg to board a different boat. Pons could not name any of the five boats.

8. Pons claimed that the crew on his boat was: a Norwegian captain and engineer, and a Russian deck-hand. The Captain and the Russian both spoke English.

9. The Norwegian Captain mentioned to Pons that he had already dropped 'people' on the English coast. Pons did not enquire further as to when this happened; he only knew that the trip was made from some point on the French coast and he thought that [the] same boat and crew were used.

10. Waldberg and Meier's boat had a crew of four or five and was larger than Pons and Kieboom's. That was all Pons could say about it. They left at

about 2 pm arriving Boulogne about five hours later. They were then taken in tow by minesweepers across the Channel.

11. Neither Pons nor Kieboom ever went to Brest: they had, however, been told by Kapitan Klapps to say, if captured, that they had come direct from Brest in a fishing boat.

Monday, 24 February 1941:

The Greek Government agrees to allow the British Army to enter the country for defence against German forces.

The British twin-engine Avro Manchester bomber makes its debut in active service. Its first mission is against warships at Brest.

Three months after the verdict on the 'Brussels Four', Lieutenant Colonel Robin Stephens at Ham Common was still very unhappy with the court verdict given to Pons. In a 'Secret' report, he wrote: 'Having escaped the gallows by some inscrutable decree of Providence, this man is slightly unnerved and has not unreasonably come to the conclusion that it would be well to cooperate with us.'[27] Stephens decided that a lot of the information gleaned from the subsidiary interrogation conducted by Goodacre and MacIntosh was of purely academic value, but nonetheless valuable as background information. Part of the interrogation, however, was not satisfactory to Stephens. He referred to point 9, where Pons claimed that the Norwegian captain had told him that he had already made one trip to the English coast and dropped 'people' there. Pons did not enquire further, but knew only that the trip was made from some point off the French coast, and he gathered that the same boat and crew had been used.

Stephens concluded that it was impossible to estimate whether this information was true. He added that while some agents had been given Dutch courage by being told that other agents had preceded them, with several parachutists informed that agents had been successfully landed in numbers, no real foundation had been found to support this. Stephens did, however, attach a great deal of importance to the 'vast' number of refugees who were appearing in Britain, and he did not have the slightest doubt that 'infiltration' had occurred.[28]

Thursday, March 27 1941:

The Home Secretary and Minister of Home Security, the Right Hon. Herbert Morrison MP, says that enemy activity has been on a small scale, both by day and by night, in the last few days. Enemy bombs had been dropped on the previous day at Yeovil, Gloucester and Overton, and Northolt Aerodrome had been machine-gunned.

In the first report of the raids on Clydeside on the 13/14 and 14/15 March, it had been stated that the casualties had been small in relation to the severity of the attack. This statement, which was inaccurate, had given rise to some feeling among the people on Clydeside, and in consequence it had been found necessary to depart from the normal rule whereby figures of casualties in particular raids were not published, and an announcement had been made that the figure of killed was 500. The latest information showed that the number killed was about 1,040. Mr McGovern, MP, had put down a question in regard to the number of casualties, and there was considerable pressure in favour of publication of a revised figure, in order to satisfy public opinion of the reliability of official figures.

In discussion, it is suggested that this showed the desirability of adhering as closely as possible to the rule of not publishing figures of casualties in particular raids.

People with little or no connection with the capture of the spies had tried to claim cash remuneration or glory by declaring an involvement that, in reality, often bore little or no relation to the truth. The capture of Carl Meier was no exception. Some three months after his execution, a Mr R. Metcalf Silvester of 16 De Cham Road, St Leonards-on-Sea, Sussex, through his MP Maurice Hely-Hutchinson, raised with the Home Office the question of reward and/or acknowledgement of the value of his services in capturing the spy:[29]

'Dear Sir,

'Whilst I was in Lydd last August I was instrumental with the aid of a friend in capturing Karl Meier the German spy who was executed at Pentonville recently.

'I wrote to the Home Secretary on Jan 7th of this year but beyond a curt circular letter informing me that my letter had been forwarded to the War Office, I have received no acknowledgement or expression of gratitude from the appropriate Government department.

'In view of the fact that my friend and I undoubtedly ran a great deal of risk in detaining this man I suggested that the £60 Meier had on him might be divided between us as some recognition of our services and also to know if another man who had not been located at the time had been arrested in case we could be of further service.

'As a member of your constituency I was advised to write to you to report what seems to me a rather deplorable lack of appreciation of a definite service to the state.

'I can, if you wish, send you a detailed account of the incident and in the meantime should be grateful if you could bring the matter before the right quarter.'

Wednesday, 2 April 1941:
At 5 pm, during a meeting of the War Cabinet held at 10 Downing Street, the Chancellor of the Exchequer, the Right Hon. Sir Kingsley Wood MP, communicates to the War Cabinet full particulars of his financial proposals for the forthcoming Budget.

Mr Silvester, replying[30] to his MP's letter dated 31 March, hinted at some financial reward for his alleged efforts in the capture of Meier, and failing that said some recognition may well be advantageous for his 'future R.A.F. career':

'Dear Sir,

'Thank you for your letter of March 31st. In order that you may be aware of the facts I enclose a statement of the facts relating to the capture of Meier.

'Quite seriously I do not expect any reward but I had an idea that the property found on a spy or prisoner could be claimed by the captor. I am probably wrong ober [sic] this.

'I did think that the capture might keep me in my future R.A.F. career and that [is] one of the reasons I venture to place the matter before you.

'Thanking you for the courtesy of your reply.'

The following[31] is the detailed explanation in which he explained his role:

'Related by R.M. Silvester.

'Karl Meier. Captured August 1940. Executed December 10 1940 at Pentonville.

'I had to visit Lydd, Kent on business and stayed with some friends at Ness Road there. Having transacted my business I suggested to my friend that we should go for a stroll and reaching the Rising Sun I suggested the heat (it was August) called for a drink. On entering we were struck by the agitation of the Landlord's wife. The reason for this was soon made clear to us. In a whisper she told us "There is a strange man in the next bar and he has been hanging about outside since 9 o'clock this morning; I'm sure he's up to no good; he came in as soon as we opened and ordered a Champagne cider and some biscuits and has been here about an hour, do please go in the Private Bar and see what you think of him." Our curiosity being aroused we at once entered the next Bar. His appearance and unusual style of clothing struck us immediately as he sat at a small table sipping his drink and munching biscuits. His clothes touched the Sea [sic] and contrasted strangely with his rather refined appearance. We perhaps were too obvious in our scrutiny of him as he looked decidedly ill at ease and gulping down his drink called for the Landlord's wife to pay for what he had consumed, [and] rising to his feet he pulled some loose change from his pocket which he regarded dubiously showing clearly that our money was strange to him. Strangely enough his accent was distinctly American and we were expecting to hear broken English as he had a most Teutonic caste of features. Pocketing his change and with a gruff "Good morning gentlemen" he made his way into the street, crossed the road and entered a small General Stores opposite.

"'Come on", said my friend, "let's follow him." We watched him purchase more biscuits and lemonade, [and upon] emerging he set off down the Dungeness Road towards the sea. We rushed to my friend's car[,] got in and drove off in the same direction, stopping a little ahead of him and alighting.

"'Can I see your Identity Card", I queried, accosting him. "I am very sorry", he said, "I have not got one yet but shall be having one shortly but you can see this", and he then handed us a passport shewing [*sic*] him to be a naturalized Dutch subject born in Coblenz, Germany. His name was given as Karl Heinrich Meier and he told us he was a Medical Student and had been to Heidelberg and other German Universities.

'He also elicited the information that he had paid the Skipper of a French Cutter, 5,000 francs for his passage and 1500 francs for a sack of food, cigarettes and Cognac.

'He had been dropped at dead of night several miles off the coast in a small rowing boat and had landed in the early hours of the morning on Dungeness Beach, [then] hidden his sack of food in a wrecked lifeboat which came off the French Liner *Normandie*, and had to our knowledge been lying on the beach for some months. He had then made his way across a long stretch of rough beach and open country, slept behind and [*sic*] empty bungalow and then made his way into Lydd town. How he managed to elude the vigilance of the sentries and patrols which are posted at frequent intervals guarding the coast, is a mystery; beaching a boat and walking over shingle must have made a great deal of noise in the still of the night.

'After a little more questioning we prevailed upon him to enter the car, turned round and took him up to Lydd Police Station.

'Meier seemed very much taken aback (this was probably due to the fact that he had not been in touch with his compatriot who had landed in the same fashion equipped with a portable wireless transmitter and both we subsequently learned had been told that if captured they would soon be released on the arrival of Hitler's Invasion troops) at being captured so soon and wanted to know what authority we had to detain him but we skipped over that and told him if he was all right we should be the ones to get into trouble ... As he entered the car he said, "You've caught me I guess and I don't mind what happens to me but I refuse to go back to Germany." He had either some good reason to fear going back or possibly having failed in his mission was in dread of some punishment. At the Police Station he was searched and found unarmed but had nearly £50 in English money on him, a small collection of foreign stamps, French coins and cigarettes and a few personal papers. These were retained by the Police.

'The Police gave him a good meal and washing facilities. We were asked to wait at the Police Station whilst they contacted Seabrook Police Station [near Hythe] for further instructions. He was asked to send the prisoner to Seabrook and we were asked to take Meier over there with Police Sergeant Tye. We set off and [passed] through Dungeness. We encountered a boy with a bicycle on which was balanced a large sack, fairly well filled. He turned out to be the Coastguard's son and he had found the sack of provisions in the derelict lifeboat as Meier had informed us. The sack was thereupon handed to Tye and was packed into the car and a little further on we stopped at the Coastguard's look-out there to learn that several other fugitives were being searched for who had reached the coast in the same manner as Meier. We were later to hear at Seabrook that another man had been found posing also as a Dutchman having in his possession over £80 in English money also revolver and ammunition.

'Passing through Dymnchurch [*sic*] our captive expressed surprise on the havoc wrought by German bombers but remarking [*sic*] that Holland had suffered much more in comparison with what little he could see. He also informed us that he had earlier in the morning been all over Lydd Church and expressed his admiration of the building.

'After a few minutes conversation he asked for permission to look in his sack and shewed [*sic*] us the contents which included Iron rations, cigarettes, French bread, cheese and other foodstuffs, and several bottles of French Cognac. A bottle of the latter he wished us to accept but Tye gave us no chance of accepting [and] he jyst [*sic*] put it back in the sack.

'Running the gauntlet of fairly intensive air activity we arrived at Seabrook Police Station. Meier there pleaded that he was a Dutch subject but was asked to complete a lengthy form which he did quite willingly until the question of signing and stating his birthplace and nationality. He here protested stating that he would be signing his death Warrant.

'This formality he was allowed to rest on a bench in the Police Court and went out into the Station yard where we saw the other "Dytchman" [*sic*] taking a little exercise with a Police guard. He like Meier seemed resigned to his fate and anxious to be on good terms with us all.'

It is interesting to note that Silvester said in his letter that his encounter with Meier took place in August, but of course this may just be an innocent mistake. His second statement mentioned the heat. Meier and his compatriots did not arrive in England until 3 September!

Thursday, 10 April 1941:
The first US combat action against Germany occurs: USS *Niblack*, a Gleaves-class destroyer, fires on a marauding German U-boat violating the US security zone.

A handwritten internal memo to MI5 (B2) requested: 'Would you kindly advise on a reply to Mr Sylvester's [*sic*] request please?'

Tuesday, 15 April 1941:
A message, designated 'Hush Most Secret', is sent from the Admiralty to C-in-C, Mediterranean, stating:

'A). It is evident that drastic measures are necessary to stabilize the position in the Middle East. After most thorough investigation it is considered that air action alone against Tripoli will not sufficiently interrupt the flow of reinforcements which are entering Libya chiefly through that port.

'B). Also taking into account the countermeasures which the Italians and Germans can use such as making their convoys pass down the Tunisian coast by day covered by dive bombers it is not considered that the interruption to their traffic which we can achieve by either submarines, surface craft working from Malta, or torpedo aircraft will suffice to stop this flow.'[32]

The handwritten internal memo from 10 April was passed by Section B2 onto B13, which stated that as they (B13) had settled the matter of Silvester's previous request, would they kindly reply to this, on behalf of Dick Goldsmith White.

Sunday 27, April 1941:
By midday, German panzers enter Athens, capital of Greece.

Regarding Silvester's claim, MI5's R.N. Speir suggested that Silvester should be informed that his request for a reward or other acknowledgement for services rendered would have been noted with other such claims, and 'will come up for consideration at the successful conclusion to present hostilities'.

Thursday, May 1 1941:
Lord Beaverbrook moves from being the Minister of Aircraft Production to Minister of State.

Friday, May 2 1941:
The British at Habbaniya in Iraq launch an attack on Iraqi forces building up outside the base.

A letter was sent to Maurice Hely-Hutchinson MP from a Richard Law regarding Silvester's part in Meier's capture and subsequent reward/recommendation.

The MP was reminded that official letters of thanks and/or monetary awards for the rendering of services such as those Silvester stated that he had made were only issued after the cessation of hostilities.

The main reason for this was that espionage trials were generally conducted in camera, and only official statements concerning them were permitted to be published. Anyone giving evidence at such trials came within the provisions of the Official Secrets Act, and must, on no account, disclose to anyone anything they had seen or heard.

In the trial of Meier – with whose arrest Silvester was concerned – the Judge made a definite order to this effect, and it would therefore not only be contrary to precedent, but also in direct opposition to an order by the High Court to issue a letter of thanks to Silvester.

The letter concluded that the authorities concerned were noting Silvester's desire for a reward or other acknowledgement with other such claims, and his case would come up for consideration at the successful conclusion of hostilities.

Thursday, 15 May 1941:
British forces launch Operation *Brevity*, an offensive to see if the German position east of Tobruk was fragile enough for the siege to be lifted without a major battle, and to push Rommel back from the border between Egypt and Libya.

Acting as an intermediary for Pons, Mary T. Kranock from Olean, New York, USA, had written a rather formal letter[33] to him. When Pons received the following letter was unknown:

'Dear Mr Pons,

'I wrote to your wife as you requested, and received a letter from W Pons, stating that your wife, mother and all are well.

'Try and write me again as they are longing for further news from you.'

Interestingly, the letter was address thus: Mr Sjoerd Pons, No 94275, Internment Camp No 006, Great Britan (*sic*), % Internees and Prisoners of War Dept., Postal and Telegraph Censorship, Liverpool, England.

Sunday, 25 May 1941:
The Royal Navy sloop HMS *Grimsby* is sunk by German aircraft off Tobruk.

On instructions from B2C, 'Robert' (again possibly Lieutenant Colonel Robin Stephens) was sent a copy of a letter from the exotically named MI5 officer Helenus Patrick Milmo to Goldsmith White. Milmo's note dealt with a selection of people for the proposed 'Black Sheep Pen' on the Isle of Man. Pons' name came to the fore. 'Robert', in particular, was getting very agitated about information being leaked to the Germans.

In a letter addressed to Goldsmith White, 'Robert' expressed concern about handing over control of spies to the Home Office for transfer to Stafford Gaol and the Isle of Man establishment 'unless there are cast iron rules calculated to prevent communication with the outside world'. 'Robert' did not want to appear to be difficult or hold up the proposed transfer, but he felt that he needed to know exactly where he stood before he gave recommendations. He thought that regulations should be laid down for both places, for it was only by such means that leakages would be prevented.

'Robert' felt that he could not help Goldsmith White with recommendations, but did highlight a point about Pons that should receive consideration, describing him as 'a difficult, dangerous and surly customer, and I do not at all like the idea he should be sent to Stafford, even as a companion'.[34]

Tuesday, 10 June 1941:
The British take the port city of Assab in Eritrea.

Aircraft examiner Horace Rendal Mansfield, of 43 Cromwell Street, Gloucester, clearly felt that he had a vested interest in Meier's arrest, and was now actively seeking recognition in another direction. Mansfield wrote[35] regarding the matter to the news editor of the *Sunday Express*, J.L. Garbutt:

'Sir,

'Last December three of four German agents who landed in this country by boat under cover of darkness were executed. Of these Carl Heinrich Meier the first to be hung was caught by me at Lydd in Kent and I attended as a witness the trial of all four men at the Old Bailey. I made a few notes and I can still remember details of the trial 'tho as time goes on I naturally am forgetting some of these details.

'What I am getting at is whether you are interested in the story for publication in your paper. If so would you be [so] good as to communicate with me as to what you would desire.'

Garbutt despatched a journalist, William Kerr Bliss, to Gloucester. Bliss was on the staff of London's *Evening Standard*, but was currently on attachment to the *Sunday Express*.

Bliss arrived at Mansfield's house at about 9 pm, explained where he had come from and produced his card and Mansfield's letter that was sent to his editor. The pair settled down in Mansfield's living room and he began to tell the journalist how he apprehended Meier. Bliss copied the story down in longhand and, at about 9.40 pm, suggested that they go out for a drink. The two men, accompanied by Mansfield's wife, retired to the New Inn Hotel. There, Mansfield handed over some pencilled notes.

Wednesday, 11 June 1941:
The RAF bomb the Ruhr and Rhineland, for the first of twenty consecutive nights.

Mansfield and Bliss met again. Bliss asked Mansfield to clarify some points, which he did. Mansfield produced the subpoena he had received to give evidence at the Old Bailey.

From his notes, Bliss wrote two articles, one long and one short. From the latter piece, he deliberately omitted, with Mansfield's approval, a number of points; for example, how suspicions were aroused leading to the arrests. Bliss destroyed his original notes 'contrary to professional practice', as a safeguard.

Saturday, 14 June 1941:
Over 15,000 Latvian citizens are deported to forced-labour camps. Families are separated and possessions confiscated.

Bliss submitted his copy to the *Sunday Express*, with the catchline 'The Kent Spies'.

Garbutt, the paper's news editor, wrote to Mansfield to update him on the situation:[36]

'Dear Mr Mansfield,

'Unfortunately, I had to send Mr Bliss of our staff away from Gloucester to Liverpool, and he was unable to re-contact you.

'The article is now awaiting the Censor's approval and we will discuss the matter of payment immediately that approval has been obtained. I hope this suits you.'

Tuesday, 24 June 1941:
The Secretary of State for Foreign Affairs, the Right Hon. Anthony Eden MP, says in the House of Commons: 'The Prime Minister, on Sunday night, told the world after his own unrivalled fashion of the decisions at which His Majesty's Government had arrived as a consequence of the German invasion of Soviet Russia ... The House and the country will, I think, desire to take a severely practical view of these matters. We keep our eye on the target; that target is Hitler's Germany. Let us pay him the compliment of understanding that he too keeps his eye on the target, and that target

is the British Empire, which he still rightly regards as the chief obstacle in his path to world dominion.'

Bliss returned to London, where he received instructions to go to the War Office and was ordered to hand over the documents dealing with the Mansfield/Meier matter to Lieutenant Colonel Hinchley Cooke, who informed him that there was a judge's order banning any publication.

Wednesday, 25 June 1941:
Luftwaffe raids over Britain continue. The Blitz has not ended, even if there has been very little activity over London since 10 May.

Bliss made a written statement at the War Office:[37]

'I am a journalist on the staff of the *Evening Standard*, temporarily attached to the *Sunday Express*.

'The letter dated 10/6/41 and signed HR Mansfield was handed to me in the course of my duties by the News Editor of the *Sunday Express* Mr JL Garbutt, with instructions to go to the address given in the letter and interview the writer. On Tuesday, 10 June, in accordance with those instructions, I went to Gloucester. I saw Mansfield at about 9 pm on that day. I told him I had come from the *Sunday Express*, produced his letter, and my card. He asked me in – he was living in rooms and told me the story of how he assisted in apprehending a German spy in the Lydd area.

'I took notes, practically all in longhand. At 9.40 pm, I suggested that we should have a drink, and he and his wife came with me to the New Inn Hotel. Little more occurred that night. I saw him again the next morning, by arrangement, and asked him to amplify certain points, which he did. On this occasion, he referred to a sheet of paper on which were certain pencil notes. This was at the New Inn Hotel.

'Either at this interview or the preceding one, he showed me the Subpoena he had received to attend the proceedings in question at the Central Criminal Court. From the notes which I had taken at the interviews, I subsequently wrote two stories, a short one and a long one, which were submitted to the *Sunday Express*. From the short story a number of points were deliberately omitted with the approval of Mr Mansfield. The original notes taken by me in pencil were destroyed subsequently by me. This is contrary to professional practice, but I did it as a safeguard.

'On my return to London, from other duties, on Tuesday, 24 June, I received instructions to call at the War Office and hand over the documents dealing with this matter to Lt Col W Hinchley Cooke. I was informed by Col Hinchley Cooke that there was a Judge's order prohibiting any disclosure of information in connection with the Trial of the persons mentioned to me by Mr Mansfield, I had no knowledge of such order having been made.'

'Robert' contacted Goldsmith White via a 'Secret' communiqué. He was incensed at another leakage of information and pointed the finger clearly at Pons. There were two letters addressed to Pons, redirected from Camp 006 in Lingfield, Surrey. 'Robert' staunchly defended his Camp 020 and claimed that as the letters were initially addressed to Camp 006, he felt that it clearly showed the letters to which they replied must have been sent from there. Furthermore, he stated that Pons had never been allowed to write or receive letters at his camp.

'Robert' cited a line in the letter, 'We are so terribly happy to have a sign of life from you', pointing out that that his family, and thus presumably the Germans, were unaware until 25 April 1941 of Pons' continued existence. He went on to say that it seemed obvious that until Pons' letters arrived, no news of his arrest or subsequent career had percolated through to the enemy, and that, as a consequence, his letters should never have been allowed to leave the country.

He ended the letter by saying that, as far as could be ascertained, no mention was made in the Press reports of the trial of Pons. The conviction of the other three was broadcast, and he hoped that the Germans would infer that Pons had turned King's Evidence, and that they themselves 'will ring his neck in due course'.[38] Just a few months after the arrival of the Brussels Four, Mansfield, in his letter to Garbutt, did mention 'four German agents who landed in this country'.

Sunday, 29 June 1941:
Oliver Lyttelton is appointed Minister of State.

Monday, 30 June 1941:
At 5 pm, a meeting of the War Cabinet is held at 10 Downing Street. The Minister of Information, the Right Hon. A. Duff Cooper MP, makes a statement saying that in his view there is need for a strong Central Propaganda Department, equipped with adequate powers to overcome the weaknesses inherent in the present arrangements. Yet the present proposals will leave the Ministry in a weaker position.

The Minister of Supply, the Right Hon. Lord Beaverbrook, supports the view taken by the Minister of Information, and says that the country requires a freer flow of news. The proposals he has made are aimed at bringing into existence an authoritative body which can give directions for propaganda in its various forms and co-ordinate a propaganda campaign.

In a 'Secret' letter sent to Goldsmith White, 'Robert' was concerned that further communications had been received en-route to Pons. They were from Amsterdam, dated 15 May 1941, and were letters from his father, mother, brother Mart and Gerda, presumably his sister. 'Robert' did not know what had happened to his letter of 26 June 1941 – there was no record of this letter – but reinforced that his sentiments expressed in the last paragraph still stood.

He enclosed for Goldsmith White the four (translated) letters[39] written to Pons. They appeared matter-of-fact and fairly innocuous, save for the issue that security protocol had been breached and the Germans may be aware that Pons had escaped the gallows. Interestingly, each family member spelt Pons' Christian name as 'Stoerd':

'Dear Stoerd,

'From America on the 11th April we received a letter from a lady who informed us that you were in England in an Internment Camp and were quite comfortable. This was the first news that we had received of you. Your letter to TO was the second. We are writing you separately as it is possible that her letter would not get through.

'The first months of this year we were very anxious and it was a relief when your letter came from America. We are writing back direct and I imagine that by the end of the month you will have news of us ... Do you need money then to buy one thing or another? Perhaps we can attend to it, at least if it can be sent. Mother, Mart and Gerda are all well. I, however, am suffering with rheumatism again. All the best; take care of yourself and write as often as you can.

'Father'

'Dear Stoerd,

'I hope that you received TO's letter. Our joy was so great when we received your letter that it was indescribable. We are looking forward to receiving your next letter soon or may you not write much? We are so glad that you are in good health. We too are well except that Father is suffering badly again, but everything will be all right in the end, as always. Stoerd, when you receive this you will have had your birthday, but probably not able to celebrate it – you are too fond of cake anyway! With a hearty kiss from your loving,

'Mother
'[PS] Greetings from Dirk.'

'Dear Stoerd,

'We were very pleased with your letter. What a troublesome time you must have had. We were in terrible anxiety; it was especially bad for TO and Mother, but at any rate the dread passed. We are longing for the war to be over and your return home. I have received three letters from JAAP via STTY (?) although I have not received any news from him for some time. I sing a lot for the radio. Can you hear me sometimes? My singing is going very well and I have plenty to do. Now Stoerd, take care of yourself.

'Goodbye, with a kiss from,

'Gerda'

'Dear Stoerd,

'Every time that you write and we receive a letter, things are better, so write often. Here everything is all right except that there is not much work. I must, however, congratulate you on your birthday. It will be much too late, but better late than never. Your motor is in the shed and I hope that I shall soon put it together. I don't know if you know that SYB GORTER has had an accident with a machine in a factory. He was struck dead. Not nice news but here follows better news. HENKMAST married his DEPPIE on May 1st. I am still unmarried and shall remain so, I think. Now Stoerd, I will close. Good luck, till we see you,

'Your brother,

'Mart'

Tuesday, 1 July 1941:

General Wavell is replaced by General Auchinleck as Commander-in-Chief, Middle East.

The Western Desert Force is reformed as the Eighth Army.

Mary Kranock's involvement with Pons through her letter of 15 May attracted the attention of MI5. They requested, via MI6, a 'Look-Up'. Their concern was that Mary 'has written to a Dutch internee having apparently been in touch with his family'.[40]

In an internal memorandum, Helenus Patrick Milmo requested a translation of a letter sent to Pons, which was written in Dutch.

Friday, 4 July 1941:

At a meeting of the War Cabinet held at 10 Downing Street at 10 am, the Lord Privy Seal, the Right Hon. C.R. Attlee MP, in the Chair, informs members that the Prime Minister has decided that instructions should be issued that all defences should be brought to the very highest state of anti-invasion efficiency by 1 September. In the meantime, no vigilance should be relaxed. Instructions had been issued in this sense by the Chiefs of Staff to their Commanders-in-Chief, and the Prime Minister asked that this direction should also be brought to the notice of all Civil Departments.

The Lord Privy Seal adds that he understands that the Prime Minister proposes to issue a suitable warning to the public before long.

The War Cabinet invites all Ministers to bring this instruction to the notice of those concerned in their Departments.

In a short discussion, it is explained that this directive is not intended to prevent the despatch of any necessary reinforcements to the Middle East.

As requested by Milmo on 1 July, a translation is made of the letters[41] sent to Pons by his wife and parents:

'Amsterdam. 25th April '41.

'Dear Boeviedik! (literally 'Fat Scallywag')

'Received your letter this morning, and you can imagine how delighted Mother, Father, Gerda, Mart & I are. We are so terribly happy to have a sign of life from you. I can't put in writing what and how much I am thinking of you. Oh, little boy, how worried I have been. I hope I shall never have to go through all this again – I couldn't stand it a second time, I was in such despair at times. But that is all over now, and you know that I love you more every day. Mother is as happy as a child! My boy will understand that, won't he! Cor and Elsa are also frightfully pleased, and have of course asked me to send their best wishes. I hope that this letter won't take so very long reaching you, as you must be bursting with impatience. Everything is alright here. We are all well, and now that we know that you are all right nothing else matters any more. Billy is all right, too – except for being a bit jealous of our new kitten. Oh, darling there's so much that I'd like to write you – only what I am thinking cannot be put in writing. I feel quite plainly that you are thinking of me a lot! You must look upon every day as one day nearer to our re-union. Mother has just said, in an anxious tone of voice: "Don't write so much now, Jo!" She's afraid that she won't get a turn – but this is only one of my jokes, really.

'Darling, I must let Mother & father write a few words now. Laddie, much love from your own little wife. It's not a good photo that I am enclosing, but it was taken to-day and I had to have one immediately. I'll send you a better one later on. Good-bye, little ragamuffin, much love and kisses (?) all from me.

'Jo'

'Dear Sjoerd,

'Oh, how glad we are that we have now heard from you that you are all right. At times it has been unbearable, but you will have gone through that, too. This has made me cry, too, but only because I was so happy. Father, Mart & Gerda & I shall write to you in a couple of days' time. One of these letters is sure to reach you. Cor & Elsa will be writing too. I shall stop now, so that Jo can post this straight away. Courage, now Sjoerd, and let's hope that everything will soon be all right again. A kiss from your loving Mother, Father, Mart & Gerda.

'Best wishes from your little niece (cousin) Willy! Also from Anny & Pa (or from Anny van Pa) etc!

'Good-bye "boeviedik" much love.'

Tuesday, 15 July 1941:
In the Soviet Union, Smolensk falls to German Army Group Centre.

Milmo sent a memo to Lieutenant Colonel Stephens at Latchmere House, admitting that the leakage of information happened at Internment Camp 006, Lingfield, where Pons was permitted to write letters. He said it had transpired that there was an intermediary involved, Mary T. Kranock, from Olean, New York, USA. At least one letter from her was sent to Pons when he was at Camp 006. Security checks on her revealed nothing, and Milmo advised Stephens that nothing more can be done 'save to take care that there is no repetition'.

Friday, 18 July 1941:
Stalin writes to Churchill, saying, 'It seems to me that the military position of the Soviet Union, as well as that of Great Britain, would be considerably improved if there could be established a front against Hitler in the West – Northern France, and in the North – the Arctic.'

Horace Mansfield was still very anxious for recognition. A flurry of letters between himself and the editor of the *Sunday Express* ensued, beginning with the following:[42]

'Dear Sir,

'I do not appear to have heard from you since your letter dated June 14th 1941.

'Have you heard from the Censor as to whether approval will be granted?

'I would appreciate hearing from you regarding the position.

'H.R. Mansfield'

Tuesday, 22 July 1941:
Japan and Vichy France agree to a mutual defence pact.

Garbutt replied to Mansfield, but the news was not very encouraging:[43]

'Dear Mr Mansfield,
   'I have to acknowledge your letter of July 18th.
   'The only information I can give you is that the matter is still under consideration by the Censor.'
                                  'Yours faithfully,
                                     'J.L. Garbutt'

Tuesday, 29 July 1941:
Lord Beaverbrook is appointed Minister for Supply.

Saturday, 6 September 1941:
In Japan, the Imperial Conference decides to accept the risk of war with the United States.

Several weeks had passed, and Mansfield was still in the dark as to whether his story would be accepted for publication and, of course, any consequent remuneration. He wrote again to Garbutt:[44]

'Dear Sir,
   'With reference to your last communication with me some few weeks ago.
   'Are you yet in a position to let me know whether or not the Censor has given approval or how long it will be before this may be anticipated?
                                  'Yours faithfully
                                     'H.R. Mansfield'

Tuesday, 9 September 1941:
Alfred Duff Cooper, British Minister of State and Chancellor of the Duchy of Lancaster, arrive in Singapore on a special mission in the Far East for the British Government.[45]

The news for Mansfield had not improved:[46]

'Dear Mr Mansfield,
   'Thank you for your letter.
   'The story is still held by the Censor, and in my judgement it will not be released until after the war.
                                  'Yours faithfully,
                                     'J.L. Garbutt'

Friday, 3 October 1941:
Hitler makes a public speech at the Berlin Sportpalast, his first since the German invasion of the Soviet Union began on 22 June. He declares that Russia is 'to a great extent' already destroyed and that Germany has the capability to 'beat all possible enemies' no matter 'how many billions they are going to spend', a remark that appears to be directed at the United States.

In a 'Secret' report issued by Lieutenant Colonel Stephens at Ham Common, he said that two further letters had arrived for Pons at Camp 020, one from his wife and another from an intermediary. The one from Pons' wife, after translation, appeared not to contain any secondary meaning, while that from the intermediary also appeared innocuous on the surface, but Stephens said he would still like them to be tested.

Friday, 10 October 1941:
German U-boat torpedoes US destroyer *Kearney*.
 RAF bombs Piraeus in Greece to prevent German heavy armour advancing.

MI5 officer Helenus Milmo had written to H.L. Smith and attached two letters, presumably destined for Pons, and requested that they be tested for secret writing. 'They may be tested to destruction,' advised Milmo.

Monday, 13 October 1941:
Hitler continues to make overtures to Britain and the British people that he wants peace between them and Germany, and that the only reason they are at war with Germany is because of Churchill.[47]

Dick Goldsmith White wrote to Captain P.E.F. Finney at MI5, sending photographs of Meier, Waldberg and Kieboom. He added, 'I hope they will serve to spur the imagination of your hearers [i.e. those who listened to Finney]!'[48]
 During mid-July 1940, Captain Finney had run the office of the North Wales branch of the British Secret Service from a modest, requisitioned property in Colwyn Bay (chosen after a nationwide search). There was a top-secret plan – *Hegira* (after the Arabic term for the prophet Muhammad's enforced departure in 622 from Mecca) – in which double agents would be evacuated from London in the event of the capital being captured after the invasion. The agents could not fall into enemy hands, so rather than shoot them and their families, they would be given a bolthole in Colwyn Bay. Finney was responsible for accommodating them there.
 H.L. Smith sent back to Milmo the two letters that had been fully tested. No secret writing was found.

Tuesday, 14 October 1941:
On the Eastern Front, fighting ends in the Vyazma Pocket, an encirclement of Soviet Red Army troops in Vyazma by the Wehrmacht's Army Group Centre.

Milmo returned to Stephens, at Camp 020, Pons' two letters which had been sent to him on 3 October. He told Stephens that no secret writing was found on either letter.

A friend of Meier, who shared a student hostel with him between April and July 1937, was now interviewed. He said that he had seen a letter from R. Metcalf Silvester regarding Meier's capture and the latter's alleged involvement. The interviewee said that in Silvester's letter, Meier had said that his fiancée was 'Scotch', and that her father was a tobacco manufacturer in Scotland. He recalled that there was a girl in the hostel who fitted that description, and added that Meier probably mentioned her to try to prove his British connections.

Sunday, 7 December 1941:
At 8 am (local time), Japan launches surprise attack on US Pacific Fleet at the US Naval Base at Pearl Harbor, Hawaii, signalling America's entry into the war and the start of the conflict in the Pacific.

Monday, 8 December 1941:
Britain and the United States declare war on Japan.

Wednesday, 10 December 1941:
Following the pre-emptive Japanese strike on Pearl Harbor, the Royal Navy cruiser HMS *Repulse* and the battleship HMS *Prince of Wales*, part of Force Z (a British naval squadron formed as a deterrent to aggression against British possessions in the Far East), are overwhelmed in the South China Sea by waves of land-based Japanese bombers and torpedo carriers.

At 11.40 am, seventeen Japanese planes appear, diving down to torpedo-release height. Nine planes attack the *Repulse* and eight the *Prince of Wales*. At 12.20 pm, twenty-six Betty torpedo bombers swoop on the *Prince of Wales*, sealing its fate. Torpedo planes also attack the *Repulse* from both sides, and the ship is struck four times. By 1.20 pm, both ships are sunk. In all, over 1,000 of the ships' crewmen were rescued, but some 840 were lost to fire, explosions or drowning.

Wednesday, 4 February 1942:
Lord Beaverbrook is appointed Minister of (War) Production.

Thursday, 5 February 1942:
Japanese planes attack convoy ships near Singapore at 11 am. At 11.05 am, SS *Empress of Asia* is hit. Twenty minutes later, the fires below decks are out of control. By 1 pm, all surviving personnel are off the ship. The crew (which numbered 416), includes seven military and eighteen naval gunners, plus 2,235 troops who are being transported. One crewman dies and fifteen troops are missing.

One of the senior secretaries at Camp 020, Miss M.H. Clegg, had taken the initiative and produced a Liquidation Report on Pons, Kieboom, Meier and Waldberg, as it was now considered an 'older case'. A Miss Dandison and Miss Yuile also used their initiative and produced Liquidation Reports on other spies.

The following is an extract of the Liquidation Report compiled by Miss Clegg:

'Kieboom was not prepared to give any information of value and only after persistent pressure the code was obtained. After midnight, Stephens re-interrogated him and many of the lies that he had told during the first interview had been rectified, according to Stephens.

'Kieboom had been frightened by the Germans to such an extent that even during interrogation he was too afraid to tell the interrogators anything because of what the Germans will do to him after they have conquered Britain. He did admit to having pushed his codes into a lavatory while he was under military guard before being turned over to the local police.

'Kieboom asserted under interrogation that it was only when he had reported in Brussels and asked for an explanation of the need for training, that he and Pons were given the option of undertaking a mission to England on behalf of Germany, or being sent to a concentration camp for smuggling currency. He tried to convince his interrogators that he accepted the first alternative in the belief that it offered him a chance of surrendering to the British authorities.

'Of the four spies, Meier showed the most readiness to give information in interrogation. Kieboom was so afraid of the Germans and of the expected invasion that information came out with difficulty and then was not always reliable.

'Considerable information on preparations for invasion, military objectives in enemy countries, the organization of the GSS [German SS] and their agents was given by these spies during their internment. Waldberg, Meier and even Kieboom, who when invasion failed to come became almost servile, all agreed to transmit messages for the British authorities.'

Thursday, 19 February 1942:
Sir Stafford Cripps is appointed Lord Privy Seal, replacing Clement Attlee.
Clement Atlee is appointed to the Dominions office.

Saturday, 7 March 1942:
The first class of five African–American Tuskegee Airmen (a group of African–American military pilots, navigators, bombardiers, mechanics, instructors, crew chiefs, nurses, cooks and other support personnel who form the 332nd Fighter Group and the 477th Bombardment Group of the United States Army Air Force) graduate.

Miss Clegg's Liquidation Report, as well as those produced by the other two secretaries, were forwarded on to ADB1 from Camp 020. Stephens thought it valuable for record purposes and of considerable interest for him in particular, 'because fresh minds have been brought to bear upon the particular problems'. He hoped that ADB1 would consider issuing instructions for distribution to the relevant files.

Thursday, 12 March 1942:
Oliver Lyttleton is appointed Minister of (War) Production.

Thursday, 19 March 1942:
R. Casey is appointed Minister Resident in the Middle East.

Thursday, 2 April 1942:
Sir Kinahan Cornwallis, the new British ambassador to Iraq, arrives in Baghdad.

More letters for Pons had arrived, which continued to give cause for concern. Lieutenant Colonel Stephens, in an internal memo to MI5's Helenus Milmo, requested that two letters he was sending him be tested for secret ink.

Saturday, 4 April 1942:
A telegram for Prime Minister Winston Churchill from General Smuts, Prime Minister of South Africa, designated 'Most Secret', is received at 1.20 pm. It states:
  'I do not wish to put spanner into the works and sincerely wish Cripps Mission all success, at same time India is now key to our whole Empire defence and putting that Key in unskilled Indian hands may have fatal results for this war.
  'Please insist that final responsibility for defence measures will rest with our High Command whatever ancillary defence powers are devolved on India.
  'Divided military control may spell ruin both to Indian and Empire defences.'

Milmo sent H.L. Smith the letters that belonged to Pons which needed to be tested for secret writing. Once again, the advice given was, 'They may be tested to destruction.'

Wednesday, 8 April 1942:

At 12 noon, at a meeting of the War Cabinet held at 10 Downing Street, the Foreign Secretary reports that arrangements have been made, and are now proceeding, for an exchange of sick and wounded prisoners with Italy in the Mediterranean. He adds that better progress is now being made with arrangements for the repatriation to Italy of Italian civilians from Ethiopia.

Smith returned Pons' two letters to Milmo after they were tested for secret writing, no evidence of it having been found. However, Smith said the letters had been tested before, presumably by the Germans. It was only between the lines of clear writing which had not been tested. There was, of course, the possibility that testing had already been carried out by British censorship, the method being essentially the same. He concluded that it was difficult to decide one way or the other.

Saturday, 11 April 1942:

The Joint Intelligence Sub-Committee produces a report on 'Enemy Intentions':

We have examined German and Japanese strategy in the light of the development of the war in Europe and in the Far East, and have reached the following conclusions, which do not differ materially from our previous views.

CONCLUSIONS.
GERMANY.

Germany's Major Offensive.
(a) Germany's first major offensive effort in 1942 will be made against Russia.
(b) It will start in the south.
(c) Its objects will be to defeat the Russian armies and to get oil.

Subsidiary Operations.
(a) Germany will maintain and intensify her attacks on allied shipping. In particular she will attack the Northern supply route to Russia by sea and air.
(b) Germany will support her forces in Libya to enable them to maintain, and if possible, to exploit their position. She will try to maintain her present air power in the Mediterranean.

Germany is unlikely to attempt, until after the defeat of Russia–

(a) An invasion of the British Isles.

(b) An occupation of the Iberian Peninsula, Sweden, or French North or West Africa.

(c) An attack on Egypt through Cyprus and Syria.

(d) An attack on Iraq and Persia through Cyprus and Syria or Turkey.

(e) An attack on Caucasia through Turkey.

(f) A move into Turkey, unless Turkey acquiesces.

JAPAN.

Japan will aim at:

(a) Consolidating as quickly as possible her East Asiatic sphere and completing it by the occupation of Burma.

(b) Achieving peace in China.

(c) Occupying bases in the South-Western Pacific to cut the sea-route from America to Australia.

(d) Compelling us to dissipate our troops and disperse our naval forces by raids and threats of raids.

Milmo had written to Lieutenant Colonel Stephens at Camp 020 to tell him that the letters destined for Pons had been tested but the results were negative.

Wednesday, 22 April 1942:

The Chiefs of Staff Committee produced a 'Note on the Transfer of Certain Training to Canada':

Consequent upon the decision to transfer to RAF transferred schools in Canada the work of all but one RAF Service Flying Training School (College) and the Polish School (No 16 (P) SFTS), it has been necessary, in agreement with the various national authorities to arrange for all Free French, Czechoslovak, Dutch, Belgian, and some Polish pupil pilots to be sent to Canada to complete their Flying Training. For the present the Polish Elementary and Service Flying Training Schools will remain in England.

Although arrangements have been made to complete the training of a few more Allied Air Observers in the United Kingdom, the rule in future will be that Air Observers, as well as pupil pilots, must complete their training in Canada.

During the period under review the following Allied pupil pilots and observers have left the United Kingdom for Canada:

Free French	10 pupil pilots.
Poles	28 pupil pilots.
	21 pupil observers.
Czechs	13 pupil pilots.
Belgians	1 pupil pilot.

Second Lieutenant J.P. de C. Day, at MI5, wrote to H.L. Smith and asked him to test a letter he had attached, which was addressed to Pons, for secret writing. Again, the advice was that it 'may be tested to destruction'.

Thursday, 23 April 1942:
Hitler is incensed when the British make a heavy bomber raid on the Baltic port of Lübeck, causing 1,000 deaths and massive destruction. He orders reprisal raids against historic British towns. In the first, against Exeter, twenty-five bombers cause widespread damage and seventy deaths.

H.L. Smith replied in a 'Secret' letter to J.P. de C. Day and said that the letter addressed to Pons had been fully tested, but no indications of secret writing had been found. However, as happened previously, the letter also showed indications of previous testing. Smith returned the letter.

Saturday, 25 April 1942:
The Würzburg Gestapo orders some 800 Jews from nineteen different sub-districts and three different counties (a total of eighty different communities) to present themselves in Platz'schen-Garten, for the purpose of 'evacuation'. Seventy-eight Jews from Würzburg are also ordered to present themselves.[49]

J.P. de C. Day informed T.L. Winn, the Camp 020 interrogator (and dentist), that Pons' letter had been submitted, as Winn requested, to a major test for secret writing, again without result. The only observation the Scientific Section had to make on it was that it showed some indications of previous testing. The letter was sent to Winn.

Sunday, 19 July 1942:
Reichsführer-SS Heinrich Himmler issues a general order to the higher SS and the Police Leader in the General Government (the area of Poland under Nazi military control) that, by 31 December 1942, SS and police authorities should 'resettle' all Jews residing in the Central Government, either to the killing centres or in closed camps located in major cities.

SIS wrote to Camp 020 and asked that certain questions be put to Pons. The questioning would take place on 22 July by Lieutenant Shanks.

Wednesday, 22 July 1942:
Treblinka extermination camp becomes operational in occupied Poland. Mass deportation of Jews from the Warsaw Ghetto to Treblinka begins.

Responding to the request by SIS to put certain questions to Pons, Lieutenant Shanks briefly interrogated the prisoner:[50]

INTERROGATION of PONS

<u>by</u> – Lieut Shanks   <u>Date</u>: 22.7.42   <u>Time</u>: 12.45–13.00 hrs.

PONS was trained in wireless every morning from 9am to 12 noon for one month at No 4, rue Stevin, Brussels.

————————————

1. Had this address a name?
   No.
2. Was there a Belgian or German doorkeeper? Can he give any details about this man?
   There was no doorkeeper employed, as the house was empty, and no property was left in the building. All apparatus etc was brought in the morning, and taken away at the end of the instruction period.
3. What other people were there in the building?
   None.
4. What formalities had to be observed in entering or leaving the building?
   None.
5. Was there a sentry posted at the front door?
   No.
6. Details about his lodgings in rue Gretry, Brussels.
   a) Number of the house?
      60 or 62 – not sure.
   b) Were other agents staying there?
      Not to his knowledge.
   c) What does he know about other lodgers there?
      Nothing. He only met one there, a refugee Austrian Jew, whose name he did not know.
   d) Who was the lodging house kept by?
      A Hungarian whose name he cannot remember.

————————————

The lodgings constitute a four-storied building, with a cafe on the bottom floor, and about 50 rooms above it. Pons and van den Kieboom had chosen these lodgings themselves, and the establishment had no connection with the Germans, as far as Pons knew.

As a consequence of Lieutenant Shanks' interrogation, Lieutenant Colonel Stephens, in a 'Secret' memo, stated that while Pons was interrogated he gave negative answers. Stephens added that, 'Pons must be regarded as unreliable.'[51]

Sunday, 22 November 1942:
Herbert Morrison is appointed Secretary of State for Home Affairs & Home Security.

Monday, 7 December 1942:
A meeting of the War Cabinet is held at 10 Downing Street at 5.30 pm. The attention of the War Cabinet is drawn to a telegram from His Majesty's Minister at Berne, stating that the International Committee had informed His Majesty's Consul at Geneva that the Germans had told the Committee officially that all prisoners would be unshackled during Christmas week. The International Committee intended to propose to both sides that this concession should be continued for an indefinite period after Christmas.

The War Cabinet takes the view that this statement provides an opportunity for ending what might otherwise become a deadlock. It is thought possible that the Germans had made the statement with the idea of bringing this procedure to an end, and that, if the shackling was suspended during Christmas week, they would be glad of an excuse for not resuming it thereafter. It is felt that, without waiting for the Swiss Government to make their appeal to both sides to unshackle their prisoners from a given day, the British Government should at once make a public statement to the general effect that, on hearing of the German proposal to unshackle British prisoners during Christmas week, it had given instructions that German prisoners in its hands should be unshackled forthwith.

R.L. Hughes returned Waldberg's transmitter to R.T. Reed (Special Agents). Hughes understood that it was lent to someone in his section 'many months ago in connection with an exercise'. He explained that the valve was burnt out and could not be replaced in England.

Chapter Eleven

Investigations Continue:
Tying Up any Loose Ends

Saturday, 6 February 1943:
Soviet troops reach the Sea of Azov (situated between Ukraine, the Crimea and Russia), isolating the German Army Group A.

Mrs K.G. Lee, Home Office (Aliens Department) wrote to Milmo, informing him that, after going through her files, she realized that she had omitted to send him a Red Cross message that was destined for Pons. She asked him if he would he be good enough to pass it on to Pons, 'If you see no objection'.

Thursday, 18 February 1943:
General von Arnim and General Rommel's forces finally meet at Kasserine in Tunisia, part of Operation *Morgenluft* (Rommel's contribution to a joint operation with von Arnim's Fifth Panzer Army against the American II Corps).

Nazis arrest White Rose leaders (a non-violent, intellectual anti-Hitler resistance group) in Munich.

At Camp 020, Lieutenant Colonel Stephens received, on behalf of Milmo, the Red Cross message for Pons, to 'dispose with as the Colonel thinks fit'.

Tuesday, 2 March 1943:
A debate is held in the House of Commons: 'The House being met, the Clerk Assistant, at the Table, informed the House of the unavoidable absence through indisposition of Mr Speaker from this day's Sitting. Whereupon Colonel Clifton ... (who conducted many questions to the House) asked the President of the Board of Trade whether in view of the excellent work done by the Scouts, he will permit them to buy uniforms free of coupons like other similar organisations?'[1]

Milmo revealed that MI5 was concerned about a serving army officer who had previous associations with one of the men who recruited the four spies – Walter Henry Praetorius. They investigated Captain Kenneth Cottam of the Intelligence Corps, who was at Southampton University with Praetorius during

1933 and 1934. Investigations had shown Cottam to be an expert in the German language and the country. Cottam's civilian occupation was a lecturer at the polytechnic in Regent Street, London. He had made several visits to Germany, including one immediately prior to the outbreak of the war for his honeymoon, and another on an earlier occasion, when, according to his own account, he served six months with a German garrison, lecturing on interpretership. He was vetted on behalf of MI1x on 3 August 1940, and again for prospective employment by MI8b on 20 August 1942. At the time, his address was given as Intelligence Training Centre, Cambridge. On both of these occasions, MI5 reported that they had nothing recorded against Cottam, despite certain vague allegations which had been made against him in 1939 and early in 1940 but, upon investigation, were not substantiated.

Saturday, 13 March 1943:
An unsuccessful assassination attempt is made on the Führer, a time bomb being found in Hitler's aircraft.

Captain B.G. Atkinson of MI5 issued a 'Secret' memo to Milmo which stated that Captain Cottam was on leave near Christchurch in Dorset, pending a posting. Atkinson travelled down to interview Cottam, but unfortunately was unable to add very much to the information that had already been obtained about Walter Praetorius.

Cottam did state that he was quite friendly with the German student whilst at university in 1933/34, and understood that he came over to Britain under the auspices of the Anglo-German Academic Bureau in Russell Square, London.

Cottam recognised Praetorius from the photograph supplied, and gave the following description of him at the time: height 5ft 6in, hair coarse, straight and fairish; eyes blue; very fresh complexion. Apart from his height, this agreed with the description previously given by Milmo's department. Cottam stated that he thought the Christian name of Praetorius was Walter, but at Southampton University he had also been known to his friends as 'Rusty' Praetorius. Praetorius was described as having a kind, gentle type of personality, and was popular with his fellow students.

Cottam reiterated what was already known, namely that Praetorius was very much a Nazi idealist and embraced the ideals of Nazism, especially what was regarded as the superiority of the German and Anglo-Saxon races over all others.

Cottam had some faint recollection of Praetorius going to Scotland on a visit during one of his vacations. So far as he could remember, Praetorius did not appear to take any unusual interest in military matters or activities. He had been a very keen cyclist, and used to spend a good deal of his time in cycling around the country. He had a camera with him and took various photographs, but these, so far as Cottam could remember, were all of an innocuous nature, such as any visitor in a foreign country might take.

Cottam, after finishing at Southampton University, won a scholarship to Berlin and Konigsberg Universities in 1934, and during the two months he was in Berlin, he stayed with the Praetorius family at Westendallee 92b.

Cottam was unaware that Praetorius Senior was of Russian extraction or that his mother of British origin, although he did recollect something being mentioned one day about distant relatives in Scotland. The Praetorius family in Berlin consisted of the mother and father – the father's name, Cottam believed, also being Walter – and an elder sister whose name he could not recollect, who would now be aged about 44, and was, in 1934, employed on some job with the civil service. He recalled that Mrs Praetorius was a rabid Nazi, very much more so than the father, who himself did not appear to take more than a superficial interest in the Nazi doctrine. Walter junior, on the other hand, was attracted to the ideology of Nazism, and after his return to Germany in 1934 became a Hitler Jugend (youth) leader, and was very keen on the physical culture side of the Nazi doctrine.

Cottam thought that Praetorius' father had at one time run some business connected with export agencies. One of the things he exported to England was lemonade straws, but Cottam could not recollect the name of the firm.

Neither could he remember any people in Southampton with whom Praetorius was particularly friendly, but he thought that his tutor, a Dr Lucas, might possibly have given further information.

Cottam apologized for remembering so few details regarding Praetorius, but as this was several years ago he found it difficult to think of any other information which may prove useful.

Although he received one or two letters from Praetorius around that time, he had not kept any of them, so Atkinson was unable to obtain a specimen of his handwriting. Cottam also stated that as far as he knew, Praetorius has not visited England since 1934, nor had Cottam heard from him.

During the interview with Cottam, Atkinson did not disclose the reason for his interest in Praetorius, nor did Cottam ask Atkinson if he was connected with MI5. Almost as an aside, Cottam did state that there was another German, an extreme Nazi whom he looked upon with much more suspicion, who was at Southampton University from 1936–37; a man named Gunter Koenjer.

Tuesday, 16 March 1943:

At 12.15 pm, a meeting of the War Cabinet is held in the Prime Minister's Room at the House of Commons.

The War Cabinet have before them a Memorandum by the Lord President of the Council, the Right Hon. Sir John Anderson MP, regarding the proposed amendment of Defence Regulation 54CA, which empowers competent authorities (mainly Supply Departments) to appoint Government directors to companies engaged in war production.

The War Cabinet are informed that this power is required to meet certain cases in the aircraft industry where the board of directors needed strengthening, but it is not considered necessary to put in a controller under the more drastic powers already conferred by Defence Regulation 55 (4).

It is explained that a Regulation giving these powers has already been made on 10 February last. What is now proposed is to substitute for this an amended Regulation which at certain points will meet some of the criticisms made against the original Regulation. The Ministers Primarily concerned are satisfied that the proposed new Regulation will be easier to defend against criticism. It is felt perhaps unfortunate that this particular Regulation should have to be debated at a time when there is general uneasiness in the House of Commons about the whole practice of legislation by Regulation; and the risk of controversy being aroused cannot be ignored. But in principle it is felt there should be no difficulty in substantiating the claim that the Government should have a right to be represented on the board of a company in which it has substantial financial interests.

Furthermore, it is deemed most inexpedient that, a Regulation having already been made giving powers to appoint Government directors to companies engaged on war production, the scheme should not be proceeded with.

A note produced on behalf of Milmo and designated 'Most Secret' contained information regarding the activities of Praetorius from the beginning of 1942 onwards:

'At the beginning of February, 1942, he arrived in Paris from Nantes in order to call on an agent known as ZIGZAG[2], having been already seconded to Nantes. In the middle of February, there was a reference of Praetorius' return from Jersey, an event which preceded a spell of leave he took on account [of] getting married. In the next three months there were indications of him travelling about between Paris and Nantes, and at the end of June that year he returned from Nantes to Paris with ZIGZAG. Towards the end of July 1942, Praetorius oversaw the training of ZIGZAG. At the end of August he was appointed permanent deputy Dienstellenleiter (Agency Chief) at Nantes. Praetorius appeared to have been concerned in some sabotage project which involved certain Bretons in Rennes. In mid-December he visited Paris together with ZIGZAG, et al. Praetorius was employed in communicating with ZIGZAG.'

Friday, 19 March 1943:

HMS *Ashanti* rescues airmen from the sea near Scapa in the Orkney Islands. A sub lieutenant and a rating gunner observer from HMS *Victorious* over-ran the flight deck when landing after a reconnaissance flight and landed in the sea. They are immediately spotted by the destroyer *Ashanti* and the crew are safely rescued. [3]

An MI5 official, on behalf of Milmo, dropped a note to Lieutenant Colonel Peter Perfect, Scottish Regional Security Officer, in Edinburgh, asking him to investigate the somewhat delicate nature of Praetorius and his Scottish mother's relatives in Dundee. It was suggested to Lieutenant Colonel Perfect that it was not necessary for him to disclose the need for information anymore than was necessary. MI5 had recently learnt that Praetorius was a fairly prominent figure in the German Secret Service in France. Southampton Police had already interviewed several people who had known Praetorius.

Apart from the fact that he used to visit Scottish relatives believed to reside at *Seathwood*, Perth Road, Dundee, there were no further particulars about these relations. However, MI5 had every confidence that Perfect and his colleagues would be able to ascertain whether the present residents lived there in 1934, and if so, whether there was any reason to regard them with suspicion. If nothing was known to their detriment, it was suggested that they should be interviewed with a view to finding out whether they knew about Praetorius, and if they could furnish any further information about him. It was explained to Perfect that although the information given to him may well be scant, the matter in hand was nevertheless of considerable importance.

Tuesday, 23 March 1943:

RESTRICTIONS IN COASTAL AREAS REQUIRED TO SAFEGUARD
PREPARATIONS FOR OFFENSIVE OPERATIONS.
MEMORANDUM BY THE HOME SECRETARY AND MINISTER OF HOME
SECURITY.

In his memorandum of the 21st March the Secretary of State for War has submitted to the War Cabinet new proposals for restrictions designed to safeguard our preparations for offensive operations.

These proposals fall into two parts – a declaration under Defence Regulation 13A of certain regulated areas, including a coastal area extending from the Humber to Penzance, and the superimposition over that part of the regulated area which extends from the Wash to Penzance of a visitors' ban.

I should say at once that I have nothing to urge against the proposed declaration of regulated areas, or the imposition within those areas by Army commanders, in consultation with Regional Commissioners, of such restrictions on comparatively small parts of each area as may be considered necessary for military purposes. In this memorandum I am concerned only with the further proposal that there should be, in addition to these restrictions, a visitors' ban over the whole of the south and east coasts from the Wash to Penzance.

It is important that we should be quite clear as to what is meant by a visitors' ban. It is not a ban on all visitors to the area to which it applies. It is merely a prohibition on entry into those areas for the purpose of a holiday, recreation or pleasure, or as a casual wayfarer. Persons who have other good reasons for entry, such as business, visits to near relatives, etc are not prohibited by the ban. The ban has hitherto applied to the coastal area from King's Lynn to Littlehampton, and the Isle of Wight, but has been lifted, over the winter months and until the 1st April, over all this area except the coastal strip from the Thames to Rye.

The proposals in the War Office memorandum are that the ban should be re-imposed over the areas to which it has hitherto been applied with the addition of an area about 10 miles deep inland, and also over an area of corresponding depth extending from Littlehampton to Penzance.

Pons was now transferred to Camp 020R. This was a duplicate reserve camp, built at Huntercombe Place, Nuffield, near Henley-on-Thames, Oxfordshire, in case of bomb damage to Camp 020. The amenities at this camp, however, left nothing to be desired and were of an exceptionally high standard, being more reminiscent of a modern hotel than an internment camp. They were far in advance of those at Camp 020. All internees were treated alike, and they were not permitted to make purchases out of their own funds; comforts were provided free. For example, from special funds, approximately £50 a month was spent on tobacco. The conditions were much more favourable to the inmates than those at Camp 020, with them being allowed considerable latitude.[4]

Camp 020R slowly became the place where enemy spies who were no longer of interest were allowed to stagnate until the end of the war. Here the prisoners learnt much about the British Constitution; they whiled away their time writing petitions to the king, the Home Secretary and judges. Sometimes they gave 'good' advice to Prime Minister Winston Churchill or Foreign Secretary Anthony Eden.[5]

Thursday, 25 March 1943:
A meeting of the War Cabinet is held in the Prime Minister's Room, House of Commons, at 12.15 pm, at which President Roosevelt's proposal for a conference on food is discussed:

'The Prime Minister emphasised the importance to this country of supplies of food at cheap rates. At the proposed Conference we were likely to find ourselves in an isolated position among delegates of producer countries.

'The Minister of Food (The Right Hon Lord Woolton), agreed that the Conference presented a number of potential dangers. Thus, it might fall into the hands of food faddists who believed that optimum nutritional standards could be applied universally to all the peoples of the world.

'A second danger was that the Conference would start dealing with currency questions or commodity control, which were outside its scope. Our delegates to the Food Conference must not get involved in discussion of these matters.

'There was a further difficulty, namely, that the interests of this country as an importing country had to be reconciled with those of the Dominions as producing countries. It was important that we should reach agreement with the Dominion representatives before the Conference, so that the delegates from the whole Empire could speak with one voice.

'At the same time, the Minister of Food thought we ought not to ignore the danger of a food shortage after the war. Consumption was increasing in many areas, owing to the rise in internal spending-power, while production in some areas had fallen off. The relief of liberated areas would be a heavy drain on food reserves.

'He thought, therefore, that it would be wise that consideration should be given to the continuance for a period after the war of an organisation on the lines of the Combined Food Board, but on a wider international basis.'

In a letter designated 'Secret', Dundee's Chief Constable requested that Lieutenant Colonel Perfect should enquire into the residents of 'Seathwood'. Perfect was informed that the house was occupied by a Mrs A. Sinclair Henderson, whose deceased husband was a partner in the firm of Alex Henderson & Sons Ltd, Jute Spinners & Manufacturers, of South Dudhope Works, Dundee. She had lived there for over forty years. Her son, who was a partner in the firm, held the rank of major in HM Forces. The Chief Constable had no doubt that she was a loyal person.

She knew Henry Praetorius simply as Walter, but thought his name was Henry Walter. He spent a holiday at her house from 7–27 August 1934 while he was at Southampton University. She thought that he had left for Germany in early September that year, and felt sure that he had not visited Scotland since, believing that he would have called upon her. She did not know what he was studying at Southampton University, but understood he was intending to be an athletics instructor. The visit had been on account of a relationship on his mother's side, Mrs Praetorius' father and Mrs Henderson's mother being cousins.

She said Walter's father's name was Richard Praetorius and he was from Riga. His mother was Hannah Thoms or Praetorius. Her father was a flax merchant near Warsaw, but was said to be a British subject on account of his father's nationality.

Mrs Henderson stated that she thought that Praetorius had a brother named Hermann and a sister, Emily. She believed that all the family had to clear out to Berlin at the time of the Russian Revolution. She had not heard anything about the family prior to the war, when a friend had visited them in Berlin and told Mrs Henderson, upon her return, that Mrs Praetorius was very ill.

Whilst on holiday at 'Seathwood', Henry Praetorius had made an entry in the visitors' book kept by Mrs Henderson: 'Had a wonderful time (from the general as well the educational point of view). Walter Praetorius.'[6]

The Chief Constable offered to send Lieutenant Colonel Perfect a photographic copy of Praetorius' handwriting, subject to Mrs Henderson's approval, should this prove to be useful.

Saturday, 27 March 1943:
German submarine U-169 is depth-charged and sunk with all hands south of Iceland.

Lieutenant Colonel Perfect sent a 'Secret' memo to H.P. Milmo, regarding Milmo's – or at least MI5's – communication of 19 March. Perfect attached a copy of the letter he had received from the Chief Constable of Dundee, dated 25 March, responding to MI5's initial enquiry. Perfect apologized for the rather sketchy nature of the information supplied, but said if Milmo wanted any point to be elaborated, he would see what he could do. Furthermore, should Milmo want a copy of Praetorius' handwriting, he should just let him know.

Wednesday, 31 March 1943:
In the House of Commons, Mr George Mathers (MP for Linlithgowshire) asks the Parliamentary Secretary to the Ministry of Food why he has fixed prices for rhubarb, which include a large proportion of inedible leaves; and whether he will make it clear to housewives that, in buying rhubarb at the controlled price, they are entitled to insist upon having the leaves cut off before weighing?[7]

Lieutenant Colonel Perfect contacted Milmo and enclosed the Police report of the interview with Mrs Sinclair Henderson. In reply, Milmo requested from Perfect a specimen of Praetorius' handwriting, possibly by photographing Praetorius' entry in Mrs Henderson's visitors' book.

Wednesday, 7 April 1943:
On the Isle of Wight, Newport town centre is attacked by German aircraft. Seventeen civilians lose their lives during the raid, with two more dying later. Also killed is an off-duty Airman with his wife who were visiting her father.[8]

Perfect wrote a 'Secret' letter to Milmo and forwarded him a copy of Praetorius' handwriting as requested.

Tuesday, 11 May 1943:
Twenty-six young women in an ATS (Auxiliary Territorial Service) hostel in Great Yarmouth, Norfolk, are killed during a Luftwaffe raid.

A letter was sent from the Red Cross Foreign Relations Department Director, Miss S.J. Warner OBE, to Major the Hon. Kenneth Younger, of 'E' Division (responsible for 'alien control' and internment), MI5. The letter said that the London Committee of the South African Red Cross Society held a Red Cross message for Charles Albert van den Kieboom but that they had been unable to trace him. They had received a notification from their headquarters in South Africa which informed them that Kieboom had been executed in England on a charge of espionage. Miss Warner wanted to know how much information should be transmitted to the Red Cross in Geneva, but said that in such cases they would normally just say that 'he died in 1940 in England'.

Thursday, 13 May 1943:
In Operation *Mincemeat*, the body of a homeless drifter, Glyndwr Michael, had been lowered into the water off the coast of Spain on 30 April. The body was dressed as a Royal Marines officer and given the identity of Major William Martin. Attached to his belt was a briefcase containing a letter that, were it to fall into the wrong hands, would reveal the Allies' plans for an imminent invasion of the Balkans.

The false documents found on the body are returned by the Spanish to the British, apparently unopened but actually shared with and copied by the Germans.

A letter on behalf of Captain Septimus Paul Brookes-Booth, MC, Section E1a (Nationals of Western Europe), was sent to Miss Warner at the British Red Cross Society, London, with reference to Kieboom's death.

Captain Brookes-Booth agreed that the suggestion that 'he died in 1940 in England' would be suitable. From a security point of view, there would be no objection to the plain facts being stated as they were fully announced in the Press at the time. However, it was advised that it might be more delicate to put it the way that the Red Cross had proposed.

Saturday, 11 September 1943:
Operation *Source* begins, using a series of attacks by X-class midget submarines to neutralize the heavy German warships *Tirpitz*, *Scharnhorst* and *Lützow* based in northern Norway. Six large submarines, each with an X-craft in tow, creep out of Loch Cairnbawn on the west coast of the Scottish Highlands and head for Kaafjord in Arctic Norway: one of their targets, *Tirpitz*, is a threat to the convoys sending vital supplies to Russia.

Friday, 24 September 1943:
Clement Atlee is now Lord President of the Council.
Sir John Anderson is appointed Chancellor of the Exchequer.

Thursday, 11 November 1943:
Lord Woolton is Minister of Reconstruction. The Prime Minister designated the new office as the focal point for all plans for the transitional period and defined its task as seeing that the plans of departments were brought into relation with each other.

Friday, 19 November 1943:
One hundred and sixty-one aircraft from the Eighth Air Force are sent to attack targets of opportunity in western Germany. No aircraft are lost.

M.R. Carden from the Internees Section of the Red Cross had sent a letter to Sjoerd Pons, c/o the Home Office, Internment Camps Division, informing him that they had received an enquiry through the International Red Cross on behalf of his parents, who stated that they had not heard from him since April 1941.

The letter added that a short personal reply may be sent to them through the same Red Cross channels. The letter concluded, 'In any case, will you be so kind as to answer this letter in order that we may know it has reached you, as the International Red Cross will repeat the enquiry until they receive some sort of answer?'[9] The letter was immediately sent on to a Mrs Lee (B2, Agents).

Monday, 22 November 1943:
A second major air raid in five days takes place on Berlin this night. The raid causes extensive damage to residential areas: 2,000 people are killed and 175,000 people rendered homeless.[10]

Mrs Lee forwarded Pons' letter to Milmo.

Wednesday, 24 November 1943:
President Roosevelt, Prime Minister Winston Churchill and China's Chiang Kai-shek meet at the Cairo Conference.

Pons' letter was sent on to Camp 020.

Friday, 26 November 1943:
Allied bombers raid Bremen. Major F.S. Gabreski, from Pennsylvania, returns with an unexploded 20mm German cannon shell which was lodged in the motor of his P-47 Thunderbolt fighter.[11]

Major Douglas 'Stimmy' Stimson, Camp 020 administrator, had written to Milmo to express concern about some of the content of Pons' letter, which he attached. Stimson understood that the MI5 man had not seen it, and suggested that the Home Office may wish to act upon some of its content. He believed that the latter part of the second paragraph contained certain implications on which the Home Office may wish to act, namely, 'In any case ... will you be so kind as to answer this letter ... as the International Red Cross will repeat the enquiry until they receive some sort of answer.'[12] It was immediately recognized that this had the propensity to become an ongoing problem.

Sunday, 12 December 1943:
The German submarine U-593 is torpedoed and sunk by British destroyers HMS *Holcombe* and *Tynedale* off the coast of Algeria.

Regarding the letter from Stimson on 26 November, Milmo stated, in a file note, that he was taking no action in connection with the last sentence, that the Home Office may wish to act in the matter. He added that all letters addressed to Pons by the International Red Cross could be ignored as there was no obligation to have any dealings with the International Red Cross on an ad-hoc basis unless, and until, that body directed some enquiry to an official quarter.

Monday, 17 July 1944:
The War Cabinet, meeting in the Cabinet War Rooms at 5.30 pm, is informed that the total casualties, both American and British, in Normandy up to 11 July were 84,000: 33,000 (4,800 killed) being British and 51,000 (7,800 killed) United States forces.

The attention of the War Cabinet is drawn to a report in the *Daily Mail* that British forces in Normandy were not receiving a sufficient ration of bread. The Secretary of State for War, the Right Hon. Sir James Grigg, undertakes to look into this question. He thinks that the solution might be to accelerate the shipment to Normandy of further mobile bakeries. Six of the twelve bakeries earmarked for this theatre are already in Normandy. It is pointed out, however, that shipping priorities are the responsibility of the Supreme Allied Commander.

Nearly four years after the arrival of the spies, inquiries have continued. Communication between MI5's Special Research Section (B1b), specifically Mrs D. Spring, and a Mr J.M. Lynch at the American Embassy reveal concerns about Meier and his association with the young American, de Vreede:[13]

'Dear Mr Lynch,
  ' ... When you came in the other day you told me that the FBI had received a copy of the handbook produced by this office on the German

Secret Service. That document does contain quite a useful summary of the case of the four boatmen which shows how Carl Meier fits into the picture.

'In addition to this, I think it would be of interest to you to have the extracts from Carl Meier's statement which disclose his recruitment and his meeting with de Vreede.

'Yours sincerely,
'Mrs D. Spring'

Wednesday, 26 July 1944:
German submarine U-214 is depth-charged and sunk in the English Channel by the British frigate HMS *Cooke*.

Major Nikolaus Fritz Adolf Ritter was interviewed at the headquarters of OC 30, Field Security Section, BLA, Hamburg. The following is a summary of the information he volunteered, which was already known to the British authorities:

- Born 8 January 1899 at Rheydt in the Rhineland, Germany. In 1917 he joined the infantry until the end of the war. Upon discharge from the German army and until 1921, he worked in the textile industry. Attended a textile school in Silesia for one year. Later he was made business manager of a factory at Laubau (Germany) until autumn, 1923.
- On New Year's Day, 1924, he arrived in New York with an immigration visa and obtained employment at H.R. Malinson silk mills, Long Island, almost immediately, and remained with the firm for two years. Thereafter, he took various odd jobs, but towards the end of 1926 he obtained work with J.J. Susmuth, West New York, New Jersey. This firm was later taken over by Manhattan Textile Works. He remained with the firm constantly until 1935, when the company went bankrupt.
- In autumn 1935, Ritter returned to Germany, with the intention of going into business in Silesia. This plan failed, however, and within three to four months he returned to the USA. He found nothing to do in the States, and failed in his efforts to succeed in establishing a business with his brother Hans. He again returned to Germany in autumn 1936.
- Ritter was offered a commission in the Wehrmacht as an auxiliary officer, effective May 1937. He accepted the commission (with the rank of captain) and was assigned to the Abwehr – Ast Hamburg. It later transpired that Herbert Wichmann was Chief of Gruppe I.
- Ritter and his wife were divorced in 1938. Mrs Ritter had custody of the children, but Ritter was permitted to see them when he was on leave, and given temporary custody of them during the summer months. His ex-wife took up employment with the American Consulate at Hamburg. Ritter

insisted that this connection had no significance as far as his Abwehr activities were concerned.

- In 1939, Ritter remarried.
- In early 1941, Ritter was given a special assignment by ABW IL (part of the OKW) to travel to Egypt to look into the possibilities of placing agents behind the British lines. He was told to contact the German Air Force in Africa and arrange for the landing of agents. Ritter described his trip as unsuccessful and a waste of time. In flying back his plane crashed on 17 July 1941, and as a result Ritter was hospitalized in Berlin for five months.
- While in hospital Ritter was interviewed regarding the arrest of around thirty-five agents in the United States. Needing a scapegoat for the Abwehr's failure in that matter, the responsibility was placed fully upon Ritter's shoulders. His Abwehr career was now at an end. Upon release from hospital, Ritter was sent to an anti-aircraft unit where he remained until the end of the war. He was eventually promoted to lieutenant colonel.

Wednesday, 22 November 1944:

The British submarine *Stratagem* is depth-charged and sunk in the Strait of Malacca between Malaya and Sumatra.

German agent Alfred Langbein was interrogated, although it is unclear by whom. Langbein was an Abwehr agent who was put ashore, by U-boat, near the village of Saint John on the Bay of Fundy coast of New Brunswick, Canada, on 14 May 1942. He spent two years in hiding without doing any spying at all, before finally turning himself in to Canadian Naval Intelligence in Ottawa in September 1944.

Langbein claimed that shortly after his arrival in Bremen, he had been approached as to whether he would accept an assignment overseas. He said that he would and, as a result, two men from Hamburg came to see him. One introduced himself as Major Ritter and the other was a hauptmann whose name Langbein could not remember. Both men wore Luftwaffe uniforms.

It was Ritter who 'opened the ball' by asking him, in English, whether he could speak English. Langbein replied, in English, that he could to a certain extent, and Ritter had instantly made up his mind by saying, 'this man will do'.

Langbein recalled that Ritter said that he needed men to go to England to obtain information concerning air force matters such as aerodromes, searchlight and gun emplacements, and numbers of aircraft. They were also very keen to have information about precautions which had been taken in England against the landing of German aircraft; they wanted to know, for instance, whether the fields had been ploughed up and whether there were any fields that could be used for landing by aircraft. Langbein was told that when he reported on the number of aircraft on an airfield, they would want to know the numbers there were of individual types.

Ritter told Langbein that the plan was to drop him into England by parachute in a region about 25 miles south-east of Bristol. He recalled that he saw the words 'Unternehmen LENA' on a file. Langbein asked what it meant, and was told it was the name of the operation in which he was to take part. Ritter told him to report to Hamburg immediately, as the mission was an urgent one and it was essential that it should be carried out quickly.

Langbein claimed that he did not actually accept the proposition.

Friday, 6 May 1945:
The aircraft carrier HMS *Formidable* is hit by kamikaze planes, but its steel decking (most US aircraft carriers had wooden decking) saves the ship from destruction.

Grand Admiral Dönitz announces that Himmler is to be relieved of all government duties.

Saturday, 7 May 1945:
The unconditional surrender of German forces is signed at Allied headquarters in Reims, France, ending the European conflict of the Second World War.

Herbert Wichmann is captured by the 21st Army Group.

Tuesday 10 May 1945:
The surrender of Germany officially takes effect at 12.01 am.

Wichmann was formally arrested in Hamburg by the Second British Army for being a member of the Abwehr.

Wednesday, 11 May 1945:
The USS *Bunker Hill* is hit by two Japanese kamikaze aircraft off Okinawa, Japan, leaving 373 dead.

The Second British Army sent a telegram to the War Rooms which stated that Wichmann had been traced to Hamburg and that 'The subject is prepared to talk'.[14]

Thursday, 12 May 1945:
German troops on Crete surrender.

Wichmann was transferred to Camp 031 at Barnstedt, near Westertimke, the same camp that would eventually welcome Heinrich Himmler.

Sunday, 22 May 1945:
The last Arctic Convoy voyage – with the designation JW67 – between Britain and Russia is nearing completion.

With the cessation of hostilities, Ritter made himself available to the Allied military authorities as a translator and consultant. He was given a certificate relating to his work, signed at Hamburg by Lieutenant Colonel (CAC) V. Rapp, Headquarters Air Defence, Investigative Liaison Officer, 21st Army Group. The certificate bore the stamp 'Air Defence Investigation, USSTAF (Rear), APO 413'.

Meanwhile, Karl Heinz Kraemer, an Abwehr officer at the German Legation in Stockholm, was interrogated at Camp 020 regarding Ritter. Kraemer had signed the usual contract at the end of September 1939, before Ritter in the General Kommando, Hamburg. Kraemer said he received his training from Ritter and when asked about cover names for various Abwehr officials, offered Ranken [*sic*] as a cover name for Ritter.

Sunday, 17 June 1945:
Japanese Thirty-Second Army's final defence line on Okinawa collapses. As a result, Japanese Admiral Ota Minoru commits ritual suicide.
    The US Sixth Army capture Naguilan in the Philippines.

The War Room sent a telegram to Major Noakes at the 21st Army Group with the following request:

'Would like Wichmann at 020. Although pressure of work precludes possibility of immediate interrogation, consider most desirable he should be segregated from colleagues and therefore suggest early transfer to UK.'[15]

Wednesday, 20 June 1945:
US Marines on Okinawa reach the southern coast of the island at several points.
    The Australian 26 Infantry Brigade capture Hill 90 on Tarakan Island in Borneo, ending organized Japanese resistance there.

Wichmann, a Category 'A' prisoner, was brought to England under the escort of Captain Hughes of the Intelligence Corps, and arrived at RAF Hendon. Owing to an administration error, however, there was no-one to meet them from Combined Services Detailed Interrogation (CSDIC) or Camp 020. An escort from No. 2 Distribution Centre, Wilton Park, eventually arrived and took him there, contrary to what was expected.

Thursday, 21 June 1945:
The Battle of Tarakan ends in an Allied victory.

The American destroyer USS *Barry* is sunk north-west of Okinawa by a Japanese kamikaze attack.

The defeat of the Japanese on Okinawa is now complete.

In 'Consolidated Interrogation Report 039', Lieutenant Findlay, Wichmann's interrogator, stated that Wichmann revealed only what he felt necessary:

> 'Wichmann has doubtless told his story honestly ... He knows that most of the facts he has given are either known or can be checked up. However, he is a wily customer who appears to be giving way on some points so as to cover his tracks on others.'[16]

Friday, 22 June 1945:
A request is made by Emperor Hirohito of Japan for peace talks: 'I desire that concrete plans to end the war, unhampered by existing policy, be speedily studied and that efforts are made to implement them.'

Surrendered German E-boats arrive at Portsmouth harbour.

Wichmann arrived at Camp 020 from the London Cage, a controversial establishment located in the heart of London at 6–7 Kensington Palace Gardens.

Wichmann was described as weak and woolly. He had been Astleiter (branch leader) of Hamburg, where he spent all but two years of his Abwehr career. Before the war, Wichmann had directed espionage against Britain, the United States and France, and in the last stages of the war, he had been nominally responsible for the creation of a stay-behind radio network in the Hamburg area. MI5 wanted to know about such efforts, hence his arrival at Ham.

Wednesday, 27 June 1945:
The new supreme military rank of Generalissimus of the Soviet Union is created for Joseph Stalin. Officially, he does not approve of the rank and continues to go by the title of Marshal.

A Liquidation Report was prepared on Pons. Robin Stephens noted that the Dutch had not asked to be supplied with a dossier on Pons, so one would not be sent to them. Furthermore, Pons' dossier had not been finally vetted, and should it be asked for later by the Dutch, it should be read through and checked first.

Sunday, 1 July 1945:
The Inner German Border (the border between East and West Germany) is established as the boundary between the Western and Soviet occupation zones.

Wichmann's case was taken over in late June by the War Room Registry (WRC1/C). A 'Monthly Summary of Cases' at Camp 020 and 020R stated that Wichmann:

> '... at once showed willingness to talk ... should prove a source of great interest ... in respect of activities ... against the United Kingdom ... before the war and in the first two years after the outbreak of war. There are ... incompletely solved cases on which Wichmann can no doubt enlighten us.'[17]

Monday, 2 July 1945:
Only 200,000 essential workers are left in Tokyo due to mass evacuation.
  The submarine USS *Barb* fires rockets on Kaihyo Island near Sakhalin, becoming the first American underwater craft to fire rockets in shore bombardment.

Deportation orders are signed, certified and served on Dutch nationals, including Pons, who was at Camp 020. Pons, along with several others, was escorted to Hendon Airport for deportation to Holland under the recommendation of HM Chief Inspector (Immigration). Pons, in particular, was deemed never to be allowed to return to the UK.

Thursday, 2 August 1945:
The Potsdam Conference ends. It was the last meeting of the 'Big Three' Allied leaders – British Prime Minister Winston Churchill, US President Franklin Roosevelt and Soviet Premier Joseph Stalin.

Wichmann was interrogated at Camp 020 about Ritter and other matters. Wichmann claimed that he was unaware of the details of the activity of I Luft officer Hauptmann Ritter (alias Rantzau). He said he knew that Ritter recruited an agent by answering an advertisement! This agent furnished information on the state of the aircraft industry.
  Ritter said he spent a few days in New York between 1937 and 1939. He used to receive information from the USA before the war about the aircraft industry from a few agents who forwarded it by mail, sometimes written in secret ink.
  In September 1941, Wichmann had put forward a proposal to Berlin that enabled agents to travel on the caravans going from Turkey to neighbouring Russian districts to obtain reports on the Russians. As it was forbidden for the

Military Intelligence Service to work with the Party Dienststelle, Berlin became involved, leaving the details to Ritter. Sums of money were granted by Berlin to finance the project.

Department I Luft had been disbanded in March 1942, and Ritter then went to North Africa.

Wichmann was willing enough to speak, but he had no specific memory of events as such, a fact confirmed by his friends and enemies alike. What facts he could remember and what information he was able to proffer was patiently, and slowly, drawn from him by his interrogators.

His espionage activities against Britain had been remarkably unsuccessful. 'All attempts to spy on England were disappointing; in spite of much effort, nothing of value was ever achieved,' Wichmann admitted.[18]

Tuesday, 7 August 1945:
Radio Tokyo reports, unspecifically, about an attack on Hiroshima on 6 August.

Wichmann continued to be interrogated at Camp 020, and now that the war with Germany was over, he was very forthcoming in disclosing agent details:

a). Agents acquired from other Dienststellen:
   Cover name 'Hubert'
   Hamburg wireless station took over this traffic from either Paris or Wiesbaden for a short time in 1944. 'Hubert' transmitted reports, in French, on troop movements in southern England.

b). Agents in England:
   i)   No 3725: Parachuted into England September 1940 by Abwehr Eins in Brussels.
        News was required and given regarding the effects of the V1 and V2 rockets. There were doubts about whether the news supplied was genuine.
   ii) Whiskey: Arrived in England via France and Spain before D-Day. Supplied information on construction and new inventions in the air industry.

Wichmann also gave information on agents in the USA and France.

Wednesday, 22 August 1945:
The Soviet assault on Maoka is completed.

Joan Paine from the War Room issued a memo bemoaning the disappointing results of Wichmann's interrogation on activities orchestrated against the

United Kingdom, prior to the outbreak of the war. The memo went on to say Ritter had 'most inconsiderately escaped interrogation' and 'he is believed to have died in 1943'.[19]

Joan had now written to John Curry at MI5, who later became the author of the first official history of the Secret Service, and enclosed a copy of the results obtained from Wichmann. She said that it was very disappointing and added little to their existing knowledge. She thought that Ritter would have proved a more fruitful source of information regarding the activities of Hamburg against Britain, but as he was thought to be dead, the chances of obtaining a more complete picture of these matters appeared to be very slight.

Sunday, 2 September 1945:
The Japanese surrender is formally signed, thereby bringing the hostilities of the Second World War to an end.

Tuesday, 11 September 1945:
Oberleutnant Praetorius, according to a report from 21st Army Group, thought that Ritter had journeyed to the USA once more before 1939. He considered Ritter to be an energetic Abwehr officer, who may have travelled a lot, but said little or nothing about his work. Praetorius thought that reports regarding Ritter's agents went to Wichmann, but did not know the contents, and he heard that there was a massive rift between Ritter and Berlin which resulted in Ritter leaving the Abwehr.

Wednesday, 12 September 1945:
A 'Secret' telegram was sent to the War Room, stating that Ritter, being on an arrest target list (as of 21 August), had been arrested and taken into custody in Germany and held by 21st Army Group. A partial interrogation report on him had been prepared by the FBI. Just a few months ago, Ritter had worked as a translator for the Allies.

Tuesday, 9 October 1945:
Lieutenant Colonel Stimson, at Camp 020, reported that Herbert Wichmann – along with eight other German nationals – was escorted to Croydon Airport for return to the British Army of the Rhine (BAOR). Wichmann, in particular, left for Buckeburg in Germany. Stimson stated that fourteen items of luggage were left behind due to excess weight. None, however, belonged to Wichmann.

Saturday, 13 October 1945:
Major John Gwyer, of MI5, wrote to the War Room regarding Nikolaus Ritter. It had been decided not to bring him over to England, but to leave him where he

was while a preliminary interrogation was conducted. Gwyer wanted to know the current position regarding Ritter's interrogation. Gwyer stated that, from the papers he personally had seen, it appeared that Ritter had not yet been interrogated by the British authorities, but only by the FBI's liaison officer.

He added that MI5's requirements were simply that Ritter should be invited to make a full statement concerning all the agents which he had despatched or controlled in the United Kingdom between 1938 and the early part of 1941, when he left for Cyrenaica.

Gwyer did not think that it was worthwhile to prepare an elaborate brief, but when a preliminary statement by Ritter was forthcoming, Gwyer would have liked to produce a detailed questionnaire dealing with any points that he had omitted or failed to cover fully.

Monday, 12 November 1945:

At 4.15 pm, and almost exactly a month after Major Gwyer's missive, a telegram,[20] designated 'Secret', was despatched from the War Room to GSI (S), BAOR, regarding Nikolaus Ritter:

'A. REFERENCE NIKOLAUS R I T T E R REPEAT R I T T E R HELD BY YOU.
'B. IF INTERROGATION NOT ALREADY COMMENCED, GRATEFUL FOR HANDLING AS FOLLOWS:-
'C. FIRST OBTAIN FROM R. A FULL STATEMENT ON AGENTS DESPATCHED TO OR CONTROLLED IN U.K.
'D. ON RECEIPT OF THIS WE WOULD BRIEF IN DETAIL ON POINTS OMITTED OR NOT FULLY COVERED.
'E. THEN OBTAIN FULL ACCOUNT OF ACTIVITIES AND PERSONNEL I LUFT HAMBURG DURING R'S TERM OF OFFICE.
'F. REGRET THIS SUGGESTION NOT MADE EARLIER THROUGH OVERSIGHT.'

Monday, 3 December 1945:

Noakes, by now a colonel, requested that a note[21] from Major Gwyer that referenced Oberstleutnant Ritter be forwarded to Major the Hon. Peter E. Ramsbotham, GSI (b), HQ BAOR. The note detailed a conversation Gwyer had with Colonel Noakes:

'I have discussed with Colonel Noakes the case of Oberstleutnant Ritter and explained that what we should like would be for Ritter, without being interrogated, to make first of all his own statement concerning his activities against this country between 1935 and 1941. On the basis of this statement we will, if necessary, prepare a detailed brief for Ritter's further questioning. I suggested, and Colonel Noakes agreed, that if Ritter were invited to make his statement at once we should be in a position to have the brief ready by the time Ritter had come to the top of the queue for actual interrogation.'

Monday, 22 March 1946:

Even after the war had ended, R. Metcalfe Silvester's mood and determination had certainly not mellowed over the years, and he had not given up his quest for recognition and glory over the capture of Meier. Silvester was not helped in his mission by the fact that his correspondence has been mislaid by the War Office:[22]

<u>MI5</u>
It is much regretted that the attached letter from R.M. Silvester had been mislaid in Registry and has only just come to light.
R.
War Office.
22.3.46.
Vic.6622/768
(Sgd) E A SALE

Silvester was far from happy. He claimed that what he had done most certainly warranted recognition, more so than that which was received by others who, in his eyes, had contributed to the nation far less than he had. Furthermore, this lack of recognition, he claimed, had damaged his career path in the Army.

The letter to the War Office from Silvester, who now resided at 3 East Ascent, St Leonards-on-Sea, read as follows:[23]

'Dear Sirs,
'<u>M.2. Karl Meier</u>
'I received a communication from the Home Office on January 15th 1941, which was sent to me whilst at Minehead, Somerset in connection with the above enemy alien who was detained and handed over to the Lydd Police by Mr Mansfield and I.

'It seems strange that after all this time I have had no acknowledgement for the service and probable risk involved in detaining this man and yet one constantly reads of dear old ladies receiving the MBE for selling Savings Stamps!

'Had I some acknowledgement from you I had hopes that this would have helped me in getting into the Army Intelligence Corps but as it was despite the fact that I volunteered for the Army I was much against my inclination consigned to the Royal Signals.

'As you have, I read in the press, lost valuable records through fire the enclosed report may be of some value to you and I should appreciate some acknowledgement in due course as so far the Police have been wrongly given the credit despite the fact that he was wandering around a garrison town with no suspicion on their part.

'Late Signalman 2598496

'Yours faithfully,

'R.M. Silvester'

By adding 'late signalman' at the end of his letter, Sylvester was possibly trying to inject a note of sarcasm to the recipient.

Wednesday, 10 April 1946:

There was ongoing concern regarding Silvester's letter, which had been delayed firstly by the Registry in the War Office losing it, and secondly by their failing to turn up the appropriate War Office file. The matter had been dealt with as far back as February 1941.

It was felt that Silvester's latest letter could have been dealt with in one of three ways:

1. a letter could have be sent to the Directorate Military Intelligence saying that careful consideration had been given to this request but that nothing could be done;
2. a minute to the War Office could have been sent representing the position;
3. a letter could come from the Director General.

The second option was favoured.

Monday, 15 April 1946:

Interestingly, in his letter of 2 April 1941 to his MP, M. Hely-Hutchinson, Silvester stated, 'I did think that the capture might keep me in my future R.A.F. career'. But, as he alluded in his letter of 22 March 1946 to the War Office, he clearly stated that he wanted to join the Army, the Intelligence Corps to be precise. Although he volunteered for the Army, against his wishes he was forced to serve in the Royal Signals instead. For this he blamed the War Office and their inaction in him not being formally recognized for his part in Meier's capture which, he thought, would have enhanced his chances of enlisting in the Intelligence Corps.

Did Silvester change his mind and join the Army? Did he ever intend to join the RAF? If so, it certainly would cast doubt upon his reliability in any testimony.

A 'Confidential' loose minute from MI5, signed by a Captain L.G. Quinlan, stated that Silvester, in 1941 and through his MP, raised with the Home Office the question of reward and/or acknowledgement of the value of his services. The matter was now referred to the War Office and it was suggested that Silvester should be informed that his claim for a reward or other acknowledgement for services rendered would be noted with other such claims and would come up for consideration.

The following[24] is an extract from a report by an officer of the Security Services, included in the loose minute. The Karl Meier referred to is, of course, Carl Heinrich Meier:

> 'There is no record of Mr Silvester having played any part in the capture of Karl Meier. It is true that he was with Mansfield, but the latter was the person who questioned Meier and asked him to produce his passport.
>
> 'Mansfield became suspicious of Meier and took him to the police station. Had Silvester done what he now alleges he did, why did he not inform the police when he went to the police station with Mansfield and Meier?
>
> 'As Silvester did nothing in the case beyond accompanying Mansfield to the police station, the question of rewarding him does not arise.'

It was suggested that a satisfactory answer to Silvester's letter would be that it was felt that the circumstances were such as not to warrant the granting of an award. It was not made clear whether Horace Mansfield had received any form of reward or not.

Friday, 9 August 1946:
W.R. Perks, HM Chief Inspector of Immigration, wrote[25] to the Immigration Officer regarding Pons, and stated that he was:

> 'one of a list of aliens who have been deported from this country at various dates. Most of them are enemy agents, and none should be allowed to land again in the United Kingdom.'

Thursday, 24 April 1947:
Several months elapsed before W.R. Perks wrote[26] to the Immigration Officer again. He stated that:

> 'Pons is a Dutch commercial traveller born 5.6.12 at Amsterdam, who arrived secretly in this country on 3.9.40. He was later detained on security grounds, and deported 2.7.45.
>
> 'He shoult [sic] not be allowed to land again in the United Kingdom.'

Tuesday, 11 May 1954:

Almost fourteen years after the four spies landed in Kent, the *Evening Standard* printed an article about the 'Brussels Four'. The headline read, 'My Secret War Trials, The FOUR MEN who LANDED in KENT', and the piece was written by Earl Jowitt. Accompanying the article, in a sketch, was a Gestapo officer sitting at his desk, facing Pons, and the officer said, 'you are Sjoerd Pons; you have made smuggling affairs'. This detailed article described the men leaving France, their intentions in England and their capture; despite the headline, no mention was made of the trial.

Earl Jowitt (1st Earl Jowitt) was the Solicitor General who, along with Laurence Byrne, acted for the prosecution during the trial of the four spies in November 1940. Considering his part in court proceedings, Jowitt ended the article somewhat unpredictably, 'These were brave men. They expected the German invasion of England to take place within a few hours of their arrival. Had it done so, they might indeed have received the high pay which they had been promised and certainly deserved.'

Friday, 28 August 1959:

By now it was virtually twenty years on from the arrival of the 'Brussels Four'. Bernard A. Hill, MI5's legal advisor, had written a 'Confidential' letter to an E.C. Barlow at the Home Office (Establishment & Organisation Division), regarding letters written by Kieboom, Waldberg and Meier. After searching their files, Hill's department regretted that they could not find either originals or copies of the spies' letters that were written in 1940. Records showed that, although they did receive the letters, there was nothing to indicate whether they were sent to the families or not; certainly no copies were kept.

Honorary Brigadier Hinchley Cooke, who dealt with these cases, unfortunately had died some years ago; therefore, Hill stated that there was nothing more that could be done.

Chapter Twelve

'All that we have known or cared for will sink into the abyss of a new Dark Age'

(Prediction by Winston Churchill in 1940, had Britain
been defeated by the Germans.[1])

T
he *raison d'être* of Operation *Lena* was to facilitate Operation *Sealion* –
the German invasion of Britain. But the three military units needed to
make *Sealion* a success could neither work in unison nor support one
another. The chiefs of the Army railed against the Navy's Grand Admiral Raeder,
while Raeder himself and his chiefs criticized the Army's plans. Göering and
the Luftwaffe made it clear that success depended on the Luftwaffe controlling
the skies. Thanks to the Royal Air Force, the Germans failed in that respect.
Furthermore, Hitler's reluctance to listen to his military commanders and
his desire to do things his own way was also significant. Hitler's intransigence
was born out of the success the military had against Poland and the nations
of Western Europe – countries Hitler attacked because he felt he instinctively
knew, or believed, Germany would win without the overwhelming support
of the military hierarchy. Because of the Luftwaffe's failure to control the
skies over the Channel and southern England, Operation *Sealion*'s indefinite
postponement was announced on Tuesday, 17 September 1940, exactly two
weeks after the 'Brussels Four' arrived on the south coast of England.

The mission of the four *Lena* men was realistically over before it had even
started. All four spies were only at large for times varying between one and
twenty-four hours after their arrival on English soil, and without a single shot
being fired. One of them was only arrested in a chance encounter with a civilian,
while another was caught after a search organized as a result of information
given by one of his companions.

At 9.30 am on 3 September, the police at Seabrook received a message from
the sergeant at Dymchurch that the military had just brought Kieboom and
Pons into custody. A report written a day later made it apparent that there was
a considerable delay between the time of these men's apprehension and their
being handed over to the police. The report recommended that this matter
should be brought to the attention of the appropriate military authority, since
'it is plain that in a case of this kind any delay may be a very serious matter'.[2]

The report concluded that in view of the possibility of further landings of this kind, this aspect of the case should be brought to the notice of those responsible for the defence of the region in order that they may satisfy themselves that all necessary precautions were taken.

The outcome not only epitomized woeful German planning, but also highlighted the vigilance of the British, fuelled by the hyper-awareness of an invasion threat that spawned an atmosphere of feverish speculation. For example, on 7 September, the Saturday following the apprehension of the men in the Kent marshes, the codeword *Cromwell* was dispatched to all units of the Home Guard, meaning that an invasion was imminent, within 24 hours. The Joint Intelligence Committee assessment which prompted this action was 'a significant item of intelligence' – very possibly from the interrogations of the 'Brussels Four'.

The manner in which the spies' expedition was planned reflected the urgency of events at the time. France had fallen, the German Army was massing at the French Channel ports for an invasion of the British Isles, the Channel Islands were occupied and the Battle of Britain was already being fought in the skies over southern England. Preparation in advance by Fifth Columnists and having spies in situ was an important feature of Nazi invasions, and the same procedure was to be expected for Britain. It is hard to believe that there were no other missions than the one described in this book. For example, Waldberg referred to a party that included Peter Schneider, which was to have landed near Plymouth but was stopped and questioned by a British Naval patrol boat. Representing themselves as fishermen, they avoided suspicion and detection, and managed to return to France.

An element of blackmail entered into the recruiting of three of the spies, shedding light on the German position at the time. The training of all of them was extremely sketchy, and instructions were at times contradictory. Equipment and intelligence was inadequate; they were, for instance, landed in a Defence Area without any civilian papers. Detailed instructions for their behaviour upon landing were completely omitted, a fact which assisted at least one speedy arrest. Invasion spies need not all be highly trained and equipped, but the lack of organization on this mission seemed to indicate a surprising state of unpreparedness on the part of the Germans. The fall of France had come unexpectedly soon, and the rapid and enormous adjustments of planning for a further invasion led to confusion and failure in technique at several points.

All four men served their purpose from the counter-espionage point of view as spectacularly as they failed in their espionage mission. The information wrested from them at Camp 020 was to prove invaluable to the British Security Service. Results of the interrogations were instantly and progressively communicated to MI5: names and descriptions of potential agents, names of English contacts and details of the German Secret Service organization, its personnel and methods. Thus, at a crucial stage in the war, there became available to the British Security Service a skeleton plan of enemy espionage activities near British shores.

Nor was the usefulness of this information limited to immediate events. When, in 1941, a certain Francois de Deeker (alias Druecke) – later to be convicted and hanged as a spy – was brought to Camp 020, one of his admissions was that he recognized a photograph of van den Kieboom, whom he said was a former employee at the Hotel Victoria in Amsterdam, a centre of German espionage activities. A later arrival at Camp 020, a seaman agent by the name of Johan Strandmoen (who arrived from Norway on the MV *Taanevik*),[3] was frightened and impressed in equal measure when his interrogators confronted him with photographs of Pons and Kieboom from the 'Obituary File' and then produced a cutting of the execution of Kieboom. Strandmoen confessed that he had been a crew member of the *Rose du Carmel* when it had brought over Pons and Kieboom. Information from other spies confirmed and amplified the details of the German Secret Service's work.

Of almost 500 prisoners who arrived at Latchmere House during the war, fifteen were shot or hanged at the Tower of London under Stephens' command. (William Joyce, the American-born Irish fascist known as Lord Haw-Haw, was interrogated there after he renounced his British citizenship and fled to Germany to broadcast Nazi propaganda over the radio; he was hanged for treason in 1946.) There were also several suicides at Camp 020.

But the number of prisoners who provided useful intelligence for the British was significant: 120 were judged to be of high value and handed over to MI5's B Division for misinformation and other counter-espionage purposes, and Stephens turned more than a dozen of them into highly successful double agents.

The calibre of the initial Operation *Lena* spies sent to Britain was extremely low; pitifully low in fact. Most of the agents who arrived as part of the operation were arrested without having come close to completing their mission 'because of their own stupidity', according to official records. They were a ragtag bunch with a remarkable lack of ability to make themselves inconspicuous. One spoke no English at all, the others fleetingly. Pons, supposedly the superior English speaker, described his mission thus, 'How the people is living, how many soldiers there are, and all the things.'[4] What information that did make its way back from the agents to their German masters was low-grade stuff. No sabotage operations of any note had been carried out. It sounds fanciful that such a scheme could ever work on the strongly guarded, heavily patrolled south coast of England, but the fact remains that, up to a point, it did work.

Their efforts may also not have been helped by the questionable loyalty of Admiral Wilhelm Canaris, head of the Abwehr, to the Nazi Party. Was his heart in it?

There are suggestions that Canaris actually went as far as to leak material to the British Government. After the war, when the diplomat Michael Soltikow asked Winston Churchill how he had been so well informed about the German plans, Churchill pointed to Ian Colvin's post-war biography of Canaris,[5] which stated, 'Well, our intelligence was not badly equipped. As you know, we had Willhelm Canaris, and that was a considerable thing.'[6]

One question that has persisted over the years is just why Pons was acquitted.

The Solicitor General, during the trial, threw doubt on Pons' claim that the Gestapo had a hold on him because of his smuggling and the spy's explanation why he did not give himself up immediately upon arrival in England.

Pons, however, was consistent in the witness box; his testament tallied with that he had told Lieutenant Colonel Hinchley Cooke in his statement. His counsel, Christmas Humphreys, maintained that his client acted while under pressure from the Nazis, and the jury was no doubt impressed when reminded that he was the only one of the four spies who told the authorities that he had a companion.

Although there was no doubt, certainly among the authorities, that Pons was as guilty as his three comrades, the jury believed his evidence, given on oath, that he had been blackmailed by the Gestapo, was under duress, and that he had gone to England with the intention of giving himself up immediately upon landing.

After the trial, the public were never told that a fourth man had been acquitted. Indeed, the British public never learned about Sjoerd Pons at all.

Whatever the reason for Pons' acquittal, it stands as an extraordinary testament to the independence of the jurors – and to the jury system itself – that Pons was acquitted as the Germans stood poised to invade. The jury was reminded daily by the sirens that their country was fighting for its life against a ferocious enemy. It was no easy thing to remain cold and dispassionate when passing judgment on men who, evidence proved, had worked for the enemy to expedite an invasion which would have changed their way of life forever. When people cast doubt on the jury system nowadays, this trial should be remembered.

This extraordinary story stands, in the end, as evidence of the only part of the invasion actually to arrive, of the appalling quality of German wartime spies, of the extraordinary fair-mindedness of a British jury, and of the first attempted Germanic conquest of Britain since the fifth century.[7]

The authorities gave the case as much publicity as they could, but there were limited facts to go on because the trial had been held *in camera* at the Old Bailey. The Press filled in the gaps with details of how the men gave themselves away or were discovered; at least three different versions were given of how the spies came to be caught, and these have found their way into various published post-war accounts.

The powers that be wanted to maintain the pretence that the men were still at large with the intention of feeding their German masters with false information. As the war developed, the British established the Double Cross system, which had its origins in the turning of spies in the First World War. In the words of J.C. Masterman, chairman of the Twenty Committee (so called because 'XX', the symbol of the Double Crossess, was the Roman numeral for twenty) that ran Britain's double agents: 'By means of the double agent system we actively ran and controlled the German espionage system in this country.'[8]

The 'Brussels Four' were among twelve Nazi spies who were sent to Britain during September 1940 as part of Operation *Lena*. All, like the four in this book, were arrested before coming anywhere near to fulfilling their mission, hampered by hapless planning and their own basic stupidity. Bearing in mind that this was one of the most important and audacious missions at a pivotal stage during the Second World War, why did the Germans – known for their efficiency and attention to detail – send such an inept bunch of individuals? It is an enduring question that has not been conclusively answered to this day.

But what might have happened if *Lena*, and the reason why *Lena* came to fruition, *Sealion*, had been successful?

The Nazis had drawn up meticulous plans for how they would rule a conquered Britain. For example, they had a 144-page *Sonderfahndungsliste GB*, or 'Black Book'. This was a list of 2,820 names of prominent politicians, writers, émigrés, known intelligence agents, scientists and artists who would be arrested after the invasion, and was drawn up by SS General Walter Schellenberg's office. Schellenberg was to become the 'Police' chief responsible for Great Britain after an invasion, with the main Gestapo offices to be based in Birmingham.

The list included, of course, Winston Churchill and members of the Government, as well as writers such as H.G. Wells, E.M. Forster and Noel Coward. Surprisingly, the Boy Scout movement was included in the 'Black Book' as it was seen as a front for the intelligence services! It was also planned to shut down the Freemasons, as freemasonry was very much treated as 'suspicious'; any other 'secret society' would either have been controlled or banned. Even the Salvation Army was seen as 'internationalist' in its outlook and therefore would be closed and its members subject to arrest.[9]

One person who was particularly concerned what would happen if the Germans invaded was Lady (Maud) Woolton, wife of the Minister of Food, Lord (Fred) Woolton. She asked her husband to buy her a small revolver, one small enough to carry in her handbag, 'I know that the Germans have a list of people who will be shot as soon as they are captured and you are on that list – and very near to Churchill who is number one.' To her husband's consternation, she added that if her husband was captured she would shoot their children before turning the gun on herself.

There seems to be little written evidence that those classed as 'wanted' would have any collective fate under a victorious German regime, although some would obviously have more to fear than others based on what was known after 1942 of the Holocaust and concentration camps, particularly Jews, Communists and ex-Nazi defectors. In 1940, there were some 450,000 persons of direct Jewish descent in the UK, all of whom would have been 'enemies' to the Nazis, as well as countless numbers with an indirect family connection.[10] Nevertheless, no arrest or incarceration would have been pleasant.

SS-Brigadeführer Dr Frank Six would have been given the job of setting up six Einsatzgruppen death squads based in London, Manchester, Birmingham, Bristol, Liverpool and Edinburgh to round up the Jews who lived in Britain in 1940. They would then have been transported to the extermination camps of Poland and Eastern Europe.[11]

According to Field Marshal Walther von Brauchitsch's 'Orders Concerning the Organization and Function of Military Government in England', drawn up by the commander-in-chief of the German Army in September 1940, 'The able-bodied male population between the ages of 17 and 45 will, unless the local situation calls for an exceptional ruling, be interned and dispatched to the Continent.'[12]

Independence, under the Reich, would have been granted to Scotland, Wales and a United Ireland, with a semi-autonomous status for the west of England. What was termed the Nationalities Plan was envisaged to weaken loyalty to the British Government, although this would have been no more than a puppet government, most likely led by David Lloyd George, an admirer of Hitler.

If a German invasion had succeeded, liberation would probably never have come about without the help of the United States. Churchill predicted that defeat in 1940 would have meant that everything, 'including all that we have known or cared for, will sink into the abyss of a new Dark Age'.

Key Personnel

Canaris, Admiral Wilhelm: Arrested by the Gestapo in July 1944 and eventually hanged at Flossenburg concentration camp on 9 April 1945 for his indirect involvement in the 20 July 1944 bomb plot conspiracy against Hitler. He was reputedly hung on a specially constructed gallows, and thin piano wire was used to deepen and prolong the agony. Canaris was quoted as saying, 'I die for my fatherland. I have a clear conscience. I only did my duty to my country when I tried to oppose the criminal folly of Hitler.'

Davison, J.A. 'Jock': Committed suicide in October 1942 immediately after resigning as Chief Constable of Kent over a matter relating to disputed expenses.

Hinchley Cooke, Lieutenant Colonel William Edward: Affectionately known by his MI5 colleagues as 'Cookie'. In 1946, Cookie received a commission from the Lord Lieutenant of the County of Kent to serve as a Deputy Lieutenant. In 1953, Cookie was awarded the Coronation Medal upon the coronation of Queen Elizabeth II. On 3 March 1955, he collapsed in the street outside his house, a victim of a massive heart attack. He was 61-years-old.

Humphreys, Travers Christmas, KC: Became involved in Buddhism in the early 1920s. He later became a judge, before his death in 1983.

Jodl, General Alfred: Jodl's wife, Irma, died on 18 April 1944. He married his former secretary and mistress, Luise Katharina von Benda, on 7 April 1945. At the end of the war, Jodl signed the instruments of unconditional surrender on 7 May in Reims, France. Upon signing, he was arrested and transferred to the prisoner of war camp at Flensburg, Schleswig-Holstein, Germany. Indicted by the Nuremberg Tribunal, Jodl was charged with conspiracy to wage a war of aggression or crimes against peace, war crimes and crimes against humanity. He was found guilty on all counts of the indictment and was hanged on 16 October 1946 in a gymnasium behind the courthouse. He was cremated at Munich and his ashes were scattered into the Isar River in Bavaria, southern Germany. In 1956, Jodl was posthumously acquitted of all charges by a German arbitrary committee because, according to the committee, he had only done his duty as a soldier.

Jowitt, 1st Earl (William Allen) PC, KC, MP: Solicitor-General who prosecuted Meier, Kieboom, Pons and Waldberg. He was elevated to peerage status 1951. In August 1942, Jowitt was prosecuted for buying animal feed without the appropriate coupons – necessary under wartime regulations – for his farm in Kent. Although he had been zealous in the prosecution of such offences, his claim that he employed a bailiff to run the farm and had no knowledge that the offence was being committed was accepted by the court. He died in August 1957.

Kieboom, Charles Albert van den: Executed at Pentonville Prison on 17 December, 1940.

Meier, Carl: Executed at Pentonville Prison on 10 December, 1940.

Pons, Sjoerd: In his file, open to all in the National Archives in London, it is noted that Pons' wife was murdered in a concentration camp in 1943. This is not true; in fact, the couple divorced in 1951, after Pons' repatriation. He remarried and moved to Spain, where he died in 1983. He had no children.

Praetorius, Walter: After the war, Praetorius was arrested and transferred to Bad Nenndorf, where he was interrogated by 'Tin Eye' Stephens. Stephens was impressed by Praetorius' Anglomania, which sat comfotably with Stephens' own raw jingoism. Praetorius was released after several months of interrogation and he settled in Goslar, West Germany, where he taught and continued his dancing.

Raeder, Erich: Sentenced to life imprisonment at Nuremburg in 1946. He was released in 1955 and died on 6 November 1960.

Ritter, Nikolaus: After the war, Ritter was interrogated by the British and held at a detention centre at Bad Nenndorf, where the commandant was 'Tin-Eye' Stephens. Ritter was eventually released back into civilian life and slipped out of sight. In the early 1970s, he resurfaced when he published his memoir, *Deckname Dr Rantzau – Die Aufzeichnungen Des Nikolaus Ritter, Offizier unter Canaris im Geheimen Nachrichtendiens* (*Code Name Dr Rantzau – The Notes of Nikolaus Ritter, Officer under Canaris in the Secret Intelligence Service*). In his book, Ritter focused on his military career, proudly detailing the ways in which the Abwehr had extracted information from their double-agents in England. Ritter died on 9 April 1974 in Germany.

Stephens, Lieutenant Colonel Robin William George 'Tin-Eye': Commandant, Camp 020. From 1945, he ran Bad Nenndorf, the Combined Services Detailed Interrogation Centre, the German version of Camp 020. While he had eschewed physical torture at Camp 020, something altered at Bad Nenndorf. Prisoners were starved, beaten and physically maltreated, and some even died. In 1948,

Stephens and three other officers from Bad Nenndorf, including the camp doctor, were court-martialed. Stephens was charged on four counts: conduct prejudicial to good order and military discipline, failure in his duty as supervisor of the facility, and two counts of disgraceful conduct of a cruel kind. Ultimately, only the doctor, Captain John Stuart Smith, was found guilty on any charges and was dismissed from the Army. Stephens was acquitted of all charges. In 1960, Robin was discharged from the Territorial Army with the honorary rank of Brigadier. Little is known of his later life and when or where he died.

Waldberg, Jose: Executed at Pentonville Prison on 10 December, 1940.

Wichmann, Herbert Christian Oscar Otto: On 9 October 1945, Wichmann was returned to Germany, where, after the war, the British gave him a job helping to rebuild the German shipping industry in Hamburg.

Wrottesley, The Hon. Mr Justice Frederic John: Judge in the case of the 'Brussels Four'. He was appointed to the King's Bench Division of the High Court in 1937, receiving the customary knighthood the same year. In 1947, he was made a Lord Justice of Appeal and appointed to the Privy Council, but was forced to retire in 1948 for health reasons. He died in 1948.

Glossary

AA   Anti-aircraft.

Abwehr   The Abwehr was an intelligence-gathering agency and dealt exclusively with human intelligence, especially raw intelligence reports from field agents and other sources.

Anschluss   The annexation of Austria by Germany in 1938. Hitler had forced the resignation of the Austrian Chancellor by demanding that he admit Nazis into his cabinet. The new Chancellor, a pro-Nazi, invited German troops to enter the country on the pretext of restoring law and order.

Arbeitsdienst   Reich Labour service. A major organization established in Nazi Germany as an agency to help mitigate the effects of unemployment on the German economy, militarize the workforce and indoctrinate it with Nazi ideology. It was the official state labour service, divided into separate sections for men and women.

ARP   Air Raid Precaution.

Cell Fourteen   A psychological contrivance at Camp 020, reminiscent of the torture chamber in George Orwell's *1984*. Room 101 itself was named after a conference room at the BBC where Orwell would have to sit through tortuously boring meetings.

D-Notice   A British government instruction preventing particular information from being made public in order to protect the country.

DSS   Defence Security Service.

Fender   A bumper used to absorb the kinetic energy of a boat or vessel berthing against a jetty, quay wall or other vessel. Fenders are used to prevent damage to boats, vessels and berthing structures.

Feldwebel   German sergeant.

Fifth Column   A clandestine subversive organization working within a country to further an invading enemy's military and political aims.

Fl	Dutch guilder.
FO	Foreign Office
Franc-tireur	A civilian, especially a guerrilla fighter or sniper.
Gefreiter	The second grade or rank to which a German enlisted man can be promoted. He had no command authority; the rank represented a raise in pay and little else.
Half-a-crown	Two shillings and six pence: 2/6 or 2s 6d.
Handelskammer	Board of Trade, Chamber of Commerce.
Inter alia	Among other things.
Jungend	As early as 13 May 1922, the National Socialist Movement in Germany began to organize youth into its growing ranks. In 1933, the Hitler Youth (Hitler Jugend, HJ) was organized into a separate and independent group that encompassed all youth related clubs in Germany.
Korvettenkapitan	German corvette captain.
Kriegsgericht	Military court; court martial.
Kriegsmarine	German Navy (officially disbanded in August 1946).
Maréchaussée	Dutch gendarmerie force performing military police and civil police duties.
ME 109	Messerschmitt 109, German fighter aircraft.
MI5	UK domestic counter-intelligence.
MI6	Secret Intelligence Service (SIS), the foreign intelligence service of the UK.
Nore	The Nore, sandbank in the Thames Estuary, extending between Shoeburyness in Essex (north) and Sheerness in Kent (south).
NSNAP	Nationaal Socialistische Nederlandsche Arbeiders-Partij, the Dutch Nazi Party.
NSDAP	The National Socialist German Workers' Party, more commonly known as the Nazi Party, was a political party in Germany between 1920 and 1945.
OKW	Oberkommando der Wehrmacht, The German Armed Forces High Command.
Opbouwdienst	Some of the Dutch forces were not demobilized when defeated in May 1940 but incorporated in the Opbouwdienst (Resurrection Service), mostly on the basis that they were unemployed in civil life, sometimes voluntarily. This force was extensively assigned to clear all the remains of obsolete defences and debris of battle and destruction.
Paravane	A device towed behind a boat at a depth regulated by its vanes or planes, so that the cable to which it is attached can cut the moorings of submerged mines.

SIS	British Secret Intelligence Service.
Sonderauftrag	Special mission (military); special order (commercial).
SS	Schutzstaffel; elite unit of the Nazi Party that served as Hitler's personal guard and special security force in Germany and the occupied countries.
Striker	A revolver. In striker-fired pistols, the striker is the component that strikes the casing, dimpling it and igniting the primer within.
Todt	German construction battalion.
Unteroffizier	German non-commissioned officer.
Vichy	Formally the French State, État Français (July 1940– September 1944). France under the regime of Marshal Philippe Pétain, from the Nazi German defeat of France to the Allied liberation.

Notes

Operation Lena: The Ascension to Heaven?
1. http://www.historylearningsite.co.uk/world-war-two/world-war-two-in-western-europe/operation-sealion.
2. Ibid.
3. MOI *The British Home Front Pocket Book 1940–1942*, pp.21–22.
4. http://tomatobubble.com/id763.html.
5. http://www.churchill-society-london.org.uk/UnknWarr.html.
6. TNA LCO 67/71.
7. Leo McKinstry, *Operation Sealion*, p.18.
8. http://tomatobubble.com/id763.html.
9. Ben Macintyre, *Agent Zigzag*, Bloomsbury, 2007 (p. 47)
10. Ben Macintyre, *Agent Zigzag* (Bloomsbury, 2007), p.47.
11. https://levinehistory.wordpress.com/2014/06/02/the-unlikely-story-of-the-german-invasion-spies/.
12. http://spartacus-educational.com/2WWfifthC.htm.

Chapter One: 'Where on Earth are we going to get hold of that many would-be suicides?'
1. TNA FO 1019/33.
2. Ibid.
3. https://ww2gravestone.com/people/jodl-alfred-gustav
4. McKinstry, *Operation Sealion*, 179
5. William B. Breuer, *Top Secret Tales of World War II*, p.11.
6. http://auschwitz.dk/Canaris/id16.htm.
7. Nicholas Booth, *Lucifer Rising* (The History Press, 2016), p.173.
8. Ibid., 62
9. William B. Breuer, *Top Secret Tales of World War II*, p.77.
10. Ibid.
11. Randall Hansen, *Disobeying Hitler*, p.19.
12. Martin Pearce, *Spymaster*, p.67.
13. Giles Macdonogh, *1938: Hitler's Gamble*, p.201.
14. Philip Oltermann, 'Botched Nazi spy mission was act of sabotage, says historian', https://www.theguardian.com/world/2014/aug/22/botched-nazi-spy-mission-sabotage-germany.
15. Macdonogh, *1938: Hitler's Gamble*, p.86.
16. Booth, *Lucifer Rising*, p.175.
17. Hugh Trevor-Roper, *The Secret World Behind the Curtain of British Intelligence In World War II and the Cold War*, p.62.
18. Macintyre, *Agent ZigZag*, p.254.

19. TNA KV 2/103.
20. Breuer, *Top Secret Tales of World War II*, p.78.
21. Ibid.
22. http://www.dailymail.co.uk/news/article-2732513/Ordering-cider-10am-cycling-wrong-road-German-sausages-luggage-Were-stupid-Nazi-spies-sent-Britain-war-act-sabotage-anti-Hitler-officials.html.
23. Peter Duffy, *Double Agent: The First Hero of World War II and how the FBI outwitted and Destroyed a Nazi Spy Ring*, p.13.
24. Booth, *Lucifer Rising*, p.173.
25. Duffy, *Double Agent*, p.14.
26. Ibid., p.15.
27. TNA KV 2/87.
28. Duffy, *Double Agent*, pp.16–17.
29. Booth, *Lucifer Rising*, 173
30. Joshua Levine, *Operation Fortitude: The Story the Spy Operation That Saved D-Day*, p.58.
31. Macintyre, *Agent ZigZag*, p.48.
32. Ibid., p.49.
33. Ibid.
34. TNA KV 2/524.
35. Ibid.
36. Gösta Caroli (codename SUMMER), a Swedish journalist, was the first of the 'Lena' men to attempt to arrive in the UK. An abortive attempt had been made to land him on the night of 1 September. The second attempt, three days after the 'Brussels Four' arrived, was, however, successful. (Public Record Office (PRO), *Camp 020 MI5 and the Nazi Spies*, p.137).

Chapter Two: The Brussels Four
 1. TNA KV 2/1452.
 2. TNA KV 2/11.
 3. TNA KV 1699.
 4. TNA KV 2/12.
 5. Ibid.
 6. Ibid.
 7. TNA KV 2/1699.
 8. TNA KV 2/12.
 9. TNA KV 2/1699
10. TNA KV 2/12.
11. Ibid.
12. Ibid.
13. TNA KV 2/1700.
14. TNA KV 2/1699.
15. TNA KV 2/1700.
16. TNA KV 2/1452.
17. TNA KV 2/13.

Chapter Three: Shaking Hands with the Devil
1. TNA KV 2/1452.
2. Ibid.
3. TNA KV 2/11.
4. TNA KV 2/107.
5. TNA KV 2/1699.
6. TNA KV 2/1452.
7. TNA KV 2/12.
8. TNA KV 2/107.
9. TNA KV 2/1700.
10. TNA KV 2/12.
11. TNA KV 2/107.

Chapter Four: Champagne Cider and a Bath
1. TNA CAB 69/1.
2. TNA KV 2/1700.
3. Ibid.
4. Ibid.
5. Ibid.
6. TNA KV 2/1452.
7. Ibid.
8. TNA KV 2-1700.
9. Ibid.
10. TNA KV 2/1452.
11. TNA KV 2/107.
12. TNA KV 2/1700.
13. TNA KV 2/107.
14. Heath, *Hitler's Girls*, p.97.
15. TNA KV 2/12.
16. TNA KV 2/1700.
17. PRO, *Camp 020*, p.42.
18. TNA KV 2/1700.
19. TNA KV 2/107.
20. TNA HO 144/21472.
21. TNA KV 2/1452.
22. TNA KV 2/107.
23. Ibid.

Chapter Five: 'Tin-Eye' and Camp 020
1. TNA KV 4/14.
2. TNA KV 4/15.
3. PRO, *Camp 020*, p.21.
4. Ibid., p.126.
5. Joshua Levine, *The Secret History of the Blitz*, p.138.
6. PRO, *Camp 020*, p.127.
7. Ibid., p.21.

8. Macintyre, *Agent Zig Zag*, pp.113–14.
9. Levine, *Operation Fortitude*, p.65.
10. Macintyre, *Agent Zig Zag*, p.136.
11. https://stmargarets.london/archives/2016/02/latchmere-house.html. Original material courtesy Martyn Day.
12. https://www.smithsonianmag.com/history/the-monocled-world-war-ii-interrogator-652794/.
13. Macintyre, *Agent Zig Zag*, p.115.
14. https://stmargarets.london/archives/2016/02/latchmere-house.html. Original material courtesy Martyn Day.
15. TNA KV 2/1699.
16. Ibid.
17. Ibid.
18. Ibid.
19. Ibid.
20. Ibid.
21. Ibid.
22. TNA KV 2/1700.
23. TNA KV 4/14.
24. TNA KV 2/11.
25. Ibid.
26. TNA KV 2/13.
27. Ibid.
28. Ibid.
29. Ibid.
30. Ibid.
31. TNA KV 2/1452.
32. TNA KV 2/1699.
33. TNA KV 2/12.

Chapter Six: Spies in Surrey

1. https://www.battleofbritain1940.net/0035.html.
2. TNA KV 2/13.
3. TNAKV 2/11.
4. TNA KV 2/1700.
5. TNA HO/144 21472.
6. TNA KV 2/13.
7. Ibid.
8. TNA KV 2/107.
9. Ibid.
10. Ibid.
11. Ibid.
12. Ibid.
13. TNA KV 2/11.
14. Ibid.
15. TNA KV 2/1452.
16. Geoffrey Wellum, *First Light*, pp.147–48.

17. TNA KV 2/12.
18. TNA KV 2/107.
19. TNA ADM 223/463 via https://www.turing.org.uk/sources/ruthless.html.
20. TNA KV 2/11.
21. Ibid.

Chapter Seven: Velvet Glove?
1. TNA KV 2/107.
2. TNA KV 2/11.
3. TNA CAB/66/12/1.
4. TNA KV 2/107.
5. Ibid.
6. Ibid.
7. http://www.nationalarchives.gov.uk/theartofwar/popup/AIR_2_5686_18C_transcript.htm.
8. McKinstry, *Operation Sealion*, p.405.
9. Ibid.
10. Ibid.
11. TNA KV 2/107.
12. TNA KV 2/11.
13. Ibid.
14. http://oldshirburnian.org.uk/bombing-of-sherborne-30-september-1940/ (courtesy Rachell Hassall, Archivist, Sherborne School).
15. TNA KV 2/11.
16. Ibid.
17. TNA KV 2/1700.
18. Goose (Karl Kurt): Dropped by parachute near Wellingborough, Northamptonshire, 3 October 1940. He was well equipped but his mission was so faulty it was doomed to failure. On completion of his mission, he was to remain in England until the proposed invasion took place, and then rejoin the invading army. Goose, lacking in initiative and courage, proved a dismal failure. TNA KV 4/15.
19. TNA KV 2/12.
20. TNA KV 2/11.
21. https://levinehistory.wordpress.com/2014/06/02/the-unlikely-story-of-the-german-invasion-spies.
22. http://www.westendatwar.org.uk/page/10_downing_street.
23. TNA KV 2/11.
24. TNA CAB 69/1.
25. TNA KV 2/1452.

Chapter Eight: Home for incurables
1. TNA KV /1452.
2. TNA CAB 69/1.
3. TNA KV 2/1700.
4. Ibid.

5. TNA CAB 69/1.
6. TNA KV 2/1452.
7. Ibid.
8. Ibid.
9. Ibid.
10. Ibid.
11. Ibid.
12. Meyrick and Ribuffi. 'There was a man called Ribuffi who kept a nightclub and a woman called Mrs Meyrick who kept a nightclub, and they had both of them given [Police] Sgt. Goddard bribes of money to allow them to break the licensing laws. Ribuffi had never seen or heard of Mrs Meyrick, and Mrs Meyrick had never seen or heard of Ribuffi and yet they were found guilty of … conspiring together.' TNA KV 2/1452. In common law, the prohibited act of conspiracy is the entry into an unlawful agreement, which need never be implemented. There need not be communication between each conspirator and every other, provided that there be a common design common to each of them all. Conspiracy is 'a difficult branch of the law, difficult in itself, and sometimes even more difficult in its application to particular facts or allegations', and it is 'necessary that the prosecution should establish, not indeed that the individuals were in direct communication with each other, or directly consulting together, but that they entered into an agreement with a common design. Such agreements may be made in various ways.' http://swarb.co.uk/rex-v-meyrick-and-ribuffi-cca-1929/.
13. TNA KV 2/1452.
14. TNA HO 144/21472.
15. TNA KV 2/1452.
16. Ibid.
17. Ibid.
18. Ibid.
19. Ibid.
20. Ibid.
21. https://merrynallingham.com/20th-century/spies-and-suspicions-on-the-home-front/.
22. TNA KV 2/1452.
23. Ibid.
24. TNA HO 144/21472.
25. TNA KV 2/1452.
26. Ibid.
27. Ibid.
28. https://ww2aircraft.net/forum/threads/this-day-in-the-war-in-europe-the-beginning.41546/page-69.
29. TNA KV 2/13.
30. TNA PCOM 9/891.
31. https://www.fleetairarmoa.org/news/on-this-day-26-november-1940.
32. TNA PCOM 9/891.
33. TNA KV 2/1452.

34. Ibid.
35. TNA HO 144/21472.
36. https://maltagc70.wordpress.com/2015/11/28/28-november-1940-convoy-bombed-as-ships-head-for-harbour/.
37. TNA KV 2/1452.
38. Ibid.
39. https://www.bbc.co.uk/news/uk-england-merseyside-34938886.
40. TNA KV 2/13.

Chapter Nine: My Name is Henri Lassudry
 1. TNA KV 2/1452.
 2. TNA PCOM 9/890.
 3. TNA HO 144/21472.
 4. CAB 69/1.
 5. TNA HO 144/21472.
 6. TNA KV 2/1452.
 7. Ibid.
 8. TNA CAB 69/1.
 9. TNA KV 2/1452.
10. TNA HO 144/21472.
11. TNA KV 2/1452.
12. TNA KV 2/107.
13. Ibid.
14. TNA HO 144/21472.
15. http://www.historyofwar.org/secondworldwar/date/1940_12_07.html.
16. TNA HO 144/21472.
17. http://www.churchillarchiveforschools.com/themes/the-themes/anglo-american-relations/just-how-special-was-the-special-relationship-in-the-Second-World-War-Part-1-1939-41/the-sources/source-2.
18. TNA KV 2/107.
19. TNA KV 2/1699.
20. Ibid.
21. TNA HO 144/21472.
22. TNA KV 2/ 1699.
23. Ibid.
24. Ibid.
25. TNA CAB 69/1.
26. https://www.secondworldwarhistory.com/operation-compass-north-africa.php.
27. TNA KV 2/1699.
28. TNA HO 144/21472.
29. TNA PCOM 9/890.
30. TNA HO 144/21472.
31. Ibid.
32. TNA PCOM 9/890/ PCOM 9/891.
33. TNA HO 144/214722.
34. TNA KV 2/13.

Chapter Ten: Epitaph for a spy

1. TNA KV 2/1452.
2. Ibid.
3. *Anni Braz-Bihen*, Operation *Seagull* was an Abwehr II/Brandenburger Regiment-sanctioned mission launched in September 1940. The object was to infiltrate the UK in preparation for Operation *Sealion*. The vessel chosen was the *Anni Braz-Bihen*. Despite being planned and launched, the mission was aborted midway during the sea crossing to Ireland. Abwehr chief Wilhelm Canaris had already issued orders that regional Abwehr stations were not to attempt to infiltrate into Britain via Ireland for the foreseeable future, due to the dismal failure of a previous attempt, Operation *Lobster I*, the previous July.
4. TNA KV 2/107.
5. TNA HO 144/21472.
6. Ibid.
7. TNA KV 2/1452.
8. TNA PCOM 9/890.
9. http://kpolsson.com/today/1213.htm.
10. TNA KV 2/1453.
11. TNA KV 2/107.
12. Ibid.
13. TNA CAB 69/1.
14. TNA KV 2/1452.
15. TNA KV 2/13.
16. TNA HO 144/21472.
17. https://maltagc70.wordpress.com/2015/12/27/27-december-1940-cold-and-wet-threatens-morale-in-malta/.
18. http://worldwartwodaily.filminspector.com/2016/12/december-30-1940-london-devastated.html.
19. http://www.historyofwar.org/secondworldwar/date/1940_12_31.html.
20. TNA HO 144/21472.
21. TNA KV 2/1452.
22. Ibid.
23. Ibid.
24. TNA KV 2/13.
25. TNA KV 2/107.
26. TNA KV 2/13.
27. Ibid.
28. Ibid.
29. TNA KV 2/12.
30. Ibid.
31. Ibid.
32. TNA CAB 69/8.
33. TNA KV 2/13.
34. Ibid.
35. TNA KV 2/1452.
36. Ibid.

37. Ibid.
38. TNA KV 2/13.
39. Ibid.
40. Ibid.
41. Ibid.
42. TNA KV 2/1452.
43. Ibid.
44. Ibid.
45. https://www.iwm.org.uk/collections/item/object/205053481.
46. TNA KV 2/1452.
47. http://www.thepeoplehistory.com/october13th.html.
48. TNA KV2/11.
49. https://www.yadvashem.org/yv/en/exhibitions/communities/wurzburg/deportation_25april.asp.
50. TNA KV 2 /13.
51. Ibid.

Chapter Eleven: Investigation Continues: Tying up loose ends
 1. https://www.theyworkforyou.com/debates/?d=1943-03-02.
 2. A British double agent by the name of Eddie Chapman. MI5's Agent ZIGZAG, he was dashing, unpredictable, a traitor and a hero; disreputable, but in a way that was rakish or appealing.
 3. https://www.iwm.org.uk/collections/item/object/205142065.
 4. TNA KV 4/102.
 5. PRO, *Camp 020*, p.47.
 6. TNA KV 2/524.
 7. https://www.theyworkforyou.com/debates/?id=1943-03-31a.176.5.
 8. http://www.isle-of-wight-memorials.org.uk/events/19430407_newport_air_raid.htm.
 9. TNA KV2/13.
10. https://www.saak.nl/battlefield%20tour/2008%20berlin/berlin%20history/berlin1943/berlin1943%20en.htm.
11. https://www.iwm.org.uk/collections/item/object/205093958.
12. TNA KV2/13.
13. TNA KV 2/12.
14. David Tremain, *Rough Justice*, p.84.
15. Ibid., p.85.
16. Ibid., p.87.
17. Ibid., p.86.
18. PRO, *Camp 020*, p.364.
19. TNA KV 2/103.
20. TNA KV 2/87.
21. Ibid.
22. TNA KV 2/12.
23. Ibid.
24. Ibid.

25. TNA KV 2/13.
26. Ibid.

Chapter Twelve: 'All that we have known or cared for will sink into the abyss of a new Dark Age'
1. Roberts, *Swastikas all the way down the Mall*.
2. TNA KV 2/11.
3. A Norwegian spying expedition organized by the Germans fetched up on Wick, in Scotland, on the M.V. *Taanevik* during April. The skipper, Henry Torgersen, naively explained to the local authorities that he had brought over a cargo of sardines which it was intended to convert by sale into whiskey, coffee, tea and other beverages needed in Norway, whither they proposed to return. The story was too simple and good to be wholly true. Torgersen and his companions, Bjarne Hansen, Hans Hansen and Johan Strandmoen, were promptly consigned to Camp 020. PRO, *Camp 020*, p.163.
4. TNA KV 2/1700.
5. Booth, *Lucifer Rising*, p.175.
6. Colvin, *Master Spy*, Foreword.
7. https://levinehistory.wordpress.com/2014/06/02/.
8. PRO, *Camp 020*, p.23.
9. Roberts, *Swastikas all the way down the Mall*.
10. Ibid.
11. Ibid.
12. Ibid.

Bibliography

The National Archives (TNA):

ADM 223/463	CAB 65/21	CAB 66/23	KV 2/524
ADM 358/3300	CAB 65/25	CAB 66/26	KV 2/1452
CAB 65/8	CAB 65/26	CAB 66/35	KV 2/1699
CAB 65/9	CAB 65/27	CAB 67/9	KV 2/1700
CAB 65/9/8	CAB 65/28	CAB 69/1	KV 4/13
CAB 65/9/15	CAB 65/33	FO 1019/9	KV 4/14
CAB 65/9/26	CAB 65/43	FO 1019/33	KV 4/15
CAB 65/9/32	CAB 65/44	HO 144/21471	KV 4/102
CAB 65/9/34	CAB 65/48	HO 144/21472	KV 4/115
CAB 65/10	CAB 66/7	KV 2/11	KV 4/324
CAB 65/14	CAB 66/12/1	KV 2/12	LCO 67/71
CAB 65/17	CAB 66/13	KV 2/13	PCOM 9/890
CAB 65/18	CAB 66/14	KV 2/87	PCOM 9/891
CAB 65/19	CAB 66/15	KV 2/103	WO 309/1701
CAB 65/20	CAB 66/17	KV 2/107	

Books:

Andrew, Christopher, *The Defence of the Realm: The Authorized History of MI5* (Penguin Books, 2010).

Booth, Nicholas, *Lucifer Rising* (The History Press, 2016).

Breuer, William B., *Deceptions of World War II* (John Wiley & Sons, Inc., 2001).

Breuer, William B., *Top Secret Tales of World War II* (John Wiley & Sons, Inc., 2000).

Breuer, William B., *Undercover Tales of World War II* (John Wiley & Sons, Inc., 1999).

Colvin, Ian, *Master Spy: The Incredible Story of Admiral Willhem Canaris, Who While Hitler's Chief of Intelligence, was a Secret Ally of the British* (McGraw-Hill, 1951).

Duffy, Peter, *Double Agent: The First Hero of World War II and How the FBI Outwitted and Destroyed a Nazi Spy Ring* (Scribner, 2014).

Farago, Ladislas, *Burn After Reading: The Espionage History of World War II* (Bluejacket Books, Naval Institute Press, 2003).

Fry, Helen, *The London Cage: The Secret History of Britain's World War II Interrogation Centre* (Yale University Press, 2017).

Goodall, Felicity, *The People's War* (David & Charles, in association with The Reader's Digest Association Ltd, 2008).

Hansen Randall, *Disobeying Hitler* (Faber & Faber, 2014).

Hayward, James, *Hitler's Spy: The True Story of Arthur Owens Double Agent Snow* (Simon & Schuster UK Ltd, 2014).

Heath, Tim, *Hitler's Girls: Doves Amongst Eagles* (Pen & Sword Military, 2019).

Hennessey, Thomas and Thomas, Claire, *Spooks: The Unofficial History of MI5 from Agent Zigzag to the D-Day Deception, 1939–45* (Amberley, 2010).

Kearns, Emily, *Mind the Gap: A London Underground Miscellany* (Summersdale Publishers Ltd, 2013).

Levine, Joshua, *Operation Fortitude: The Story of the Spy Operation that Saved D-Day* (Harper Collins, 2011).

Levine, Joshua, *The Secret History of the Blitz* (Simon & Schuster UK Ltd, 2015).

Macdonogh, Giles, *1938: Hitler's Gamble* (Constable & Robinson Ltd, 2010).

Macintyre, Ben, *Agent Zigzag* (Bloomsbury, 2007).

Macrakis, Kristie, *Prisoners, Lovers & Spies: The Story of Invisible Ink from Herodotus to al-Qaeda* (Yale University Press, 2014).

McKinstry, Leo, *Operation Sealion* (John Murray, 2014).

Milton, Giles, *Churchill's Ministry of Ungentlemanly Warfare: The Mavericks who plotted Hitler's defeat* (John Murray, 2017).

Ministry of Information, *The British Home Front Pocket-Book 1940–1942* (Conway, 2010).

Murphy, Christopher J., *Security and Special Operations: SOE and MI5 During the Second World War* (Palgrave Macmillan, 2006).

Overy, Richard, *The Bombing War Europe 1939–1945* (Penguin Group, 2013).

Pearce, Martin, *Spymaster* (Transworld Publishers, 2016).

Public Record Office Secret History Files, Oliver Hoare (Intro), *Camp 020: MI5 and the Nazi Spies* (Public Record Office, 2000).

Roland, Paul, *The Nazis: The Rise and Fall of History's Most Evil Empire* (Arcturus Publishing Ltd, 2018).

Saward, Dudley, *Bomber Harris* (Sphere Books Ltd, 1985).

Sitwell, William, *Eggs or Anarchy* (Simon Schuster, 2017).

Thomas, Gordon, *Inside British Intelligence: 100 Years of MI5 and MI6* (JR Books, 2010).

Tremain, David, *Rough Justice: The True Story of Agent Dronkers, the Enemy Spy Captured by the British* (Amberly, 2016).

Trevor-Roper, Hugh, *The Secret World: Behind the Curtain of British Intelligence in World War II and the Cold War* (I.B. Tauris & Co Ltd, 2014).

Wellum, Geoffrey, *First Light* (Penguin Books, 2009).

West, Nigel (ed.), *The Guy Liddell Diaries Vol. 1, 1939–1942* (Routledge, 2005)

Winter, Paul, *Defeating Hitler: Whitehall's Secret Report on Why Hitler Lost the War* (Continuum International Publishing Group, 2012).

Articles and websites:

http://2001-2009.state.gov

http://auschwitz.dk/Canaris/id16.htm

https://www.battleofbritain1940.net/0035.html

http://www.bbc.co.uk/history/historic_figures/eden_anthony.shtml

https://www.bbc.co.uk/news/uk-england-merseyside-34938886

https://blog.nationalarchives.gov.uk/blog/remembering-city-benares-tragedy/
http://www.britannica.com/biography/Wilhelm-Canaris
https://www.britannica.com/biography/Roger-Casement
http://www.capitalpunishmentuk.org/hangmen.html
http://www.churchillarchiveforschools.com/themes/the-themes/anglo-american-relations/just-how-special-was-the-special-relationship-in-the-Second-World-War-Part-1-1939-41/the-sources/source-2
http://www.churchill-society-london.org.uk/UknnWarr.html
https://codenames.info/operation/abigail-rachel/
http://www.dailymail.co.uk/news/article-2223831/How-Britain-tortured-Nazi-PoWs-The-horrifying-interrogation-methods-belie-proud-boast-fought-clean-war.html
http://www.dailymail.co.uk/news/article-2732513/Ordering-cider-10am-cycling-wrong-road-German-sausages-luggage-Were-stupid-Nazi-spies-sent-Britain-war-act-sabotage-anti-Hitler-officials.html
https://www.fleetairarmoa.org/news/on-this-day-26-november-1940
https://www.forces-war-records.co.uk/hitlers-black-book
http://www.german-helmets.com/HITLER%20YOUTH%20Main.htm
http://histclo.com/essay/war/ww2/air/eur/bob/bob-osl.html
https://www.history.co.uk/article/operation-mincemeat-how-a-dead-tramp-and-the-author-of-james-bond-helped-the-allies-take
http://www.historylearningsite.co.uk/world-war-two/world-war-two-in-western-europe/operation-sealion/
https://history.howstuffworks.com/world-war-ii
https://history.howstuffworks.com/world-war-ii/nazi-germany-conquers-france6.htm
http://www.historyofwar.org/secondworldwar/date/1940_12_07.html
http://www.historyofwar.org/secondworldwar/date/1940_12_31.html
http://hydrastg.library.cornell.edu/fedora/objects/nur:00573/datastreams/pdf/content
https://intelnews.org/2014/08/25/01-1540/#more-11276
https://ipfs.io/ipfs/QmXoypizjW3WknFiJnKLwHCnL72vedxjQkDDP1mXWo6uco/wiki/Alfred_Jodl.html
https://www.islandnet.com/~kpolsson/ww2hist/ww21940jun.htm
http://www.isle-of-wight-memorials.org.uk/events/19430407_newport_air_raid.htm
https://www.iwm.org.uk/collections/item/object/205053481
https://www.iwm.org.uk/collections/item/object/205093958
https://www.iwm.org.uk/collections/item/object/205142065
https://www.iwm.org.uk/history/the-polish-pilots-who-flew-in-the-battle-of-britain
http://www.jewishvirtuallibrary.org/wilhelm-canaris
http://www.josefjakobs.info/2014/01/governor-of-wandsworth-prison-major.html
http://www.josefjakobs.info/2015/11/the-german-spymaster-and-alabama.html
http://kpolsson.com/today/1213.htm

http://lawcollections.library.cornell.edu/nuremburg/catalog/nur:00573

https://levinehistory.wordpress.com/2014/06/02/the-unlikely-story-of-the-german-invasion-spies/

https://maltagc70.wordpress.com/2015/12/27/27-december-1940-cold-and-wet-threatens-morale-in-malta/

https://maltagc70.wordpress.com/2015/11/28/28-november-1940-convoy-bombed-as-ships-head-for-harbour/

https://merrynallingham.com/20th-century/spies-and-suspicions-on-the-home-front/

http://moebius.freehostia.com/ranks.htm

http://nationalarchives.gov.uk

http://www.nationalarchives.gov.uk/theartofwar/popup/AIR_2_5686_18C_transcript.htm

http://oldshirburnian.org.uk/bombing-of-sherborne-30-september-1940

https://www.onthisday.com/date/1940/

https://www.pinterest.co.uk/pin/453667362436353274/

https://www.rafmuseum.org.uk/research/online-exhibitions/history-of-the-battle-of-britain/operation-sealion.aspx

https://www.revolvy.com/main/index.php?s=Operation%20Seagull%20(Ireland)

https://www.saak.nl/battlefield%20tour/2008%20berlin/berlin%20history/berlin1943/berlin1943%20en.htm

https://www.secondworldwarhistory.com/1940-ww2-events-timeline.asp

https://www.secondworldwarhistory.com/britain-ww2-events-timeline.asp

https://www.secondworldwarhistory.com/operation-compass-north-africa.php

https://www.smithsonianmag.com/history/the-monocled-world-war-ii-interrogator-652794/

http://spartacus-educational.com/2WWfifthC.htm

http://spartacus-educational.com/FWWm5.htm

http://spartacus-educational.com/GERcanaris.htm

https://stmargarets.london/archives/2016/02/latchmere-house.html

http://sussexhistoryforum.co.uk/index.php?PHPSESSID=fbh77btj0vujndivgrnkn29vj2&topic=3351.30

http://swarb.co.uk/rex-v-meyrick-and-ribuffi-cca-1929/

https://www.thefamouspeople.com/profiles/alfred-jodl-3565.php

https://www.theguardian.com/world/2014/aug/22/botched-nazi-spy-mission-sabotage-germany

http://www.thepeoplehistory.com/october13th.html

https://www.theyworkforyou.com/debates/?d=1943-03-02

https://www.theyworkforyou.com/debates/?id=1943-03-31a.176.5

http://tomatobubble.com/id763.html

https://www.tracesofwar.com/persons/38491/Jodl-Alfred-Josef-Ferdinand.htm?c=aw

https://www.turing.org.uk/sources/ruthless.html

https://www.warhistoryonline.com/war-articles/operation-sealion-impaired-nazi-intelligence.html

http://www.waroverholland.nl/index.php?page=the-capitulation-ceremony---
15-may

http://www.westendatwar.org.uk/page/10_downing_street

http://worldwartwodaily.filminspector.com/2016/12/december-30-1940-
london-devastated.html

https://www.ww2aircraft.net/forum/threads/this-day-in-the-war-in-europe-
the-beginning.41546/page-69

https://ww2db.com/event/today/05/06/1945

https://ww2gravestone.com/people/jodl-alfred-gustav

http://ww2timeline.info/ww21941.htm

https://www.yadvashem.org/yv/en/exhibitions/communities/wurzburg/
deportation_25april.asp

Harris, Robert, 'The Heroic Appeaser', *The Week*, 30 September 2017, pp.52–53.

Jones, Nigel, 'Would we have collaborated with Hitler?', The *Daily Telegraph*, 20
February 2017.

Origo, Iris, 'In Enemy Territory', The *Telegraph Magazine*, 14 October 2017,
pp.47–49, extracted and abridged from *A Chill in the Air* (Pushkin Press, 2017).

Roberts, Andrew, 'Swastikas all the way down the Mall', The *Sunday Telegraph*,
19 February 2017.